CIVILIZATION'S QUOTATIONS

CIVILIZATION'S QUOTATIONS

Life's Ideal

RICHARD ALAN KRIEGER

Algora Publishing
New York

© 2002 by Algora Publishing.
All Rights Reserved.
www.algora.com

No portion of this book (beyond what is permitted by
Sections 107 or 108 of the United States Copyright Act of 1976)
may be reproduced by any process, stored in a retrieval system,
or transmitted in any form, or by any means, without the
express written permission of the publisher.
Softcover ISBN 1-892941-76-7
Hardcover ISBN 1-892941-77-5

Library of Congress Cataloging-in-Publication Data 2002006368

Civilization's quotations : life's ideal / [compiled] by Richard Alan
Krieger.
   p. cm.
 ISBN 1-892941-76-7 (alk. paper)
 1. Quotations, English. I. Krieger, Richard Alan.
 PN6081 .C49 2002
 082—dc21
                        2002006368

Printed in the United States

Table of Contents by Category

To my loving parents

Introduction

Life's Ideal

Volumes of touching, edifying, and inspiring sound-bites have been collected throughout history; why put together another one, now? This book cannot pretend to be an exhaustive compendium of the world's most original expressions; rather, I have collected observations and maxims that seemed to me to be particularly striking, and I present them to the reader in a "poetic quotation" style that may provide pleasant reading in reflective moments as well as serving as a resource to help find the right words for a special moment. It is more than a reference book; it is an invitation to walk with me through all the stages and facets of life, together savoring some of the insights and adages that civilization has bestowed upon us for each moment.

We are born into this life and our journey begins. Our sense of self grows, while we become aware of the world around us. As we progress along our path, our experiences help us to define our character. A destiny is woven into our being, and luck too comes into play as we move through our cycle of time. We express our love, which produces a happiness that motivates us to be good. As truth is revealed to us, it gradually builds into an inner wisdom, and our mind expands as we encounter the various ideas of philosophy. The power of words shows us the value of education, which is never ending. The need for prudence, gratitude, forgiveness and charity become clear as we see how these attributes help us to create a sense of peace. Faith in our dreams motivates our will to move forward and gives us the courage to turn our inner genius into action. As we work, we help to create opportunities that may bring success, wealth, power. We learn that with growth comes responsibility, and we gain a greater appreciation of how justice is to be applied in the development of civilization.

Meeting diverse people along the way, we receive inspiration from others; we discover our true love and together form a family, and we enjoy new and ongoing friendships. With a greater sense of freedom, we find the time to explore all the beauty that exists around us. As we age, we come to respect the four seasons of life, as expressed in humanity and the abundant Earth we inhabit, and we appreciate every age as each time period for what it represents. We do our best to maintain our natural health, knowing that this is always our greatest treasure as we travel on life's journey. Our exploration of science builds a better understanding of reality, of the world and the universe in which we live.

And as we make our way through life, we prize the timeless insights bequeathed us in the proverbs and witticisms of every era and every culture. In this book, I present to you a hand-picked selection of eternal truths and pithy sayings from around the globe and across the breadth of human experience, with the wish that they will be as useful, intriguing and inspiring for you as they have been for me.

— Richard Alan Krieger

LIFE

"Life isn't about finding yourself. Life is about creating yourself." — George Bernard Shaw

"Life is what you make it." — Grandma Moses

"Life is either a daring adventure, or it is nothing." — Helen Keller

"Life moves on, whether we act as cowards or heroes." — Henry Miller

"Let me not look for allies in life's battlefield but to my own strength." — Buddha

"Life, like a dome of many-colored glass, stains the white radiance of eternity." — Shelley

"Life imitates art far more than art imitates life." — "The secret of life is an art." — Oscar Wilde

"Man's main task in life is to give birth to himself." — Erich Fromm

"To be what we are, and to become what we are capable of becoming is the only end of life." — Robert Louis Stevenson

"The time of life is short; to spend that shortness basely were too long." — "Simply the thing I am shall make me live." — Shakespeare

"What counts is not to live, but to live aright." — "The unexamined life isn't worth living." — Socrates

"There are two things to aim at in life: first, to get what you want; and, after that, to enjoy it. Only the wisest of mankind achieve the second." — Logan Pearsall Smith

"The longer I live, the more beautiful life becomes." — Frank Lloyd Wright

"Life's journey is the reward." — Chinese proverb

"People for the sake of getting a living forget to live." — Margaret Fuller

"There is more to life than increasing its speed." — Gandhi

"We are here to add what we can to, not to get what we can from, life." — Sir William Osler

"The most important things in life aren't things." — Anonymous

"What is important in life is life, and not the result of life." — Goethe

"Life is not so much a matter of position as of disposition." — Andrew Carnegie

"There are two ways to live your life. One is as though nothing is a miracle. The other is as though everything is a miracle." — Einstein

"Plunge boldly into the thick of yearning." — Anonymous

"It's a funny thing about life; if you refuse to accept anything but the best, you very often get it." — W. Somerset Maugham

"The mass of men lead lives of quiet desperation and go to the grave with the song still in them." — "Our life is frittered away by detail . . . .Simplify, simplify." — Thoreau

"Here is a test to see if your mission on earth is finished. If you are alive, it isn't." — "Choose the life that is most useful, and habit will make it the most agreeable." — Sir Francis Bacon

"Man lives by habits, indeed, but what he lives for is thrills and excitements." — William James

"Life is a game of cards. The hand you are dealt is determinism; the way you play it is free will." — Nehru

"With most people life is like backgammon — half skill and half luck." — Oliver Wendell Holmes

"Life is like a play! It's not the length, but the excellence of the acting that matters." — "While we are postponing, life speeds by." — Seneca

"Life is what happens to us while we are making others plans." — Thomas La Mance

"Love to live, and live to love." — English proverb

"Yes, that's right . . . love should come before logic . . . Only then will man come to understand the meaning of life." — Fyodor Dostoevsky

"That life is worth living is the most necessary of assumptions, and were it not assumed, the most impossible of conclusions." — Santayana

"Life can only be understood backwards; but it must be lived forwards." — Soren Kierkegaard

"Change is the law of life. And those who look only to the past or present are certain to miss the future." — John F. Kennedy

"Learn from yesterday, live for today, hope for tomorrow." — Anonymous

"Nothing is beneath you if it is in the direction of your life." — "Life is a succession of lessons which must be lived to be understood." — Emerson

"The life so short, the craft so long to learn." — Hippocrates

"Life is the art of drawing sufficient conclusions from insufficient premises." — Samuel Butler

"Life is really simple, but we insist on making it complicated." — Confucius

"To the wise, life is a solution; to the fool, a problem." — Martial

"Life is 'trying things to see if they work.'" Ray Bradbury

"Such is life — seven times down, eight times up!" Japanese proverb

"Almost every man wastes part of his life in attempts to display qualifications which he does not possess." — "It matters not how a man dies, but how he lives." — Samuel Johnson

"Live your own life, for you will die your own death." — "Let us live while we live." — Latin proverbs

"And in the end, it is not the years in your life that count. It's the life in your years." — Abraham Lincoln

"A long life may not be good enough, but a good life is long enough." — Benjamin Franklin

"Live as if you expected to live forever; live as if you were to die tomorrow." — Algerian proverb

"The art of living well and the art of dying well are one." — Epicurus

"It is nothing to die; it is frightful not to live." — Victor Hugo

"So live your life that the fear of death can never enter your heart." — Wabasha Indian proverb

"Do not act as if you had a thousand years to live." — Marcus Aurelius

"Manage all your actions, words, and thoughts accordingly, since you can at any moment quit life." — Far Eastern saying

"No one at all can be living forever, and we must be satisfied." — John Millington Synge

"The surest test if a man be sane is if he accepts life whole, as it is." — Lao-tse

"If existence had not been better than non-existence, there would have been no being." — Kahlil Gibran

"Life is life and without it we would be dead." — Milton

"Do not take life too seriously. You will never get out of it alive." — "The best way to prepare for life is to begin to live." — Elbert Hubbard

"Live your life and forget your age." — Vincent Norman Peale

"In three words I can sum up everything I've learned about life: It goes on." — Robert Frost

"Life is a bridge; enjoy while crossing, but don't build a castle upon it." — The Upanishads

"The whole life of a man is but a point of time; let us enjoy it, therefore, while it lasts, and not spend it to no purpose." — Plutarch

"He who has a why for which to live can bear with almost any how." — "Is not life a hundred times too short for us to bore ourselves?" Nietzsche

"We are so engaged in doing things to achieve purposes of outer value that we forget that the inner value, the rapture that is associated with being alive, is what it's all about." — Joseph Campbell

"The proper function of man is to live, not exist." Jack London

"Joys are not the property of the rich alone: nor has a man lived ill, who at his birth and at his death has passed unnoticed." — Horace

"The mere sense of living is joy enough." — "I shall not live in vain if I can ease one life the aching or cool one pain." — Emily Dickinson

"He who saves one life saves the world entire." — The Talmud

"May you live your life as if the maxim of your actions were to become universal law." — Immanuel Kant

"Man did not weave the web of life: he is merely a strand in it. Whatever he does to the web, he does to himself." — Chief Seattle

"How far you go in life depends on your being tender with the young, compassionate with the aged, sympathetic with the striving and tolerant of the weak and strong. Because someday in your life you will have been all of these." — George Washington Carver

"Every one desires to live long, but no one would be old." — "May you live all the days of your life." — Jonathan Swift

Life as a Journey

"The purpose is not the end, but the journey." — Old proverb

"The journey of a thousand leagues begins with a single step." — Lao-tse

"The distance is nothing; it is only the first step which counts." — Madame du Deffand

"What is the use of running when we are not on the right road?" German proverb

"If we don't change our direction, we are likely to wind up where we are headed." — Chinese proverb

"If you are reluctant to ask the way, you will be lost." — Malay proverb

"Better ask twice than lose your way once." — Danish proverb

"Every road has two directions." — Russian proverb

"It is a long road that has no turning." — Irish proverb

"If you don't know where you are going, any road will get you there." — Lewis Carroll

"A man without convictions is a tramp on the road that leads to the land of nowhere." — Evangelist

"The people who make no roads are ruled out from intelligent participation in the world's brotherhood." — Michael Fairless

"I have become better acquainted with the country from having had the good luck sometimes to lose my way." — Horne Tooke

"Two roads diverged in a wood and I — I took the one less traveled by, and that has made all the difference." — Robert Frost

"One who walks in another's tracks leaves no footprints." — Old proverb

"Do not go where the path may lead: go instead where there is no path and leave a trail." — Emerson

"We will be known forever by the tracks we leave." — Native American proverb

"A man should learn to sail in all winds." — Italian proverb

"Vessels large may venture more, but little boats should keep near shore." — Benjamin Franklin

"One doesn't discover new lands without consenting to lose sight of the shore for a very long time." — André Gide

"If one wishes to be sure of the road he treads on, he must close his eyes and walk in the dark." — St. John

"Before people can come to Utopia, they must learn the way there." — H. G. Wells

"I am going in search of the great perhaps." — Rabelais

"Strong and content I travel the open road." — Whitman

"The soul of a journey is liberty, perfect liberty, to think, feel, and do just as one pleases." — William Hazlitt

"A rolling stone gathers no moss." — Publilius Syrus

"He who travels much, knows much." — Thomas Fuller

"Better one safe way than a hundred on which you cannot reckon." — Aesop

"The middle path is the safe path." — German proverb

"Don't cross the bridge until you have come to it." — Old proverb

"Every path has its puddle." — English proverb

"The path is smooth that leadeth on to danger." — Shakespeare

"The last mile is always the hardest." — Old proverb

"He who is outside his door has the hardest part of his journey behind him." — Dutch proverb

"Who travels for love finds a thousand miles not longer than one." — Japanese proverb

"Who walks a road with love will never walk that road alone again." — Charles Thomas Davis

"Pursue some path, however narrow and crooked, in which you can walk with love and reverence." — Thoreau

"There is the path of fear and the path of love. Which will you follow?" Buddha

"A traveler without observation is a bird without wings." — Far Eastern saying

"They change their climate, not their disposition or soul, who run beyond the sea." — Horace

"Keep out of ruts; a rut is something which if traveled in too much, becomes a ditch." — Arthur Guiterman

"They are short-sighted who look only on the path they tread." — Kahlil Gibran

"To go beyond is as wrong as to fall short." — Confucius

"There are many paths to the top of the mountain, but the view is the same once you get there." — Hawaiian proverb

"The map is not the territory." — Alfred Korzbyski

"There is a great deal of unmapped country within us." — George Eliot

"There is only one journey. Going inside yourself." — Rainer Maria Rilke

"No man ever steps in the same river twice, for it's not the same river and he is not the same man." — Heraclitus

"A man travels the world over in search of what he needs and returns home to find it." — George Moore

"And the end of all our exploring will be to arrive where we started and know the place for the first time." — T. S. Eliot

Self Discovery

"Self-preservation is the first law of nature." — Donne

"Self-love is the instrument of our preservation." — Voltaire

"Self-defense is nature's eldest law." — John Dryden

"Self-reflection is the school of wisdom." — Baltasar Gracian

"Self-knowledge is an everlasting task." — Christopher Harvey

"Be so true to thyself as thou be not false to others." — Sir Francis Bacon

"Know Thyself." — Solon

"'Know thyself' means this, that you get acquainted with what you know, and what you can do." — Menander of Athens

"Know thyself? If I knew myself, I'd run away." — Goethe

"I know all save myself alone." — François Villon

"Many men are wise about many things, and ignorant about themselves." — St. Bernard

"They are most cheated who cheat themselves." — Old proverb

"One is a fool that praises himself, and one is mad who speaks ill of himself." — Danish proverb

"A man who finds no satisfaction in himself seeks for it in vain elsewhere." — La Rochefoucauld

"We carry with us the wonders we seek without us." — Sir Thomas Browne

"The supreme fall of falls is this, the first doubt of one's self." — Comtesse de Gasparin

"There are three Things extremely hard; Steel, a Diamond, and to know one's self." — Benjamin Franklin

"One's own self is the most difficult to master." — Far Eastern saying

"Nothing is so difficult as not deceiving oneself." — Wittgenstein

"There is no man so low down that the cure for his condition does not lie strictly within himself." — Thomas Lansing Masson

"No man is the worse for knowing the worst of himself." — "Drown not thyself to save a drowning man." — Thomas Fuller

"You must take the beam from your eye before you can see well enough to remove the splinter from your brother's." — Bible, Matthew 7:3

"There is always someone worse off than yourself." — Aesop

"You are only what you are when no one is looking." — Robert Edwards

"We are what we pretend to be, so we must be careful what we pretend to be." — Kurt Vonnegut, Jr.

"Seem, as you are, yourself . . . be, as you seem to be." — Mevlana

"To know oneself, one should assert oneself." — Albert Camus

"First say to yourself what you would be; and then do what you have to do." — Epictetus

"Resolve to be thyself: and know that he who finds himself loses his misery." — Matthew Arnold

"I propose to show my fellow-mortals a man in all the integrity of nature; and this man shall be myself." — Rousseau

"I have made myself what I am." — Tecumseh

"You've got to do your own growing, no matter how tall your grandfather was." — Irish proverb

"They who know themselves best esteem themselves the least." — "A man must have a just esteem of himself without being proud." — Old proverbs

"The greatest thing in the world is to know how to belong to oneself." — Montaigne

"What others say of me matters little, what I myself say and do matters much." — Elbert Hubbard

"Don't bother just to be better than your contemporaries or predecessors. Try to be better than yourself." — William Yeats

"There is nothing noble about being superior to some other man. The true nobility is in being superior to your previous self." — Hindustani proverb

"Observe thyself as thy greatest enemy would do, so shalt thou be thy greatest friend." — Jeremy Taylor

"I am grateful to those who, by their opposition, often help me to remain true to myself." — Jean Rostand

"Everything that irritates us about others can lead us to an understanding of ourselves." — Carl Jung

"When we see men of a contrary character, we should turn inwards and examine ourselves." — Confucius

"What you see in yourself is what you see in the world." — Afghan proverb

"It takes courage to grow-up and become who you really are." — e. e. cummings

"If you want good service, serve yourself." — Spanish proverb

"Of all mankind, each loves himself the best." — Terence

"In one thing people of all ages are alike; they have believed obstinately in themselves." — Friedrich Jacobi

"The inner self never stops caressing itself." — Anonymous

"Borrow from yourself." — Cato

"Never trouble another for what you can do yourself." — Thomas Jefferson

"A man who lives only for himself is truly dead to others." — Publilius Syrus

"None of us liveth to himself." — Bible, Romans 14:7

"People seldom improve when they have no model but themselves to copy after." — Oliver Goldsmith

"The most amiable men are those who least wound the self-love of others." — Jean de La Bruyère

"Who knows himself knows others." — Chinese proverb

"One may understand the cosmos, but never the ego; the self is more distant than any star." — G. K. Chesterton

"When everything is known as the Self, not even an atom is seen as other than the Self." — Shankara

"There is little that can withstand a man who can conquer himself." — Louis XIV

"Better to conquer yourself than to conquer thousands in battle." — Buddha

"Let they that would move the world first move themselves." — Socrates

"Above all things, reverence yourself." — "No man is free who cannot command himself." — Pythagoras

"Most powerful is he who has himself in his own power." — Seneca

"Lord of oneself, though not of lands; and having nothing, yet hath all." — Sir Henry Wotton

"There's only one corner of the universe you can be certain of improving, and that's your own self." — Aldous Huxley

"If you seek to understand the whole universe, you will understand nothing at all. If you seek only to understand yourself, you will understand the whole universe." — Native American proverb

"To thy own self be true . . . Then to all others, you will be too." — "Self-love is not so vile a sin as self-neglect." — Shakespeare

"It is as hard to see one's self as to look backwards without turning around." — "What lies behind us and what lies ahead of us are tiny matters compared to what lives within us." — Thoreau

"So much is a man worth as he esteems himself." — "How shall I be able to rule over others, and not have full power and command of myself?" Rabelais

"One who knows others is learned; One who knows himself is wise." — "If I keep from imposing on people, they become themselves." — "Conquering others requires force. Conquering oneself requires strength." — Lao-tse

"The precept, 'Know yourself,' was not solely intended to obviate the pride of mankind; but likewise that we might understand our own worth." — Cicero

"The man who makes everything that leads to happiness depend upon himself, and not upon others, has adopted the very best plan for living happily." — Plato

"When you come right down to it, all you have is your self. Your self is a sun with a thousand rays in your belly. The rest is nothing." — Picasso

"That kind of life is most happy which affords us most opportunities of gaining our own self-esteem." — "Self-confidence is the first requisite to great undertakings." — Samuel Johnson

"Your self consists of two selves; one imagines that it knows himself and the other that the people know him." — Kahlil Gibran

"Remember, you cannot abandon what you do not know. To go beyond yourself, you must know yourself." — Sri Nisargadatta Maharaj

"No conflict is so severe as his who labors to subdue himself." — "Be not angry that

you cannot make others as you wish them to be, since you cannot make yourself
as you wish to be." — Thomas à Kempis

"We cannot forgive another for not being ourselves." — "Wherever we go, whatever
we do, self is the sole subject we study and learn." — "Make the most of
yourself, for that is all there is of you." — Emerson

"Remember who you are." — Lewis Carroll

Purpose

"The secret of success is constancy to purpose." — Disraeli

"Always place a definite purpose before thee." — Thomas à Kempis

"A place for everything, everything in its place." — "Let us then be up and doing, and
doing to the purpose." — Benjamin Franklin

"They too serve a certain purpose who only stand and cheer." — Henry Adams

"This is the true joy in life, the being used for a purpose recognized by yourself as a
mighty one." — George Bernard Shaw

"Great minds have purposes, others have wishes." — Washington Irving

"Do not miss the purpose of this life, and do not wait for circumstance to mold or
change your fate." — Ella Wheeler Wilcox

"The greatest work has always gone hand in hand with the most fervent moral
purpose." — Sidney Lanier

"Man would sooner have the void for his purpose than be void of purpose." —
Nietzsche

"Lack of something to feel important about is almost the greatest tragedy a man may
have." — Arthur Morgan

"We know what we are, but know not what we may be." — Shakespeare

"Nothing is so terrible than activity without insight." — Carlyle

"Everyone excels in something in which another fails." — Publilius Syrus

"Accomplishment of purpose is better than making a profit." — Hausa proverb

"There is a purpose for everything that happens in life." — Old proverb

"As far as we can discern, the sole purpose of human existence is to kindle a light in
the darkness of mere being." — Carl Jung

"The purpose of life seems to be to acquaint a man with himself." — Emerson

"Let every man abide in the same calling wherein he is called." — Bible, I Corinthians
7:20

"All things — and I mean all things — have their own will and their own purpose;
this is what is to be respected." — "Every being has an identity and a purpose.
To live up to his purpose, every being has the power of self-control, and that's
where spiritual power begins." — Rolling Thunder

"Fortunate is the man who has developed the self-control to steer a straight course
toward his objective in life, without being swayed from his purpose by either
commendation or condemnation." — Napoleon Hill

"Many men have the wrong idea about what constitutes true happiness. It is not attained through self-gratification but through fidelity to a worthy purpose." — Helen Keller

Cause

"In a just cause the weak will beat the strong." — Sophocles

"Everything is the cause of itself." — Emerson

"A man is a lion in his own cause." — Scottish proverb

"Happy the soul who has been able to understand the causes of things." — Virgil

"The best cause requires a good pleader." — Dutch proverb

"I assert that nothing ever comes to pass without a cause." — Jonathan Edwards

"The probability that we may fail in the struggle ought not to deter us from the support of a cause we believe to be just." — Abraham Lincoln

"No man is worth his salt who is not ready at all times to risk his body, to risk his well-being, to risk his life, in a great cause." — Theodore Roosevelt

CHARACTER

"Character is Destiny." — "A man's character is his guardian divinity." — Heraclitus

"Character is the basis of happiness and happiness the sanction of character." — Santayana

"Character is the result of two things: Mental attitude and the way we spend our time." — Elbert Hubbard

"Character is the governing element of life, and is above genius." — Frederick Saunders

"Character is made by what you stand for; reputation by what you fall for." — Alexander Woollcott

"Character and personal force are the only investments that are worth anything." — Whitman

"Character must be kept bright, as well as clean." — Lord Chesterfield

"Characters do not change. Opinions alter, but characters are only developed." — Disraeli

"Character building begins in our infancy and continues until death." — Eleanor Roosevelt

"A character is a perfectly formed will." — Novalis

"A lost wife can be replaced, but the loss of character spells ruin." — Malay proverb

"A man who makes character makes foes." — Edward Young

"A man's character always takes its hue, more or less, from the form and color of things about him." — Frederick Douglass

"Every man is the architect of his own character." — George Boardman

"You cannot dream yourself into a character; you must hammer and forge one for yourself." — James Froude

"By constant self-discipline and self-control you can develop greatness of character." — Grenville Kleiser

"Simplicity of character is no hindrance to subtlety of intellect." — John Viscount Morley

"Not education, but character, is a man's greatest need and a man's greatest safeguard." — Herbert Spencer

"Society affects to estimate men by their talents, but really feels and knows them by their character." — Thoreau

"There is nothing so fatal to character as a half-finished task." — David George

"Weakness of character is the only defect which cannot be amended." — La Rochefoucauld

"No man can climb out beyond the limitations of his own character." — John Morley

"A man who damages the character of another damages his own." — African proverb

"A man of character will make himself worthy of any position he is given." — Gandhi

"A man's character is the arbiter of every man's fortune." — Publilius Syrus

"It is not what one has, or even what one does, which expresses the worth of a man, but what he is." — Henri Amiel

"Our character is but the stamp on our souls of the free choices of good and evil we have made through life." — John Geikie

"Only what we have wrought into our character during life can we take away with us." — Baron Alexander von Humboldt

"Character is like a tree and reputation is like its shadow. The shadow is what we think of it; the tree is the real thing." — Abraham Lincoln

"Character is higher than intellect." — "Men of character are the conscience of the society to which they belong." — "No change of circumstances can repair a defect of character." — Emerson

"Character is much easier kept than recovered." — "Reputation is what men and women think of us; character is what God and angels know of us." — Thomas Paine

"Character cannot be developed in ease and quiet. Only through experience of trial and suffering can the soul be strengthened, vision cleared, ambition inspired, and success achieved." — Helen Keller

"Character is simply habit long continued." — "Of two who made love to his daughter, he preferred the man of worth to the one who was rich, saying he desired a man without riches, rather than riches without a man." — Plutarch

"Character is doubtless of far more importance than mere intellectual opinion." — "If I take care of my character, my reputation will take care of itself." — Dwight Moody

"Character may almost be called the most effective means of persuasion." — "Our characters are the result of our conduct." — Aristotle

"Character is built out of circumstances. From exactly the same material one man builds palaces, while another man builds hovels." — George Lewes

"Character is in oneself; the reputation others have of you is their opinions." — "Happiness is not the end of life: character is." — Henry Ward Beecher

"A man's character never changes radically from youth to old age. What happens is that circumstances bring out characteristics which have not been obvious to the superficial observer." — Hesketh Pearson

"It is not money, nor is it mere intellect, that governs the world; it is moral character, and intellect associated with moral excellence." — Theodore Woolsey

"Talents are best nurtured in solitude; character is best formed in the stormy billows of the world." — "There is nothing by which men display their character so much as in what they consider ridiculous or laugh at." — Goethe

"You can tell the character of every man when you see how he receives praise." — "There is the need for someone against which our characters can measure themselves. Without a ruler, you won't make the crooked straight." — Seneca

"I shall not evaluate men by their fortunes, but by their moral character. Everyone gives himself his own moral character; status is assigned by chance." — Macrobius

"There are three marks of a superior man: being virtuous, one is free from anxiety; being wise, one is free from perplexity; being brave, one is free from fear." — Confucius

Honor

"Honor is purchased by the deeds we do; Honor is not won until some honorable deed be done." — Christopher Marlowe

"Honor and ease are seldom bedfellows." — John Clarke

"A prophet is not without honor, save in his own country." — Bible, Matthew 8:57

"Honors change manners." — Virgil

"Act well your part, there all the honor lies." — Alexander Pope

"The shortest and surest way to live with honor in the world, is to be in reality what we would appear to be." — Socrates

"It is better to deserve honors and not have them than to have them and not deserve them." — Mark Twain

"True honor is acquired by nothing but good conduct." — Sir Richard Steele

"What is fitting is honorable, and what is honorable is fitting." — Cicero

"What is most honorable is also safest." — Livy

"No amount of ability is of the slightest avail without honor." — "All honor's wounds are self-inflicted." — Andrew Carnegie

"It is the fashion to seek honor for disgraceful conduct." — Plautus

"The louder they talked of their honor, the faster we counted our spoons." — Emerson

"The most tragic thing in the world is a man of genius who is not a man of honor." — George Bernard Shaw

"A man that desires honor is not worthy of honor." — William Secker

"It is a worthier thing to deserve honor than to possess it." — Thomas Fuller

"The honor we receive from those that fear us is not honor; those respects are paid to royalty and not to me." — Montaigne

"No cost is too heavy for the preservation of one's honor." — Gandhi

"In a large sense we cannot dedicate, we cannot hallow this ground. The brave men, living and dead, who struggled here, have consecrated it far above our poor power to add or detract." — Abraham Lincoln

"Better to die ten thousand deaths than wound my honor." — Joseph Addison

"My honor is dearer to me than my life." — Cervantes

"Seek Honor first, and Pleasure lies behind." — Thomas Chatterton

"Pleasures are mortal, honors immortal." — Periander

"Let honor be to us as strong an obligation as necessity is to others." — Pliny the Elder

"The love of honor alone is untouched by age." — Thucydides

"What is left when honor is lost?" Publilius Syrus

"Leave not a stain in thine honor." — Apocrypha, Ecclesiasticus 33:22

"Nobody can acquire honor by doing what is wrong." — Thomas Jefferson

"Be noble! Our own heart, and not other men's opinions forms our true honor." — "No man was ever honored for what he received, but for what he gave." — Samuel Coleridge

"Mine honor is my life; both grow in one; take honor from me and my life is done." — "See that you come not to woo honor, but to wed it." — Shakespeare

"Who is honored? One who honors others." — The Talmud

"Honor all men." — Bible, I Peter 2:17

Virtue

"Virtue is the truest nobility." — Cervantes

"Virtue is its own reward." — Ovid

"Virtue is a like a rich stone, best plain set." — Sir Francis Bacon

"Virtue is fairer far than beauty." — English proverb

"Virtue is the performance of pleasant actions." — James Stephens

"Virtue was sufficient of herself for happiness." — Diogenes Laertius

"Virtue consists in action." — Old proverb

"Virtue alone is the unerring sign of a noble soul." — Nicolas Boileau-Despreaux

"Virtue debases itself in justifying itself." — "Men are equal; it is not birth but virtue that makes the difference." — Voltaire

"Virtue never dwells alone; it always has neighbors." — Chinese proverb

"Virtue has many preachers, but few martyrs." — Claude Helvetius

"Virtue consists not in abstaining from vice, but in not desiring it." — George Bernard Shaw

"Virtue and riches seldom settle on one man." — Machiavelli

"Virtues are virtues only to those who can appreciate them." — Panchatantra

"Virtue is certainly the most noble and secure possession a man can have." — Richard Savage

"Recommend to your children virtue; that alone can make them happy, not gold." — Ludwig van Beethoven

"And virtue, though in rags, will keep me warm." — John Dryden

"There never was yet a truly great man that was not at the same time truly virtuous." — Benjamin Franklin

"All virtue is summed up in dealing justly." — Aristotle

"Few men have virtue to withstand the highest bidder." — George Washington

"The highest proof of virtue is to possess boundless power without abusing it." — Lord Macaulay

"There are virtues which become crimes by exaggeration." — Alexandre Dumas the Elder

"We should cease to grow the moment we cease to discriminate between virtue and vice." — Gandhi

"To flee vice is the beginning of virtue." — Horace

"There is much vice and misery in the world, I know; but more virtue and happiness, I believe." — Thomas Jefferson

"To be innocent is to be not guilty; but to be virtuous is to overcome our evil feelings and intentions." — William Penn

"I always admired virtue — but I could never imitate it." — Charles II

"No virtue is safe that is not enthusiastic." — Sir John Seeley

"Who follows not virtue in youth cannot fly sin in old age." — Italian proverb

"There is no road or ready way to virtue." — Sir Thomas Browne

"Always, in times of stress, it is the simple virtues that really count." — John Winant

"The virtue lies in the struggle, not in the prize." — Richard Milnes

"Silver and gold are not the only coin; virtue too passes current all over the world." — Euripides

"If you can be well without health, you may be happy without virtue." — Edmund Burke

"Even virtue followed beyond reason's rule may stamp the just man knave, the sage a fool." — Horace

"Moderation is the greatest virtue." — Cleobulus

"Birth is nothing where virtue is not." — Molière

"The origin of all men is the same and virtue is the only nobility." — Seneca

"In all circumstances, try to cultivate virtue." — Buddha

"If it be usual to be strongly impressed by things that are scarce, why are we so little impressed by virtue?" La Bruyère

"The most virtuous of all men is he that contents himself with being virtuous without seeking to appear so." — Plato

"Many wish not so much to be virtuous, as to seem to be." — "The existence of virtue depends entirely upon its use." — Cicero

"It is in virtue that happiness consists, for virtue is the state of mind which tends to make the whole of life harmonious." — Zeno

"Virtue is bold, and goodness never fearful." — "Our virtues lie in the interpretation of the time." — "We rarely like the virtues we have not." — "Virtue itself turns vice, being misapplied." — Shakespeare

"Virtue is not to be considered in the light of mere innocence, or abstaining from harm; but as the exertion of our faculties in doing good." — Joseph Butler

"Virtue is action in accord with the laws of man's own nature." — "Blessedness is not the reward of virtue but virtue itself." — Spinoza

"Virtue is a state of war, and to live in it we have always to combat with ourselves." — Rousseau

"Virtue requires a rough and stormy passage; she will have either outward difficulties to wrestle with, or internal difficulties." — Montaigne

"Virtue is not given by money, but that from virtue comes money and every other good of a man, public as well as private." — "All human virtues increase and strengthen themselves by the practice and experience of them." — Socrates

"To be able under all circumstances to practice five things constitutes perfect virtue; these five are gravity, generosity of soul, sincerity, earnestness, and kindness." — "The superior man thinks always of virtue; the common man thinks of comfort." — Confucius

"The simple virtues of willingness, readiness, alertness and courtesy will carry a young man farther than mere smartness." — Henry Davison

"The virtuous man cannot be hurt, the misery that his enemy would inflict comes back on them." — "The path of virtue lies in the renunciation of arrogance and pride." — "The best policy for a man is not to boast of his virtues." — Far Eastern sayings

"What is a weed? A plant whose virtues have not yet been discovered." — "The only reward of virtue is virtue." — "The less a man thinks or knows about his virtues the better we like him." — Emerson

"The virtue of a man ought to be measured not by his extraordinary exertions, but by his everyday conduct." — Pascal

The Noble Spirit

"Nobility is the one and only virtue." — Juvenal

"Virtue is the first title of nobility." — Molière

"Dignity and nobility does not consist in possessing honors, but in deserving them." — Aristotle

"It is not wealth, nor ancestry, but honorable conduct and a noble disposition that make men great." — Ovid

"Put more trust in nobility of character than in an oath." — Solon

"If a man be endued with a generous mind, this is the best kind of nobility." — Plato

"The nobler a man, the harder it is for him to suspect inferiority in others." — Cicero

"Truly noble and resolved spirit raises itself; and becomes more conspicuous in times of disaster and ill fortune." — Plutarch

"Let one nobly live or nobly die." — Sophocles

"True nobility is exempt from fear." — "Sweet mercy is nobility's true badge." — Shakespeare

"It is better to be nobly remembered than nobly born." — John Ruskin

"The aids to noble life are all within." — M. Arnold

"True nobility is invulnerable." — Old proverb

"He who requires urging to do a noble act will never accomplish it." — Kahlil Gibran

"Every noble work is at first impossible." — Carlyle

"Every noble activity makes room for itself." — Emerson

"The greatest word in any language is nobility." — Buddha

"He who is lord of himself, and exists upon his own resources, is a noble but a rare being." — Sir Samuel Brydges

"I long to accomplish a great and noble task, but it is my chief duty to accomplish small tasks as if they were great and noble." — Helen Keller

"One hour of life, crowded to the full with glorious action, and filled with noble risks, is worth whole years of those mean observances of paltry decorum." — Sir Walter Scott

"A tragic situation exists precisely when virtue does not triumph but when it is still felt that a man is nobler than the forces which destroy him." — George Orwell

"Men do not care how nobly they live, but only how long, although it is within the reach of everyone to live nobly, but within no man's power to live long." — Seneca

Morality

"Morality is the basis of things and truth is the substance of all morality." — Gandhi

"Morality is religion in practice; religion is morality in principle." — Wardlaw

"Morality knows nothing of geographical boundaries or distinctions of race." — Herbert Spencer

"Morality is the best of all devices for leading mankind by the nose." — Nietzsche

"Everything has got a moral, if only you can find it." — Lewis Carroll

"Void of purity in morals, faith is but a hypocrite of words." — Martin Tupper

"Without consistency there is no moral strength." — John Owen

"A straight line is the shortest in morals as in mathematics." — Maria Edgeworth

"I shall endeavor to enliven morality with wit, and to temper wit with morality." — Joseph Addison

"True eloquence takes no heed of eloquence, true morality takes no heed of morality." — Pascal

"Men committing acts in obedience to law or habit are not being moral." — Wystan Auden

"What is moral is what you feel good after and what is immoral is what you feel bad after." — Ernest Hemingway

"In matters of prudence, last thoughts are best; in matters of morality, first thoughts." — Robert Hall

"Learn what a people glory in, and you may learn much of both the theory and practice of their morals." — James Martineau

"The success of any great moral enterprise does not depend upon numbers." — William Garrison

"The greatest secret of morals is love." — Shelley

"Only morality in our actions can give beauty and dignity to life." — Einstein

"It is difficult to moralize about any matter, as ideas of conventional morality differ from age to age and country to country." — Nehru

"Moral qualities rule the world, but at short distances the senses are despotic." — "There can be no high civility without a deep morality." — Emerson

Conscience

"Conscience is a man's compass." — Vincent van Gogh

"Conscience is the inner voice which warns us that someone may be looking." — H. L. Mencken

"Conscience is the nest where all good is hatched." — Welsh proverb

"Conscience is the root of all true courage; if a man would be brave, let him obey his conscience." — James Freeman Clarke

"Conscience without judgment is superstition." — Benjamin Whichcote

"Conscience is the voice of the soul; the passions of the body." — Rousseau

"A clear conscience is far more valuable than money." — Philippine proverb

"A clear conscience and the respect of one's fellow citizens are still worth striving for." — Anonymous

"A clear conscience can bear any trouble." — Old proverb

"A clear conscience never fears midnight knocking." — Chinese proverb

"A clear conscience is a soft pillow." — German proverb

"A quiet conscience sleeps in thunder." — English proverb

"A good conscience is a choice companion." — Old proverb

"We cannot live better than in seeking to become better, nor more agreeably than in having a clear conscience." — Socrates

"The foundation of true joy is in the conscience." — "The conscience of well-doing is an ample reward." — Seneca

"A man of integrity will never listen to any plea against conscience." — Henry Home

"It is neither safe nor prudent to do aught against conscience." — Martin Luther

"Never do anything against conscience, even if the state demands it." — Einstein

"The worst man is least troubled by his conscience." — A. Maclaren

"He that loses his conscience has nothing left that is worth keeping." — Coussin

"Nothing is more wretched than the mind of one conscious of guilt." — Plautus

"A guilty conscience is a hidden enemy." — Hindu proverb

"He who sacrifices his conscience to ambition burns a picture to obtain the ashes." — Chinese proverb

"There is no witness so terrible — no accuser so powerful as conscience which dwells within us." — Sophocles

"What we call conscience, is, in many instances, only a wholesome fear of the police." — Christian Bovee

"Let their tormentor conscience find them out." — Milton

"My dominion ends where that of conscience begins." — Napoleon

"Put your hand in your conscience and see if it does not come out as black as pitch." — Dutch proverb

"If simple conscience rest content, thy livelihood is lawful." — Martin Tupper

"The man who acts never has any conscience; no one has any conscience but the man who thinks." — Goethe

"Trust that man in nothing who has not a conscience in everything." — Laurence Sterne

"Endeavor to keep alive in your breast that spark of heavenly fire called conscience." — George Washington

"Conscience is the voice of the soul, as the passions are the voice of the body. No wonder they often contradict each other." — Rousseau

"An evil conscience breaks many a men's neck." — "A guilty conscience never thinketh itself safe." — "A good conscience is the best divinity." — Thomas Fuller

"Of a truth, knowledge is power, but it is a power reined by scruple, having a conscience of what must be and what may be." — George Eliot

"A guilty conscience never feels secure." — "A scar on the conscience is the same as a wound." — "Even when there is no law, there is conscience." — Publilius Syrus

"One will easily be content and at peace, whose conscience is pure." — "An evil conscience is always fearful and unquiet." — "The glory of the good is in their consciences." — Thomas à Kempis

Principles

"Principle is a passion for truth and right." — Hazlitt

"Nothing can bring you peace but the triumph of principles." — Emerson

"Back of every noble life there are principles which have fashioned it." — George Lorimer

"One may be better than his reputation, but never better than his principles." — Nicolas de Latena

"People of principle may be the principal people." — Old proverb

"Every principle contains in itself the germs of a prophecy." — S. T. Coleridge

"Do not be sick or despairing if you do not always succeed in acting from right principles." — Marcus Aurelius

"Expedients are for the hour; principles for the ages." — Henry Ward Beecher

"If you don't stand for something, you will fall for something." — African proverb

"We must be prepared to displease the dearest ones for the sake of principle." — Gandhi

"Everywhere the basis of principle is tradition." — Oliver Wendell Holmes, Jr.

"Independence of principle consists in having no principle on which to depend." — C. C. Colton

"No single principle can answer all of life's complexities." — Felix Frankfurter

"Important principles may and must be flexible." — Abraham Lincoln

"It is not talking nonsense that offends, but talking it in the name of principles." — Jean Rostand

"Principles can not mainly influence even the principled; we talk on principle, but we act on interest." — W. S. Landor

"It is easier to fight for one's principles than to live up to them." — Alfred Adler

"We lament the mistakes of a good man, and do not begin to detest him until he affects to renounce his principles." — Junius

"The deepest principle in human nature is the craving to be appreciated." — "As-if principle: If you want a quality, act as if you already had it." — William James

"Our principles are the springs of our actions; our actions, the springs of our happiness or misery." — Philip Skelton

"One who merely knows right principles is not equal to those who love them." — "Men of principle are sure to be bold, but those who are bold may not always be men of principle." — Confucius

Honesty

"Honesty is the first chapter in the book of wisdom." — Thomas Jefferson

"Honesty is the best policy." — "The bird that is not honest foulest its own nest." — English proverbs

"Honesty is exact to a penny." — "Honesty in little things is not a little thing." — Old proverbs

"Honesty's praised, then left to starve." — Juvenal

"What is dignity without honesty?" Cicero

"No legacy is so rich as honesty." — Shakespeare

"A man is not honest, simply because he never had a chance to steal." — Hebrew proverb

"Make yourself an honest man, and then you may be sure that there is one less rascal in the world." — Carlyle

"An honest man is not the worse because a dog barks at him." — Old proverb

"No one believes the sincere except the honest." — Kahlil Gibran

"Of all crafts, to be an honest man is the master-craft." — Old proverb

"An honest man's word is as good as his bond." — Cervantes

"The best standard by which to judge the honesty of nations as well as people is whether they keep their word." — Schwellenbach

"I hope I shall always possess firmness and virtue enough to maintain what I consider the most enviable of all titles, the character of an honest man." — George Washington

Humility

"Humility is the solid foundation of all the virtues." — Confucius

"Humility is a virtue all preach, none practice; and yet everybody is content to hear." — John Selden

"Humility is the most difficult of all virtues to achieve; nothing dies harder than the desire to think well of oneself." — T. S. Eliot

"Humility is the surest sign of strength." — Thomas Merton

"Humility, that low, sweet root from which all heavenly virtues shoot." — Thomas Moore

"Humility, like darkness, reveals the heavenly lights." — Thoreau

"Life is a long lesson in humility." — Sir James Matthew Barrie

"Before honor is humility." — Bible, Proverbs 15:33

"Without humility there can be no humanity." — Sir John Buchan

"After crosses and losses men grow humbler and wiser." — Benjamin Franklin

"Appear always what you are and a little less." — Greek proverb

"Aim high in your career but stay humble in your heart." — Korean proverb

"The loftiest towers rise from the ground." — Chinese proverb

"The sun will set without thy assistance." — The Talmud

"And whosoever exalt himself shall be humbled; and he that shall humble himself shall be exalted." — Bible, Matthew 23:12

"Be humble if thou wouldst attain to Wisdom." — Old proverb

"We come nearest to the great when we are great in humility." — Rabindranath Tagore

"The first test of a truly great man is his humility." — John Ruskin

"Do nothing from selfishness or conceit but in humility count others better than yourselves." — Bible, Philippians 2:3

"Too humble is half proud." — Hebrew proverb

"One may be humble out of pride." — Montaigne

"It was pride that changed angels into devils; it is humility that makes men as angels." — Augustine of Hippo

"Sense shines with a double luster when set in humility." — William Penn

"Be utterly humble and you shall hold to the foundation of peace." — Lao-tse

"A man not humble in his own sight will never be exalted in the sight of others." — Far Eastern saying

"It is no great thing to be humble when you are brought low; but to be humble when you are praised is a great and rare attainment." — Bernard of Clairvaux

Modesty

"Modesty is the color of virtue." — Diogenes

"Modesty is the citadel of beauty and virtue." — Demades

"Modesty is a shining light; it prepares the mind to receive knowledge, and the heart for truth." — François Guizot

"Modesty is not only an ornament, but also a guard to virtue." — Joseph Addison

"Modesty seldom resides in a breast that is not enriched with nobler virtues." — Oliver Goldsmith

"Modesty once extinguished knows not how to return." — Seneca

"A false modesty is the meanest species of pride." — Edward Gibbon

"False modesty is the refinement of vanity. It is a lie." — Jean de La Bruyère

"A modest man seldom fails to gain the good will of those he converses with, because nobody envies a man who appears to be pleased with himself." — Sir Richard Steele

Manners

"Manners make the man." — A. Barclay

"Manners are not idle, but the fruit of loyal nature and of noble mind." — Tennyson

"Manners are of more importance than laws." — Edmund Burke

"Manners easily and rapidly mature into morals." — Horace Mann

"Manners — the final and perfect flower of noble character." — William Winter

"Manner is everything with some people, and something with everybody." — Conyers Middleton

"Good manners are a part of good morals; and it is as much our duty as our interest to practice both." — John Hunter

"Good manners and good morals are sworn friends and fast allies." — Cyrus Bartol

"Bad manners are a species of bad morals; a conscientious man will not offend in that way." — Christian Bovee

"Bad manner spoils everything, even reason and justice." — Baltasar Gracian

"Much of good-doing was destroyed for lack of tact and manner." — Martin Tupper

"Better to show too much civility than too little." — Old proverb

"Every man's manners makes his fortune." — Cornelius Nepos

"A man's own manner and character is what most becomes him." — Cicero

"Manners must adorn knowledge and smooth its way through the world." — "A man's own good breeding is the best security against other people's ill manners." — Lord Chesterfield

"Good breeding consists in having no particular mark of any profession, but a general elegance of manners." — Samuel Johnson

"All the education young people receive will be in vain if they do not learn good manners." — Gandhi

"Manners make the fortune of the ambitious youth." — "Manners are the happy ways of doing things." — "Fine manners need the support of fine manners in others." — "Good manners are made of petty sacrifices." — "Your manners are always under examination, and by committees little suspected, a police in citizens clothes, — but are awarding or denying you very high prizes when you least think of it." — Emerson

"Good manners is the art of making those people easy with whom we converse; whoever makes the fewest people uneasy, is the best bred man in company." — Swift

"Don't shake hands too eagerly." — Pythagoras

"Other times, other manners." — Pindar

Politeness

"Politeness is merely the art of choosing among your thoughts." — Madame de Stael

"Politeness is good nature regulated by good sense." — Sydney Smith

"Politeness is to do and say the kindest thing in the kindest way." — Ludwig Lewisohm

"Politeness is the ritual of society, as prayers are of church." — Emerson

"Politeness comes from within, from the heart." — John Hall

"Politeness goes far, yet costs nothing." — Samuel Smiles

"Politeness costs nothing, and gains everything." — Lady Mary Montagu

"Politeness smoothes wrinkles." — "Politeness is the flower of humanity." — Joubert

"Politeness has been well defined as benevolence in small things." — Thomas Macaulay

"One never loses anything by politeness." — Vincent Lean

"If a man be gracious and courteous to strangers, it shows he is a citizen of the world." — Sir Francis Bacon

"A want of tact is worse than a want of virtue." — Disraeli

"With hat in hand, one gets on in the world." — German proverb

"The true effect of genuine politeness seems to be rather ease than pleasure." — Samuel Johnson

"True politeness is perfect ease and freedom. It simply consists in treating others just as you love to be treated yourself." — Lord Chesterfield

Courtesy

"Life is not so short but that there is always time enough for courtesy." — Emerson

"The greater the man, the greater the courtesy." — Tennyson

"There is no outward sign of true courtesy that does not rest on a deep moral foundation." — Goethe

"Approved valor is made precious by natural courtesy." — Sir Philip Sidney

"The courteous man learns his courtesy from the discourteous." — Turkish proverb

"Even among intimate friends there should be courtesy." — Japanese proverb

"How beautiful is humble courtesy!" Sir Rabindranath Tagore

"The small courtesies sweeten life; the greater, ennoble it." — Christian Bovee

"Hail, ye small, sweet courtesies of life! For smooth do ye make the road of it." — Laurence Sterne

Charm

"Charm is more than beauty." — Hebrew proverb

"Charm is getting the answer yes without asking a clear question." — Albert Camus

"Charm strikes the sight, but merit wins the soul." — Alexander Pope

"Without charm there can be no fine literature, as there can be no perfect flower without fragrance." — Arthur Symons

"Fair and softly goes far." — Cervantes

"What thou wilt, thou must rather enforce it with thy smile, than hew to it with thy sword." — Shakespeare

"If you have charm, you don't need to have anything else; and if you don't have it, it doesn't matter what else you have." — Sir James Matthew Barrie

(Self) Respect

"Respect a man, he will do the more." — James Howell

"Respect yourself if you would have others respect you." — Baltasar Gracian

"All must respect those who respect themselves." — Disraeli

"Our reverence is good for nothing if it does not begin with self-respect." — Oliver Wendell Holmes

"Self-respect, that corner-stone of all virtue." — Sir John Herschel

"Self-reliance and self-respect are about as valuable commodities as we can carry in our pack through life." — Luther Burbank

"Without feelings of respect, what is there to distinguish men from beasts?" Confucius

"The power of dress is very great in commanding respect." — Sir Richard Steele

"The only man to me who is not respectable is the man who consumes more than he produces." — Elbert Hubbard

"When you are content to be simply yourself and don't compare or compete, everybody will respect you." — Lao-tse

"Give credit where credit is due." — Old proverb

"Men are respectable only as they respect." — Emerson

"He who wants a rose must respect the thorn." — Arabian proverb

"We do not possess our home, our children, or even our own body. They are only given to us for a short while to treat with care and respect." — Buddha

"Never esteem anything as of advantage to thee that shall make thee break thy word or lose thy self-respect." — Marcus Aurelius

Reputation

"Reputation is often got without merit and lost without fault." — English proverb

"No ruins are so irreparable as those of reputation." — Sir Richard Steele

"He who fears losing his reputation is sure to lose it." — Napoleon

"A broken reputation is like a broken vase — it may be mended, but it always shows where the break was." — Josh Billings

"The reputation of a thousand years may be determined by the conduct of one hour." — Japanese proverb

"Many a man's reputation would not know his character if they met on the street." — Elbert Hubbard

"How many worthy men have we known to survive their own reputation!" Montaigne

"You can't build a reputation on what you are going to do." — Henry Ford

"It matters not what you are thought to be, but what you are." — Publilius Syrus

"First impressions are the most lasting." — Congreve

"The good seaman is known in bad weather." — Old proverb

"In all the affairs of this world, so much reputation is, in reality, so much power." — John Tillotson

"The way to gain a good reputation is to endeavor to be what you desire to appear." — Socrates

"Associate with men of good quality, if you esteem your own reputation; it is better to be alone than to be in bad company." — George Washington

Name

"A good name is rather to be chosen than great riches." — Bible, Proverbs 22:1

"A good name in men and women is the immediate jewel of their souls." — Shakespeare

"Have regard for your name, since it will remain for you longer than a great store of gold." — Apocrypha, Ecclesiasticus 41:12

"A good name keeps its luster in the dark." — English proverb

"Good will, like a good name, is got by many actions, and lost by one." — Lord Jeffrey

"Good men must die, but death cannot kill their names." — Spanish proverb

"Life is for one generation; a good name is forever." — Japanese proverb

"A good name is a sound inheritance." — Old proverb

"The beginning of wisdom is to call things by their right names." — Chinese proverb

Conduct

"Conduct has the loudest tongue." — Old proverb

"Conduct is three-fourths of our life and its largest concern." — Matthew Arnold

"Conduct is the great profession. What a man does tells us what he is." — Frederick Huntington

"The force that rules the world is conduct, whether it be moral or immoral." — Nicholas Butler

"After all, what counts is not creed but conduct." — Sir Sarvepalli Radhakrishnan

"Almost all absurdity of conduct arises from the imitation of those whom we can not resemble." — Samuel Johnson

"Depend not on fortune, but on conduct." — Publilius Syrus

"The superior man wishes to be slow in his words, and earnest in his conduct." — Confucius

"Let your conduct be marked by truthfulness in word, deed, and thought." — Taittiriya Upanishad

"So conduct yourself that during life you will be praised, and in death, beatified." — Periander

"Rules of conduct, whatever they may be, are not sufficient to produce good results unless the ends sought are good." — Bertrand Russell

Responsibility

"Responsibilities gravitate to the man who can shoulder them; power flows to the man who knows how." — Elbert Hubbard

"He who weighs his responsibilities can bear them." — Martial

"We have to do the best we can. This is our sacred human responsibility." — Einstein

"Man has responsibility, not power." — Native American proverb

Rights

"Men, their rights, and nothing more; women, their rights, and nothing less." — Susan B. Anthony

"If you don't know your rights, you don't have any rights." — Anonymous

"Every right implies a responsibility." — John Davison Rockefeller Jr.

"No man has a right to do as he pleases, except when he pleases to do right." — Charles Simmons

Example

"Example is the best precept." — Aesop

"Example is better than precept." — J. Mirk

"Precepts may lead — but examples draw." — Old proverb

"We live in an age that hath more need of good examples than precepts." — George Herbert

"Example is the school of mankind; they will learn at no other." — Edmund Burke

"Example is not the main thing in life — it is the only thing." — Albert Schweitzer

"Noble examples stir us up to noble actions." — Seneca

"Be silent; and prove thy maxim by example." — "Be sparing of advice by words, but teach thy lesson by example." — Martin Tupper

"Imitation is the sincerest form of flattery." — Charles Caleb Colton

"In others take an example for yourselves." — Terence

"I have given you an example, that you should do as I have done unto you." — Bible, John, 13:15

"The three highest titles that can be given a man are those of a martyr, hero or a saint." — William Gladstone

"The only rational way of educating is to be an example — if one can't help it, a warning example." — Einstein

DESTINY

"Destiny leads the willing, but drags the unwilling." — Seneca

"Destiny has more resources than the most imaginative composer of fiction." — Frank Moore

"Destiny has two ways of crushing us — by refusing our wishes and by fulfilling them." — Amiel

"Destiny, or karma, depends upon what the soul has done about what it has become aware." — Edgar Cayce

"A man is asked to make of himself what he is supposed to become to fulfill his destiny." — Paul Tillich

"In your own self lies destiny." — Ella Wheeler Wilcox

"What you are comes to you." — Emerson

"This day we fashion Destiny, our web of Fate we spin." — Whittier

"One meets his destiny often in the road he takes to avoid it." — French proverb

"No man of woman born, coward or brave, can shun his destiny." — Homer

"A consistent man believes in destiny, a capricious man in chance." — Disraeli

"Not to accept destiny is to face death blindfolded." — Lao-tse

"Our destiny exercises its influence over us even when, as yet, we have not learned its nature." — Nietzsche

"Lead me, O Zeus and thou, O Destiny, Lead thou me on, to whatsoever task thou sendest me." — Cleanthes

"We are but as the instrument of Heaven. Our work is not design, but destiny." — Tennyson

"How easy 'tis, when Destiny proves kind, with full-spread sails to run before the wind!" John Dryden

"No wind favors them who have no destined port." — Montaigne

"If a man is destined to drown, he will drown even in a spoonful of water." — Hebrew proverb

"But ah, who can deceive his destiny?" Spenser

"'Tis vain to quarrel with our destiny." — Thomas Middleton

"Each man suffers his own destiny." — Virgil

"Greater dooms win greater destinies." — Heraclitus

"Where destiny blunders, human prudence will not avail." — Publilius Syrus

"Who cannot but see oftentimes how strange the threads of our destiny run?" Cervantes

"If the wise man achieves something, it is well; if he achieves nothing, it is also well; he recognizes destiny." — Confucius

"We are not permitted to choose the frame of our destiny. But what we put into it is ours." — Dag Hammarskjold

"Life must be dedicated to a destiny in order to have meaning." — Jose Ortega y Gasset

"Everything comes gradually and at its appointed hour." — Ovid

"Destiny is not a matter of chance, it is a matter of choice; it is not a thing to be waited for, it is a thing to be achieved." — William Bryan

"The characteristic of the good man is to delight in and to welcome what befalls and what is being spun for him by destiny." — Marcus Aurelius

"Let a man accept his destiny." — "He who glories in his luck may be overthrown by destiny." — Epictetus

"The real test of a man is not how well he plays the role he has invented for himself, but how well he plays the role that destiny assigned to him." — Jan Patoka

"Every man supposes that he directs his life and governs his actions, when his existence is irretrievably under the control of destiny." — Goethe

"Sow a Thought, and you reap an Act; Sow an Act, and you reap a Habit; Sow a habit, and you reap a Character; Sow a Character, and you reap a Destiny." — James Allen

"Shunless destiny." — "There's a divinity that shapes our ends, rough-hew them how we will." — "Are you up to your destiny?" Shakespeare

Fate

"Fate is the friend of the good, the guide of the wise, the tyrant of the foolish, the enemy of the bad." — William Alger

"Fate laughs at probabilities." — Bulwer-Lytton

"Fate has terrible power. You cannot escape it by wealth or war. No fort will keep it out, no ships outrun it." — Sophocles

"Whatsoever we perpetrate, we do but row, we are steered by fate." — Samuel Butler

"I claim not to have controlled events, but confess plainly that events have controlled me." — Abraham Lincoln

"What is ordained is master of the gods and thee." — "Necessity is harsh. Fate has no reprieve." — Euripides

"One hour is marked, and no one can claim a moment of life beyond what fate has predestined." — Napoleon

"Even-handed fate hath but one law for small and great: that ample urn holds all men's names." — Horace

"The handsome gifts that fate and nature lend us most often are the very ones that end us." — Chaucer

"Better not to know the future and to await with patience the calamities of fate." — Iamblichus

"There is no armor against fate." — James Shirley

"Nor sitting by his hearth at home doth a man escape his appointed doom." — Aeschylus

"If fate means you to lose, give him a good fight anyhow." — William McFee

"If we must fall, we should boldly meet our fate." — Tacitus

"Thy fate is the common fate of all; into each life some rain must fall." — Longfellow

"For fate has wove the thread of life with pain." — Homer

"Our nature such, ill choice ensures ill fate." — Edward Young

"We are spinning our own fates, good or evil, never to be undone." — William James

"I am the master of my fate; I am the captain of my soul." — William Ernest Henley

"For humans are humans and masters of their own fate." — Tennyson

"A man must stand very tall to see his own fate." — Danish proverb

"Heaven from all creatures hides the book of fate." — Alexander Pope

"Even the Sun will not overstep his measures; if he does, the Erinyes or the Fates, the minions of Justice, will find him out." — Heraclitus

"*Que Sera, Sera* . . . Whatever will be, will be." — Spanish proverb

"What goes around comes around." — American proverb

"Merchant today, beggar tomorrow." — German proverb

"Leave things of the future to fate." — Charles Swain

"All is created and goes according to order, yet over our lifetime rules an uncertain fate." — Goethe

"Nothing happens by chance or accident." — Edgar Cayce

"No snowflake ever falls in the wrong place." — Zen proverb

"It is the fate of the coconut husk to float, for the stone to sink." — Malayan proverb

"Fate finds for every man his share of misery." — "The man who sticks it out against his fate shows spirit, but the spirit of a fool." — "Nothing happens to any man which he is not fitted by nature to bear." — "Whatever may befall thee, it was preordained for thee from eternity." — Marcus Aurelius Antoninus

"Fate, then, is a name for facts not yet passed under the fire of thought; for causes which are unpenetrated." — "The element running through entire nature, which we call fate, is known to us as limitation." — "Whatever limits us, we call Fate." — Emerson

"I do not believe in a fate that falls on people however they act; but I do believe in a fate that falls on them unless they act." — G. K. Chesterton

"We cannot conquer fate and necessity, yet we can yield to them in such a manner as to be greater than if we could." — Walter Savage Landor

"The cosmos is no accident in Time; there is meaning in each play of Chance, there is freedom in each face of Fate." — Sri Aurobindo

"The man who submits to his fate calls it the will of God; the man who puts up a hopeless and exhausting fight is more apt to see the devil in it." — Carl Jung

"Our fate is decreed, and things do not happen by chance, but every man's portion of joy or sorrow is predetermined." — "What must be shall be; and that which is a necessity to him that struggles, is little more than a choice to him that is willing." — Seneca

"Men, at some time, are masters of their fates. The fault, dear Brutus, is not in our stars, but in ourselves, that we are underlings." — "What fates impose, that me must needs abide; it boots not resist both wind and tide." — Shakespeare

"Keep thine eyes open, or Fate will open them for thee." — "A misfortune that
· cometh from on high cannot be averted; caution is useless against the decrees of Fate." — "Put yourself frankly into the hands of Fate, and let her spin you out the fortune she pleases." — Far Eastern sayings

"Learn to love your fate." — Nietzsche

Providence

"Providence is always on the side of the big battalions." — Madame de Sevigne

"We must follow, not force, providence." — Shakespeare

"I have seen fools resist Providence before and I have seen their destruction." — Woodrow Wilson

"As a wise man, if wiser, would deal with himself, so the Divine Providence deals with him." — "Even in small things there is great providence." — Old proverbs

"When good befalls a man he calls it providence, when evil, fate." — Knut Hamsun

"Fear not, but trust in providence, wherever thou may'st be." — Thomas Hayne Bayly

"Fate is not the ruler, but the servant of Providence." — Bulwer-Lytton

"If Providence bolts the door do not go through the window." — Old proverb

"The well of Providence is deep. It's the buckets we bring to it that are small." — Mary Webb

"The winds of grace blow all the time. All we need to do is set our sails." — Ramakrishna

Luck

"Luck affects everything." — "There is something in omens." — Ovid

"Luck is always on the side of the last reserve." — Napoleon

"Luck is like having a rice dumpling fly into your mouth." — Japanese proverb

"Luck is loaned, not owned." — Norwegian proverb

"Luck has a slender anchorage." — English proverb

"Luck never made any man wiser." — Seneca

"Luck is not chance — it's toil — fortune's expensive smile is earned." — Emily Dickinson

"Luck is infatuated with the efficient." — "Go and wake up your luck." — Persian proverbs

"Diligence is the mother of good luck." — Benjamin Franklin

"It is better to be born lucky than rich." — J. Clarke

"Have but luck, and you will have the rest; be fortunate, and you will be thought great." — Victor Hugo

"The lucky man passes for a genius." — Euripides

"One ounce of good luck is better than a ton of brains." — Yugoslavian proverb

"Good luck beats early rising." — "There is no luck except where there is discipline." — Irish proverbs

"I'm a great believer in luck, and I find the harder I work the more I have of it." — Thomas Jefferson

"The public man needs but one patron, namely, the lucky moment." — Bulwer-Lytton

"A man does not seek his luck, luck seeks him." — Turkish proverb

"Guests bring good luck with them." — Kurdish proverb

"The third time is lucky." — Scottish proverb

"Pitch a lucky man into the Nile and he will come up with a fish in his mouth." — Arabian proverb

"One man can burn water, whereas another cannot even burn oil." — Kashmiri proverb

"As long as we are lucky we attribute it to our smartness; our bad luck we give the gods credit for." — Josh Billings

"The dice of Zeus have ever lucky throws." — Sophocles

"If heaven drops a date, open your mouth." — Chinese proverb

"The only sure thing about luck is that it will change." — Wilson Mizner

"No blessing lasts forever." — Plautus

"Ill-luck, you know, seldom comes alone." — "A stout heart breaks bad luck." — Cervantes

"When ill luck falls asleep, let none wake her." — Italian proverb

"Do not reveal your thoughts to every man, lest you drive away your good luck." — Apocrypha, Ecclesiasticus 8:19

"The only good luck many great men ever had was being born with the ability and determination to overcome bad luck." — Channing Pollock

"In the queer mess of human destiny the determining factor is Luck. For every important place in life there are many men of fairly equal capacities. Among them Luck decides who shall accomplish the great work, who shall be crowned with laurel, and who shall fall back into obscurity and silence." — William E. Woodward

"True luck consists not in holding the best of the cards at the table: Luckiest is one who knows just when to rise and go home." — John Hay

"Better a pound of luck than a pound of gold." — "Intelligence is not needed for luck, but luck is needed for intelligence." — "When a man has luck, even his ox calves." — Jewish proverbs

"They that are afraid of bad luck will never know good." — "Do not be born good or handsome, but be born lucky." — Russian proverbs

Fortune

"Fortune is a prize to be won. Adventure is the road to it. Chance is what may lurk in the shadows at the roadside." — O. Henry

"Fortune is not for the faint-hearted." — Sophocles

"Fortune sides with those who dare." — Virgil

"Fortune favors the brave." — Simonides

"Fortune favors the bold but abandons the timid." — Latin proverb

"Fortune commands men, and not men fortune." — Herodotus

"Fortune does not change men; it only unmasks them." — Marie Riccoboni

"They dance well whom fortune pipes." — Italian proverb

"When fortune comes, seize her in front with a sure hand, because behind she is bald." — Leonardo da Vinci

"When fortune knocks upon the door, open it widely." — Spanish proverb

"When Fortune smiles, I smile to think how quickly she will frown." — Robert Southwell

"So conscience chide me not, I am prepared for Fortune as she wills." — Dante

"As we are, so we do; and as we do, so is it done to us; we are the builders of our fortunes." — Emerson

"To be thrown upon one's own resources is to be cast into the very lap of fortune." — Benjamin Franklin

"Every man is the architect of his own fortune." — Appius Claudius

"We make our fortunes, and we call them fate." — Disraeli

"Private information is practically the source of every large modern fortune." — Oscar Wilde

"However rich or elevated we may be, a nameless something is always wanting to our imperfect fortune." — Horace

"This is the posture of fortune's slave: one foot in the gravy, one foot in the grave." — James Thurber

"When the fountain has gone up, it comes down." — Persian proverb

"Trust not fortune." — Sophist saying

"Don't trust in fortune until you are in heaven." — Philippine proverb

"Blessings do not come in pairs; misfortunes never come singly." — Chinese proverb

"From fortune to misfortune is but a step; from misfortune to fortune is a longer way." — Hebrew proverb

"There is in the worst of fortune the best of chances for a happy change." — Euripides

"Learn to bear the changes of fortune." — Cleobulus

"Endeavor to bear the ignorance of fortune with patience." — "Affairs sleep soundly when fortune is present." — Greek proverbs

"In good fortune be moderate, in bad, prudent." — Periander

"'Tis better to be fortunate than wise." — John Webster

"Good fortune will elevate even petty minds, and give them the appearance of a certain greatness and stateliness." — Plutarch

"The greatest evil which fortune can inflict on a man is to endow him with small talents and great ambition." — Marquis de Vauvenargues

"If you are too fortunate, you will not know yourself. If you are too unfortunate, nobody will know you." — Thomas Fuller

"If fortune give thee less than she has done, then make less fire, and walk more in the sun." — Sir R. Baker

"Fortune brings in some boats that are not steered." — "There is a tide in the affairs of men, which, taken at the flood, leads on to fortune." — "Will fortune never come with both hands full?" "A hazard of new fortunes." — "For 'tis a question left us yet to prove, whether love lead fortune, or else fortune love." — Shakespeare

"Fortune is like glass — the brighter the glitter, the more easily broken." — "Fortune makes a fool of him whom she favors too much." — "A man's own character is the arbiter of his fortune." — Publilius Syrus

"Fortune never appears so blind as to those to whom she does no good." — "The most brilliant fortunes are often not worth the littleness required to gain them." — "We need greater virtues to sustain good fortune than bad." — La Rochefoucauld

"Fortune is like the market, where many times, if you can stay a little, the price will fall." — "Chiefly the mold of a man's fortune is in his own hands." — Sir Francis Bacon

"Fortune dreads the brave, and is only terrible to the coward." — "A great fortune is a great slavery." — "A man should not fear fortune, for a man counts not only chattels, property, and high office, but even his body, his eyes, his hands, and everything whose use makes life dearer to us, nay, even his very self, to be things whose possession is uncertain; he lives as though he had borrowed them, and is ready to return them cheerfully whenever they are claimed." — Seneca

"Fortune may have yet a better success in reserve for you, and they who lose today may win tomorrow." — "A brave man craves out his fortune, and every man is the child of his own work." — "Diligence is the mother of good fortune." — Cervantes

"A great fortune depends on luck, a small one on diligence." — "When fortune is good, you rule over the devils; when fortune is bad, they rule over you." — Chinese proverbs

"Fortune is blind, but not invisible." — "Fortune is a woman; if you neglect her today, do not expect to regain her tomorrow." — French proverbs

"The power of fortune is confessed only by the miserable, for the happy impute all their success to prudence or merit." — Swift

"I say again that this is most true, and all history bears witness to it, that men may second Fortune, but they cannot thwart her — they may weave her web, but they cannot break it." — Machiavelli

"Someone who is willing to work, and unable to find work, is perhaps the saddest sight that fortune's inequality exhibits under the sun." — Carlyle

"For a man who understandeth thoroughly the teachings which he hath received, it is the same whether he meets with good fortune or with bad fortune." — Buddha

Chance

"Chance governs all." — Milton

"Chance favors a prepared mind." — Louis Pasteur

"Chance, fate, nurturing an inner preparedness for change and direction — how can one disentangle them?" Sigmund Freud

"Chance usually favors the prudent man." — Joubert

"Chance fights ever on the side of the prudent." — Euripides

"Chance contrives better than we ourselves." — Menander

"Chance is always powerful. Let your hook be always cast; in the pool where you least expect it, there will be a fish." — Ovid

"Chance makes a football of a man's life." — "Who chance often passes by, it finds at last." — "Everything may happen." — Seneca

"Chance happens to all, but to turn chance to account is the gift of few." — Bulwer-Lytton

"A wise man turns chance into good fortune." — Thomas Fuller

"Chance is a word void of sense; nothing can exist without a cause." — "Almost all human life depends on probabilities." — Voltaire

"Chances rule men and not men chances." — Herodotus

"What Chance has made yours is not really yours." — Lucilius

"What we anticipate seldom occurs; what we least expect generally happens." — Disraeli

"How often events, by chance, and quite unexpectedly, come to pass, which you had not dared even to hope for!" Terence

"Nobody owes anybody a living, but everybody is entitled to a chance." — Jack Dempsey

"One chance is all you need." — Jesse Owens

"A man that leaveth nothing to chance will do few things ill, but he will do very few things." — Edward F. Halifax

"Something must be left to chance; nothing is sure in a sea fight beyond all others." — Horatio Nelson

"Enjoy yourself, drink, call the life you live today your own, but only that; the rest belongs to chance." — Euripides

"It's all fate and chance." — Arabian proverb

"Make chance essential." — Paul Klee

"For we know in part, and we prophesy in part." — Bible, I Corinthians 13:9

"Thou mayest take small heed, thou hast counted it a chance; but that which now hath flowered, groweth on old roots." — Martin Tupper

"Work and acquire, and thou hast chained the wheel of chance." — Emerson

"Every possession and every happiness is but lent by chance for a uncertain time, and may therefore be demanded back the next hour." — Schopenhauer

"Theoretical considerations of cause and effect often look pale and dusty in comparison to the practical results of chance." — "Synchronicity is a Meaningful Coincidence." — Carl Jung

"I have set my life upon a cast, and I will stand the hazard of the die." — Shakespeare

"Take a chance! All life is a chance. The man who goes farthest is generally the one who is willing to do and dare." — Dale Carnegie

TIME

"Time is the seed of the universe." — Mahabharata

"Time is the soul of this world." — Pythagoras

"Time is the image of eternity." — "In time shape, fortune, name, and nature all decay." — Plato

"Time and space are fragments of the infinite for the use of finite creatures." — Henri Frederic Amiel

"Time is but the stream I go fishing in." — "As if you could kill time without injuring eternity!" Thoreau

"Time is infinite movement without rest." — Tolstoy

"Time is the most valuable thing a man can spend." — Theophrastus

"Give thy purse rather than thy time." — "The greatest expense we can be at is that of our time." — Old proverbs

"You can ask me for anything you like, except time." — Napoleon

"Time is what we want most, but what, alas! We use worst." — William Penn

"Time is a great healer." — Menander

"Time heals what reason cannot." — "Whatever begins, also ends." — Seneca

"Time heals griefs and quarrels, for we change and are no longer the same persons." — Pascal

"Time in its aging course teaches all things." — "Time brings all things to pass." — Aeschylus

"Time is the rider that breaks youth." — George Herbert

"Time will rust the sharpest sword." — Sir Walter Scott

"Time is the longest distance between two places." — Tennessee Williams

"Time and words can't be recalled." — "He lives long that lives well, and time misspent is not lived, but lost." — Thomas Fuller

"Time flies over us, but leaves its shadow behind." — Nathaniel Hawthorne

"Time makes more converts than reason." — "These are the times that try men's souls." — Thomas Paine

"Time does not become sacred to us until we have lived it." — John Burroughs

"Time will discover everything to posterity; it is a babbler, and speaks even when no question is put." — Euripides

"Time, that aged nurse, rocked me to patience." — John Keats

"Time, the subtle thief of youth." — Milton

"Time goes, you say? Ah no! Alas, Time stays, we go." — Henry Austin Dobson

"Time destroys the speculations of man and omen, but it confirms the judgment of nature." — Cicero

"Time preserves nothing that you make without its help." — Anatole France

"Times change and we with the time." — Lyly

"Be ruled by time, the wisest counselor of all." — Plutarch

"We always have time enough, if we will but use it aright." — Goethe

"Nothing flows faster than the years, daughters of time." — Leonardo da Vinci

"Everything happens to everybody sooner or later if there is time enough." — George Bernard Shaw

"Nothing is more precious than time, yet nothing less valued." — Old proverb

"What I most value next to eternity is time." — Anne Swetchine

"An inch of time cannot be bought with an inch of gold." — Chinese proverb

"What greater crime than loss of time?" Old proverb

"To let time slip is a reverseless crime. You may have time again, but not the same time." — Sir R. Baker

"We take no note of time but from its loss." — "The time that bears no fruit deserves no name." — Edward Young

"In the short life of a man no lost time can be afforded." — Old proverb

"To kill time is, by definition, to murder it." — Anonymous

"A wise man redeemeth his time that he may improve his chances." — Martin Tupper

"A stone thrown at the right time is better than gold given at the wrong time." — Persian proverb

"Punctuality is the politeness of princes." — Louis XVIII

"It is not enough to run, one must start in time." — French proverb

"Anytime means no time." — Old proverb

"You will never 'find' time for anything. If you want time, you must make it." — Charles Buxton

"Our souls traverse spaces in Life which are not measurable by Time, that invention of man." — Kahlil Gibran

"Let the measure of time be spiritual, not mechanical." — Emerson

"Our judgments about things vary according to the time left us to live — that we *think* is left us to live." — André Gide

"Great Time makes all things dim." — Sophocles

"The grand Instructor, Time." — Edmund Burke

"Time and tide wait for no one." — "Time is a file that wears and makes no noise." — "Time trieth truth." — "Time flies when you're having fun." — "Time lost is gone forever." — "Time will tell." — English proverbs

"Time, . . . is the author of authors." — "One who is young in years may be old in hours, if he has lost no time." — "To choose time is to save time." — Sir Francis Bacon

"Time is money." — "Dost thou love life, then do not squander time, for that's the stuff life is made of." — "Lose no time; be always employed in something useful. Keep out of all unnecessary action." — Benjamin Franklin

"Time is too Slow for those who wait, too Swift for those who Fear, too Long for those who Grieve, too Short for those who Rejoice, but for those who Love, Time is not." — Henry van Dyke

"Time, which strengthens friendship weakens love." — "Those who make the worst use of their time are the first to complain of its brevity." — La Bruyère

"Time is precious, but truth is more precious than time." — "There is no waste of time in life like that of making explanations." — "Time will teach more than all our thoughts." — Disraeli

"Time will bring to light whatever is hidden; it will conceal and cover up what is now shining with the greatest splendor." — Horace

"Time, which changes people, does not alter the image we have retained of them." — "The time which we have at our disposal every day is elastic; the passions that we feel it, those that we inspire contract it; and habit fills up what remains." — Marcel Proust

"Time is a sort of river of passing events, and strong is its current; no sooner is a thing brought to sight than it is swept by and another takes its place, and this too will be swept away." — Marcus Aurelius

"Time is a sandpile we run our fingers in." — "Time is the coin of your life. It is the only coin you have, and only you can determine how it will be spent. Be careful lest you let other people spend it for you." — Carl Sandburg

"Time is the most undefinable yet paradoxical of things; the past is gone, the future has not come, and the present becomes the past even while we attempt to define it, and, like the flash of the lightning, at once exists and expires." — Charles Colton

"Time ripens all things. No man's born wise." — "There's a time for some things, and a time for all things; a time for great things, and a time for small things." — Cervantes

"I wasted time, and now doth time waste me." — "Time's glory is to calm contending kings, to unmask falsehood and bring truth to light." — "The inaudible and noiseless foot of Time." — Shakespeare

"The greatest loss of time is delay and expectation, which depend upon the future. We let go the present, which we have in our power, and look forward to that which depends upon chance, — and so relinquish a certainty for an uncertainty." — Seneca

"That which is proven by time cannot be assailed by man, while that which is disproved by time cannot be justified by man." — Confucius

"Pastime is a word that should never be used but in a bad sense; it is vile to say a thing is agreeable because it helps to pass the time." — William Shenstone

"Still, in a way, nobody sees a flower, really, it is so small; we haven't time, and to see takes time, like to have a friend takes time." — Georgia O'Keefe

"Lost wealth may be replaced by industry, lost knowledge by study, lost health by temperance, but lost time is gone for ever." — Samuel Smiles

"The trouble is that you think you have time." — "Whatever we cultivate in time of ease, we gather as strength for time of change." — Buddha

"To every thing there is a season, and a time to every purpose under the heaven. A time to be born, and a time to die. A time to weep, and a time to laugh; a time to mourn, and a time to dance; a time to keep silence, and a time to speak; a time to love, and a time to hate; a time of war and a time of peace." — Bible, Ecclesiastes 3:1-7

The Past

"Those who do not remember the past are condemned to repeat it." — Santayana

"If you want the present to be different from the past, study the past." — Baruch Spinoza

"Study the past if you would divine the future." — Confucius

"The best prophet of the future is the past." — Lord Byron

"The past is never, never dead. It's not even past." — William Faulkner

"The past is certain; that which is to come is obscure." — Pittacus

"Not heaven itself upon the past has power; But what has been, has been, and I have had my hour." — John Dryden

"The next day is never as good as the day before." — Publilius Syrus

"Ah, how they glide by, the years, the swift years!" Horace

"The years teach much which the days never know." — Emerson

"The time will come when winter will ask us: What were you doing all the summer?" Bohemian proverb

"We have seen better days." — "Past, and to come, seems best; things present, worst." — Shakespeare

"So sad, so fresh, the days that are no more." — Tennyson

"We take no note of time but from its loss: to give it then a tongue is wise in a man." — Edward Young

"The mill cannot grind with the water that is past." — T. Drake

"Things past cannot be recalled." — H. Medwall

"The beauty of the past belongs to the past." — Margaret Bourke-White

"The further backward you can look, the farther forward you are likely to see." — Churchill

"Our yesterdays follow us; they constitute our life, and they give character and force and meaning to our present deeds." — Parker

The Present

"There's no time like the present." — English proverb

"The present is a gift of the moment." — Anonymous

"The present time has one advantage over every other — it is our own." — Charles Caleb Colton

"One who does not fear the future may enjoy the present." — Thomas Fuller

"Look not to the future with fear, nor to the past with anger, but be in the present with awareness." — James Thurber

"Real generosity toward the future lies in giving all to the present." — Albert Camus

"In spring no one thinks of the snow that fell last year." — Swedish proverb

"Every man's life lies within the present; for the past is spent and done with, and the future is uncertain." — Marcus Aurelius

"The present hour is man's alone." — "The future is purchased by the present." — Samuel Johnson

"Often, the precious present is wasted in visions of the future." — Martin Tupper

"By losing present time we lose all time." — Old proverb

"When you walk, just walk; when you eat, just eat." — Buddha

"A happy man is too satisfied with the present to dwell too much on the future." — Einstein

"In rivers, the water that you touch is the last of what has passed and the first of that which comes: so with time present." — Leonardo da Vinci

The Moment

"Seize the moment." — Latin proverb

"Live for the moment." — Old proverb

"All life is but a moment in time." — Plutarch

"The butterfly counts not months but moments, and has time enough." — Rabindranath Tagore

"Every moment is a golden one for those who have the vision to recognize it as such." — Henry Miller

"Every situation — nay, every moment — is of infinite worth; for it is the representative of a whole eternity." — Goethe

"In tragedy every moment is eternity; in comedy, eternity is a moment." — Christopher Fry

"Who makes quick use of the moment is a genius of prudence." — Johann Kaspar Lavater

"Remember the sole life which one can lose is that which he is living at the moment." — Marcus Aurelius

"Allowing the is-ness of the moment is allowing the experience of freedom." — Ishvara

"My friend, let's not think of tomorrow, but let's enjoy this fleeting moment of life." — Omar Kyyam

"All the treasures of earth cannot bring back one lost moment." — French proverb

"All my possessions for one moment of time." — Queen Elizabeth I

"We are being born and dying at every moment." — Dogen

"You must live in the present, launch yourself on every wave, find your eternity in each moment." — Thoreau

"One moment in eternity is as important as another moment, for eternity changeth not, neither is one part better than another part." — Far Eastern saying

"If you take care of each moment, you will take care of all time." — "Give up all hope for results and be in the moment." — Buddha

"Life is all memory, except for the one present moment that goes by so quick you hardly catch it going." — Tennessee Williams

"Life is no brief candle to me. It is a sort of splendid torch which I have got a hold of for the moment, and I want to make it burn as brightly as possible before handing it on to future generations." — George Bernard Shaw

Now

"Now's the time." — Old proverb

"Now is the accepted time." — Bible, II Corinthians 6:2

"Now is now-here, but tomorrow's nowhere." — Old proverb

"Seize now and here the hour that is, nor trust some later day!" Horace

"Be here now." — Anonymous

"That which is time, is timeless, is found now." — Buddha

"Improve your opportunities, every hour lost now is a chance of future misfortune." — Napoleon

"Eternity itself cannot restore the loss struck from the minute." — Old proverb

"The hours perish and are laid to our charge." — Inscription at Oxford College

"I'm working to improve my methods, and every hour I save is an hour added to my life." — Ayn Rand

"To each thing belongs its measure. Occasion is best to know." — Pindar

"There is no cure for birth and death save to enjoy the interval." — Santayana

"The year does nothing else but open and shut." — Danish proverb

"Now is the constant syllable ticking from the clock of time." — "Now is the watchworld of the wise; Now is on the banner of the prudent." — Martin Tupper

"Now is the result of all your yesterdays and the basis of all our tomorrows, so why don't you just pay attention to what's happening now?" Eli Ywahoo

Today

"Today is the first day of the rest of your life." — "Each day provides its own gifts." — American proverbs

"Today is yesterday's pupil." — "The morning has gold in its mouth." — Benjamin Franklin

"Today gold — tomorrow dust." — Old proverb

"Today let me live well; none knows what it may be tomorrow." — Palladas

"Today's egg is better than tomorrow's hen." — Turkish proverb

"The immortal spirit of one happy day." — Wordsworth

"Everyday is a little life, and our whole life is but a day repeated." — Old proverb

"Every day cannot be a feast of lanterns." — Chinese proverb

"One day well spent is to be preferred to an eternity of error." — Cicero

"The day is short and the work is long." — Old proverb

"Every man hath his ill day." — "What one day gives, another takes." — George Herbert

"Give me today, and take tomorrow." — St. John Chrysostom

"Give me insight into today, and you may have the antique and future worlds." — Nietzsche

"For there is no day however beautiful which has not its night." — Anonymous

"Many seek good nights and lose good days." — Dutch proverb

"Consider that this day never dawns again." — Dante

"Each day is the scholar of yesterday." — "Every day should be passed as if it were to be our last." — Publilius Syrus

"We know nothing of tomorrow; our business is to be good and happy today." — Sydney Smith

"If you won't do better today, you'll do worse tomorrow." — "The remedy of tomorrow is too late for the evil of today." — Old proverbs

"Here today, gone tomorrow." — Old proverb

"Tomorrow's life comes late; live, then, today." — Martial

"Tomorrow is the reaping of today." — W. S. Partridge

"And if tomorrow shall be sad, or never come at all, I've had at least today!" Edward Hersey Richards

"What a day may bring a day may take away." — Thomas Fuller

"One day is as good as two for he who does everything in its place." — "One day at a time." — Old proverbs

"One shall rise up at the voice of the bird." — Bible, Ecclesiastes 12:4

"The early riser is healthy, cheerful and industrious." — "It is not the early rising, but the well spending of the day." — Old proverbs

"Every day learns from the one that went before, but no day teaches the one that follows." — Russian proverb

"Unborn is tomorrow and dead is yesterday." — F. Scott Fitzgerald

"Each day the world is born anew for those who take it rightly." — James Russell

"A day is a miniature eternity." — "Progress is the activity of today and the assurance of tomorrow." — "Write it on your heart that every day is the best day in the year." — Emerson

"Rome was not built in one day." — "Make hay while the sun shines." — "One of these days is none of these days." — "Never put off till tomorrow what may be done today." — "One today is worth many tomorrows." — English proverbs

"Take no thought of the morrow, for the morrow shall take thought for the things of itself. Sufficient unto the day is the evil thereof." — Bible, Matthew 6:34

"No matter how difficult the past, you can always begin today." — "Each morning we are born again. What we do today is what matters most." — Buddha

"Strength for today is all we need, for there never will be a tomorrow; For tomorrow will prove but another today with its measure of joy and of sorrow." — Anonymous

"Each day is a little life." — "Do not shorten the morning by getting up late; look upon it as the quintessence of life, as to a certain extent sacred." — Schopenhauer

"If any count on two days, or any more, to come, they are a fool; for a man has no morrow, till with good luck he has got through today." — Sophocles

"For yesterday is but a dream, and tomorrow is only a vision. Look well therefore to this day! Such is the Salutation of the Dawn." — Hindu proverb

Tomorrow

"Tomorrow is a new day." — English proverb

"All the flowers of all the tomorrows are in the seeds of today and yesterday." — Chinese proverb

"It may be a fire — tomorrow it will be ashes." — Arabic proverb

"Use not today what tomorrow will need." — Old proverb

"Life is made up of tomorrows." — French proverb

"We consume our tomorrows fretting about our yesterdays." — Persius

"We are tomorrow's past." — Mary Webb

"Tomorrow is often the busiest day of the week." — Spanish proverb

"Tomorrow never comes." — English proverb

"Only put off until tomorrow what you are willing to die having left undone." — Picasso

"Let tomorrow take care of tomorrow." — Charles Swain

"Often, the painful present is comforted by flattering the future, and kind tomorrow beareth half the burdens of today." — "Tomorrow's victory shall crown the conflict of today." — Martin Tupper

"If you wait for tomorrow, tomorrow comes. It you don't wait for tomorrow, tomorrow comes." — Senegalese proverb

"The man least dependent upon the morrow goes to meet the morrow most cheerfully." — Epicurus

The Future

"When all else is lost, the future still remains." — Christian Bovee

"The only way to predict the future is to have the power to shape the future." — Eric Hoffer

"There is a past which is gone forever; but there is a future which is still our own." — Old proverb

"If you do not think about the future, you cannot have one." — John Galsworthy

"We should all be concerned about the future because we will have to spend the rest of our life there." — Charles Kettering

"If we open a quarrel between the past and the present, we shall find that we have lost the future." — Churchill

"Till the Future dares forget the Past, this fate and fame shall be an echo and a light unto eternity!" Shelley

"I never think of the future. It comes soon enough." — Einstein

"The future you shall know when it has come; before then, forget it." — Aeschylus

"The future struggles that it may now become the past." — Publilius Syrus

"That man is prudent who neither hopes nor fears anything from the uncertain events of the future." — Anatole France

"Let us not go over the old ground, let us rather prepare for what is to come." — Marcus Cicero

"If a man takes no thought about the distant, he will find sorrow near at hand." — Confucius

"A day to come shows longer than a year's that's gone." — Thomas Fuller

"The afternoon knows what the morning never suspected." — Swedish proverb

"The best thing about the future is that it only comes one day at a time." — Abraham Lincoln

"I hold that a man is in the right who is most closely in league with the future." — Henrik Ibsen

"I believe the future is only the past again, entered through another gate." — Sir Arthur Wing Pinero

"The future enters into us, in order to transform itself in us, long before it happens." — Rainer Maria Rilke

"The wave of the future is coming and there is no fighting it." — Anne Morrow Lindbergh

"The enemies of the Future are always the very nicest of people." — Christopher Morley

"When man speaks of the future, the gods laugh." — Chinese proverb

"The future influences the present just as much as the past." — "It is our future that lays down the law of our today." — Nietzsche

"The future is something which every man reaches at the rate of sixty minutes an hour, whatever he do, whoever he is." — Clive Staples Lewis

The Age/Era

"Nothing is impossible in the long lapse of ages." — Herodotus

"Every man of us has all the centuries in him." — John Viscount Morley

"For each age is a dream that is dying, or one that is coming to birth." — Arthur O'Shaughnessy

"The altar of an eon is the doormat of the next." — Mark Twain

"The philosophies of one age have become the absurdities of the next, and the foolishness of yesterday has become the wisdom of tomorrow." — Sir William Osler

"An age more curious than devout is more fond to fix the place of heaven, or hell, than studious this to shun, or that to secure." — Edward Young

"They who have not the spirit of their age, of their age have all the misery." — "Every man is the creature of the age in which he lives; very few are able to raise themselves above the ideas of the times." — Voltaire

"To each age belongeth its own book." — The Koran, 8:38

"The heresy of one age becomes the orthodoxy of the next." — Helen Keller

"Every age confutes old errors and begets new." — Thomas Fuller

"Perfections of means and confusion of goals seem in my opinion, to characterize our age." — Einstein

"Living for ages in the night-realm, we dream that our darkness is full of day." — Far Eastern saying

"Every age appears to souls who live in it most unheroic." — Elizabeth Barrett Browning

"From the days of the first grandfather, every man has remembered a golden age behind him!" James Russell Lowell

"The golden age never was the present age." — Benjamin Franklin

"The golden time of Long Ago." — William Winter

"Time will run back and fetch the Age of Gold." — Milton

"The world's great age begins anew, the golden years return." — Shelley

"The Golden Age upon earth once more may live." — "Much will rise again that has long been buried, and much become submerged which is held in honor today." — Horace

"The corruption of the age is made up by the particular contribution of every individual; some contribute treachery, others injustice, irreligious, tyranny, avarice, cruelty, according to their power." — Montaigne

"You know that the dark age is like a knife, which kings handle like butchers. Justice has taken wing and flown away. The darkness of untruth obscures even the light of the moon which cannot be seen." — Guru Kanak

"This age of darkness will constantly proceed in it's decay until the beginning of a new era." — Vishnu Purana 4:24

LOVE

"Love makes the world go round." — Lewis Carroll

"Love is something eternal; the aspect may change, but not the essence." — Vincent van Gogh

"Love is a great thing." — "Love is fulfilling the law." — "Love rejoiceth in the truth." — Bible, Romans

"Love is Nature's second sun." — George Chapman

"Love is a canvas furnished by Nature and embroidered by imagination." — "Love those who love you." — Voltaire

"Love is an Art, and the greatest of the Arts." — Edward Carpenter

"Love is all we have, the only way that each can help the other." — Euripides

"Love is the greatest refreshment of life." — Picasso

"Love is sweet, but tastes best with bread." — Jewish proverb

"Love is a state in which a man sees things most decidedly as they are not." — Nietzsche

"Love is an attempt to change a piece of a dream into reality." — Theodor Reik

"Love is the irresistible desire to be irresistibly desired." — Robert Frost

"Love is composed of a single soul inhabiting two bodies." — Aristotle

"Love is the egotism of two." — Henri La Salle

"Love is as strong as death." — Bible, Solomon 8:6

"Love is a product of habit." — Lucretius

"Love is the lord and the slave of all!" George MacDonald

"Love makes obedience lighter than liberty." — William Alger

"Love makes the music of the blest above, Heaven's harmony is universal love." — William Cowper

"Love sacrifices all things to bless the thing it loves." — Lord Lytton

"Love goes without that another may have." — "All goodness grows from love." — Rev. J. M. Gibbon

"Love in your heart wasn't put to stay. Love isn't love till you give it a way." — Oscar Hammerstien

"Love without return is like a question without an answer." — Old proverb

"Love that's wise will not say all it means." — Edwin Arlington Robinson

"Love built on beauty, soon as beauty, dies." — John Donne

"Love thou the rose, yet leave it on its stem." — Edward Robert Bulwer-Lytton

"Love doth ever shed rich healing where it nestles." — Cobbett

"Love can neither be bought nor sold; its only price is love." — Old proverb

"Love, and a cough, cannot be hid." — George Herbert

"Love's night is noon." — Persian proverb

"Love will find a way." — T. Deloney

"Love knows hidden paths." — German proverb

"Love never fails." — Bible, I Corinthians 13:4

"Love has its instinct." — Balzac

"Love conquers all; let us surrender to love." — Virgil

"Love rules without a sword, and binds without a cord." — Old proverb

"Love, and not armies, must guard the men of great." — Periander

"Love rules without rules." — "One who is not impatient is not in love." — Italian proverbs

"Love with life is heaven; and life unloving, hell." — Martin Tupper

"Love is not without bitterness." — Old proverb

"Love me when I least deserve it because that is when I really need it." — Swedish proverb

"Love covers all transgressions." — Bible, Proverbs 10:12

"Love means never having to say you're sorry." — Erich Segal

"Love was the first motion." — John Woolman

"Love, I say, is energy of life." — Robert Browning

"Love's gift cannot be given, it waits to be accepted." — Rabindranath Tagore

"Lovers know what they want, but not what they need." — Publilius Syrus

"Love like the light silently wrapping all." — "I never could explain why I love anybody, or anything." — Whitman

"Love has many ways of expressing itself, but in general the ways are two — the practical and the sentimental." — Ferral

"Love consists in this, that two solitudes protect and touch and greet each other." — Rainer Maria Rilke

"Love does not consist in gazing at each other, but looking outward together in the same direction." — Antoine de Saint-Exupéry

"Love knows not labor." — "Love knows no limits." — "Love demands faith and faith firmness." — "Love will creep where it cannot go." — "Love grows with obstacles." — "Love betters what is best." — "Love levels all inequalities." — "Love has no thought of self." — Old proverbs

"Our first love, and last love is self-love." — Christian Bovee

"In love, losing ourselves we find ourselves." — "Truth individualizes, love unites." — Thomas Lynch

"What a man loves, a man is." — St. Augustine

"We are shaped and fashioned by what we love." — Goethe

"Do we not always grow to the likeness of what we love." — "The strongest evidence of love is sacrifice." — Caroline Fry

"To love for the sake of being loved is human, but to love for the sake of loving is angelic." — Alphonse de Lamartine

"But through love be servants of one another." — Bible, Galatians 5:13

"Owe no one anything, but to love one another." — Bible, Romans

"To love is to be useful to yourself; to cause love is to be useful to others." — Beranger

"All for love, and nothing for reward." — Edmund Spenser

"As you give love, you will have love." — Old proverb

"It is better to love than to be loved." — St. Francis

"There is more pleasure in loving than in being beloved." — "Absence sharpens love, presence strengthens it." — Thomas Fuller

"Being deeply loved by someone gives you strength while loving someone deeply gives you courage." — Lao-tse

"All love is sweet, given or returned." — Shelley

"How do I love thee? Let me count the ways." — Elizabeth Barrett Browning

"But we loved with a love that was more than love." — Poe

"Deeper than speech our love, stronger than life our tether." — Kipling

"The sweetest of all sounds is that of the voice of the one we love." — La Bruyère

"Pleasant words are the food of love." — Ovid

"When one is truly in love, one not only says it, but shows it." — Longfellow

"Let us not love in word, nor in tongue, but in deed and in truth." — Bible, I John 3:18

"The first duty of love is to listen." — Paul Tillich

"For love enters a man through his eyes, and a woman through her ears." — Polish proverb

"To love is to place our happiness in the happiness of another." — Leibnitz

"Two persons who love each other are in a place more holy than the interior of a church." — William Phelps

"For love is heaven, and heaven is love." — Sir Walter Scott

"Matches are made in heaven." — Robert Burton

"Mutual love, the crown of all our bliss." — Milton

"It's a couple's world." — "It takes two to tango." — Old proverbs

"Why do you take by force that which you could obtain by love?" Powhatan

"Make Love! Not War." — A saying from the Vietnam War protests

"All's fair in love and war." — Lyly

"Either take away, O Eros, all wish for love, or let me be loved! Take away all desire, or satisfy it." — Lucilius

"Many waters cannot quench love, neither can the floods drown it." — Bible, Solomon 8:7

"Nothing kills love like an overdose of it." — Oscar Wilde

"There is no remedy for love but to love more." — Thoreau

"Hot love is soon cold." — "An honest love is not afraid to frown." — Edward Young

"They love us truly who correct us freely." — Old proverb

"Pleasure of love lasts but a moment, pain of love lasts a lifetime." — Jean Pierre Claris De Florian

"But of all pains, the greatest pain it is to love, but love in vain." — Abraham Cowley

"One word frees us of all the weight and pain of life. That word is love." — Sophocles

"There is no fear in love; but perfect love casteth out fear." — Bible, John 4:18

"Nuptial love maketh mankind; friendly love perfecteth it; but wanton love corrupteth and embaseth it." — Sir Francis Bacon

"Eunuchs, abortive Platonists and priests speak always very wisely about love." — Theodore Spencer

"Books cannot teach you love's marvelous lore." — Hafiz of Persia

"Reason is not what directs love." — Molière

"Who ever loved, that loved not at first sight?" Christopher Marlowe

"I think true love is never blind." — Phoebe Cary

"Nobody's sweetheart is ugly." — Dutch proverb

"We must know a person thoroughly before we can love." — Martial D'Auvergne

"[There's] No folly like being in love." — Latin proverb

"Let love be without hypocrisy." — Greek proverb

"Before you love, learn to run through snow leaving no footprint." — Turkish proverb

"Then fly betimes, for only they conquer love that run away." — Thomas Carew

"The only victory over love is flight." — Napoleon

"Not loving is but a long dying." — Ti Wu

"A loveless life is a living death." — Old proverb

"If nobody loves you, be sure it is your own fault." — Philip Dryden

"People while they love are never quite depraved." — Charles Lamb

"Let no one who loves be called altogether unhappy. Even love unreturned has its rainbow." — Sir James Matthew Barrie

"Don't cry because love is over, smile because it happened." — Anonymous

"Who loves well is slow to forget." — Old proverb

"The heart that has truly loved never forgets." — Thomas Moore

"Only love makes me remember, it alone stirs my heart." — Leonardo da Vinci

"True love never grows old." — Old proverb

"Nothing is more beautiful than the love that has weathered the storms of life." — J. K. Jerome

"Never change when love has found its home." — Propertius

"In love is no lack." — Old proverb

"When poverty comes in at the door, love flies out of the window." — Caxton

"To love is the great Amulet that makes this world a garden." — Robert Louis Stevenson

"Gravitation cannot be held responsible for people falling in love." — Einstein

"Who would give a law to lovers? Love is unto itself a higher law." — Boethius

"The law of love is better than the love of law." — "The life of love is better than the love of life." — Old proverbs

"You have lived if you have loved." — A. de Musset

"The Eskimos had fifty-two names for snow because it was important to them: there ought to be as many for love." — Margaret Atwood

"Love is something so divine, description would but make it less. 'Tis what I feel, but can't define, 'tis what I know, but can't express." — Beilby Porteus

"Love makes the time pass. Time makes love pass." — "Try to reason about love, and you will lose your reason." — "In love, there is always one who kisses and one who offers the cheek." — French proverbs

"Love is a trembling happiness." — "Passionate love is a quenchless thirst." — "Love knows not its depth till the hour of separation." — "Love, like death, changes everything." — "It is wrong to think that love comes from long companionship and persevering courtship. Love is the offspring of spiritual affinity and unless that affinity is created in a moment, it will not be created for years or even generations." — Kahlil Gibran

"Love that ends is the shadow of love; true love is without beginning or end." — "With love, even the rocks will open." — Hazrat Inayat Khan

"Love me little, love me long." — "They love too much that die for love." — "Do when ye may, or suffer ye the nay, in love 'tis the way." — "They who love most are least valued." — "Kisses that are easily obtained are easily forgotten." — "Where love fails we espy all faults." — English proverbs

"Love without veneration and enthusiasm is only friendship." — "There is only one happiness in life, to love and be loved." — George Sand

"Love is perfect kindness." — "So through the eyes love attains the heart: for the eyes are the scouts of the heart." — Guiraut de Borneilh

"Love never claims, it ever gives. Love ever suffers, never resents, never revenges itself." — "A coward is incapable of exhibiting love; it is the prerogative of the brave." — "Where there is love there is life." — Gandhi

"Love, and you shall be loved. All love is mathematically just, as much as the two sides of an algebraic equation." — "Who drinks of Cupid's nectar cup loveth downward, and not up." — "All mankind loves a lover." — Emerson

"Love reckons hours for months, and days for years; and every little absence is an age." — "Fool, not to know that love endures no tie, and Jove but laughs at lovers' perjury." — John Dryden

"Love really has nothing to do with wisdom or experience or logic. It is the prevailing breeze in the land of youth." — Rudolph Block

"Love in the past is only a memory. Love in the future is a fantasy. Only here and now can we truly love." — "Do not seek perfection in a changing world. Instead, perfect your love." — Buddha

"Love is never security; love is a state in which there is no desire to be secure; it is a state of vulnerability." — "Love, and don't be caught in opinions and ideas about what love is or should be." — J. Krishnamurti

"Love is the rule for fulfilling all rules." — "Love understands, and therefore waits." — "Nothing is a hardship to love, and nothing is hard." — "You will find as you look back upon your life that the moments when you have truly lived are the moments when you have done things in the spirit of love." — Henry Drummond

"Love is the medicine of all moral evil." — "Young love is a flame; very pretty, often very hot and fierce, but still only light and flickering. The love of the older and disciplined heart is as coals, deep burning, unquenchable." — Henry Ward Beecher

"Love is the only sane and satisfactory answer to the problem of human existence." — "Immature love says: 'I love you because I need you.' Mature love says: 'I need you because I love you.'" "While every human being has a capacity for love, its realization is one of the most difficult achievements." — "Love is an act of faith, and whoever is of little love is of little faith." — Erich Fromm

"Love's great miracle is the curing of coquetry." — "True love is like ghosts, which everybody talks about and few have seen." — "We always love those who admire us; we do not always love those whom we admire." — "The reason why lovers are never weary of one another is this — they are always talking of themselves." — "There is no disguise which can for long conceal love where it exists or simulate it where it does not." — La Rochefoucauld

"Love sought is good, but given unsought, is better." — "The course of true love never did run smoothly." — "Love reasons without reason." — "They do not love who do not show their love." — "What's mine is yours, and what is yours is mine." — "But love is blind, and lovers cannot see the pretty follies that themselves commit." — "My love's richer than my tongue." — "Speak low, if you speak love." — "A heaven on earth I have won, by wooing thee." — "Love is merely a madness." — Shakespeare

"Love is not altogether a delirium, yet it has many points in common therewith." — "Love is ever the beginning of Knowledge, as fire is of light." — Carlyle

"Love is blind." — "For neither birth, nor wealth, nor honors, can awaken in the minds of men the principles which should guide those who from their youth aspire to an honorable and excellent life, as Love awakens them." — Plato

"Love, free as air at sight of human ties, spreads its light wings, and in a moment flies." — "It is very natural for a young friend and a young lover to think the persons they love have nothing to do but to please them." — "Who love too much hate in the same extreme." — Alexander Pope

"Where there is love there is pain." — "When love is not madness, it is not love." — "Works and not words are the proof of love." — "Love is like war: you begin when you like and leave off when you can." — Spanish proverbs

"Love and war are the same thing." — "Lovers are commonly industrious to make themselves uneasy." — "Absence, that common cure of love." — "Everything disturbs the absent lover." — "The eyes those silent tongues of love." — Cervantes

"There was never any yet that wholly could escape love, and never shall there be any, never so long as beauty shall be, never so long as eyes can see." — Longu

"Love is something far more than desire for sexual intercourse; it is the principal means of escape from the loneliness which afflicts most men and women throughout the greater part of their lives." — Bertrand Russell

"'Tis better to have loved and lost, than never to have loved at all." — "When we fall out with those we love and kiss again with tears." — "As love, if love be perfect, casts out fear." — Tennyson

"If Jack's in love, he's no judge of Jill's beauty." — "He that falls in love with himself will have no rivals." — "If you would be loved, love and be lovable." — "Those who love deeply never grow old. They may die of old age, but they die young." — Benjamin Franklin

"The magic of first love is our ignorance that it can ever end." — "Romance has been elegantly defined as the offspring of fiction and love." — Disraeli

"One cannot clothe love into words, for love is the same as bliss, a state without a place. It is imperishable and cannot be shaped or manipulated into what it is not." — "Love is the instrument with which one may spread the eternal force that can never be extinguished, which overcomes death and spreads light, which embodies the poise of wisdom, peace and all that exceeds understanding." — Semjase

"If you are to be loved, be worthy to be loved." — "Let one who does not wish to be idle, fall in love." — "Love is born of idleness and, once born, by idleness is fostered." — "Love is a kind of warfare." — Ovid

"As love without esteem is capricious and volatile, esteem without love is languid and cold." — "That which is to be loved long is to be loved with reason rather than with passion." — Dr. Johnson

"Like everybody who is not in love, they imagined that one chose the person whom one loved after endless deliberations and on the strength of various qualities and advantages." — Marcel Proust

"We are not the same persons this year as last; nor are those we love. It is a happy chance if we, changing, continue to love a changed person." — W. Somerset Maugham

"It is possible that a man can be so changed by love as hardly to be recognized as the same person." — "The quarrel of lovers is the renewal of love." — Terence

"When one is in love one always begins by deceiving oneself, and one always ends by deceiving others. That is what the world calls romance." — "To love oneself is the beginning of a life long romance." — Oscar Wilde

"The supreme happiness of life is the conviction of being loved for yourself, or, more correctly, being loved in spite of yourself." — Victor Hugo

"We conceal it from ourselves in vain — we must always love something. In those matters seemingly removed from love, the feeling is secretly to be found, and people cannot possibly live for a moment without it." — Pascal

"You carry a part of my life. If I love you, it must be because we shared, at some moment, the same imaginings, the same madness, the same stage." — "The only abnormality is the incapacity to love." — Anais Nin

"They sin who tell us love can die; With life all other passions fly, all others are but vanity . . . Love is indestructible." — Robert Southey

The Heart

"There is no instinct like that of the heart." — Lord Byron

"A loving heart is the truest wisdom." — Dickens

"It is wisdom to believe the heart." — Santayana

"The heart has reasons that reason does not understand." — Pascal

"For as he thinketh in his heart, so is he." — Bible, Proverbs 23:7

"For where your treasure is, there will your heart be also." — Bible, Matthew 6:21

"To give pleasure to a single heart by a single kind act is better than a thousand head-bowings in prayer." — Saddi

"Some people come into our lives, leave footprints on our hearts, and we are never the same." — Franz Schubert

"A kind heart is a fountain of gladness, making everything in its vicinity to freshen into smiles." — Washington Irving

"A merry heart maketh a cheerful countenance." — Bible, 15:13

"He that are of a merry heart hath a continual feast." — Bible, Proverbs 15:15

"It is a poor heart that never rejoices." — Marryat

"Woe to him whose heart has not learned while young to hope, to love — and to put its trust in life!" Joseph Conard

"The heart is forever inexperienced." — Thoreau

"The heart that is soonest awake to the flowers is always the first to be touched by the thorns." — Thomas Moore

"Never morning wore to evening, but some heart did break." — Tennyson

"Never love with all your heart, it only ends in breaking." — English proverb

"A broken hand works, but not a broken heart." — Persian proverb

"If thy heart fails thee, climb not at all." — Queen Elizabeth

"Half heart is no heart." — Old proverb

"The teeth are smiling, but is the heart?" Congolese proverb

"Sacrifice not thy heart upon every altar." — Thomas Fuller

"Riches that are in the heart cannot be stolen." — Russian proverb

"Nothing is less in our power than the heart, and far from commanding we are forced to obey it." — Rousseau

"All who know their own minds do not know their own hearts." — La Rochefoucauld

"Culture of the mind must be subservient to the heart." — Gandhi

"Great thoughts come from the heart." — Luc de Clapiers

"An honest heart being the first blessing, a knowing head is the second." — Thomas Jefferson

"Where the heart lies, let the brain lie also." — Robert Browning

"The heart is the best logician." — Wendell Phillips

"A good heart is better than all the heads in the world." — Bulwer-Lytton

"The prudence of the best heads is often defeated by the tenderness of the best of hearts." — Henry Fielding

"It is the inclination and tendency of the heart which finally determines the opinions of the mind." — Christoph Luthardt

"Men, as well as women, are much oftener led by their hearts than by their understandings." — Lord Chesterfield

"When the heart is won, the understanding is easily convinced." — Charles Simmons

"One ought to hold on to one's heart; for if one lets it go, one soon loses control of the head too." — Nietzsche

"All the knowledge I possess everyone else can acquire, but my heart is all my own." — Goethe

"A man's heart changes his countenance, either for good or for bad." — Apocrypha, Ecclesiasticus 13:25

"It is hard to contend against one's heart's desire; for whatever it wishes to have it buys at the cost of the soul." — Heraclitus

"The heart of fools is in their mouth and the mouth of wise ones is in their hearts." — Apocrypha, Ecclesiasticus 21:29

"The heart seldom feels what the mouth expresses." — Jean Galbert de Campistron

"When the heart speaks, glory itself is an illusion." — Napoleon

"What commands they utter from the heart come to pass." — Yoga Sutras II:36

"They did it with all their heart and prospered." — Bible, II Chronicles

"I carry your heart . . . in my heart." — e. e. cummings

"We were two and had but one heart between us." — François Villon

"Two souls with but a single thought, two hearts that beat as one." — Von Munch Bellinghausen

"The same heart beats in every human breast." — Matthew Arnorld

"All our actions take their hue from the complexion of the heart, as landscapes their variety from light." — Sir Francis Bacon

"The ways of the heart, like the ways of providence, are mysterious." — Henry Ware

"The heart is great which shows moderation in the midst of prosperity." — Seneca

"Thou shalt rest sweetly if thy heart condemn thee not." — Thomas à Kempis

"Our own heart always exceeds us." — Rainer Maria Rilke

"Men's hearts ought not to be set against one another, but set with one another, and all against evil only." — Carlyle

"Win hearts, and you have all men's hands and purses." — William Henry Burleigh

"What comes from the heart goes to the heart." — Old proverb

"The heart that loves is always young." — Greek proverb

"There is an awful warmth about my heart like a load of immortality." — John Keats

"There is no pleasure above the joy of the heart." — Apocrypha, Ecclesiasticus 30:16

"Keep thy heart with all diligence; for out of it are the issues of life." — Bible, Proverbs 3:23

"Nothing is impossible to a willing heart." — Old proverb

"The best and most beautiful things in the world cannot be seen, nor heard, nor touched . . . but are felt in the heart." — Helen Keller

"Joy and openness come from our own contented heart." — "The heart is like a garden. It can grow compassion or fear, resentment or love. What seeds will you plant there?" "Weigh the true advantages of forgiveness and resentment to the heart. Then choose." — Buddha

"When the knot of the heart, which is ignorance, is loosed, all doubts are dissolved, all evil effects of deeds are destroyed." — "He who sees the Self revealed in his heart belongs to eternal bliss." — The Upanishads

"Go to your bosom; Knock there, and ask your heart what it doth know." — "What is a stronger breastplate than a heart untainted?" "Is there any cause in nature that makes these hard hearts?" Shakespeare

"There is as much in that space within the heart, as there is in the whole world outside. Heaven, earth, fire, wind, sun, moon, stars; whatever is and whatever is not, everything is there." — Chhandogya-Upanishad

"Some reckon time by the stars, and some by hours; Some measure days by dreams, and some by flowers; My heart alone records my days and hours." — Madison Cawein

"The heart of a wise man should resemble a mirror, which reflects every object without being sullied by any." — "Wheresoever you go, go with all your heart." — Confucius

Compassion

"Compassion will do more than passion." — Old proverb

"We must understand the meaning of compassion . . . which is to "suffer with." — Anonymous

"The dew of compassion is a tear." — Lord Byron

"Of all noble qualities, loving compassion is the noblest." — Lao-tse

"He who actually loves even those that do not love him in return is compassionate." — Bhagavad-gita

"The mind is no match with the heart in persuasion; constitutionality is no match with compassion." — Everett Dirksen

"If you want others to be happy, practice compassion. If you want to be happy, practice compassion." — 14th Dalai Lama

"Our sorrows and wounds are healed only when we touch them with compassion." — "Begin each day with the idea of being able to generate compassion and understanding the whole day through." — Buddha

"The purpose of human life is to serve and to show compassion and the will to help others. Until we extend the circle of compassion to all living things, humanity will not find peace." — Albert Schweitzer

"As you travel through life, offer good wishes to each being you meet." — Buddha

Feeling

"Feeling in the young precedes philosophy, and often acts with a better and more certain aim." — William Carleton

"Our feelings are our most genuine paths to knowledge." — Audre Lorde

"Only feeling understands feeling." — Heinrich Heine

"Never apologize for showing feelings. When you do so, you apologize for truth." — Disraeli

"Seeing is believing, but feelings the truth." — Thomas Fuller

"Half our mistakes in life arise from feeling where we ought to think, and thinking where we ought to feel." — John Collins

"Trust not thy feeling, for whatever it be now, it will quickly be changed." — Thomas à Kempis

"Human affairs inspire in noble hearts only two feelings — admiration or pity." — Anatole France

"We want people to feel with us more than to act for us." — George Eliot

"The value of a sentiment is the amount of sacrifice you are prepared to make for it." — John Galsworthy

Emotion

"Emotion has taught mankind to reason." — Marquis de Vauvenargues

"Emotion is the surest arbiter of a poetic choice, and it is the priest of all supreme unions in the mind." — Max Eastman

"Emotion turning back on itself, and not leading on to thought or action, is the element of madness." — John Sterling

"Emotions become more violent when expression is stifled." — Philo

"When a man is prey to his emotions, he is not the master, but lies at the mercy of fortune." — Spinoza

"People don't ask for facts in making up their minds. They would rather have one good, soul-satisfying emotion than a dozen facts." — Robert Keith Leavitt

"Emotion is not something shameful, subordinate, second-rate; it is a supremely valid phase of humanity at its noblest and most mature." — Joshua Liebman

HAPPINESS

"Happiness is the only good." — Old proverb

"Happiness is unrepented pleasure." — Socrates

"Happiness is like a sunbeam, which the least shadow intercepts." — Chinese proverb

"Happiness is not a station you arrive at, but a manner of traveling." — Margaret Lee Runbeck

"Happiness is not a goal, it is a by-product." — Eleanor Roosevelt

"Happiness is no other than soundness and perfection of mind." — Antoninus

"Happiness is speechless." — George William Curtis

"Happiness is not a horse, you cannot harness it." — Russian proverb

"Happiness is a warm puppy." — Charles Shultz

"Happiness is possible even in pain and suffering. But pleasure alone can never create happiness." — Paul Tillich

"Happiness depends, as nature shows, less on exterior things than most suppose." — William Cowper

"Happiness does not depend on outward things, but on the way we see them." — Leo Tolstoy

"Happiness consists in the attainment of our desires, and in our having only right desires." — Augustine of Hippo

"Happiness grows at our own firesides, and is not to be picked in strangers' gardens." — Douglas Jerrold

"Happiness lies, first of all, in health." — George Curtis

"Happiness makes up in height for what it lacks in length." — Robert Frost

"Happiness hates the timid." — Eugene O'Neill

"Happy the man who early learns the wide chasm that lies between his wishes and his powers!" Goethe

"Happy are they who learn the causes of things and who put beneath their feet all fears." — Virgil

"Happy the people whose annals are blank in history-books." — Carlyle

"Being happy is a virtue too." — Ludwig Borne

"Assuredly, all nature informs us that mankind is born for happiness." — André Gide

"The right to happiness is fundamental." — Anna Pavlova

"Every one of these hundreds of millions of human beings is in some form seeking happiness." — H. G. Wells

"We all live with the objective of being happy; our lives are all different and yet the same." — Anne Frank

"O happiness! Our being's end and aim! For which we bear to live, or dare to die." — Alexander Pope

"The common course of things is in favor of happiness; happiness is the rule, misery the exception." — Paley

"As we are now living in an eternity, the time to be happy is today." — Grenville Kleiser

"The only ones among you who will be really happy are those who will have sought and found how to serve." — Albert Schweitzer

"The time to be happy is now, the place to be happy is here, the way to be happy is to make others so." — Robert Ingersoll

"All who joy would win must share it — happiness was born a twin." — Byron

"The supreme happiness of life is the conviction that we are loved." — Victor Hugo

"The days that make us happy make us wise." — John Masefield

"Wisdom is the most important part of happiness." — Sophocles

"Happy is the man that findeth wisdom . . . and every man who retaineth it." — Bible, Proverbs

"Talk happiness. The world is sad enough without your woe. No path is wholly rough." — Ella Wheeler Wilcox

"Be happy while you're living, for you're a long time dead." — Scottish proverb

"No man is happy who does not think himself so." — Publilius Syrus

"Most of us are just about as happy as we make up our minds to be." — Abraham Lincoln

"There is an hour wherein a man might be happy all his life could he find it." — George Herbert

"How bitter a thing it is to look into happiness through another man's eyes." — Shakespeare

"We torment ourselves rather to make it appear that we are happy than to become so." — La Rochefoucauld

"It is the chiefest point of happiness that a man is willing to be what he is." — Desiderius Erasmus

"To be happy is not the purpose of our being, but to deserve happiness." — Fichte

"There can be no real and abiding happiness without sacrifice." — H. W. Sylvester

"Knowledge of the possible is the beginning of happiness." — Santayana

"The secret of happiness is not in doing what one likes, but in liking what one has to do." — Sir James Matthew Barrie

"There is no happiness except in the realization that we have accomplished something." — Henry Ford

"Get happiness out of your work or you may never know what happiness is." — Elbert Hubbard

"The happiness of the outward life arises from honest action and temperate living." — Solon

"The loss of wealth is loss of dirt, as sages in all times assert; The happy man is without a shirt." — John Heywood

"We cannot find happiness until we forget to seek for it." — Henry Van Dyke

"Everyone chases after happiness, not noticing that happiness is at his heels." — Bertolt Brecht

"Seek not happiness too greedily, and be not fearful of unhappiness." — Lao-tse

"A great obstacle to happiness is to expect too much happiness." — Bernard de Fontenelle

"There is no more mistaken path to happiness than worldliness, revelry, high life." — Schopenhauer

"The more we limit and concentrate happiness, the more certain we are of securing it." — Deverant

"If thou wouldst be happy . . . have an indifference for more than what is sufficient." — William Penn

"Very little is needed to make a happy life. It is all within yourself, in your way of thinking." — Marcus Aurelius

"Most people ask for happiness on condition. Happiness can only be felt if you don't set any condition." — Arthur Rubinstein

"Happiness is the meaning and purpose of life, the whole aim and end of human existence." — "Happiness depends upon ourselves." — "Happiness seems to require a modicum of external prosperity." — Aristotle

"Happiness is that state of consciousness which proceeds from the achievement of one's values." — "No one's happiness but my own is in my power to achieve or to destroy." — Ayn Rand

"Happiness comes most to persons who seek her least, and think least about it. It is not an object to be sought; it is a state to be induced. It must follow and not lead. It must overtake you, and not you overtake it." — "The secret of happiness is something to do." — John Burroughs

"Happiness is as a butterfly, which, when pursued, is always beyond our grasp, but which, if you will sit down quietly, may alight upon you." — Nathaniel Hawthorne

"Happiness is to feel that one's soul is good; there is no other, in truth, and this kind of happiness may exist even in sorrow." — Joubert

"Happiness is not being pained in body or troubled in mind." — "Our greatest happiness does not depend on the condition of life in which chance has placed us, but is always the result of a good conscience, good health, occupation, and freedom in all just pursuits." — "It is neither wealth nor splendor, but tranquillity and occupation, which give happiness." — Thomas Jefferson

"The U. S. Constitution doesn't guarantee happiness, only the pursuit of it. You have to catch up with it yourself." — "There are two ways of being happy; we may either diminish our wants or augment our means." — Benjamin Franklin

"To me there is no duty we so underrate as the duty of being happy. By being happy, we sow anonymous benefits upon the world." — "The habit of being happy enables one to be freed, or largely freed, from the domination of outward conditions." — "To forget oneself is to be happy." — Robert Louis Stevenson

"The happy only are truly great." — "Most true a wise man will never be sad; but neither will sonorous, bubbling mirth, a shallow stream of happiness betray." — "No man every found a happy life by chance, or yawned it into being with a wish." — "Were all people happy, reveling would cease." — Edward Young

"The happiest is one who suffers the least pain; the most miserable, one who enjoys the least pleasure." — "The thirst after happiness is never extinguished in the heart of man." — Rousseau

"A great part of the happiness of life consists not in fighting battles, but in avoiding them. A masterly retreat is in itself a victory." — Longfellow

"A few bear fruit in happiness; the others go awry." — "That man is happiest who lives day to day and asks no more, garnering the simple goodness of a life." — Euripides

"We have no more right to consume happiness without producing it than to consume wealth without producing it." — "Give a man health and a course to steer, and he'll never stop to trouble about whether he's happy or not." — George Bernard Shaw

"You have to believe in happiness, or happiness never comes . . . Ah, that's the reason a bird can sing — On his darkest day he believes in Spring." — Douglas Malloch

"In the depth of winter, I finally learned that within me there lay an invincible summer." — "To be happy, we must not be too concerned with others." — Albert Camus

"We take greater pains to persuade others that we are happy than in endeavoring to be so ourselves." — "But where to find that happiest spot below, who can direct, when all pretend to know?" Oliver Goldsmith

"True happiness has no localities, no tones provincial, no peculiar garb." — "The song of mirth is soon past, for happiness counts not the hours." — Pollok

"It is better to be happy for a moment and be burned up with beauty than to live a long time and be bored all the while." — Don Marquis

"The great lesson to be learned is that Happiness is within us. No passing amusement, no companionship, no material possession can permanently satisfy." — Phil A. Ledger

"One who is not happy with nothing, will not be happy with anything." — "Learn to let go. That is the key to happiness." — "Simplicity brings more happiness than complexity." — "Praise and blame, gain and loss, pleasure and sorrow come and go like the wind. To be happy, rest like a great tree in the midst of them all." — Buddha

"Three grand essentials to happiness in this life are something to do, something to love, and something to hope for." — Joseph Addison

"There is only one way to happiness, and that is to cease worrying about things which are beyond the power of our will." — Epictetus

"When one door of happiness closes, another opens; but often we look so long at the closed door that we do not see the one that has been opened for us." — Helen Keller

"If you ever find happiness by hunting for it, you will find it as the old woman did her lost spectacles safe on her own nose all the time." — Josh Billings

Cheerfulness

"Cheerfulness in a man is that which when people meet him makes others happy." — Henry Ward Beecher

"Cheerfulness and content are great beautifiers and are famous preservers of youthful looks." — Dickens

"Cheerfulness opens, like spring, all the blossoms of the inward man." — J. P. Richter

"Cheerfulness in most cheerful people is the rich and satisfying result of strenuous discipline." — Edwin Percy Whipple

"Cheerfulness is an excellent wearing quality." — "Cheerfulness has been called the bright weather of the heart." — "Cheerfulness gives harmony to the soul and is a perpetual song without words." — "Cheerfulness enables nature to recruit its strength." — "Cheerfulness smoothes the road of life." — Old proverbs

"Wondrous is the strength of cheerfulness." — Carlyle

"A Cheerful life is what Muses love, a soaring spirit is their prime delight." — John Keats

"The best of healers is good cheer." — Pindar

"Welcome is the best cheer." — Greek proverb

"Be cheerful, one of care; for great is the multitude of chances." — Martin Tupper

"A cheerful spirit moveth quick — a grumbler in the mud will stick." — "Be always as cheerful as ever you can." — "Always walk on the sunny side of the street." — Old proverbs

"Burdens become light when cheerfully borne." — Ovid

"The cheerful live longest in years, and afterwards in our regards. Cheerfulness is the off-shoot of goodness." — Christian Bovee

"Lay aside life-harming heaviness and entertain a cheerful disposition." — Shakespeare

"So of cheerfulness, or a good temper, the more it is spent, the more it remains." — "That which befits us is cheerfulness and courage." — Emerson

"The true source of cheerfulness is benevolence. The soul that perpetually overflows with kindness and sympathy will always be cheerful." — Parke Godwin

Joy

"Joy is not in things; it is in us." — Richard Wagner

"Joy comes not to those who seek it for themselves, but to those who seek it for other people." — H. W. Sylvester

"Joys shared with others are more enjoyed." — Old proverb

"Joy increases as you give it, and diminishes as you try to keep it for yourself." — Vincent Norman Peale

"Joys are our wings; sorrows our spurs." — Richter

"Rejoice evermore." — Bible, I Thessalonians 5:16

"Every season brings its own joy." — Spanish proverb

"The joyfulness of a man will prolongeth his days." — Apocrypha, Ecclesiasticus 30:22

"Always have the support of a joyful mind in all situations." — Buddha

"We're here to learn to go with joy among the sorrows of the world." — Joseph Campbell

"It seldom happens that any felicity comes so pure as not to be tempered and allayed by some mixture of sorrow." — Cervantes

"Sorrows remembered sweeten present joy." — Pollok

"How much better is it to weep at joy than to joy at weeping." — Shakespeare

"Where there is joy there is creation. Where there is no joy there is no creation: know the nature of joy." — The Upanishads

"There is no joy above the joy of the heart." — Apocrypha, Ecclesiasticus

"Every life has its joy; every joy its law." — Old proverb

"Restraint is the golden rule of enjoyment." — Letitia Landon

"There is the true joy of life, to be used by a purpose recognized by yourself as a mighty one." — George Bernard Shaw

"On with dance, let joy be unconfined, is my motto; whether there's any dance to dance or any joy to unconfine." — Mark Twain

"Variety is the mother of Enjoyment." — Disraeli

"Tranquil pleasures last the longest; we are not fitted to bear long the burden of great joys." — Christian Bovee

"Much joy not only speaks small happiness, but happiness that shortly must expire." — Edward Young

"The most profound joy has more of gravity than of gaiety in it." — Montaigne

"Gladness of the heart is the life of people." — Apocrypha, Ecclesiasticus 30:23

"One of gladness seldom falls into madness." — Anonymous

"Labor and trouble one can always get through alone, but it takes two to be glad." — Ibsen

"The moe the merrier." — English proverb

"Sometimes your joy is the source of your smile, but sometimes your smile is the source of your joy." — Thich Nhat Hanh

"There is no beautifier of complexion, or form, or behavior, like the wish to scatter joy and not pain around us." — Emerson

"I have always said and felt that true enjoyment cannot be expressed in words." — Rousseau

"Enjoy yourself. It's later than you think." — Chinese proverb

"Learn how to feel joy." — Seneca

"The soul should always stand ajar, ready to welcome the ecstatic experience." — Emily Dickinson

"Man is the merriest, the most joyous of all the species of creation. Above and below man all are serious." — Joseph Addison

"I love such mirth as does not make friends ashamed to look upon one another the next morning." — Izaak Walton

"Joy can be real only if people look upon their lives as a service, and have a definite object in life outside themselves and their personal happiness." — Leo Tolstoy

"Human felicity or happiness is produced not so much by great pieces of good fortune that seldom happen, as by little advantages that occur every day." — Benjamin Franklin

Wonder

"Wonders will never cease." — H. Bates

"The world will never starve for wonder; but only for want of wonder." — G. K. Chesterton

"We can't survive without enchantment . . . the loss of it is killing us." — Thomas Moore

"He who can no longer pause to wonder and stand rapt in awe, is as good as dead; his eyes are closed." — Einstein

"Everything has its wonders, even darkness and silence, and I learn, whatever state I may be in, therein to be content." — Helen Keller

"Listen to the wonder! How wonderful: to stand outside as well as in, to grasp and be grasped, to look on and at the same time be the seen itself, to hold and be held — that is the aim." — Eckehart

Pleasure

"Pleasure is the greatest good." — Epicurus

"Pleasure is the object, the duty, and the goal of all rational creatures." — Voltaire

"Pleasure is due only when all duty's done." — Pollok

"Pleasure once tasted satisfies less than the desire experienced for its torments." — Joseph Roux

"Pleasure comes, but not to stay; even this shall pass away." — Theodore Tilton

"Pleasure's couch is virtue's grave." — Augustine Duganne

"One half the world can not understand the pleasures of the other." — Jane Austen

"People seek but one thing in life — their pleasure." — M. Somerset Maugham

"Choose such pleasures as recreate much and cost little." — Thomas Fuller

"Few people want the pleasures they are free to take." — Ovid

"To make pleasures pleasant, shorten them." — Charles Buston

"Don't mistake pleasure for happiness. They're a different breed of dog." — Josh Billings

"We lose the peace of years when we hunt after the rapture of moments." — Bulwer-Lytton

"Most people pursue pleasure with such breathless haste that they hurry past it." — Soren Kierkegaard

"Selfish pleasure as an end is always a disappointment." — Martin Tupper

"Oft ill diseases spring from trivial pleasure." — Cato

"In diving to the bottom of pleasures we bring up more gravel than pearls." — HonorJ de Balzac

"Let pleasure be ever so innocent, the excess is always criminal." — W. Dodd

"One buys honey too dear who licks it from thorns." — Old proverb

"After pleasant scratching comes unpleasant smarting." — Danish proverb

"Sweet is pleasure after pain." — "A very merry, dancing, drinking, laughing, quaffing, and unthinking time." — John Dryden

"Fly the pleasure that bites tomorrow." — George Herbert

"All worldly pleasure is correspondent to a like measure of anxiety." — Francis Osborn

"When Pleasure is at the bar the jury is not impartial." — "Consider pleasures as they depart, not as they come." — Aristotle

"It is not abstinence from pleasures that is best, but mastery over them without being worsted." — Aristippus

"Make the coming hour over flow with joy, and pleasure drown the brim." — Shakespeare

"No pleasure endures unseasoned by variety." — Publilius Syrus

"The sweetest pleasures are those which do not exhaust hope." — Gaston de Levis

"We tire of those pleasures we take, but never of those we give." — John Petit-Senn

"Lose no chance of giving pleasure." — F. R. Havergal

"The most delicate, the most sensible of all pleasures, consists in promoting the pleasure of others." — Jean de La Bruyère

"The greatest pleasure of life is love." — Sir William Temple

"Life is not life at all without delight." — Coventry Patmore

"Follow your bliss and doors will open where you didn't know doors existed." — Joseph Campbell

"Pleasure is very seldom found where it is sought. Our brightest blazes are commonly kindled by unexpected sparks." — "In all pleasure hope is a considerable part." — "Men become friends by a community of pleasures." — Samuel Johnson

"Pleasures are alike, simply considered in themselves. He that take pleasure to hear sermons enjoys himself as much as he that hears a play." — "Pleasure is nothing else but the intermission of pain." — John Selden

"Pleasure is deaf when told of future pain." — "Pleasure admitted in undue degree enslaves the will, nor leaves the judgment free." — William Cowper

"All fits of pleasure are balanced by an equal degree of pain or languor; 'tis like spending this year part of the next year's revenue." — Swift

"Though sages may pour out their wisdom's treasure, there is no sterner moralist than pleasure." — "With pleasure drugged, they almost longed for woe." — Lord Byron

"The man of pleasure little knows the perfect joy he loses for the disappointing gratifications which he pursues." — Joseph Addison

"The man of pleasure, by a vain attempt to be more happy than any other man can be, is often more miserable than most men are." — Charles Caleb Colton

"In life there is nothing more unexpected and surprising than the arrivals and departures of pleasure. If we find it in one place today, it is vain to seek it there tomorrow. You can not lay a trap for it." — Alexander Smith

"A perpetuity of bliss is bliss." — "Bliss is too great to lodge within an hour — duration is essential to the name." — "Reverberated pleasures fire the breast." — Edward Young

"There is little pleasure in the world that is true and sincere beside the pleasure of doing our duty and doing good. I am sure no other is comparable to this." — John Tillotson

"Pleasure dies at the very moment when it charms us most." — "To know how to despise pleasure is itself a pleasure." — "Enjoy present pleasures in such a way as not to injure future ones." — Seneca

Joking

"My way of joking is telling the truth; that is the funniest joke in the world." — George Bernard Shaw

"A comedian can only last till he either takes himself serious or his audience takes him serious." — Will Rogers

"The crisis of today is the joke of tomorrow." — H. G. Wells

"It is no joke to bear with someone who is all jokes." — "A joke not only can make an enemy, but often loses a friend." — Old proverbs

"Many a friend was lost through a joke, but none was ever gained so." — Czech proverb

"A joker is near akin to a buffoon; and neither of them is the least related to wit." — Lord Chesterfield

"A poor joke must invent its own laughter." — Latin proverb

"Clumsy jesting is no joke." — Aesop

"A difference of tastes in jokes is a great strain on the affections." — George Eliot

"Jokes of the proper kind, properly told, can do more to enlighten questions of politics, philosophy, and literature than any number of dull arguments." — Isaac Asimov

"It is requisite for the relaxation of the mind that we make use, from time to time, of playful deeds and jokes." — Thomas Aquinas

"Even the gods love jokes." — Plato

"A man reveals his character by nothing so clearly as the joke he resents." — G. C. Lichtenberg

"If they can't take a joke . . . forget them!" Anonymous

"Take a joke as a joke, and it will not provoke." — Old proverb

Jesting

"Jests that give pains are no jests." — Cervantes

"Jesting is not unlawful if it trespasseth not in quantity, quality, or reason." — Thomas Fuller

"A jest breaks no bones." — Samuel Johnson

"A jest driven home too far brings home hate." — "One that would jest must take a jest, else to let it alone were best." — Old proverbs

"The jest loses its point when one who makes it is the first to laugh." — Schiller

"The saddest ones are those that wear the jester's motley garb." — Donald Marquis

"There is no jesting with edge tools." — John Fletcher

"Many a true word is spoken in jest." — English proverb

"Jesters do oft prove to be prophets." — "A jest's prosperity lies in the ear of him that hears it, never in the tongue of him that makes it." — "They jest at scars, that never felt a wound." — Shakespeare

"If you be a jester, keep your wit till you have use for it." — "Fear not a jest. If one throws salt at you, you will not be harmed unless you have sore places." — Latin proverbs

Humor

"Humor is emotional chaos remembered in tranquillity." — James Thurber

"Humor is falling downstairs ¾ if you do it while in the act of warning someone else." — Kenneth Bird

"Humor is a drug which it's the fashion to abuse." — William Gilbert

"Humor is the only test of gravity, and gravity of humor; for a subject which will not bear raillery is suspicious, and a jest which will not bear serious examination is false wit." — Aristotle

"Humor is mankind's greatest blessing." — "The secret source of humor itself is not joy, but sorrow." — Mark Twain

"Keep good humor still, whatever we lose." — Alexander Pope

"True humor springs not more from the head than from the heart." — Carlyle

"If I had no sense of humor, I would long ago have committed suicide." — Gandhi

"The longer I live, the more I think of humor as in truth the saving sense." — Jacob Riis

"In the present state of the world it is difficult not to write lampoons." — Juvenal

"The perception of the comic is a tie of sympathy with other people." — Emerson

"People will confess to treason, murder, arson, false teeth, or a wig. How many of them will own up to a lack of humor?" Frank Moore Colby

Wit

"Wit is the only wall between us and the dark." — Mark Van Doren

"Wit is the salt of conversation, not the food." — William Hazlitt

"Wit is a form of lightning calculation; humor the exploitation of disproportion." — Russell Green

"Wit makes its own welcome, and levels all distinctions." — Emerson

"Wit should be used as a shield for defense rather than as a sword to wound others." — Thomas Fuller

"Wit ill applied is a dangerous weapon." — Edward Young

"Brevity is the soul of wit." — "Always the dullness of the fool is the whetstone of the wits." — Shakespeare

"A man of wit would often be at a loss were it not for the company of fools." — La Rochefoucauld

"The impromptu reply is precisely the touchstone of a man of wit." — Molière

"Melancholy men of all others are most witty." — Aristotle

"Great wits are sure to madness near allied, and thin partitions do their bounds divide." — John Dryden

"A man who has provoked the shaft of wit cannot complain that he smart from it." — Samuel Johnson

"Don't screw your wit beyond the compass of good manners." — Colley Cibber

"Satire! Thou shining supplement of public laws." — Edward Young

"The well of true wit is truth itself." — George Meredith

"True satire is not the sneering substance that we know, but satire that includes the satirist." — Frank Moore Colby

"Wit is a treacherous dart. It is perhaps the only weapon with which it is possible to stab oneself in one's back." — Geoffrey Bocca

Laughter

"Laughter is the music of the soul." — "Laughter is the best medicine." — Old proverbs

"Laughter is the tonic, the relief, the surcease for pain." — Charlie Chaplin

"Laughter is not at all a bad beginning for a friendship, and it is far the best ending for one." — Oscar Wilde

"Laugh, if thou art wise." — Martial

"Man alone suffers so excruciatingly in the world that we were compelled to invent laughter." — Nietzsche

"Excellent authority tells us that the right laughter is medicine to weary bones." — Carl Sandburg

"A good laugh is sunshine in a house." — William Thackeray

"A smile is the whisper of a laugh." — Anonymous

"I like the laughter that opens the lips and the heart, that shows at the same time pearls and the soul." — Victor Hugo

"They deserve Paradise who makes their companions laugh." — The Koran

"If you're not allowed to laugh in heaven, I don't want to go there." — Martin Luther

"With the fearful strain that is on me night and day, if I did not laugh I should die." — Abraham Lincoln

"I make myself laugh at everything, for fear of having to weep." — Pierre de Beaumarchais

"I shall laugh myself to death." — Shakespeare

"It better befits a man to laugh at life than to lament over it." — Seneca

"Excess of sorrow laughs. Excess of joy weeps." — William Blake

"A laugh's the wisest, easiest answer to all that's queer." — Herman Melville

"People who believe in little laugh at little." — Leonard Feeney

"No man who has once heartily and wholly laughed can be altogether and irreclaimably depraved." — Carlyle

"In laughter there is always a kind of joyousness that is incompatible with contempt or indignation." — Voltaire

"That laughter costs too much which is purchased by the sacrifice of decency." — Quintilian

"He is not laughed at that laughs at himself first." — Thomas Fuller

"You grow up the day you have the first real laugh — at yourself." — Ethel Barrymore

"A man isn't poor if he can still laugh." — Raymond Hitchcock

"The most utterly lost of all days is that in which you have not once laughed." — Sebastien Chamfort

"Against the assault of laughter, nothing can stand." — Mark Twain

"We are all here for a short spell, so get all the good laughs you can." — "Everything is funny as long as it is happening to somebody else." — Will Rogers

"He who laughs last, laughs best." — "Better the last smile than the first laughter." — English proverbs

Play

"Play so that you may be serious." — Anacharsis

"To the art of working well a civilized race would add the art of playing well." — Santayana

"It is a happy talent to know how to play." — Emerson

"In our play we reveal what kind of people we are." — Ovid

"You can discover more about a man in an hour of play than in a year of conversation." — Plato

"It is better to play than do nothing." — Confucius

"I am a great friend to public amusements; for they keep people from vice." — Samuel Johnson

"The nearer death's day, the more should old people play." — Old proverb

"Enjoy the game and you will play better vs. if you play better, you will enjoy the game." — Anonymous

"Though the most be players, some must be spectators." — Ben Jonson

"I dance to the tune that is played." — Spanish proverb

"A little nonsense now and then is relished by the wisest of men." — Anonymous

"After a certain point, money is meaningless. It ceases to be the goal. The game is what counts." — Aristotle Onassis

"The game isn't over till it's over." — Yogi Berra

"It's not whether you win or lose, it's how you play the game." — Old proverb

"What is sport to the cat is death for the mouse." — German proverb

"Those who'll play with cats must expect to be scratched." — Cervantes

"Don't play with the bear if you don't want to be bit." — "After the game, the king and pawn go into the same box." — Italian proverbs

"The chessboard is the world; the pieces are the phenomena of the universe; the rules of the game are what we call laws of nature." — Thomas Huxley

"The true object of all human life is play." — G. K. Chesterton

"One man in his time plays many parts." — "If all the year were playing holidays, to sport would be as tedious as to work." — Shakespeare

"No man is really depraved who can spend half an hour by himself on the floor playing with his little child's electric train." — Simeon Strunsky

Leisure

"Leisure offers a marvelous opportunity for freedom." — Robert Lee

"Leisure is a beautiful garment, but it will not do for constant wear." — Anonymous

"The end of labor is to gain leisure." — Aristotle

"A life of leisure and a life of laziness are two things." — "Employ thy time well if thou meanest to get leisure." — Benjamin Franklin

"One hath no leisure who useth it not." — George Herbert

"To a hasty demand a leisure reply." — Old proverb

"Dionysius the Elder, being asked whether he was at leisure, replied, 'God forbid that it should ever befall me!'" Plutarch

"When I rest, I rust." — German proverb

"Too much rest is rust." — Sir Walter Scott

"It would be glorious to see man at leisure for once. It is nothing but work, work, work." — Thoreau

"I hope I shall have leisure to make good." — Shakespeare

"There is luck in leisure." — G. Meriton

"Easy come, easy go." — English proverb

"A working man ought to have leisure in proportion to the wear and tear of his strength." — Leo XIII

"All intellectual improvement arises from leisure." — Samuel Johnson

"A poor life this is if, full of care, we have no time to stand and stare." — William Henry Davies

"Man is never less at leisure than when at leisure." — "Man does not seem to me to be a free man who does not sometimes do nothing." — Cicero

GOODNESS

"Goodness is the only investment that never fails." — "Be not merely good; be good for something." — Thoreau

"Goodness is the supreme beauty." — Caroline Fry

"Goodness is easier to recognize than to define." — Wystan Hugh Auden

"Good temper, like a sunny day, sheds a brightness over everything." — Washington Irving

"Good order is the foundation of all things." — Edmund Burke

"One good turn deserves another." — English proverb

"Seek not good from without: seek it within yourselves, or you will never find it." — Epictetus

"A good man does good merely by living." — Bulwer-Lytton

"It is his nature, not his standing, that makes the good man." — Publilius Syrus

"We may be as good as we please, if we please to be good." — Isaac Barrow

"Prove all things; hold fast that which is good." — Bible, I Thessalonians 5:21

"The greatest good is to do the present thing well." — Pittacus

"Crown every passing day with some good action daily." — Martin Tupper

"The good and the pleasant approach a man; the wise prefers the good to the pleasant." — Katha-Upanishad

"The more you associate yourself with good, the better." — Plautus

"Do good and care not to whom." — Old proverb

"You can only make others better by being good yourself." — Hugh R. Hawies

"What I hold good for self, I should for all." — Zoroaster

"Look round the habitable world: how few know their own good, or knowing it, pursue it?" Juvenal

"We know the good, we apprehend it clearly. But we can't bring it to achievement." — Euripides

"Oh yet we trust that somehow good will be the final goal of ill!" Tennyson

"Many foxes grow, but few grow good." — Benjamin Franklin

"It is very hard to be simple enough to be good." — "A good intention clothes itself with power." — Emerson

"To be good I would be good. To the not-good I would also be good in order to make them good." — Lao-tse

"Be not overcome with evil, but overcome evil with good." — Bible, Romans 12:21

"Bear with evil and expect good." — "A good bone does not always come to a good dog." — French proverbs

"To make one good action succeed another is the perfection of goodness." — Ali-Ibn-Abi-Talib

"It is good to be zealously affected always in a good thing." — Bible, Galatians 4:18

"Reverence the good." — Sophist saying

"A good thing if you know it — do it." — "A good thing is soon snatched up." — "A good thing is all the sweeter when won with pains." — "A ragged colt may make a good horse." — "A good horse never lacks a saddle." — "There is as much greatness in owning a good turn as in doing it." — Old proverbs

"Do good by stealth, and blush to find it fame." — Alexander Pope

"One that does good for good's sake seeks neither praise nor reward, but he is sure of both in the end." — William Penn

"For the good are always merry." — William Butler Yeats

"That which is striking and beautiful is not always good; but that which is good is always beautiful." — Ninon de l'Enclos

"All are presumed good till they are found in a fault." — George Herbert

"We hardly find any men of good sense save those who agree with us." — La Rochefoucauld

"A good life keeps off wrinkles." — Old proverb

"Better good than pious." — Hebrew proverb

"Experience makes us see an enormous difference between piety and goodness." — Pascal

"No news is good news." — James I

"A word or a nod from the good, has more weight than the eloquent speeches of others." — Plutarch

"Refrain not to speak when there is occasion to do good." — Apocrypha, Ecclesiasticus

"A good archer is not known by his arrows, but his aim." — English proverb

"A man's good intentions seldom add to his income." — Old proverb

"There is no good that doth not cost a price." — "The best things are not bought and sold." — Walter Smith

"Men prone to tears are good." — Greek proverb

"Be good, and let heaven answer for the rest." — Edward Young

"Real goodness does not attach itself merely to this life — it points to another world." — Webster

"A good beginning makes a good ending." — Old proverb

"All good things must come to an end." — Chaucer

"Beauty will fade, but not goodness." — Philippine proverb

"The scene changes but the aspirations of men of good will persist." — Vannevar Bush

"Postpone not a good action." — Irish proverb

"Don't make excuses — make good." — Elbert Hubbard

"Do not forget to be good." — Bible, Hebrews 13:16

"Can we ever have too much of a good thing?" Cervantes

"You can have too much of a good thing." — B. Burgh

"Too much of a good thing is wonderful." — Mae West

"You are not only good yourself, but the cause of goodness in others." — "The only good is knowledge and the only evil is ignorance." — "Living or dead, to a good man there can come no evil." — Socrates

"Health, beauty, vigor, riches, and all the other things called good, operate equally as evils to the vicious and unjust, as they do as benefits to the just." — "Excellent things are rare." — Plato

"Good has two meanings: it means that which is good absolutely and that which is good for somebody." — "Quite often good things have hurtful consequences. There are instances of men who have been ruined by their money or killed by their courage." — Aristotle

"To be doing good is man's most glorious task." — "In season, all is good." — "Who does not befriend himself by doing good?" Sophocles

"It is hard for the good to suspect evil, as it is for the bad to suspect good." — "Whatever befalls in accordance with nature should be accounted good." — Cicero

"Waste no more time arguing what a good man should be. Be one." — "What is not good for the swarm is not good for the bee." — Marcus Aurelius

"Let no man think lightly of good, saying in his heart, 'It will not come nigh me.' By the falling of waterdrops a pot is filled; the wise man becomes full of good, even if he gather it little by little." — Buddha

"In the huge mass of evil as it rolls and swells, there is ever some good working toward deliverance and triumph." — Carlyle

"One who returns a good for evil obtains the victory." — "When thy hand hath done a good act, ask thy heart whether it was well done." — Thomas Fuller

"Philosophers and clergymen are always discussing why we should be good — as if anyone doubted that we ought to be." — George Trevelyan

"Do not act as if you had ten thousand years to throw away. Death stands at your elbow. Be good for something, while you live, and it is in your power." — Far Eastern saying

"Do all the good you can, by all the means you can, in all the ways you can, in all the places you can, at all the times you can, to all the people you can, as long as you can." — John Wesley

Kindness

"Kindness begets kindness." — Greek proverb

"Kindness it is that which brings forth kindness always." — Sophocles

"Kindness is the golden chain by which society is bound together." — Goethe

"Kind words don't wear out the tongue." — Old proverb

"Kind looks foretell a kind heart within." — Pollok

"A kind face is a beautiful face." — "All kindness begins in purpose." — Old proverbs

"What wisdom can you find that is greater than kindness?" Rousseau

"Kindness is more important than wisdom, and the recognition of this is the beginning of wisdom." — Theodore Isaac Rubin

"We cannot be just unless we are kindhearted." — Marquis de Vauvenargues

"A kindness is never wasted." — Aesop

"Be kind, for every man you meet is fighting a hard battle." — Plato

"Life is so hard, how can we be anything but kind?" Buddha

"You can accomplish by kindness what you cannot do by force." — Publilius Syrus

"[There's] No enmity so hard and fierce, that kindness cannot melt." — Martin Tupper

"Try these: a kind thought, a kind word, and a good deed." — Elbert Hubbard

"My religion is very simple ¾ my religion is kindness." — 14th Dalai Lama

"The unfortunate need people who will be kind to them; the prosperous need people to be kind to." — Aristotle

"Little deeds of kindness, little words of love, help to make earth happy like the heaven above." — Julia A. Fletcher Carney

"A laugh, to be joyous, must flow from a joyous heart, for without kindness there can be no true joy." — Carlyle

"To cultivate kindness is a valuable part of the business of life." — Samuel Johnson

"To be amiable is to be satisfied with one's self and others." — William Hazlitt

"I had rather never receive a kindness, than never bestow one." — Seneca

"The best portion of a good man's life are his nameless, unremembered acts of kindness and love." — Wordsworth

"If you stop to be kind, you must swerve often from your path." — Mary Webb

"Ask yourself daily, to how many ill-minded persons you have shown a kind disposition." — Marcus Aurelius

"A part of kindness consists in loving people more than they deserve." — Joubert

"Forget injuries, never forget kindness." — Chinese proverb

"One can pay back the loan of gold, but one dies forever in debt to those who are kind." — Malayan proverb

"In hospitality it is the spirit that counts." — Greek proverb

"Write injuries in sand, kindnesses in marble." — French proverb

"Always try to be a little kinder than is necessary." — Sir James Matthew Barrie

"Have you had a kindness shown? Pass it on." — Henry Burton

"Let us be kinder to one another." — Aldous Huxley

Purity

"Purity and impurity belong to oneself; no one can purify another." — Buddha

"Unto the pure all things are pure." — Bible, Titus 1:15

"The words of the pure are pleasant words." — Bible, Proverbs

"Whatever purifies fortifies the heart." — Blair

"The night rinses what the day has soaped." — Swiss proverb

"My strength is as the strength of ten, because my heart is pure." — Tennyson

"The sun shines on the dung but is not tainted." — Diogenes

"Keep oneself unspotted from the world." — Bible, James 1:27

"Better keep yourself clean and bright: you are the window through which you must see the world." — George Bernard Shaw

"Purity of motive and nobility of mind shall rarely condescend to prove its rights, and prate of wrongs, or evidence its worth to others." — Martin Tupper

Innocence

"Innocence is a desirable thing." — Dorothy Parker

"Innocence is never accustomed to blush." — Molière

"Innocence is like polished armor; it adorns and defends." — Robert South

"Innocence, most often, is a good fortune and not a virtue." — Anatole France

"In our obsession with original sin, we do often forget . . . original innocence." — Pope Innocent of Assisi

"He that knows no evil will suspect none." — Ben Johnson

"But innocence has nothing to dread." — Jean Baptiste Racine

"There is no courage but in innocence; no constancy but in an honest cause." — Thomas Southerne

Right

"Right is right only when entire." — Victor Hugo

"Righteousness is a straight line, and is always the shortest distance between two points." — W. H. Howe

"Do right and fear no one." — Scottish proverb

"Be always sure you are right — then go ahead." — Davy Crockett

"I would rather be right than be President." — Henry Clay

"Always do right. This will gratify some people, and astonish the rest." — Mark Twain

"Choose always the way that seems the best, however rough it may be; custom will soon render it easy and agreeable." — Pythagoras

"Better is a little with righteousness, than great revenues with injustice." — Bible, proverbs

"The fear of doing right is the grand treason in times of danger." — Henry Ward Beecher

"Because right is right, to follow right where wisdom is the scorn of consequence." — Tennyson

"We cannot freely and wisely choose the right way for ourselves unless we know both good and evil." — Helen Keller

"It is not enough to do good; one must do it the right way." — John Viscount Morley

"You say it is needful: Is it therefore right?" Edward Young

"I will follow the right side even to the fire, but excluding the fire if I can." — Montaigne

"Doing what's right is no guarantee against misfortune." — William McFee

"Blessed are they which do hunger and thirst after righteousness: for they shall be filled." — Bible, Matthew 5:6

"Any man more right than his neighbors constitutes a majority of one." — Thoreau

"The time is always right to do what is right." — Martin Luther King, Jr.

"It takes less time to do a thing right than it does to explain why you did it wrong." — Longfellow

"I think and think for months and years. Ninety-nine times, the conclusion is false. The hundredth time I am right." — Einstein

"Let us have faith that right makes might, and in that faith, let us to the end, dare to do our duty, as we understand it." — Abraham Lincoln

Greatness

"Great men are rarely isolated mountain-peaks; they are the summits of ranges." — Thomas W. Higginson

"Great men are meteors designed to burn so that the earth may be lighted." — Napoleon

"Great men are able to do great kindnesses." — Cervantes

"Great men are not always wise." — Bible, Job 32:9

"Great and good are seldom the same man." — Thomas Fuller

"Great beings hallow a whole people, and lift up all who live in their time." — Sydney Smith

"Great engines turn on small pivots." — English proverb

"Greater things are believed of those who are absent." — Tacitus

"Greatness lies not in being strong, but in the right using of strength." — Henry Ward Beecher

"The price of greatness is responsibility." — Churchill

"Nothing can be truly great which is not right." — Samuel Johnson

"Everything great is not always good, but all good things are great." — Demosthenes

"They're only truly great who are truly good." — George Chapman

"There is no greatness where there is not simplicity, goodness, and truth." — Leo Tolstoy

"We can do not great things; only small things with great love." — Gandhi

"If any man seeks for greatness, let him forget greatness and ask for truth, and he will find both." — Horace Mann

"The truly great man is one who would master no one, and one who would be mastered by none." — Kahlil Gibran

"A man is great enough that is his own master." — Joseph Hall

"Whoever tries for great objects must suffer something." — Plutarch

"Whosoever wants to be great among you, must be the servant of the rest." — Bible, Matthew 20:26

"Deeds, not stones, are the true monuments of the great." — American proverb

"I would sooner fail than not be among the greatest." — John Keats

"As the greatest are, in their simplicity sublime." — Tennyson

"The great man is the man who does a thing for the first time." — Alexander Smith

"No man was ever great by imitation." — Samuel Johnson

"How great a matter a little fire kindleth!" Bible, James 3:5

"It is a great thing to do a little thing well." — "The greatest things are done by the help of small ones." — Old proverbs

"Find the great in the small and the many in the few." — Lao-tse

"There is nothing insignificant...nothing." — Samuel Coleridge

"It is to be lamented that great characters are seldom without a blot." — George Washington

"The renown of great men should always be measured by the means which they have used to acquire it." — La Rochefoucauld

"One is greatest who is most often in men's good thoughts." — Samuel Butler

"None think the great unhappy, but the great." — Edward Young

"It is the nature of a man to rise to greatness if greatness is expected of him." — Steinbeck

"Small people think they are small; great people never know they are great." — Chinese proverb

"We feel that we are greater than we know." — Wordsworth

"A great man is one who never loses his child's-heart." — Mencius

"Strike at a great man and you will miss." — Sophocles

"Every man has a fair turn to be as great as he pleases." — Jeremy Collier

"All excellent things are as difficult as they are rare." — Spinoza

"Health is the greatest gift, contentment the greatest wealth and faithfulness the greatest relationship." — Buddha

"There is only one road to true human greatness: through the school of hard knocks." — Einstein

"It is not the strength, but the duration of great sentiments that makes great men." — Nietzsche

"No man is truly great who is great only in his lifetime. The test of greatness is the page of history." — William Hazlitt

"Perfection is attained by slow degrees; it requires the hand of time." — Voltaire

"Anything great requires time, patience, and perseverance." — W. J. Wilmont Buxton

"Every calling is great when greatly pursued." — Oliver Wendell Holmes, Jr.

"Accept thy privilege to be great." — Charles Leonard Moore

"In every generation there are some outstanding chiefs." — Somaoan proverb

"Greatness knows itself." — "Some are born great, some achieve greatness, and some have greatness thrust upon them." — Shakespeare

"Great men are the commissioned guides of mankind, who rule their fellows." — "All greatness is unconscious, or it is little and naught." — Carlyle

"No great thing is created suddenly." — "For with slight efforts how should we obtain great results? It is foolish even to desire it." — Epictetus

"One who intends to be a great man ought to love neither himself nor his own things, but only what is just, whether it happens to be done by himself or by another." — Plato

"It is a rough road that leads to the heights of greatness." — "He who would do great things should not attempt them alone." — Seneca

"The heights by great men reached and kept were not attained by sudden flight, but they while their companions slept, were toiling upward in the night." — "Lives of great men all remind us we can make our lives sublime and, departing, leave behind us footprints in the sands of time." — Longfellow

"The greatest efforts of the race have always been traceable to the love of praise, as its greatest catastrophes to the love of pleasure." — John Ruskin

"The happy man must prepare ahead for evil days that are to come; and when he does, let the thought that every good and great man has been made to suffer at some time." — "One who patiently endures injury, and maintains a blameless life — is a great man indeed!" Far Eastern sayings

"Keep away from small people who try to belittle your ambitions. Small people always do that, but the really great make you feel that you, too, can become great." — Mark Twain

"A great man does not lose his self-possession when he is afflicted; the ocean is not made muddy by the falling in of its banks." — Panchatantra

"To be great is to be misunderstood." — "To be simple is to be great." — "He is great who is what he is from Nature, and who never reminds us of others." — "Not in one's goals but in one's transitions is a man great." — "No great man ever complains of want of opportunity." — Emerson

"Do not despise the bottom rungs of the ladder in the ascent to greatness. It takes a long time to bring excellence to maturity." — Publilius Syrus

The Golden Rule

"Do not to others as you would not like done to yourself." — Confucius

"Do not to others what ye do not wish done to yourself." — Mahabharata, Hinduism

"Do not do to your fellow people what is hateful to you." — The Talmud

"Do as you would want done to you." — Vdana-Varga, Buddhism

"Whatsoever ye would have others do to you, do ye even so to them." — Bible, Matthew 7:12, Christianity

"No one of you is a believer until he desire for their brother that which he desire for himself." — The Koran, Islam

"Blessed are those who prefer others before themselves." — Baha'i Faith

"Regard all creatures as you would regard your own self." — Jainism

"Whatever is disagreeable to yourself do not do unto others." — Zoroastrian proverb

"Do not do unto others what angers you if done to you by others." — Isocrates

"Refrain from doing what you do not want them to do to you." — Thales

"We should behave to our friends as we would wish our friends to behave to us." — Aristotle

"If you accommodate others, you will be accommodating yourself." — Chinese proverb

TRUTH

"Truth is always the strongest argument." — Sophocles

"Truth is stranger than fiction." — Lord Byron

"Truth is stranger than fiction, but not so popular." — Anonymous

"Truth is more important than the facts." — Frank Lloyd Wright

"Truth is established by investigation and delay; falsehood prospers by precipitancy." — Tacitus

"Truth is completely spontaneous. Lies have to be taught." — Buckminster Fuller

"Truth is not only violated by falsehood; it may be equally outraged by silence." — Henri Amiel

"Truth is generally the best vindication against slander." — "I am not bound to win, but I am bound to be true." — Abraham Lincoln

"Truth is simply the complete coherence of the universe in relation to every point contained within it." — Teilhard de Chardin

"Truth is on the march and nothing can stop it." — Emile Zola

"Truth alone conquers." — Mundaka-Upanishad

"Truth seeks no corners." — Old proverb

"Truth has a handsome countenance but torn garments." — German proverb

"Truth always lags last, limping along on the arm of time." — Baltasar Gracian

"Truth stood on one side and ease on the other; it has often been so." — Theodore Parker

"Truth finds foes where it makes none." — Old proverb

"Truth lies at the bottom of the well." — Lactantius

"Truth and oil always come to the surface." — Spanish proverb

"Truth will out." — Latin proverb

"Truth will come to light." — Shakespeare

"Truth fears no trial." — "Craft must have clothes, but truth loves to go naked." — Thomas Fuller

"Truth comes into the world with two faces: sad suffering and laughs. But it is the same face." — The Talmud

"Truth often suffers more by the heat of its defenders than from the arguments of its opposers." — William Penn

"Truths turn into dogmas the moment they are disputed." — Gilbert Chesterton

"The truth! The many eyes that look on it! The diverse things they see." — George Meredith

"If it is the truth what does it matter who says it?" Anonymous

"It is a matter of perfect indifference where a thing originated; the only question is: 'Is it true in and for itself?'" Hegel

"You will know the truth and the truth shall set you free." — Bible, John 8:32

"Great is truth, and mighty above all things." — Apocrypha, I Esdras 4:41

"Great is truth. Fire cannot burn, nor water drown it." — Alexandre Dumas the Elder

"It is a man who makes truth great, not truth which makes a man great." — Confucius

"There is no truth existing which I fear, or would wish unknown to the whole world." — Thomas Jefferson

"Live truly, and thy life shall be a great and noble creed." — H. Bonar

"For it is noble to seek truth, and it is beautiful to find it." — Sydney Smith

"The path of truth is the path of progress." — Harold Ickes

"The seeker after truth should be humbler than the dust." — Gandhi

"The deepest truths are the simplest and the most common." — Frederich Robertson

"There is nothing so strong or safe in an emergency of life as the simple truth." — Dickens

"The pure and simple truth is rarely pure and never simple." — Oscar Wilde

"He who would distinguish the true from the false must have an adequate idea of what is true and false." — Spinoza

"Every truth has two sides; it is well to look at both, before we commit ourselves to either." — Aesop

"A hair perhaps divides the False and True." — Omar Kyyam

"Would that I could discover truth as easily as I can uncover falsehood." — Cicero

"All I want is the truth, just give me some truth!" John Lennon

"There is nothing so powerful as truth, — and often nothing so strange." — Webster

"Unless you expect the unexpected you will never find 'truth,' for it is hard to discover and hard to attain." — Heraclitus

"When you have eliminated the impossible, whatever remains, however improbable, must be the truth." — Sir Arthur Conan Doyle

"What a man sees only in his best moments as truth is truth in all moments." — Joseph Cook

"From shadows and symbols into the truth." — John Henry Newman

"Speak the truth, but leave immediately after." — Slovenian proverb

"If thou art in company with others, be not ashamed of Truth." — Martin Tupper

"It would be wrong to put friendship before truth." — Aristotle

"I am therefore to become your enemy because I tell you the truth?" Bible, Galatians 4:16

"The truth is not always what we want to hear." — "How many will listen to the truth when you tell them?" Jewish proverbs

"The truth hurts." — Old proverb

"So absolutely good is truth, truth never hurts the teller." — Robert Browning

"I must speak the truth, and nothing but the truth." — Cervantes

"One should utter the truth." — Dhammanpada 224

"A truth spoken before its time is dangerous." — Greek proverb

"The poorest truth is better than the richest lie." — Old proverb

"Anything more than the truth would be too much." — Robert Frost

"The will steadfast to the truth — this is fidelity." — Old proverb

"Buy the truth, and sell it not." — Bible, Proverbs 23:23

"There are truths which are not for all people, nor for all times." — "One who seeks truth should be of no country." — Voltaire

"The way of truth is like a great road. It is not difficult to know it. The evil is only that men will not seek it." — Mencius

"But men do not seek the truth. It is truth that pursues men who run away and will not look around." — Lincoln Steffens

"People must love the truth before they thoroughly believe it." — Robert South

"The people have a right to the truth as they have a right to life, liberty and the pursuit of happiness." — Frank Norris

"But such is the irresistible nature of truth, that all it asks, and all it wants, is the liberty of appearing." — Thomas Paine

"All great truths begin as blasphemies." — George Bernard Shaw

"Man approaches the unattainable truth through a succession of errors." — Aldous Huxley

"It is the customary fate of new truths to begin as heresies and to end as superstitions." — Thomas Henry Huxley

"If the world goes against truth, then Athanasius goes against the world." — Athanasius the Great

"I believe that in the end the truth will conquer." — John Wycliffe

"Peace if possible, but truth at any rate." — Martin Luther

"The only thing one cannot embellish without causing its death is truth." — Jean Rostand

"Nothing that was worthy in the past departs; no truth or goodness realized by man ever dies, or can die." — Carlyle

"All things perish, Truth alone remains." — Katha-Upanishad

"Truth is not introduced into the individual from without, but was within them all the time." — "I know the truth only when it becomes life in me." — Soren Kierkegaard

"Truth is a jewel which should not be painted over; but it may be set to advantage and shown in a good light." — Santayana

"Truth is as impossible to be soiled by any outward touch as the sunbeam." — "Of truth, in word mightier than they in arms." — Milton

"Truth is brighter than the sun; truth is the sunny day of Reason, and falsehood the mind's dark night." — "Daily practical wisdom consists of four things: To know the root of Truth, the branches of Truth, the limit of Truth, and the opposite of Truth." — "All has an end, and will pass away. Truth alone is immortal, and lives forever." — "By truth alone is man's mind purified, and by right discipline it doth become inspired." — Far Eastern sayings

"Truth is stranger than fiction, but it is because Fiction is obliged to stick to possibilities; Truth isn't." — "If you tell the truth you don't have to remember anything." — Mark Twain

"Truth is the daughter of time, not authority." — "Men prefer to believe what they prefer to be true." — "No pleasure is comparable to the standing upon the vantage ground of truth." — "Truth comes out of error more readily than out of confusion." — "There are three parts in truth: first, the inquiry, which is the wooing of it; secondly, the knowledge of it, which is the presence of it; and thirdly, the belief, which is the enjoyment of it." — Sir Francis Bacon

"Truth is the summit of being; justice is the application of it to affairs." — "Truth is the property of no individual but is the treasure of all people." — "The greatest homage we can pay to truth is to use it." — "No man thoroughly understands a truth until he has contended against it." — Emerson

"Truth is its own reward." — "Seven years of silent inquiry are needful for a man to learn the truth, but fourteen in order to learn how to make it known to his fellow humans." — Plato

"Truth-telling, I have found, is the key to responsible citizenship. The thousands of criminals I have seen in forty years of law enforcement have had one thing in common: Every single one was a liar." — J. Edgar Hoover

"The truth is found when people are free to pursue it." — "Eternal truths will be neither true or eternal unless they have fresh meaning for every new social situation." — Franklin D. Roosevelt

"People occasionally stumble over the truth, but most of them pick themselves up and hurry off as if nothing had happened." — Churchill

"Some modern zealots appear to have no better knowledge of truth, nor better manner of judging it, than by counting noses." — Swift

"To all appearances, fiction is the native dialect of man, and the truth as esoteric language as yet but imperfectly learned and little loved." — Carl Van Doren

"Seize upon truth, wherever it is found, amongst your friends, amongst your foes, on Christian or on heathen ground; the flower's divine wherever it grows." — Isaac Watts

"Fundamental truths should be both clear and familiar truths; self-evident truths are a solid foundation for reasoning." — Charles Simmons

"I speak the truth, not so much as I would, but as much as I dare; and I dare a little the more, as I grow older." — Montaigne

"The individual absorbs knowledge, but Truth absorbs the individual." — "Perception = Examination = Reflection = Reasoning = Knowledge = Wisdom = Truth." — Manly P. Hall

"Not every sheer truth is the better for showing her face. Silence also many times is the wisest thing for a man to have in his mind." — Pindar

"Believe those who are seeking the truth; doubt those who find it." — "To love the truth is to refuse to let oneself be saddened by it." — Gide

"Rather then love, than money, than fame, give me truth." — "It takes two to speak the truth — one to speak and another to hear." — Thoreau

"How can one attempt seeing truth without knowing falsehood. It is the attempt to see the light without knowing darkness. It cannot be." — Frank Herbert

"Truth is a deep kindness that teaches us to be content in our everyday life and share with the people the same happiness." — "Say not, "I have found the truth," but rather, "I have found a truth." — "The truth that needs proof is only half true." — Kahlil Gibran

"Ethical axioms are found and tested not very differently from the axioms of science. Truth is what stands the test of experience." — "If you are out to describe the truth, leave elegance to the tailor." — Einstein

"The love of truth has its reward in heaven and even on earth." — "Convictions are more dangerous enemies of truth than lies." — Nietzsche

"The greatest enemy of any one of our truths may be the rest of our truths." — "The ultimate test for us of what a truth means is the conduct it dictates and inspires." — William James

"I do not know what I may appear to the world; but to myself I seem to have been only like a boy playing on the seashore, and diverting myself in now and then finding a smoother pebble or a prettier shell than ordinary, whilst the great ocean of truth lay all undiscovered before me." — Newton

"We know the truth, not only by the reason, but by the heart." — "There would be too great a darkness, if truth had not visible signs." — Pascal

"Cows are of many colors, but milk is of one color, white; so the proclaimers who proclaim the Truth use many varying forms to put it in, but yet the Truth enclosed in all is One." — The Upanishads

"The nearer one approaches the Truth, the happier one becomes. For the essential nature of Truth is positive Absolute Bliss." — Sivananda

"Every man wishes to have truth on his side, but it is not every man that sincerely wishes to be on the side of truth." — Richard Whately

"You will observe with concern how long a useful truth may be known and exist, before it is generally received and practiced on." — Benjamin Franklin

"Do not expect truth to prevail in all situations." — "Foolish to think that truth is in untruth, equally foolish that untruth is in truth — truth is always truth, untruth always untruth." — "If you can't find the truth right where you are, where else do you think you will find it?" Buddha

Trust

"Trust thyself only, and another shall not betray thee." — Thomas Fuller

"Trust men and they will be true to you; treat them greatly and they will show themselves great." — Emerson

"Trust them little who praises all, those less who censures all, and them least who are indifferent about all." — Johann Kaspar Lavater

"Trust everybody, but cut the cards." — Finley Peter Dunne

"Trust your ears less than your eyes." — "Men trust their ears less than their eyes." — Herodotus

"Hear willingly, but trust not hastily." — Cleobulus

"Men cannot be trusted always to know their true rational interests." — Plato

"I wonder of people who dare trust themselves with others." — Shakespeare

"They who mistrusts the most should be trusted the least." — Theognis

"It is an equal failing to trust everybody, and to trust nobody." — Old proverb

"To trust is a virtue. It is weakness that begets distrust." — Gandhi

"The trust which we put in ourselves causes us to feel trust in others." — La Rochefoucauld

"He who doesn't trust himself can never really trust anyone else." — Cardinal De Retz

"Just trust yourself, then you will know how to live." — Goethe

"To be trusted is a greater compliment than to be loved." — James MacDonald

"You may be deceived if you trust too much, but you will live in torment if you do not trust enough." — Frank Crane

"The man who trusts men will make fewer mistakes than they who distrusts them." — Conte Camillo ci Cavour

"The soul and spirit that animates and keeps up society is mutual trust." — Robert South

"I think that we may safely trust a good deal more than we do. We may waive just so much care of ourselves as we honestly bestow elsewhere." — Thoreau

"The only way to make a man trustworthy is to trust him; and the surest way to make him untrustworthy is to distrust him and show your distrust." — Henry Lewis Stimson

"People who can be relied upon are always in demand. The scarcest thing in the world is a thoroughly reliable person." — Hetty Green

Sincerity

"Sincerity and truth are the basis of every virtue." — Confucius

"Sincerity, thou first of virtues." — Lord Kames

"Men of weak character cannot be sincere." — La Rochefoucauld

"Self-suffering is the truest test of sincerity." — Gandhi

"A man often hopes that his friends are more sincere than himself." — William Allingham

"Sincerity is to speak as we think, to do as we pretend and profess, to perform what we promise, and really to be what we would seem and appear to be." — John Tillotson

Ideals

"Ideals are the world's masters." — Josiah Gilbert Holland

"Idealism increases in direct proportion to one's distance from the problem." — John Galsworthy

"The ideal life is in our blood and never will be still." — Phillips Brooks

"You can tell the ideals of a nation by its advertisements." — George Norman Douglas

"Our sense of fatal habits of reasoning, paralyze us, we need the impulse of the pure ideal." — Heraclitus

"All men are prepared to accomplish the incredible if their ideals are threatened." — Hermann Hesse

"If you believe in an ideal, you don't own you, it owns you." — Raymond Chandler

"Beauty passes, but perfection remains with us." — Turkish proverb

"Ideals are like stars; you will not succeed in touching them with your hands. But like the seafaring man on the desert of waters, you choose them as your guides, and following them you will reach your destiny." — Carl Schurz

"It's really a wonder that I haven't dropped all my ideals, because they seem so absurd and impossible to carry out. Yet I keep them, because in spite of everything, I still believe that people are really good at heart." — Anne Frank

"Each time a man stands for an ideal, or acts to improve the lot of others, or strikes out against injustice, he sends forth a tiny ripple of hope." — Robert F. Kennedy

"No man can be perfectly free till all are free; no man can be perfectly moral till all are moral; no man can be perfectly happy till all are happy." — Herbert Spencer

"If you have built castles in the air, your work need not be lost; that is where they should be. Now put the foundations under them." — Thoreau

WISDOM

"Wisdom is the principal thing; therefore get wisdom; and with all thy getting get understanding." — Bible, Proverbs 4:7

"Wisdom is better than rubies. And all the things that may be desired are not to be compared to her." — Bible, Proverbs 8:11

"Wisdom is knowing what to do next; virtue is doing it." — David Jordan

"Wisdom is always an overmatch for strength." — Phaedrus

"Wisdom is the wealth of the wise." — "Wisdom is a good purchase though we pay dear for it." — Old proverbs

"Wisdom is ofttimes nearer when we stoop than when we soar." — Wordsworth

"Wisdom is the gray hair unto the old." — Apocrypha, Wisdom of Solomon 4:9

"Wisdom is not harsh-voiced and frowning, but benignant and approachable." — Thomas Lynch

"Wisdom is not vicarious." — W. H. Howe

"Wisdom is not a product of schooling but of the lifelong attempt to acquire it." — Einstein

"Wisdom is not wisdom when it is derived from books alone." — "Dare to be wise." — "Wisdom at times is found in folly." — Horace

"Wisdom excelleth folly, as far as light excelleth darkness." — Bible, Ecclesiastes I, 2:13

"Wisdom begins in wonder." — Socrates

"Wisdom comes by disillusionment." — Santayana

"Wisdom comes alone through suffering." — "It is a high advantage for a wise man not to seem wise." — Aeschylus

"Wisdom without goodness is craft and treachery." — Sir Richard Steele

"Wisdom is a loving spirit." — "Whoso watcheth for wisdom shall quickly be without care." — Apocrypha, Book of Wisdom

"Wise men plead causes, but fools decide them." — Anacharsis

"Wise men care not for what they cannot have." — Old proverb

"Wise men, even if all the laws were abolished, would still lead the same lives." — Aristophanes

"The learned differ from the unlearned in the wise have a good hope." — Chilon

"A wise man's country is the world." — Aristippus

"That man alone is wise who keeps the mastery of himself." — Far Eastern saying

"The wisest men follow their own direction." — Euripides

"Lips never err when Wisdom keeps the door." — Delaune

"The mouth of the righteous speaketh wisdom." — Bible, David

"A wise man is known by few words." — Bible, Proverbs 10:14

"A wise man will hold his tongue till he sees opportunity." — Apocrypha, Ecclesiasticus

"The wise man has long ears and a short tongue." — German proverb

"The wise man wishes to be slow in his words, and earnest in his conduct." — Confucius

"A single conversation with a wise man is better than a month's study of books." — Chinese proverb

"A word to the wise is enough." — Dunbar

"Converse with the wise." — "Be a lover of wisdom." — "Emulate wisdom." — Sophist sayings

"Sciences may be learned by rote, but wisdom not." — Laurence Sterne

"Not by years but by disposition is wisdom acquired." — "No man is wise enough by himself." — Plautus

"The first point of wisdom is to discern that which is false; the second, to know that which is true." — Lactantius

"It is the duty of a wise man to foresee evil and to prevent it." — Pittacus

"The function of wisdom is to discriminate between good and evil." — Cicero

"What is not wisdom is danger." — Old proverb

"It is a characteristic of wisdom not to do desperate things." — Thoreau

"The art of being wise is the art of knowing what to overlook." — William James

"It is not wise to be wiser than is necessary." — Quinault

"Nine-tenths of wisdom consists in being wise in time." — Theodore Roosevelt

"Some are wise, and some are otherwise." — Benjamin Franklin

"He is not wise that is not wise for himself." — English proverb

"The weakest spot in every man is where he thinks himself to be the wisest." — Nathaniel Emmons

"Many men might have attained to wisdom had they not assumed that they already possessed it." — Seneca

"Knowledge is proud that one has learned so much; Wisdom is humble that one knows no more." — William Cowper

"What is it to be wise? 'Tis but to know how little can be known — to see all other's faults and feel our own." — Alexander Pope

"Let not the wise man glory in his wisdom!" Bible, Jeremiah

"Not all people are wise; indeed, very few are." — Guicciardini

"Every man is a damn fool for at least five minutes every day; wisdom consists in not exceeding the limit." — Elbert Hubbard

"A wise man does not strive, the ignorant man ties himself up." — Taoist proverb

"In seeking wisdom thou art wise; in imagining that thou hast attained it thou art a fool." — Simon Ben Azzai

"A sensible man is wiser than he knows, while a fool knows more than is wise." — Lao-tse

"A wise man's day is worth a fool's life." — Arabian proverb

"In the world we live in, one fool makes many fools, but one sage only a few sages." — G. C. Lichtenberg

"If wise men were hairs, the world would need a wig." — Austin O'Malley

"No wise man stands behind an ass." — Terence

"The wise learn from adversity; the foolish merely repeat it." — Old proverb

"I don't think much of a man who is not wiser today than he was yesterday." — Abraham Lincoln

"Let us raise a standard to which the wise and honest can repair." — George Washington

"It takes a wise man to recognize a wise man." — Xenophanes

"Nothing indeed in this world purifies like wisdom." — Bhagavad-gita

"The truest wisdom is a resolute determination." — Napoleon

"Be ye therefore wise as serpents, and harmless as doves." — Bible, Matthew 10:16

"Knowledge comes but wisdom lingers." — Tennyson

"Knowledge becomes Understanding, which becomes Wisdom." — Old proverb

"In youth and beauty, wisdom is rare." — Homer

"Youth is the time to study wisdom; old age is the time to practice it." — Rousseau

"The aged in council, the young in action." — Danish Proverb

"Days should speak and multitude of years should teach wisdom." — Bible, Job

"Pain is the father, and love the mother, of wisdom." — Ludwig Borne

"Nothing in human life is more to be lamented, than that a wise man who should have so little influence." — Herodotus

"I am not very keen for doves or hawks. I think we need more owls." — George Aiken

"The wisest man is generally one who thinks himself the least so." — Nicolas Boileau-Despreaux

"Defer not till tomorrow to be wise, tomorrow's sun to thee may never rise." — William Congreve

"The sublimity of wisdom is to do those things living which are to be desired when dying." — Jeremy Taylor

"Therefore the desire of wisdom brings one to the everlasting Kingdom." — Apocrypha, Wisdom 6:21

"The beginning of wisdom is the knowledge that what is old is new." — Anonymous

"Where ignorance is bliss 'tis folly to be wise." — Thomas Gray

"No man so wise but has a little folly to spare." — Old proverb

"Mingle just a little folly with wisdom." — French proverb

"Wisdom rises upon the ruins of folly." — "A wise man may look ridiculous in the company of fools." — "There is not a wise man that cannot play the fool upon occasion." — "'Tis not knowing much, but what is useful, that makes a man wise." — Thomas Fuller

"Wisdom is a loving spirit. Her conversation hath no bitterness." — "Despise not the discourse of the wise, but acquaint thyself with their proverbs." — Apocrypha, Ecclesiasticus

"Wisdom is to the soul what health is to the body." — "It is easier to be wise on behalf of others than to be so for ourselves." — La Rochefoucauld

"Perfect wisdom hath four parts; wisdom, the principle of doing things aright; justice, the principle of doing things equally in public and private; fortitude, the principle of not flying danger, but meeting it; and temperance, the principle of subduing desires and living moderately." — Plato

"Wisdom resteth in the heart of one that hath understanding." — "Incline thine ear unto wisdom." — "How much better is it to get wisdom than gold!" "Say unto wisdom: Thou art my brother." — "He shall be commended according to his wisdom." — "He that getteth wisdom loveth his own soul." — "Get wisdom, get understanding; forget it not." — "It is more easy to be wise for others than for thyself." — "If thou be wise, thou shalt be wise for thyself." — "Go to the ants . . . consider their ways, and be wise!" "He that walketh with wise men shall be wise." — "The lips of the wise shall preserve them." — "Wisdom is too high for a fool." — Bible, Proverbs

"Wise men profit more by fools, than fools by wise men; for a wise man avoids the faults of fools, but that fool would not imitate the good example of a wise man." — Cato

"Men can acquire knowledge but not wisdom. Some of the greatest fools ever known were learned men." — "It is better to weep with wise ones than to laugh with fools." — Spanish proverbs

"Wise it is to comprehend the whole." — "A man of wisdom is a man of years." — "Wealth may seek us; but wisdom must be sought, sought before all; but how unlike all else we seek on earth, 'tis never sought in vain." — "Be wise today; 'tis madness to defer." — Edward Young

"Life is a festival only to the wise." — "Go where he will, the wise man is at home, his hearth the earth, — his hall the azure dome." — "Wise men are not wise all the time." — Emerson

"He is not called wise who knows good and ill, but he who can recognize the two evils the lesser." — "A wise man hears one word and understands two." — "The wise man, even when he holds his tongue, says more than the fool when he speaks." — Jewish proverbs

"A wise man tighteneth his tongue, speaking less than thinking." — "Thou art wise, if thou beat off petty troubles, nor suffer their stinging to fret thee." — "A wise man scorneth nothing, be it never so small or homely." — Martin Tupper

"In much wisdom is much pain." — "Wisdom is better than strength . . . and better than weapons of war." — "Better is a poor and wise child than an old and foolish king." — Bible, Ecclesiastes

"It is unwise to be too sure of one's own wisdom. It is healthy to be reminded that the strongest might weaken and the wisest might err." — Gandhi

"Great wisdom consists in not demanding too much of human nature, and yet not altogether spoiling it by indulgence." — Lin Yutang

"From the errors of others a wise man corrects his own." — "They bid fair to grow wise who have discovered that they are not so." — Publilius Syrus

"Socrates the first and wisest of them all professed to know this only, that he nothing knew." — "To know that which before us lies in daily life is the prime wisdom." — Milton

"Though a soul be wise, it is no shame for him to live and learn." — "How terrible is wisdom when it brings no profit to the man that is wise!" Sophocles

"To feel one's ignorance is to be wise; to feel sure of one's wisdom is to be a fool." — "Unenduring are youth, beauty, life, wealth, lordship, the society of the beloved; let not the wise be deluded by these." — Far Eastern sayings

"He who learns the rules of wisdom without conforming to them in his life is like someone who ploughs in his field but does not sow." — Sa'di

"The road to wisdom? Well, it's plain and simple to express: Error and error and error and error again but less and less and less." — Piet Hein

"They that be wise shall shine as the brightness of the firmament; and they that turn many to righteousness as the stars for ever and ever." — Bible, Daniel

"It is part of a wise man to feed himself with moderate pleasant food and drink, and to take pleasure with perfumes, with the beauty of growing plants, dress, music, sports, and theaters." — Spinoza

"The wise old owl sat on an oak, the more he saw the less he spoke; the less he spoke the more he heard; why aren't we like that wise old bird?" Edward Hersey Richards

"It is the part of a wise man to keep himself today for tomorrow, and not to venture all his eggs in one basket." — Miguel de Cervantes

"The latter part of a wise man's life is taken up in curing the follies, prejudices, and false opinions he had contracted in the former." — "Some people take more care to hide their wisdom than their folly." — "No wise man ever wished to be younger." — "A wise man is never less alone than when he is alone." — Swift

"A wise man never loses anything if he has himself." — "The most manifest sign of wisdom is a continual cheerfulness." — Montaigne

"A wise man associating with the vicious becomes an idiot; a dog traveling with good man becomes a rational being." — Arabian proverb

"The fool doth think he is wise, but the wise man knows himself to be a fool." — "When clouds are seen a wise man puts on his coat." — "So wise, so young, they say, do never live long." — Shakespeare

"How can a wise man, knowing the unity of life, seeing all creatures in himself, be deluded or sorrowful." — Chhandogya-Upanishad

"In wisdom be a lamp, a light unto yourself." — "We do not need more knowledge but more wisdom. Wisdom comes from our own attention." — "Even death is not to be feared by he who has lived wisely." — Buddha

Knowledge

"Knowledge is power." — Sir Francis Bacon

"Knowledge is the food of the soul." — Plato

"Knowledge is the true organ of sight, not the eyes." — Panchatantra

"Knowledge is the eye of desire and can become the pilot of the soul." — Will Durant

"Knowledge is but folly unless it is guided by grace." — George Herbert

"Knowledge is more than equivalent to force." — Samuel Johnson

"Knowledge is the intellectual manipulation of carefully verified observations." — Sigmund Freud

"Knowledge exists to be imparted." — Emerson

"Knowledge humbleth the great man, astonisheth the common man, and puffeth up the little man." — Old proverb

"Knowledge and timber should not be much used until they are seasoned." — Oliver Wendell Holmes

"Knowledge the clue to life can give: Then wherefore hesitate to live." — Martial

"Knowledge the wing wherewith we fly to heaven." — Shakespeare

"Knowledge, like religion, must be 'experienced' in order to be known." — Edwin Percy Whipple

"Knowledge, in truth, is the great sun in the firmament. Life and power are scattered with all beams." — Webster

"All our knowledge has its origins in our perceptions." — "The desire to know is natural to good men." — Leonardo da Vinci

"True knowledge is not attained by thinking. It is what you are; it is what you become." — Sri Aurobindo

"One that would know what shall be must consider what hath been." — Thomas Fuller

"All wish to possess knowledge, but few, comparatively speaking, are willing to pay the price." — Juvenal

"That the soul be without knowledge, it is not good." — Bible, Proverbs 19:2

"My people are destroyed for lack of knowledge." — Bible, Hosea 4:6

"It is knowledge that ultimately gives salvation." — Mahatma Gandihi

"A man of knowledge increaseth strength." — Bible, Proverbs 24:5

"A man who does not know one thing knows another." — Kenyan proverb

"It is better, of course, to know useless things than to know nothing." — Seneca

"One part of knowledge consists in being ignorant of such things as are not worthy to be known." — Crates

"It is better to know many things than to be ignorant of all." — Cleobulus

"The first step to knowledge is to know that we are ignorant. As for me, all I know is that I know nothing." — Socrates

"Behold, we know not anything." — Tennyson

"It is better to know nothing than to know what ain't so." — Josh Billings

"Beware of false knowledge; it is more dangerous than ignorance." — George Bernard Shaw

"A little knowledge is a dangerous thing." — Alexander Pope

"If a little knowledge is dangerous, where is the man who has so much as to be out of danger?" Thomas Huxley

"The more you know, the less you understand." — Tao Te Ching

"The more you know, the less you need." — Aboriginal Australian proverb

"We may with advantage at times to forget what we know." — Publilius Syrus

"Let those who claim to know a lot produce their knowledge." — Hawaiian proverb

"To be proud of knowledge is to be blind with light." — American proverb

"Those who know do not tell, those who tell do not know." — Lao-tse

"One who knows little quickly tells it." — Italian proverb

"Who knows most speaks least." — Spanish proverb

"The things we know best are the things we haven't been taught." — Marquis de Vauvenargues

"Knowledge which is acquired under compulsion obtains no hold on the mind." — Plato

"Never any knowledge was delivered in the same manner it was invented." — Sir Francis Bacon

"Sweet food of sweetly uttered knowledge." — Sir Philip Sidney

"What harm in getting knowledge even from a sot, a pot, a fool, a mitten, or an old slipper?" Rabelais

"In many things it is not well to say, 'Know thyself'; it is better to say, 'Know others.'" Menander of Athens

"The seeds of knowledge may be planted in solitude, but must be cultivated in public." — Samuel Johnson

"Zeal without knowledge is like fire without light." — English proverb

"If you have knowledge, let others light their candles at it." — Thomas Fuller

"To know and yet not to do, is in fact not to know." — Wang Yang Ming

"The end of all knowledge should be in virtuous action." — Sir Sydney Smith

"A tree is known by its fruit." — Bible, Matthew 12:33

"As knowledge increases, wonder deepens." — Charles Morgan

"The desire of knowledge, lies the thirst of riches, increases ever with the acquisition of it." — Laurence Sterne

"One that knoweth all that may be known is as a God among people." — Pythagoras

"To know all things is not permitted." — Horace

"Those who busy themselves in vain knowledge resemble owls which see only in the night, but are blind in the light." — Bias

"The ignorant go everywhere and learn little; the wise go within and learn everything there is to know." — George King

"No man can reveal to you aught but that which already lies half a sleep in the dawning of your knowledge." — Kahlil Gibran

"If you lack knowledge, what do you have? If you have knowledge, what do you lack?" Old proverb

"All men by nature desire knowledge." — "Some men are just as sure of the truth of their opinions as are others of what they know." — Aristotle

"That jewel knowledge is great riches, which is not plundered by kinfolk, nor carried off by thieves, nor decreased by giving." — Bhavabhuti

"It is the ancient feeling of the human heart — that knowledge is better than riches; and it is deeply and sacredly true!" Sydney Smith

"An investment in knowledge always pays the best interest." — "Proclaim not all thou knowest, all thou owest, all thou hast, nor all thou can'st." — Benjamin Franklin

"Since we cannot be universal and know all that is to be known of everything, we ought to know a little about everything." — Pascal

"A taste of every sort of knowledge is necessary to form the mind, and is the only way to give the understanding its due improvement to the full extent of its capacity." — Locke

"There is no purifier like knowledge in this world: time makes one find himself in his heart." — "The raft of knowledge ferries the worst sinner to safety." — Bhagavad-gita 4

"When you know a thing, to hold that you know it, and when you do not know a thing, to allow that you do not know it: this is knowledge." — "The essence of knowledge is, having it, to apply it; not having it, to confess your ignorance." — "Real knowledge is to know the extent of one's ignorance." — Confucius

"The more extensive a man's knowledge of what has been done, the greater will be his power of knowing what to do." — Disraeli

Understanding

"Understanding begins with love and respect." — Rolling Thunder

"Understanding is a two-way street." — Eleanor Roosevelt

"Only when you stop liking and disliking will all be clearly understood." — Zen proverb

"To understand everything is to forgive everything." — Buddha

"I have learned not to mock, lament or execrate, but to understand human actions." — Spinoza

"O Lord, help me not to despise or oppose what I do not understand." — William Penn

"All the glory of greatness has no luster for men who are in search for understanding." — Pascal

"I want, by understanding myself, to understand others." — Katherine Mansfield

"Our dignity is not in what we do, but what we understand. The whole world is doing things." — Santayana

"Men may be made to follow a path of action, but they may not be made to understand it." — Confucius

"They seeing, see not; and hearing, they hear not, neither do they understand." — Bible, Matthew

"They damn what they do not understand." — Cicero

"To understand all makes us very indulgent." — Madame de Stael

"To depart from evil is understanding." — Bible, Job 38:28

"Good understanding giveth favor." — Bible, Proverbs

"All I know is that one understands, only what one loves." — Marc Chagall

"I shall light a candle of understanding in thine heart, which shall not be put out." — Apocrypha, II Esdras 4:8

"Tell me and I'll forget; show me and I may remember; involve me and I'll understand." — Chinese proverb

"Every man supposes himself not to be fully understood or appreciated." — "It is a luxury to be understood." — Emerson

"There is a great difference between knowing a thing and understanding it. You can know a lot about something and not really understand it." — Charles Kettering

"If one master one thing and understands one thing well, one has at the same time, insight into and understanding of many things." — Vincent van Gogh

"If thou seest a man of understanding, get thee betimes unto him, and let thy foot wear the steps of his door." — Apocrypha, Ecclesiasticus

"People are of three different capacities: one understands intuitively, another only understands so far as it is explained, and a third understands neither of himself nor by explanation: the first is excellent, the second commendable, and the third altogether useless." — Niccolo Machiavelli

"O foolish people, and without understanding; which have eyes and see not; which have ears and hear not." — Bible, Jeremiah 5:21

"The improvement of the understanding is for two ends; first, our own increase of knowledge; secondly, to enable us to deliver that knowledge to others." — Locke

"What is not fully understood is not possessed." — "A man doesn't learn to understand anything unless he loves it." — Goethe

Advice

"Advice is a sacred thing." — Plato

"Advice is easier than helping." — Old proverb

"Advice is like snow; the softer it falls, the longer it dwells upon, and the deeper its sinks into the mind." — Samuel Coleridge

"Advice is seldom welcome. Those who need it most, like it least." — Philip Stanhope

"Advice should be viewed from behind." — Swedish proverb

"Advise not what is most pleasant, but what is most useful." — Solon

"Good advice is beyond all price." — Old proverb

"The advice of the aged will not mislead you." — Welsh proverb

"One who seeks advice seldom errs." — Filipino proverb

"Ask for advice but do what you think is best." — Greek proverb

"No man can give you wiser advice than yourself." — "Dare to give true advice with all frankness." — Cicero

"In giving advice I advise you, be short." — Horace

"Never trust the advice of someone in difficulties." — Aesop

"No enemy is worse than bad advice." — Sophocles

"Do not ask advice of the ignorant." — Tamil proverb

"A wise man doesn't need advice, and a fool won't take it." — Elbert Hubbard

"Many receive advice, few profit from it." — Publilius Syrus

"A man asks for advice in vain who will not follow it." — French proverb

"A man who won't be advised, can't be helped." — Old proverb

"The worst men often give the best advice." — Philip James Bailey

"Men give away nothing so liberally as their advice." — La Rochefoucauld

"Who cannot give good counsel? 'Tis cheap, it costs them nothing." — Robert Burton

"I realize that advice is worth what it costs — that is nothing." — Gen. Douglas MacArthur

"Don't offer me advice; give me money." — Spanish proverb

"No man is wise enough to advise himself." — "Good counsel never comes too late." — German proverbs

"If the counsel be good, take it no matter who gave it." — Old proverb

"Friendly counsel cuts off many foes." — Shakespeare

"In the multitude of counselors there is safety." — Bible, Proverbs 11:14

"Reproofs of instruction are the way of life." — Bible, Proverbs

"You can give a piece of advice, but not good luck along with that." — Norwegian proverb

"Advice when most needed is least heeded." — "There is nothing which we receive with so much reluctance as advice." — English proverbs

"Advice after injury is like medicine after death." — "A man who builds to every one's advice will have a crooked house." — "The best advice is found on the pillow." — Danish proverbs

"Give neither counsel nor salt till you are asked for it." — "Be slow of giving advice, ready to do a service." — "Write down the advice of those who love you, though you like it not at present." — Italian proverbs

"Seek counsel of them who makes you weep, and not of them who makes you laugh." — "Never give advice in a crowd." — Arabian proverbs

"It is easy to sit in the sunshine and talk to the man in the shade. It is easy to float in a well-trimmed boat, and point out the places to wade." — Ella Wheeler Wilcox

"When Thales was asked what was difficult, he said, 'To know one's self.' And what was easy, 'to advise another.'" Diogenes Laertius

Mind

"Mind over matter." — Old proverb

"Minds are conquered not by force, but by love and high-mindedness." — Spinoza

"The mind is its own place, and in itself can make a heaven of Hell, a hell of Heaven." — Milton

"The mind is fickle and hard to be checked." — "The mind is the slayer of the real." — Bhagavad-gita

"The mind contains all possibilities." — Buddha

"The mind covers more ground than the heart but goes less far." — Chinese proverb

"The mind that would be happy must be great." — Edward Young

"The mind ought sometimes to be amused, that it may return the better to thinking." — Phoedrus

"The mind grows narrow in proportion as the soul grows corrupt." — Rousseau

"The human mind is our fundamental resource." — John F. Kennedy

"It is the mark of an educated mind to be able to entertain a thought without accepting it." — Aristotle

"There is nothing so much worth as a mind well instructed." — Apocrypha, Ecclesiasticus

"Where is the love, beauty and truth we seek, but in our mind?" Shelley

"Let every man be fully persuaded in his own mind." — Bible, Romans 14:5

"The mind of each man is the man himself." — Cicero

"Ten people, ten minds." — Japanese proverb

"Remember when life's path is steep to keep your mind even." — Horace

"The mind is like a bright mirror standing. Take care to wipe it all the time, and allow no dust to cling." — Taoist proverb

"The perfect man employs his mind as a mirror. It grasps nothing; it refuses nothing. It receives, but does not keep." — Chuang-tzu

"It is not enough to have a good mind; the main thing is to use it well." — Descartes

"Where brains are what you need, force will not succeed." — Jewish proverb

"Our minds have unbelievable power over our bodies." — Andre Maurois

"One good head is better than a hundred strong hands." — Thomas Fuller

"In the beginner's mind there are many possibilities, in the expert's mind there are few." — Shunryu Suzuki

"The wisest mind has something yet to learn." — Santayana

"Old minds are like old horses; you must exercise them if you wish to keep them in working order." — John Quincy Adams

"Few minds wear out; more rust out." — Christian Bovee

"Free your mind." — "Keep an open mind." — Anonymous

"The resolved mind hath no cares." — George Herbert

"If a cluttered desk signs a cluttered mind, of what, then, is an empty desk a sign?" Einstein

"Empty thy mind of evil, but fill it with good." — Far Eastern saying

"It is the mind that maketh good or ill, that maketh wretch or happy, rich or poor." — Edmund Spenser

"The two great movers of the human mind are the desire of good, and the fear of evil." — Samuel Johnson

"The greatest minds are capable of the greatest vices as well as of the greatest virtues." — Rene Descartes

"Our purses shall be proud, our garments poor: for 'tis the mind that makes the body rich." — Shakespeare

"Great minds discuss ideas, average minds discuss events, small minds discuss people." — Eleanor Roosevelt

"Little things affect little minds." — Disraeli

"Little things please little minds." — Ovid

"A common mind perceiveth not beyond his eyes and ears." — Martin Tupper

"Commonplace minds usually condemn what is beyond the reach of their understanding." — La Rochefoucauld

"A man cannot develop his mind by simply writing and reading or making speeches all day long." — Gandhi

"A mind conscious of integrity scorns to say more than it means to perform." — Robert Burns

"I not only use all the brains I have, but all I can borrow." — Woodrow Wilson

"No state of mind once gone can recur and be identical with what it was before." — William James

"One need not a house; The brain has corridors surpassing material place." — Emily Dickinson

"No matter where this body is, the mind is free to go elsewhere." — William Henry Davies

"The mind of man is capable of anything, because everything is in it, all the past as well as the future." — Joseph Conrad

"The highest, most varied and lasting pleasures are those of the mind." — Schopenhauer

"Mind is the great lever of all things; human thought is the process by which human ends are ultimately answered." — Webster

"To the dull mind all of nature is leaden. To the illumined mind the whole world sparkles with light." — "A chief event of life is the day in which we have encountered a mind that startled us." — Emerson

"Let us train our minds to desire what the situation demands." — "A good mind possesses a kingdom." — "As the soil, however rich it may be, cannot be productive without culture, so the mind without cultivation can never produce good fruit." — "The mind is never right but when it is at peace within itself." — Seneca

"Strongest minds are often those of whom the noisy world hears least." — "Minds that have nothing to confer find little to perceive." — Wordsworth

"Of all the tyrannies on human kind, the worst is that which persecutes the mind." — "A narrow mind begets obstinacy; we do not easily believe what we cannot see." — John Dryden

"Between the poles of the conscious and the unconscious, there has the mind made a swing. Thereon hang all beings and all worlds, and that swing never ceases its sway." — Kabir

"A mind stretched to a new idea never goes back to its original dimensions." — Oliver Wendell Holmes

Intellect

"Intellect alone is a dry and rattling thing." — Ilka Chase

"Intellectual passion drives out sensuality." — Leonardo da Vinci

"Intelligence is shown by good judgment." — "Intelligence is not shown by witty words, but by wise acts." — Far Eastern sayings

"To perceive things is the gem of intelligence." — Lao-tse

"If a man's eye is on the Eternal, his intellect will grow." — Emerson

"An intellectual is someone whose mind watches itself." — Albert Camus

"It is only intellect that keeps me sane; perhaps this makes me overvalue intellect against feeling." — Bertrand Russell

"The pleasures of the intellect are permanent, the pleasures of the heart are transitory." — Thoreau

"We should take care not to make intellect our god; it has, of course, powerful muscles, but no personality." — Einstein

"We pay a high price for being intelligent. Wisdom hurts." — Euripides

"Many complain of their looks, but none of their brains." — Hebrew proverb

"One does not gain much by mere cleverness." — Marquis de Vauvenargues

"Clever men are good, but they are not the best." — Carlyle

"The use of intelligence is the highest privilege and the deadliest menace of humanity." — Joseph Jastrow

"Give me the young man who has brains enough to make a fool of himself." — Robert Louis Stevenson

"Intelligence increases mere physical ability one half. The use of the head abridges the labor of the hands." — Henry Ward Beecher

"The difference between intelligence and an education is this — that intelligence will make you a good living." — Charles Kettering

"Man has a great aversion to intellectual labor." — Samuel Johnson

"If you don't use your head, you'll use your pocketbook." — Belgian proverb

"Intelligence appears to be the thing that enables a man to get along without education. Education appears to be the thing that enables a man to get along without the use of his intelligence." — Albert Edward Wiggam

"No great intellectual thing was ever done by great effort; a great thing can only be done by a great man, and he does it without effort." — John Ruskin

Thinking

"Thinking is the essence of wisdom." — Persian proverb

"Thinking is the talking of the soul with itself." — Plato

"Thinking is like loving and dying, each of us must do it for himself." — Josiah Royce

"I think; therefore I am — Cogito, ergo sum" Descartes

"To act is easy; to think is hard." — Goethe

"To meditate is to labor; to think is to act." — Victor Hugo

"They can do all because they think they can." — Virgil

"To think great thoughts you must be heroes, as well as idealists." — Oliver Wendell Holmes, Jr.

"I was a freethinker before I knew how to think." — George Bernard Shaw

"I cannot teach anybody anything, I can only make them think." — Socrates

"To most people nothing is more troublesome than the effort of thinking." — James Bryce

"Most people would rather die than think; in fact, most do." — Bertand Russell

"Two heads are better than one." — English proverb

"The rich are too indolent, the poor too weak, to bear the insupportable fatigue of thinking." — William Cowper

"The real problem is not whether machines think but whether men do." — B. F. Skinner

"Fore-think, though you cannot fore-tell." — "As you think of others, others will think of you." — Old proverbs

"There is nothing either good or bad, but thinking makes it so." — Shakespeare

"Life has taught me to think, but thinking has not taught me how to live." — Alexander Herzen

"Think for yourselves and let others enjoy the privilege to do so too." — "Those who think are excessively few; and those few do not set themselves to disturb the world." — Voltaire

"Where all think alike, no one thinks very much." — Walter Lippmann

"Thinking is the hardest work there is, which is the probable reason why so few engage in it." — "If you think you can or can't . . . you are right." — Henry Ford

"It is astonishing what an effort it seems to be for many people to put their brains definitely and systematically to work. They seem to insist on somebody else doing their thinking for them." — Thomas Edison

"If you make people think they're thinking, they'll love you. If you really make them think they'll hate you." — Donald Marquis

"A great many people think they are thinking when they are merely rearranging their prejudices." — "A thing is important if any one think it important." — William James

"The great thinker is seldom a disputant. He answers other men's arguments by stating the truth as he sees it." — Daniel March

"While thou thinkest of many things thou thinkest of nothing; while thou wouldst go many ways thou standest still." — Anonymous

"People like to imagine that because all our mechanical equipment moves so much faster, that we are thinking faster too." — Christopher Morley

"Those who have finished by making all others think with them, have usually been those who began by daring to think for themselves." — Charles Colton

"What I must do is all that concerns me, not what some people think." — "A man is what he thinks about all day long." — "What is the hardest task in the world? To think." — Emerson

"Whatsoever things are true, whatsoever things are honest, whatsoever things are just, whatsoever things are pure, whatsoever things are lovely, whatsoever things are of good report; if there be any virtue, and if there be any praise, think on these things." — Bible, Philippians 4:8

Thought

"By thought I embrace the universal." — Pascal

"Even a thought, even a possibility, can shatter us and transform us." — Nietzsche

"Great thoughts come from the heart." — Marquis de Vauvenargues

"The greatest events of an age are its best thoughts. It is the nature of thought to find its way into action." — Christian Bovee

"Change your thoughts and you change your world." — Norman Vincent Peale

"Fully to understand a grand and beautiful thought requires, perhaps, as much time as to conceive it." — Joseph Joubert

"Stung by the splendor of sudden thought." — Robert Browning

"A mind forever voyaging through strange seas of thought, alone." — Wordsworth

"I have found power in the mysteries of thought." — "Second thoughts are ever wiser." — Euripides

"Expression is the dress of thought." — Old proverb

"Liberty of thought is the life of the soul." — Voltaire

"The dome of thought, the palace of the soul." — Lord Byron

"Have an open face but conceal our thoughts." — Italian proverb

"It is the hardest thing in the world to be a good thinker without being a good self-examiner." — Lord Shaftesbury

"Take thy thoughts to bed with thee, for the morning is wiser than the evening." — Russian proverb

"There's something so beautiful in coming on one's very own inmost thoughts in another." — Olive Schreiner

"An egg before an eagle, a thought before a thing." — Martin Tupper

"As soon as thoughts are ordered they begin to seem less sincere." — Jean Rostand

"Live thy better, let thy worst thoughts die." — Sir Walter Raleigh

"Earnest men never think in vain though their thoughts may be errors." — Bulwer-Lytton

"Learning without thought is labor lost; thought without learning is perilous." — Confucius

"Thoughts rule the world." — "The key to every man is his thoughts." — "The ancestor of every action is a thought." — "Every thought which genius and piety throw into the world alters the world." — "Good thoughts are no better than good dreams, unless they be executed!" Emerson

"Thought is invisible nature; nature, visible thought." — "The thought precedes the deed as the lightning the thunder." — "Wise men think out their thoughts; fools proclaim them." — Heinrich Heine

"Our thoughts are epochs in our lives; all else is but as a journal of the winds that blow while we are here." — Thoreau

"Let one strive to purify his thoughts, what a man thinks, that he is: this is an old secret." — "The subtle self is to be known by thought alone." — Far Eastern sayings

"We are what our thoughts have made us; so take care about what you think. Words are secondary. Thoughts live; they travel far." — Swami Vivekananda

"The possibilities of thought training are infinite, its consequence eternal, and yet few take the pains to direct their thinking into channels that will do them good, but instead leave all to chance." — Marden

"The epitome of the human realm is to be stuck in a huge traffic jam of discursive thought." — Chogyam Trungpa

"A man would do well to carry a pencil in his pocket, and write down the thoughts of the moment. Those that come unsought for are commonly the most valuable, and should be secured, because they seldom return." — Sir Francis Bacon

"If a man speaks or acts with pure thought, happiness follows him like a shadow that never leaves him." — "All that we are is the result of what we have thought: it is founded on our thoughts, it is made up of our thoughts." — "Our own worst enemy cannot harm us as much as our unwise thoughts. No man can help us as much as our own compassionate thoughts." — Buddha

"Thought is free." — "Nimble thought can jump both sea and land." — "Love's heralds should be thoughts, which ten times faster glide than the sun's beams." — "When to the sessions of sweet silent thought I summon up remembrance of things past, I sigh the lack of many a thing I sought." — "Thoughts are but dreams till their effects be tried." — Shakespeare

"The happiness of your life depends upon the quality of your thoughts, therefore guard accordingly; and take care that you entertain no notions unsuitable to virtue and reasonable nature." — "Our life is what our thoughts make it." — Marcus Aurelius

Logic

"Logic works; metaphysics contemplates." — Joseph Joubert

"Logic is neither a science nor an art, but a dodge." — Benjamin Jowett

"Logic, like whiskey, loses its beneficial effect when taken in too large quantities." — Lord Dunsany

"Logical consequences are the scarecrows of fools and the beacons of wise men." — Thomas Huxley

"The mind has its own logic but does not often let others in on it." — Bernard De Voto

"Logic and rhetoric make men able to contend. Logic differeth from rhetoric as the fist from the palm; the one close, the other at large." — Sir Francis Bacon

"Logic and metaphysics make use of more tools than all the rest of the sciences put together, and they do the least work." — Charles Colton

"Ethics make one's soul mannerly and wise, but logic is the armory of reason, furnished with all offensive and defensive weapons." — Thomas Fuller

"It was a saying of the ancients, that 'truth lies in a well'; and to carry on the metaphor, we may justly say, that logic supplies us with steps whereby we may go down to reach the water." — Isaac Watts

"One of the best things to come out of the home computer revolution could be the general and widespread understanding of how severely limited logic really is." — Frank Herbert

"'Contrariwise,' continued Tweedle-dee, 'if it was so, it might be; and if it were so, it would be; but as it isn't, it ain't. That's logic.'" Lewis Carroll

PHILOSOPHY

"Philosophy is the art of living." — Plutarch

"Philosophy is the science which considers truth." — "Wonder is the first cause of philosophy." — Aristotle

"Philosophy is reason with the eyes of the soul." — Sims

"Philosophy is the rational expression of genius." — Lamartine

"Philosophy is nothing but discretion." — John Selden

"Philosophy is the knowledge of the limits of our knowledge." — Immanuel Kant

"Philosophy is the microscope of thought." — Victor Hugo

"Philosophy is queen of the arts and the daughter of heaven." — Burke

"Philosophy goes no further than probabilities, and in every assertion keeps a doubt in reserve." — James Froude

"Philosophy triumphs easily over past evils and future evils; but present evils triumph over it." — La Rochefoucauld

"Philosophy may teach us to bear with equanimity the misfortunes of our neighbors." — Oscar Wilde

"Philosophy, when superficially studied, excites doubt; when thoroughly explored, it dispels it." — Sir Francis Bacon

"Philosophy's work is finding the shortest path between two points." — Kahlil Gibran

"Make philosophy thy journey." — Quarles

"Wonder is the feeling of a philosopher, and philosophy begins in wonder." — Socrates

"Wonder is the foundation of all philosophy, inquiry the progress, ignorance the end." — Montaigne

"Every philosophy is the philosophy of some stage of life." — Nietzsche

"The business of philosophy is to circumnavigate human nature." — Hare

"Whence? Whither? Why? How? These questions cover all philosophy." — Joseph Joubert

"A great memory does not make a philosopher, any more than a dictionary can be called a grammar." — John Newman

"Truth is the object of philosophy, but not always of philosophers." — John Collins

"Be a philosopher; but amidst all your philosophy be still a man." — David Hume

"To make light of philosophy is to be a true philosopher." — Pascal

"The gold of the philosophers with which the wise are enriched is not that gold which is coined." — Theophrastus Paracelsus

"The people who are not interested in philosophy need it most urgently; they are most helplessly in its power." — Ayn Rand

"A man has one thing to fear, that is to die before he becomes a philosopher." — Solon

"There is nothing so strange and so unbelievable that it has not been said by one philosopher or another." — Descartes

"There are more things in heaven and earth, Horatio, than are dreamt of in your philosophy." — Shakespeare

"The chief intellectual characteristic of the present age is its despair of any constructive philosophy." — John Dewey

"Until philosophers are kings . . . cities will never cease from ill, nor the human race." — Plato

"Philosophy did not find Plato already a noble man, it made him one." — "Philosophy is the art and law of life." — "Philosophy is the health of the mind." — "It is the bounty of nature that we live, but of philosophy, that we live well; which is, in truth, a greater benefit than life itself." — Seneca

"Philosophy is such an impertinently litigious lady that a man had as good be engaged in lawsuits as have to do with her." — Newton

"Philosophers have done wisely when they have told us to cultivate our reason rather than our feelings, for reason reconciles us to daily things of existence; our feelings teach us to yearn after the far, the difficult, the unseen." — Bulwer-Lytton

"Philosophy, if rightly defined, is nothing but the love of wisdom." — "To study philosophy is nothing but to prepare one's self to die." — Cicero

"What is it to be a philosopher? Is it not to be prepared against events?" "The first business of philosophy is to part from self-conceit. For it is impossible for any man to begin to learn what he thinks he already knows." — "All philosophy lies in two words, sustain and abstain." — Epictetus

"To be a philosopher is not merely to have subtle thoughts; but to so love wisdom as to live according to its dictates." — Thoreau

"The philosopher is Nature's pilot. And there you have the difference: to be in hell is to drift; to be in heaven is to steer." — George Bernard Shaw

"The besetting sin of philosophers is that, being human, they endeavor to survey the universe from the standpoint of gods." — Alfred North Whitehead

"My definition of a philosopher is of a man in a balloon, with his family and friends holding the ropes which confine him to earth and trying to haul him down." — Louisa May Alcott

"The philosopher is one to whom the highest has descended and the lowest has mounted up; who is the equal and kindly brother of all." — Carlyle

"The maxim 'Think for yourself,' is basic; but the further maxim, 'Think socially,' must be added if philosophy is to do its whole duty." — Edgar Brightman

"All the persecutors declare against each other mortal war, while the philosopher, oppressed by them all, contents himself with pitying them." — "The discovery of what is true, and the practice of that which is good, are the two most important objects of philosophy." — Voltaire

"When Aristotle was asked what he gained from philosophy, he answered, 'To do without being commanded what others do from fear of the laws.'" Diogenes

Reason

"Reason is the triumph of the intellect." — James Schouler

"Reason never has failed man. Only force and repression have made the wrecks in the world." — William White

"Reason was given to people to help them escape reality." — Leo Tolstoy

"Reason can wrestle and overthrow terror." — Euripides

"Reason has a natural and rightful authority over desire and affection." — Plato

"Reason only controls individuals after emotion and impulse have lost their impetus." — Carlton Simon

"True virtue is life under the direction of reason." — Spinoza

"If we would guide by the light of reason, we must let our minds be bold." — Louis Brandeis

"Wouldst thou subject all things to thyself? Subject thyself to thy reason." — Seneca

"When reason rules money is a blessing." — Publilius Syrus

"Good reasons must, of force, give place to better. Strong reasons make strong actions." — Shakespeare

"Let reason go before every enterprise, and counsel before every action." — Apocrypha, Ecclesiasticus

"When a man has not a good reason for doing a thing, he has one good reason for letting it alone." — Sir Walter Scott

"We are all very proud of our reason, and yet we guess at fully one-half we know." — Anonymous

"When folly passes by, reason draws back." — Japanese proverb

"Error of opinion may be tolerated where reason is left free to combat it." — Thomas Jefferson

"'Tis in vain to speak reason where it will not be heard." — Thomas Fuller

"Where can I find a man governed by reason instead of habits and urges?" Kahlil Gibran

"Nothing is ever accomplished by a reasonable man." — American proverb

"Neither great poverty nor great riches will hear reason." — Henry Fielding

"It is useless to attempt to reason a man out of a thing he was never reasoned into." — Swift

"Never reason from what you do not know." — Andrew Ramsay

"The golden rule is to test everything in the light of reason and experience, no matter from whom it comes." — Gandhi

"Human reason needs only to will more strongly than fate, and she is fate." — Thomas Mann

"Happy is the man who lets reason be his guide." — Mozart

"Wise men are instructed by reason; men of less understanding, by experience; the most ignorant, by necessity; and beasts by nature." — Cicero

"One that will not reason is a bigot; one that cannot reason is a fool; and one that dares not reason is a slave." — William Drummond

"Human reason is like a drunken man on horseback; set it up on one side, and it tumbles over on the other." — "Reason is the enemy of faith." — Martin Luther

"Let us not dream that reason can ever be popular. Passions, emotions, may be made popular, but reason remains ever the property of the few." — Goethe

"There is nothing that has been created without some reason, even if human nature is incapable of knowing precisely the reason for them all." — John Chrysostom

"There need not be in religion, or music, or art, or love, or goodness, anything that is against reason; but never while the sun shines will we get great religion, or music, or art, or love, or goodness, without going beyond reason." — Harry Emerson Fosdick

Theory

"Theory helps us to bear our ignorance of facts." — Santayana

"Indeed, I hold that what cannot be proved in practice cannot be sound in theory." — Gandhi

"The supreme misfortune is when theory outstrips performance." — Leonardo da Vinci

"A theory must be tempered with reality." — Nehru

"Creating a new theory is not like destroying an old barn and erecting a skyscraper in its place. It is rather like climbing a mountain, gaining new and wider views, discovering unexpected connections between our starting point and its rich environment." — Einstein

Consciousness

"Constantly maintain alertness of consciousness in walking, in sitting, in eating, and in sleeping." — Buddha

"The reason we like precious jewels so much is they remind us of planes of consciousness we've lived on, where those are the pebbles." — Aldous Huxley

"The world of our present consciousness is only one out of many worlds of consciousness that exist." — William James

"A plane of being is not a place of being, but a state of being." — Anonymous

"There is no coming to consciousness without pain." — Carl Jung

"The consciousness that creates the problem cannot be the consciousness that solves it." — Einstein

Sense

"Common sense is the knack of seeing things as they are, and doing things as they ought to be done." — Calvin Stowe

"Common sense and nature will do a lot to make the pilgrimage of life not too difficult." — W. Somerset Maugham

"Common sense is in spite of, not the result of, education." — Victor Hugo

"Common sense is not so common." — Voltaire

"There's no sense so uncommon as common sense." — Old proverb

"Nothing astonishes men so much as common sense and plain dealing." — Emerson

"That great stream of all common sense: compromise." — William Bolitho

"If Poverty is the Mother of Crimes, want of Sense is the Father." — Jean de La Bruyère

"A rising tide lifts all boats." — John F. Kennedy

"No stream rises higher than its source." — Frank Lloyd Wright

"Still waters run deep." — T. Draxe

"To go fast, row slowly." — Vincent Norman Peale

"A man who stands on tiptoe does not stand firm." — Lao-tse

"A man gazing on the stars is proverbially at the mercy of the puddles in the road." — Alexander Smith

"No man regards what is before his feet; we all gaze at the stars." — Quintus Ennius

"Keep your eyes on the stars, and your feet on the ground." — Theodore Roosevelt

"'Tis looking downward that makes one dizzy." — Robert Browning

"Never is a long time." — Chaucer

"Eagles don't catch flies." — Erasmus

"Lightning never strikes the same place twice." — P. H. Myers

"The sharper the storm, the sooner it's over." — Seneca

"It ain't no use putting up your umbrella till it rains." — Alice Rice

"You don't need a weatherman to know which way the wind blows." — Bob Dylan

"Beware of the young doctor and the old barber." — Benjamin Franklin

"There is a time and place for everything." — "You cannot shift an old tree without it dying." — A. Barclay

"Good seed makes a good crop." — W. Wager

"You cannot make an omelet without breaking eggs." — T. P. Thompson

"You cannot put an old head on young shoulders." — H. Smith

"A man must keep his mouth open a long while before a roast pigeon flies into it." — Thomas Lynch

"Every tub must stand on its own bottom." — W. Bullein

"Don't throw out your dirty water until you get in fresh." — W. Painter

"Don't throw the baby out with the bath-water." — J. Kepler

"Don't go near the water until you learn how to swim." — H. G. Bohn

"A drowning man will clutch at a straw." — J. Prime

"It is the last straw that breaks the camels back." — J. Bramhall

"The last drop makes the cup run over." — Thomas Fuller

"You don't get something for nothing." — Disraeli

"Always take things by their smooth handle." — Thomas Jefferson

"Resolve slowly, act swiftly; a quiet eye for the quick hand." — Martin Tupper

"Better shun the bait than struggle in the snare." — John Dryden

"Think in the morning, act in the noon, eat in the evening, sleep at night." — William Blake

"Live your life, do your work, then take your hat." — Thoreau

"Everything should be made as simple as possible, but not simpler." — Einstein

"The most solid stone in the structure is the lowest one in the foundation." — Kahlil Gibran

"Use it or lose it." — Anonymous

"Begin at the beginning and go till you come to the end; then stop." — Lewis Carroll

"Well begun is half done." — Horace

"What's done cannot be undone." — Sophocles

"What's done is done." — "Great floods have flown from simple sources." — "If two ride on a horse, one must ride behind." — "Let Hercules himself do what he may, the cat will mew and dog will have his day." — "One fire drives out one fire; one nail, one nail." — "The ripest fruit first falls." — "Such as we are made of, such we be." — "Have more than thou showest, speak less than thou knowest, lend less than thou owest." — "If it be now, 'tis not to come; if it be not to come, it will be now; if it be not now, yet it will come; the readiness is all." — "Love all, trust a few, do wrong to none." — Shakespeare

"Our senses, as our reason, are divine." — "Plain sense but rarely leads us far astray, of plain, sound sense, life's current coin is made." — "There are forty men of wit to one of sense." — "Too low they build, who build beneath the stars." — Edward Young

"There is nobody so irritating as somebody with less intelligence and more sense than we have." — Don Herold

"Not to have control over the senses is like sailing in a rudderless ship, bound to break to pieces on coming in contact with the very first rock." — Gandhi

"Common sense is only a modification of talent. Genius is an exaltation of it. The difference is, therefore, in degree, not nature." — Baron Lytton

"Believe nothing, no matter where you read it, or who said it — even if I said it — unless your own reason and your own common sense agree." — Buddha

"Two footsteps do not make a path." — "A single tree can not make a forest." — "There are forty kinds of lunacy, but only one kind of common sense." — African proverbs

"No river can return to its source, yet all rivers must have a beginning." — "When you are in the water you swim." — "The rain falls on the just and the unjust." — "One finger cannot lift a pebble." — Native American proverbs

"Don't fix it if it ain't broke." — American proverb

"The larger a man's roof, the more snow it collects." — "A drowning man is not troubled by rain." — "Stretch your foot to the length of your blanket." — "The wise man sits on the hole in his carpet." — Arabian proverbs

"A sheep was never known to climb a tree." — "What you can not avoid, welcome." — Chinese proverbs

"Though the birds may fly over your head, let them not make their nest in your hair." — "Fire and straw soon make flame." — Danish Proverbs

"Better lose the anchor than the whole ship." — "Best not to trade horses while crossing in mid-stream." — Dutch proverbs

"Better short of pence than short of sense." — "Don't set the cart before the horse." — "A bird in the hand is better than two in the bush." — "Big fish eat the little fish." — "Where there is smoke there is fire." — "That hit the nail on the head." — English proverbs

"One flower will not make a garland." — "No smoke without fire." — French proverbs

"An ass loaded with gold still eats thistles." — "Even the lion has to defend himself against flies." — "Not every spring becomes a stream." — German proverbs

"Wood that grows warped can never be straightened." — "In baiting a mousetrap with cheese, always leave room for the mouse." — "Seize the end and you will hold the middle." — "Add not fire to fire." — "Act quickly, think slowly." — "Age brings experience, and a good mind wisdom." — Greek proverbs

"An ox remains an ox, even if driven to Vienna." — Hungarian proverb

"A bird never flew on one wing." — "Never bolt your door with a boiled carrot." — "Anything will fit a naked man." — "It is almost as good as bringing good news not to bring bad." — "It is not fish until it is on the bank." — "The day of the storm is not the time for thatching." — "When the apple is ripe it will fall." — Irish proverbs

"Tell not all you know, believe not all you hear, do not all you are able." — "It is easy to frighten a bull from the window." — "Empty sacks will never stand upright." — "Land was never lost for want of an heir." — "No pear falls into a shut mouth." — "There is no need to bind up one's head before it is broken." — "When the sun is highest it casts the least shadow." — Italian proverbs

"A fog cannot be dispelled by a fan." — "Darkness reigns at the foot of the lighthouse." — Japanese proverbs

"Time and words can't be recalled, even if it was only yesterday." — "Before you start up a ladder, count the rungs." — "Look down if you would know how high you stand." — "At the baths, all are equal." — Jewish proverbs

"One that hath wax for a head must not walk in the sun." — "If there is no wind, row." — Latin proverbs

"Although it may rain, cast not away the watering pot." — "A piece of incense may be as large as the knee, but unless burnt emits no fragrance." — "Though a tree grow ever so high, the falling leaves return to the root." — "Kick away the ladder and one's feet are left dangling." — Malayan proverbs

"An ant on the move does more than a dozing ox." — "It's not enough to know how to ride — you must also know how to fall." — Mexican proverbs

"When the explorer is ready, the guide will appear." — Nepalese proverb

"When the mouse laughs at the cat there is a hole nearby." — Nigerian proverb

"Do not drink from a well and throw a stone into it." — "Knock on the door before entering." — "One hand can't clap." — Palestinian proverbs

"One pound of learning requires ten pounds of common sense to apply it." — Persian proverb

"Into the closed mouth the fly does not get." — Philippine proverb

"Even a clock that is not going is right twice a day." — "The bell is loud because it is empty." — "Do not push the river, it will flow by itself." — Polish proverbs

"Visits always give a pleasure; if not the arriving, so the departing." — "The fish dies by its mouth." — "Where the iron goes, there goes also rust." — "Never cut what can be untied." — Portuguese Proverbs

"After the head is off, one does not cry over the hair." — "It is easy to undress the naked." — "A lizard on a cushion will still seek leaves." — "The hammer shatters glass but forges steel." — "A jug that has been mended lasts two hundred years." — Russian proverbs

"Better to bend than to break." — "There's many a good cock that comes out of a tattered bag." — "It is ill fishing if the hook is bare." — "Better wear out shoes than sheets." — Scottish proverbs

"A handful of common sense is worth a bushel of learning." — "In a calm sea every man is a pilot." — "Who ties well, unties well." — "What belongs to everybody belongs to nobody." — "Stars are not seen by sunshine." — "Every cask smells of the wine it contained." — "Drink nothing without seeing it; Sign nothing without reading it." — "Visit your aunt and uncle, but not every day of the year." — Spanish proverbs

"A boat doesn't go forward if each man is rowing his own way." — Swahili proverb

"Don't throw away the old bucket until you know whether the new one holds water." — "During the calm waters, every ship has a great Captain." — Swedish proverbs

"Eat according to the limits of your provisions; walk according to the length of your step." — Tibetan proverb

"One arrow does not bring down two birds." — "Two watermelons cannot be held under one arm." — Turkish proverbs

"If the shoe fits, wear it." — "A little oil may save a great deal of friction." — "What goes up must come down." — Old proverbs

Ideas

"Ideas are the roots of creation." — Ernest Dimnet

"Ideas control the world." — James Garfield

"A new idea is delicate." — Charles D. Brower

"The simplest things give me ideas." — Joan Miro

"An idea is a feat of association." — Robert Frost

"Don't despair of a student if he has one clear idea." — Nathaniel Emmons

"The man with a new idea is a crank until the idea succeeds." — Mark Twain

"The difficulty lies not so much in developing new ideas as in escaping from old ones." — Keynes

"Man's fear of ideas is probably the greatest dike holding back human knowledge and happiness." — Morris Ernst

"A healthful hunger for a great idea is the beauty and blessedness of life." — Jean Ingelow

"The best ideas are common property." — Seneca

"An Idea isn't responsible for the people who believe in it." — Donald Marquis

"Out beyond the ideas of right-doing or wrong-doing there is a field — I'll meet you there." — Rumi

"Nothing else in the world . . . not all the armies . . . is so powerful as an idea whose time has come." — Victor Hugo

"Ideas must work through the brains and the arms of good and brave men, or they are no better than dreams." — "It is a lesson which all history teaches wise men, to put trust in ideas, and not in circumstances." — Emerson

"An idea, to be suggestive, must come to the individual with the force of a revelation." — "A new idea is first condemned as ridiculous and then dismissed as trivial, finally, it becomes what everyone knows." — William James

Opinion

"Opinion ultimately governs the world." — Woodrow Wilson

"Opinion is ultimately determined by the feelings, and not by the intellect." — Herbert Spencer

"Opinions cannot survive if one has no chance to fight for them." — Thomas Mann

"A mass of men equals a mass of opinions." — Latin proverb

"So many men, so many opinions." — Terence

"As our inclinations so our opinions." — Goethe

"One who is master of all opinions can never be the bigot of any." — Willim Alger

"A man's opinions are generally of much more value than his arguments." — Oliver Wendell Holmes

"The masses procure their opinions ready made in open market." — Charles Colton

"The dissenting opinions of one generation become the prevailing interpretation of the next." — Burton J. Hendrick

"Predominant opinions are generally the opinions of the generation that is vanishing." — Disraeli

"The men of the past had convictions, while we moderns have only opinions." — Heinrich Heine

"Public opinion in this country is everything." — Abraham Lincoln

"Public opinion's always in advance of the Law." — John Galsworthy

"It is not only arrogant, but profligate, for a man to disregard the world's opinion of himself." — Cicero

"If one man says to thee, 'Thou art a donkey,' pay no heed. If two speak thus, purchase a saddle." — The Talmud

"Ultimately what we really are matters more than what other people think of us." — Nehru

"The greatest deception men suffer is from their own opinions." — Leonardo da Vinci

"Those who never retract their opinions love themselves more than they love truth." — Joseph Joubert

"The most difficult secret for a man to keep is his own opinion of himself." — Marcel Pagnol

"We think very few people sensible, except those who are of our opinion." — La Rochefoucauld

"He who has no opinion of his own, but depends upon the opinion and taste of others, is a slave." — Friedrich Klopstock

"Don't keep searching for the truth, just let go of your opinions." — Buddha

"The history of human opinion is scarcely anything more than the history of human errors." — Voltaire

"No error of opinion can possibly be dangerous in a country where opinion is left free to grapple with them." — William Simms

"The feeble tremble before opinion, the foolish defy it, the wise judge it, the skillful direct it." — Madame Roland

"Every difference of opinion is not a difference in principle." — Thomas Jefferson

"Opinion is the main thing which does good or harm in the world. It is our false opinions of things which ruin us." — Marcus Aurelius

"One has of course the right to change opinion, but on condition of not fraudulently adjusting the new to the old." — Jean Rostand

"There never was in the world two opinions alike, no more than two hairs or two grains. The most universal quality is diversity." — Montaigne

"It is difference of opinion that makes horse races." — "Loyalty to petrified opinion never yet broke a chain or freed a human soul." — Mark Twain

"Whatever your opinions are, don't make them a prison. Always leave some space to change your mind and your system of the world." — Anonymous

"He that never changes his opinions never corrects his mistakes, and will never be wiser on the morrow than he is today." — Tryon Edwards

"If a man should register all his opinions upon love, politics, religion, learning, etc., beginning from his youth, and so go on to old age, what a bundle of inconsistencies and contradictions would appear at last." — Swift

Memory

"Memory is the treasury and guardian of all things." — Aeschylus

"Memory is the diary that we all carry about with us." — Oscar Wilde

"Memory tempers prosperity, mitigates adversity, controls youth, and delights old age." — Lactantius

"Memory is not wisdom; idiots can by rote repeat volumes. Yet what is wisdom without memory?" Martin Tupper

"Memory [is] the warder of the brain." — Shakespeare

"Memories are all we really own." — Elias Lieberman

"The true art of memory is the art of attention." — Samuel Johnson

"We do not remember days, we remember moments." — Cesare Pavese

"Every man can remember that which has interested himself." — Plautus

"The ax forgets but the cut log does not." — African proverb

"Joy's recollection is no longer joy, while sorrow's memory is sorrow still." — Lord Byron

"What is hard to bear is sweet to remember." — Portuguese proverb

"The things we remember best are those better forgotten." — Balthasar Gracian

"What one knows is sometimes useful to forget." — Latin proverb

"Better by far you should forget and smile than that you should remember and be sad." — Christina G. Rossetti

"We have all forgot more than we remember." — Thomas Fuller

"Can anybody remember when the times were not hard and money not scarce?" Emerson

"The world does not require so much to be informed as to be reminded." — Hannah More

"A man's real possession is his memory. In nothing else is he rich, in nothing else is he poor." — Alexander Smith

"What we learn with pleasure we never forget." — Charles Mercier

"When it comes to memory . . . .try to remember the good things." — Anonymous

"How vast a memory has Love!" Alexander Pope

"Recollection is the only paradise here on earth from which we cannot be turned out." — Richter

"Memory is the cabinet of imagination, the treasury of reason, the registry of conscience, and the council chamber of thought." — Basil

"A memory without blot or contamination must be an exquisite treasure, an inexhaustible source of pure refreshment." — Charlotte Brontë

WORDS

"Words are tools which automatically carve concepts out of experience." — Julian Huxley

"Words do not fall into the void." — Zohar

"Words often do more than blows." — German proverb

"Words are the clothes that thoughts wear — only the clothes." — Samuel Butler

"Words are but the shadows of actions." — Democritus

"Words are meaningless till translated into action." — Guru Nanak

"Words are like leaves; and where they most abound, much fruit of sense beneath is rarely found." — Alexander Pope

"Words are the counters of wise men, and the money of fools." — Thomas Hobbes

"Words should be weighed and not counted." — Hebrew proverb

"Words have the power to destroy or heal. When words are both true and kind, they can change the world." — Buddha

"In the beginning was the word." — Bible; John 1:1

"All miracles at the beginning of the world were made by the word." — Roger Bacon

"Thy word is a lamp unto my feet, and a light unto my path." — Bible, Psalms 119:105

"Their words burned like a lamp." — Apocrypha, Ecclesiasticus 48:1

"The pleasure and excitement of words is that they are living and generation things." — Christopher Fry

"A soul wise in words shall make himself beloved." — Apocrypha Ecclesiasticus 20:3

"And the words of my mouth shall be such as may please." — Bible, Psalms 18:15

"Good words cost no more than bad." — "Good words cost nothing and are worth much." — Old proverbs

"A good word maketh the heart glad." — Bible, Proverbs

"A word in due season — how good it is!" Bible, Proverbs 15:23

"A word spoken in season, at the right moment, is the matter of ages." — Carlyle

"How forcible are right words!" Bible, Job 6:25

"Proper words in the proper places, make the true definition of a style." — Swift

"Kind words can be short and easy to speak but their echoes are truly endless." — Mother Teresa

"Grammar . . . knows how to control even kings." — Molière

"With words we govern people." — Disraeli

"Buffaloes are held by cords, people by their words." — Malay proverb

"An agreement is more valuable than money." — Russian proverb

"Longer than deeds liveth the word." — Pindar

"Keep your word." — Apocrypha, Ecclesiasticus 29:3

"The best way to keep your word is not to give it." — Napoleon

"Be careful of what you say or the words will come back to haunt you." — Old proverb

"Sticks and stones may break my bones but words will never hurt me." — Old English Rhyme

"A flow of words is no proof of wisdom." — "A word, once out, flies everywhere." — Old proverbs

"It is with a word as with an arrow — once let it loose and it does not return." — Abd-el-Kader

"What you keep by you, you may change and mend; but words, once spoken, can never be recalled." — Wentworth Dillon

"A witty saying proves nothing." — Voltaire

"Fine words butter no parsnips." — J. Clarke

"Be not the slave to Words." — Carlyle

"A thousand words will not leave so deep an impression as one deed." — Ibsen

"One who is scared by words has no heart for deeds." — Old proverb

"Be doers of the word and not hearers only, deceiving your own selves." — Bible, James 1:22

"Good words do not last long until they amount to something." — Chief Joseph

"Few were their words, but wonderfully clear." — Homer

"Much wisdom often goes with fewest words." — Sophocles

"The most valuable of all talents is that of never using two words when one will do." — Thomas Jefferson

"Every word that is unnecessary only pours over the side of a brimming mind." — Cicero

"The finest words in the world are only vain sounds, if you can not comprehend them." — Anatole France

"Words are merely the vehicle on which thoughts ride; and when the vehicle creaks too loudly in the wheels it distracts attention from the cargo." — James Adams

"Such as thy words are, such will thy affections be esteemed; and such will thy deeds as thy affections, and such thy life as thy deeds." — Socrates

"Like a beautiful flower, full of color, but without scent, are the fine but fruitless words of those who do not act accordingly." — Far Eastern saying

"A word out of season may mar a whole lifetime." — "Whatever kind of word thou speakest the like shalt thou hear." — Greek proverbs

"Men suppose their reason has command over their words; still it happens that words in return exercise authority on reason." — Sir Francis Bacon

"Although words exist for the most part for the transmission of ideas, there are some which produce such violent disturbance in our feelings that the role they play in transmission of ideas is lost in the background." — Einstein

"When I use a word," said Humpty Dumpty, in rather a scornful tone, "it means just what I choose it to mean — neither more nor less." — Lewis Carroll

"Noise, anger, explosive tones, superlatives, exaggerations of passion, add nothing to the force of what we say, but rather rob our words of the power that belongs to them." — Gladden

"A little word in kindness spoken, a motion or a tear, has often healed the heart that's broken, and made a friend sincere." — Daniel Clement Colesworthy

"The difference between the right word and the almost right word is the difference between lightning and the lightning bug." — Mark Twain

"The North — the East — the West — the South — whence, according to some curious etymologists, comes the magical word NEWS." — Thomas De Quincey

"Scientists tell us that the words spoken by Abraham and Elijah are still influencing the air; that the atmosphere is a mighty library, on whose pages human actions and utterances have all been impressed." — Morgan

"When words are scarce they are seldom spent in vain." — "Men of few words are the best men." — "These words are razors to my wounded heart." — "What's in a name? That which we call a rose by any other name would smell as sweet." — Shakespeare

"No one has a prosperity so high or firm, but that two or three words can dishearten it; and there is no calamity which right words will not begin to redress." — Emerson

Speech

"Speech is civilization itself." — Thomas Mann

"Speech is the mirror of action." — Solon

"Speech is a mirror of the soul: as a man speaks, so he is." — Publilius Syrus

"Speech is the entry to the palace of love." — Jami of Persia

"Speech is the index of the mind." — Seneca

"Speech ventilates our intellectual fire." — Edward Young

"Speech finely framed delighteth the ears." — Apocrypha, II Maccabees 15:39

"Speeches measured by the hour, die by the hour." — Thomas Jefferson

"Speeches cannot be made long enough for the speakers, nor short enough for the hearers." — James Perry

"Speak clearly if you speak at all; Carve every word before you let if fall." — O. W. Holmes

"Speak softly and carry a big stick; you will go far." — Theodore Roosevelt

"Speak of the moderns without contempt, and of the ancients without idolatry." — Philip Stanhope

"Speak ill of no man, but speak all the good you know of everybody." — Benjamin Franklin

"Speak well of all." — Sophist saying

"Speak less than thou knowest." — Shakespeare

"Speaking much is a sign of vanity." — Sir Walter Raleigh

"Sayings remain meaningless until they are embodied in habits." — Kahlil Gibran

"A superior man is modest in his speech, but exceeds in his actions." — Confucius

"They said little, but to the purpose." — Lord Byron

"Better say nothing than nothing to the purpose." — English proverb

"Let your speech be always with grace, seasoned with salt." — Bible, Colossians 4:6

"To speak kindly does not hurt the tongue." — French proverb

"When I want to speak, let me think first. Is it true? Is it kind? Is it necessary? If not, let it be left unsaid." — Babcock

"First learn the meaning of what you say, and then speak." — Epictetus

"Do not say all that you know, but always know what you say." — Claudius

"Let thy speech be short, comprehending much in few words." — Bible, Ecclesiaticus 33:8

"Say only a little but say it well." — Celtic proverb

"Nothing is said now that has not been said before." — Terence

"Let no man say that I have said nothing new; the arrangement of the subject is new." — Pascal

"This is such a serious world that we should never speak at all unless we have something to say." — Carlyle

"It is better not to speak a word at all than to speak more words than we should." — Thomas à Kempis

"They knew the precise psychological moment when to say nothing." — Oscar Wilde

"If you don't say it, you'll not have to unsay it." — "If you don't have something good to say, don't say it." — Old proverbs

"Let thy speech be better than silence or be silent." — Dionysius the Elder

"More have repented of speech than silence." — "The heart does not think all the mouth says." — Old proverbs

"Ten men who speak make more noise than ten thousand who are silent." — Napoleon

"A wise man reflects before he speaks. A fool speaks, and then reflects on what was uttered." — French proverb

"A man may teach another to speak; but none can teach another to hold his peace." — Pollok

"He can never speak well, who knows not how to hold his peace." — Plutarch

"If you think twice before you speak once, you will speak twice the better for it." — Anonymous

"Blessed is the man who, having nothing to say, abstains from giving wordy evidence of the fact." — George Eliot

"Half a brain is enough for one who says little." — Italian proverb

"Few men speak humbly of humility, chastely of chastity, skeptically of skepticism." — Pascal

"In general those who nothing have to say contrive to spend the longest time in doing it." — James Lowell

"Let any man speak long enough, and he will get believers." — Robert Louis Stevenson

"There is that speaking rashly that is like the piercings of a sword." — Bible, Proverbs

"Out of the mouth proceeds blessing and cursing." — Bible, James 3:10

"Let no evil speech proceed from your mouth." — Bible, Ephesians 4:29

"Do not speak harshly to any man; those who are so spoken to will answer thee in the same way." — Far Eastern saying

"If you say a bad thing, you may soon hear a worse thing said about you." — Hesiod

"What people say behind your back is your standing in the community." — Edgar Watson Howe

"How awful to reflect that what people say of us is true!" Logan Pearsall Smith

"Never rise to speak till you have something to say; and when you have said it, cease." — John Witherspoon

"Brevity is the best recommendation of speech, whether in a senator or an orator." — Cicero

"Never say more than is necessary." — Richard Sheridan

"Think all you speak, but speak not all you think. Thoughts are your own; your words are so no more." — Patrick Delany

"No man means all he says, and yet very few say all they mean." — Henry Adams

"I not only speak so that I can be understood, but so that I cannot be misunderstood." — Cobbett

"Everything that can be said can be said clearly." — Wittgenstein

"We speak little if not egged on by vanity." — "True eloquence consists in saying all that is necessary, and nothing but what is necessary." — La Rochefoucauld

"The music that can deepest reach, and cure all ill, is cordial speech." — "Use what language you will, you can never say anything but what you are." — "It is proof of high culture to say the greatest matters in the simplest way." — Emerson

"Sooner throw a pearl at hazard than an idle or useless word; and do not say little in many words, but a great deal in a few." — Pythagoras

"Nature has given us two ears, two eyes, and but one tongue, to the end that we should hear and see more than we speak." — Socrates

"It really lies in this: the one describes what has happened, the other what might. Hence poetry speaks of what is universal, history of what is particular." — Aristotle

"As a vessel is known by the sound, whether it be cracked or not, so men are proved by their speeches whether they be wise or foolish." — Demosthenes

"I like better for one to say some foolish thing upon important matters than to be silent. That becomes the subject of discussion and dispute, and the truth is discovered." — Denis Diderot

"All the fun is in how you say something." — "Half the world is composed of people who have something to say and can't, and the other half who have nothing to say and keep on saying it." — Robert Frost

"Neither speak well nor ill of yourself. If well, people will not believe you; if ill, they will believe a great deal more than you say." — Anonymous

"The real art of conversation is not only to say the right thing at the right place but to leave unsaid the wrong thing at the tempting moment." — Dorothy Nevill

"Let thy speech be short, comprehending much in few words; be as one that knoweth and yet holdeth his tongue." — Apocrypha, Ecclesiasticus

"My method is to take the utmost trouble to find the right thing to say, and then to say it with the utmost levity." — George Bernard Shaw

"Discretion of speech is more than eloquence; and to speak agreeably to one with whom we deal with is more than to speak in good words, or in good order." — Sir Francis Bacon

"I disapprove of what you say, but I will defend to the death your right to say it." — Voltaire

Talking

"Talk does not cook rice." — Chinese proverb

"Talk like Robin Hood when you can shoot with his bow." — Anonymous

"Talkers are no good doers." — Shakespeare

"Walk your talk." — Anonymous

"How can you get wisdom . . . when your talk is of bullocks?" Apocrypha, Ecclesiasticus 38:25

"Too much talk will include errors." — Burmese proverb

"They always talk who never think." — Matthew Prior

"They think too little who talk too much." — John Dryden

"He is a wonderful talker, who has the art of telling you nothing in a great harangue." — Molière

"Must we always talk for victory, and never once for truth, for comfort, and joy?" Emerson

"A civil guest will no more talk all, than eat all the feast." — George Herbert

"Answer not before thou hast heard the cause: neither interrupt men in the midst of their talk." — Apocrypha, Ecclesiasticus 11:8

"No man would listen to you talk if he didn't know it was his turn next." — Ed Howe

"It is easy for men to talk one thing and think another." — Publilius Syrus

"There is only one rule for being a good talker: learn to listen." — Christopher Morley

"There is only one thing in the world worse than being talked about, and that is not being talked about." — Oscar Wilde

"Whether it be to friend or foe, talk not of other people's lives." — Apocrypha, Ecclesiasticus 19:8

"People who know little are usually great talkers, while people who know much say little." — Rousseau

"Do you know that conversation is one of the greatest pleasures in life? But it wants leisure." — W. Somerset Maugham

"To talk well and eloquently is a very great art, but that an equally great one is to know the right moment to stop." — Mozart

"Talkative men who wish to be loved are hated; when they desire to please, they bore; when they think they are admired, they are laughed at; they injure their friends, benefit their enemies, and ruin themselves." — Plutarch

"As it is the characteristic of great wits to say much in few words, so it is of small wits to talk much and say nothing." — "We talk little when vanity does not make us." — La Rochefoucauld

"The worst part of an eminent man's conversation is, nine times out of ten, to be found in that part which he means to be clever." — Bulwer-Lytton

"A dog is not considered good because of his barking, and a man is not considered clever because of his ability to talk." — Chuang-tzu

"A wise man talks because he has something to say; fools, because they would like to say something." — "As empty vessels make the loudest sound, so they that have least wit are the greatest babblers." — "The more the pleasures of the body fade away, the greater to me is the pleasure and charm of conversation." — Plato

"There can be no fairer ambition than to excel in talk." — Robert Louis Stevenson

The Tongue

"A man that can rule his tongue shall live without strife." — Apocrypha, Ecclesiasticus

"A sharp tongue is the only edge tool that grows keener with constant use." — Washington Irving

"A man is hid under his tongue." — Ali Ibn-Abi-Talib

"Don't tie a knot in your tongue that you cannot untie with your teeth." — Portuguese proverb

"The tongue is a little member and boasteth great things." — St. James

"The tongue of a fool is the key of his counsel, which, in a wise man, wisdom hath in keeping." — Socrates

"The tongue is not steel — yet it cuts." — Old proverb

"The tongue wounds more than a lance." — Persian proverb

"Every kind of animal can be tamed, but not the tongue of a man." — Philippine proverb

"A tame tongue is a rare bird." — Old proverb

"The tamed tongue subdues the adversary." — Gladden

"Men govern nothing with more difficulty than their tongues." — Spinoza

"Let not thy tongue run before thy mind." — Chilon

"It hurteth not the tongue to give fair words." — English proverb

"Better that the feet slip than the tongue." — Old proverb

"The body pays for a slip of the foot and gold pays for a slip of the tongue." — Malayan proverb

"Where the tongue slips, it speaks the truth." — Irish proverb

"A tongue talks at the head's cost." — Old proverb

"An unlucky word dropped from the tongue, cannot be brought back again by a coach and six horses." — Chinese proverb

"We cannot control the evil tongues of others; but a good life enables us to disregard them." — Cato the Younger

"The tongue can no man tame; it is an unruly evil full of deadly poison." — Bible, James 3:8

"Keep your tongue from evil and your lips from speaking wicked." — Bible, Psalms 33:14

"They have sharpened their tongues like a serpent; the venom of asps is under their lips." — Bible, Psalms 139:4

"Woe for the misery and crime an aggravating tongue can cause!" Martin Tupper

"Thistles and thorns prick sore, but evil tongues prick more." — Old proverb

"For the tongue is a smoldering fire, and excess of speech a deadly poison." — Baha'u'llah

"A man of an ill tongue is dangerous in his city." — Apocrypha, Ecclesiasticus 9:18

"Give your tongue more holiday than your hands or eyes." — Rabbi Ben Azai

"No man can safely speak who does not willingly hold his tongue." — Thomas à Kempis

"A still tongue makes a wise head." — English proverb

"No man ever repented of having held his tongue." — "He cannot speak well who cannot hold his tongue." — "One knows much who knows how to hold his tongue." — "Who has not a good tongue ought to have good hands." — "A bridle for the tongue is a necessary piece of furniture." — Old proverbs

"The heart of the fool is in his tongue; the tongue of the wise is in their heart." — "Vinegar does not catch a fly, but honey. A sweet tongue draweth the snake from the earth." — Far Eastern sayings

"The tongue is more to be feared than the sword." — "The tongue is but three inches long, yet it can kill a man six feet tall." — Japanese proverbs

"A wound from a tongue is worse than a wound from a sword; for the latter affects only the body, the former the spirit." — Pythagoras

"Many have fallen by the edge of the sword but not so many as have perished by their own tongue." — Bible, Ecclesiastes 28:22

"By examining the tongue, physicians find out the diseases of the body; and philosophers, the diseases of the mind and heart." — Justin

"Men's fortunes are oftener made by their tongues than by their virtues; and more men's fortunes overthrown thereby than by their vices." — Sir Walter Raleigh

"Whoso keepeth their mouth and their tongue, keepeth their soul from troubles." — "The tongue of the righteous is as choice silver." — "Death and life are in the power of the tongue." — Bible, Proverbs

"The tongue is, at the same time, the best part of a man, and the worst: with good government, none is more useful; without it, none is more mischievous." — Anacharsis

LISTENING

"It is better to love to listen than to love to speak." — Cleobulus

"He that hath ears to hear, let him hear." — Bible, Mark 9:9

"Many a one hears, but hears It not." — Rig-Veda

"From listening comes wisdom, and from speaking repentance." — Italian proverb

"Be swift to hear, and with patience give answer." — Apocrypha, Ecclesiaticus

"A wooer should open his ears more than his eyes." — Norwegian proverb

"Though the speaker be a fool, let the hearer be wise." — Old proverb

"When I did well, I heard it never; when I did ill, I heard it ever." — Anonymous

"A man who says what he likes, must hear what he does not like." — Old proverb

"I like to listen. I have learned a great deal from listening carefully. Most people never listen." — Ernest Hemingway

"Those who are meant to hear will understand. Those who are not meant to understand will not hear." — Confucius

"If you wish to know the mind of a man, listen to his words." — Chinese proverb

"Who speaks, sows; who listens, reaps." — Old proverb

"Take time everyday to sit quietly and listen." — Buddha

"If thou love to hear, thou shalt receive understanding." — Apocrypha, Ecclesiasticus

"Hear the meaning within the word." — "Give everyone thine ear, but few thy voice: Take each man's censure, but reserve thy judgment." — Shakespeare

Writing

"Write what you know." — Old proverb

"If one has no heart, one cannot write for the masses." — John Keats

"Look, then, into thine heart and write." — Longfellow

"No tears in the writer, no tears in the reader." — Robert Frost

"Of all that is written, I love only what a man hath written with his blood." — Nietzsche

"The difficulty of literature is not to write, but to write what you mean." — Robert Louis Stevenson

"You don't write because you want to say something; you write because you've got something to say." — F. Scott Fitzgerald

"A writer is not a confectioner, a cosmetic dealer, or an entertainer. He is a man who has signed a contract with his conscious and his sense of duty." — Anton Chekhov

"The poet gives us his essence, but prose takes the mold of the body and mind entire." — Virginia Woolf

"To have one's page alive the author must be alive himself, constantly acquiring fresh thought." — Matthews

"The only reason for the existence of a novel is that it does attempt to represent life." — Henry James

"A pure style in writing results from the rejection of everything superfluous." — Albertine de Saussure

"The writer is more concerned to know than to judge." — W. Somerset Maugham

"Amuse the reader at the same time that you instruct him." — Horace

"What I like in a good author is not what he says, but what he whispers." — Logan Pearsall Smith

"True ease in writing comes from art, not chance, as those move easiest who have learned to dance." — Alexander Pope

"Of all those arts in which the wise excel, nature's chief masterpiece is writing well." — John Sheffied

"From writing rapidly it does not result that one writes well, but from writing well it results that one writes rapidly." — Quintilian

"The writer does the most who gives his reader the most knowledge and takes from them the least time." — Sydney Smith

"If you would be a reader, read; if a writer, write." — Epictetus

"I write when I'm inspired, and I see to it that I'm inspired at nine o'clock every morning." — Peter De Vries

"It's not the college degree that makes a writer. The great thing is to have a story to tell." — Polly Adler

"Most writers mend their tattered thoughts with patches from dictionaries." — Kahlil Gibran

"I always do the first line well, but I have trouble doing the others." — Molière

"One who proposes to be an author should first be a student." — J. Montgomery

"'Tis easy to write epigrams nicely, but to write a book is hard." — Martial

"The profession of book-writing makes horse racing seem like a solid, stable business." — John Steinbeck

"And Famous isn't good for a writer. You don't observe well when you're being observed." — Ken Kesey

"A writer needs three things, experience, observation, and imagination, any two of which, at times any one of which, can supply the lack of the others." — "The writer's only responsibility is to his art." — William Faulkner

"When writing a novel, a writer should create living people; people, not characters. A character is a caricature." — "Easy writing makes hard reading." — Ernest Hemingway

"Nothing goes by luck in composition. It allows of no tricks. The best you can write will be the best you are." — "Write while the heat is in you. The writer who postpones the recording of his thoughts uses an iron which has cooled to burn a hole with. ne cannot inflame the minds of his audience." — Thoreau

"In good writing, words become one with things." — "People do not deserve good writing, they are so pleased with the bad." — Emerson

"People have lost sight of distant horizons. Nobody writes for humanity, for civilization; they write for their country, their sect; to amuse their friends or annoy their enemies." — Norman Douglas

"Newspapers are unable, seemingly, to discriminate between a bicycle accident and the collapse of civilization." — George Bernard Shaw

"I fear three newspapers more than a hundred thousand bayonets." — "There are only two powers in the world, the sword and the pen; and in the end the former is always conquered by the latter." — Napoleon

"The pen is mightier than the sword." — Bulwer-Lytton

"I would rather be attacked than unnoticed. For the worst thing you can do to an author is to be silent as to his work." — Samuel Johnson

"A man who leaves memoirs, whether well or badly written, provided they be sincere, renders a service to future psychologists and writers." — Henryk Sienkiewicz

"Employ your time in improving yourself by other people's writings so that you shall come easily by what others have labored hard for." — Socrates

Poetry

"Poetry is the mirror of the soul." — English proverb

"Poetry is vocal painting, as painting is silent poetry." — Simonides

"Poetry is thoughts that breathe, and words that burn." — Thomas Gray

"Poetry is not the thing said but a way of saying it." — Alfred Housman

"Poetry is a counterfeit creation, and makes things that are not, as though they were." — John Donne

"Poetry is a man's rebellion against being what he is." — James Branch Cabell

"Poetry is something more philosophical and more worthy of serious attention than history." — Aristotle

"Poetry is forged slowly and patiently, link by link, with sweat and blood and tears." — Sir Lord Alfred Douglas

"Poetry is a comforting piece of fiction set to more or less lascivious music." — Henry Mencken

"Poetry ought to be as well written as prose." — "All great poetry gives the illusion of a view of life." — T. S. Eliot

"Poets are all who love, who feel great truths, and tell them; and the truth of truths is love." — Philip James Bailey

"Poets are men who despise money except what they need for today." — Sir James Matthew Barrie

"Poetic license may be forgiven to the tellers of unusual stories." — Eliphas Levi

"A poem begins in delight and ends in wisdom." — "A poem begins with a lump in the throat." — Robert Frost

"A poet is, before anything else, a person who is passionately in love with language." — Wystan Auden

"One merit of poetry few people will deny; it says more, and in fewer words, than prose." — Voltaire

"There is a pleasure in poetic pains which only poets know." — William Cowper

"The great poet draws his creations only from out of his own reality." — Nietzsche

"If poetry comes not as naturally as leaves to a tree it had better not come at all." — John Keats

"Science sees signs; Poetry the thing signified." — Augustus and Julius Hare

"Science is for those who learn; poetry, for those who know." — Joseph Roux

"The function of the poet is not to be inspired himself, but to create inspiration in his readers." — Valry

"The important thing about a poem is the reader." — Mark Van Doren

"To have great poets, there must be great audiences, too." — Whitman

"A poet can survive everything but the misprint." — Oscar Wilde

"Nothing is more confident than a bad poet." — Martial

"A good poet's made as well as born." — Ben Jonson

"One who, in an enlightened and literary society, aspires to be a great poet, must first become a little child." — Thomas Macaulay

"Truth shines the brighter clad in verse." — Alexander Pope

"We can read poetry, and recite poetry, but to live poetry — is the symphony of life." — S. Frances Foote

"The great things in poetry are song at the core, but externally mere speech." — Arthur Symons

"Poetry is simply the most beautiful, impressive and widely effective mode of saying things, and hence its importance." — Matthew Arnold

"Poetry is like painting: one piece takes your fancy if you stand close to it, another if you keep at some distance." — "Poets desire either to teach or to give pleasure." — Horace

"Poetry is a language which tells us, through a more or less emotional reaction, something that cannot be said." — Edwin Robinson

"Poetry is the spontaneous overflow of powerful feelings: It takes its origin from emotion recollected in tranquilly." — "The Poet binds together by passion and knowledge the vast empire of human society, as it is spread over the whole earth, and over all time." — Wordsworth

"Poetry comes nearer to vital truth than history." — "Poets utter great and wise things which they do not themselves understand." — "At the touch of love, everyone becomes a poet." — Plato

"Poetry is a flash of lightning; it becomes mere composition when it is an arrangement of words." — "The poet is one who makes you feel, after reading his poems, that his best verses have not yet been composed." — Kahlil Gibran

"Poetry is the record of the best and happiest moments of the happiest and best minds." — "Poets are the unacknowledged legislators of the world." — "Poet's food is love and fame." — Shelley

"Poetry alone imagines, and imagining creates the world that people can wish to live in and make true." — "A poem should not mean but be." — Archibald MacLeish

"When power leads people towards arrogance, poetry reminds them of their limitations. When power narrows the areas of a people's concern, poetry reminds them of the richness and diversity of their existence. When power corrupts, poetry cleanses." — John F. Kennedy

"You arrive at truth through poetry; I arrive at poetry through truth." — "You will not find poetry anywhere unless you bring it with you." — Joseph Joubert

"All that is best in the great poets of all countries is not what is national in them, but what is universal." — "Many a poem is marred by a superfluous verse." — Longfellow

"A vein of poetry exists in the hearts of all men." — "A poet without love were a physical and metaphysical impossibility." — Carlyle

"Cheerfulness, without which no man can be a poet — for beauty is his aim." — "The finest poems of the world have been expedients to get bread." — "There are two classes of poets — the poets by education and practice, these we respect; and poets by nature, these we love." — Emerson

"Good poetry seems too simple and natural a thing that when we meet it we wonder that all men are not always poets. Poetry is nothing but healthy speech." — Thoreau

"I decided that it was not wisdom that enabled poets to write their poetry, but a kind of instinct or inspiration, such as you find in seers and prophets who deliver all their sublime messages without knowing in the least what they mean." — Socrates

"With me poetry has been not a purpose, but a passion; and the passions should be held in reverence." — "I would define, in brief, the Poetry of words as the Rhythmical Creation of Beauty. Its sole arbiter is Taste." — Edgar Allan Poe

"Farther than the arrow, higher than wings, fly poet's song and prophet's word." — Roscoe C. E. Brown

Style

"Style is a way in which great minds think." — Frank Harris

"Style is a man's own; it is a part of his nature." — Comte de Buffon

"Style is the gossamer on which the seeds of truth float through the world." — George Bancroft

"Style is the dress of thoughts." — Philip Stanhope

"Style may be defined, 'proper words in proper places.'" Jonathan Swift

"In what they leave unsaid I discover a master of style." — Schiller

"Simple style is like white light. It is complex but its complexity is not obvious." — Anatole France

"A man's style in any art should be like his dress — it should attract as little attention as possible." — Samuel Butler

"Fashion can be bought. Style one must possess." — Edna Chase

"Find a subject you care about and which you feel others should care about. It is this genuine caring, and not your games with language which will be the most compelling and seductive element in your style." — Kurt Vonnegut, Jr.

Quotations

"A quotation at the right moment is like bread to the famished." — The Talmud

"The wisdom of the wise, and the experience of ages, may be preserved by quotations." — Disraeli

"Life itself is a quotation." — Jorge Luis Borges

"Proverbs are the lamp of speech." — Arabian proverb

"Proverbs are short sentences drawn from long experiences." — Miguel de Cervantes

"The genius, wit, and spirit of a nation are discovered in its proverbs." — Sir Francis Bacon

"A country can be judged by the quality of its proverbs." — German proverb

"By necessity, by proclivity, and by delight, we all quote." — Emerson

"Famous remarks are very seldom quoted correctly." — Simeon Strunsky

"Quotations such as have point and lack triteness from the great old authors are an act of filial reverence on the part of the quoter, and a blessing to a public grown superficial and external." — Louise Imogen Guiney

"'Familiar quotations' . . . are more than familiar; they are something of a part of us . . . These echoes from the past have two marked characteristics — a simple idea, and an accurate rhythmic beat." — Carroll A. Wilson

Language

"Language is the archive of history." — Emerson

"Language is the road of a culture. It tells you where its people come from and where they are going." — Rita Mae Brown

"Language is as much an art and as sure a refuge as painting or music or literature." — Jane Ellen Harrison

"A man's language is an unerring index of his mind." — Laurence Binyon

"The language denotes the man." — Christian Bovee

"The function of language is twofold: to communicate emotion and to give information." — Aldous Huxley

"Think like a wise man but communicate in the language of the people." — William Butler Yeats

"Everyone smiles in the same language." — Old proverb

"Translation is at best an echo." — James Bone

"An idea does not pass from one language to another without change." — Miguel de Unamuno

"That is not a good language that all understand not." — Anonymous

"There were no ill language were it not ill taken." — Old proverb

"Slovenly language corrodes the mind." — James Adams

"Ice is the silent language of the peak; and fire the silent language of the star." — Conrad Aiken

"There's a language in her eye, her cheek, her lip." — "But for my own part, it was Greek to me." — Shakespeare

"Use what language you will, you can never say anything to others but what you are." — Emerson

"We shall never understand one another until we reduce the language to seven words." — Kahlil Gibran

"One of the difficulties in the language is that all our words from loose use have lost their edge." — Ernest Hemingway

"If you wish to learn the highest truths, begin with the alphabet." — Japanese proverb

"Perhaps of all the creations of mankind language is the most astonishing." — Lytton Strachey

"Be the same thing that ye want to be called." — Scottish proverb

"Do not call a fly an elephant." — Old proverb

"If names are not correct and language be not in accordance with the truth of things, affairs cannot be carried on to success." — Confucius

"Every legend, moreover, contains its residuum of truth, and the root function of language is to control the universe by describing it." — James Baldwin

EDUCATION

"Education has for its object the formation of character." — Herbert Spencer

"Education is the apprenticeship of life." — Robert Willmott

"Education is helping a child realize his potentialities." — Erich Fromm

"Education is not filling a bucket, but lighting a fire." — William Yeats

"Education is the ability to listen to almost anything without losing your temper or your self-confidence." — Robert Frost

"Education should be as gradual as the moonrise, perceptible not in progress but in result." — George John Whyte-Melville

"Education sows not seeds in you, but makes your seeds grow." — Kahlil Gibran

"Educate your daughters as you do your sons." — Cleobulus

"It made me glad to be getting some education, it being like a big window opening." — Mary Webb

"Rest assured that literary education is no good without character." — Gandhi

"Character development is the great, if not the sole, aim of education." — William O'Shea

"The first thing education teaches you is to walk alone." — Alfred Horn

"Better build schoolrooms for 'the children' than cells and gibbets for the 'grown-ups.'" Eliza Cook

"The very spring and root of honesty and virtue lie in the felicity of lighting on good education." — Plutarch

"It is only the ignorant who despise education." — Publilius Syrus

"Only the educated are free." — Epictetus

"Very few can be trusted with an education." — Louise Guiney

"The great difficulty in education is to get experience out of ideas." — Santayana

"When you don't have an education, you've got to use your brains." — Anonymous

"I have never let my schooling interfere with my education." — Mark Twain

"The best education in the world is that got by struggling to get a living." — Wendell Phillips

"Self-education is, I firmly believe, the only kind of education there is." — Isaac Asimov

"Too much and too little education hinder the mind." — Pascal

"A university . . . by its very name professes to teach universal knowledge." — John Newman

"A human being is not, in any proper sense, a human being till he is educated." — Horace Mann

"The wise are instructed by reason; ordinary minds, by experience; the stupid, by necessity; and brutes by instinct." — Cicero

"The education of a man is never completed until he dies." — Robert E. Lee

"What sculpture is to a block of a marble, education is to the soul." — Joseph Addison

"Education is an ornament in prosperity and a refuge in adversity." — "The roots of education are bitter, but the fruit is sweet." — Aristotle

"The secret of education lies in respecting the pupil." — "The things taught in schools and colleges are not an education, but the means of education." — Emerson

"Education . . . has produced a vast population able to read but unable to distinguish what is worth reading." — George Macaulay Trevelyan

"Our progress as a nation can be no swifter than our progress in education." — "A child mis-educated is a child lost." — John F. Kennedy

"All who have meditated on the art of governing mankind have been convinced that the fate of empires depends upon the education of youth." — Aristotle

"In the education of children there is nothing like alluring the interest and affection; otherwise you only make so many asses laden with books." — Montaigne

"The most important method of education always has consisted of that in which the pupil was urged to actual performance." — Einstein

"For every one pupil who needs to be guarded from a weak excess of sensibility there are three who need to be awakened for the slumber of cold vulgarity. The task of the modern educator is not to cut down jungles but to irrigate deserts." — C. S. Lewis

"On one occasion Aristotle was asked how much an educated man was superior to one who was uneducated: 'As much,' said he, 'as the living are to the dead.'" Diogenes

"By nature all men are alike, but by education widely different." — "If you are planning for a year, sow rice. If you are planning for a decade, plant trees. If you are planning for a lifetime, educate a man." — Chinese proverbs.

Teaching

"Teach the art of living well." — "While we teach we learn." — Seneca

"Teach me to live, that I may dread the grave as little as my bed." — Bishop Thomas Ken

"Teach us that wealth is not elegance, that profusion is not magnificence, that splendor is not beauty." — Disraeli

"Teaching is not a lost art, but the regard for it is a lost tradition." — Jacques Barzun

"To teach is to learn." — Japanese proverb

"One who learns, teaches." — African proverb

"A teacher affects eternity; he can never tell where his influence stops." — Henry Adams

"To know how to suggest is the art of teaching." — Amiel

"It is the supreme art of the teacher to awaken joy in creative expression and knowledge." — Einstein

"A good teacher is better than many books." — German proverb

"The students' minds must not be caged, nor for that matter those of the teachers." — Gandhi

"The object of teaching a child is to enable him to get along without his teacher." — Elbert Hubbard

"Instruction in things moral is most necessary to the making of the highest type of citizenship." — Theodore Roosevelt

"Many a teacher, lacking judgment, hindereth his own lessons." — Martin Tupper

"Need teaches a plan." — Irish proverb

"Hunger is the teacher of many." — Greek proverb

"What smarts, teaches." — Anonymous

"When the pupil is ready, the teacher appears." — Far Eastern saying

"The one exclusive sign of a thorough knowledge is the power of teaching." — Aristotle

"Teachers open the door, but you must enter by yourself." — "Give a man a fish, and you feed him for a day. Teach a man to fish, and you feed him for a lifetime." — Chinese proverbs

"Do not teach children learning by force and harshness; but direct them to it by what amuses their minds, so that you may be the better able to discover with accuracy the peculiar bent of the genius of each." — Plato

"Let our teaching be full of ideas. Hitherto it has been stuffed only with facts." — "The whole art of teaching is only the art of awakening the natural curiosity of young minds for the purpose of satisfying it afterwards." — Anatole France

"The method of teaching which approaches most nearly to the method of investigation, is incomparably the best." — Edmund Burke

"The best teacher is the one who suggests rather than dogmatizes, and inspires his listener with the wish to teach themselves." — Bulwer-Lytton

"If we wish to teach, we must stop to think the scholar's thoughts." — "The teacher who has forgotten his childhood will have poor success." — A. Maclaren

"When you wish to instruct, be brief; that men's minds take in quickly what you say, learn its lesson, and retain it faithfully." — Cicero

"The teacher who is attempting to teach without inspiring the pupil with a desire to learn is hammering on cold iron." — Horace Mann

"Modern cynics and skeptics . . . see no harm in paying those to whom they entrust the minds of their children a smaller wage than is paid to those to whom they entrust the care of their plumbing." — John F. Kennedy

"All great teachings have the single purpose of controlling the ego to create a better world." — "A man should first direct himself in the way he should go. Only then should he instruct others." — Buddha

"If a man keeps cherishing his old knowledge, so as continually to be acquiring new, he may be a teacher of others." — Confucius

Scholars

"The ink of the scholar is more sacred than the blood of the martyr." — Mohammed

"A table is not blessed if it has fed no scholars." — Jewish proverb

"Iron sharpens iron; scholar, the scholar." — The Talmud

"The more scholastically educated a man is generally, the more he is an emotional boor." — D. H. Lawrence

"The world's great people have not commonly been great scholars, nor its great scholars great people." — Oliver Wendell Holmes

"The wisest mind hath something to learn." — Santayana

"The knowledge of words is the gate of scholarship." — John Wilson

"How often when they find a sage as sweet as Socrates or Plato they hand him hemlock for his wage, or bake him like a sweet potato!" Donald Marquis

"The office of the scholar is to cheer, to raise, to guide people by showing them facts amidst appearances." — Emerson

Learning

"Learning is there for every man." — French proverb

"Learning is a treasure that will follow its owner everywhere." — Chinese proverb

"Learning is an ornament in prosperity, a refuge in adversity, and a provision in old age." — Aristotle

"Learning is a scepter to some, a bauble to others." — Old proverb

"Learn what you are and be such." — Pindar

"Learn as though you would never be able to master it; hold it as though you would be in fear of losing it." — Confucius

"Learn to live, and live to learn, ignorance like a fire doth burn, little tasks make large return." — Bayard Taylor

"Learning makes a man fit company for himself." — Thomas Fuller

"Learning teaches how to carry things in suspense, without prejudice, till you resolve." — Sir Francis Bacon

"A lesson that is never learned can never be too often taught." — "My joy in learning is partly that it enables me to teach." — Seneca

"One who has no inclination to learn more will be very apt to think that he knows enough." — Sir John Powell

"To be proud of learning is the greatest ignorance." — Jeremy Taylor

"A man, though wise, should never be ashamed of learning more, and must unbend his mind." — Sophocles

"It is impossible for any man to begin to learn what he thinks he already knows." — Epictetus

"It is surely harmful to souls to make it a heresy to believe what is proved." — Galileo

"A little learning is a dangerous thing; Drink deep, or taste not the Pierian spring." — Alexander Pope

"There are lessons to be learned from a stupid man." — Horace

"I have learnt silence from the talkative, toleration from the intolerant, and kindness from the unkind." — Kahil Gibran

"It is less painful to learn in youth than to be ignorant in age." — Anonymous

"Whoso neglects learning in his youth, loses the past and is dead for the future." — Euripides

"What one knows is, in youth, is of little moment; he knows enough who knows how to learn." — Henry Adams

"The only thing that interferes with my learning is my education." — Einstein

"Much learning does not teach understanding." — Heraclitus

"Some will never learn anything because they understand everything too soon." — Sir Thomas Pope Blount

"It is easy to learn something about everything, but difficult to learn everything about anything." — Nathaniel Emmons

"I still am learning." — "I go to school that I may continue to learn." — Michelangelo

"I am always doing something I can not do, in order that I may learn how to do it." — Picasso

"You learn something everyday." — Old proverb

"Be not weary of learning." — Sophist saying

"You cannot learn to fly by flying. First you must learn to walk, to run, to climb, to dance." — Nietzsche

"All men should try to learn before they die what they are running from, and to, and why." — James Thurber

"It is better to learn late than never." — Publilius Syrus

"In every man there is something wherein I may learn from him, and in that I am his pupil." — Emerson

"That learning is most requisite which unlearns evil." — Antisthenes

"There are no national frontiers to learning." — Japanese proverb

"Seeing much, suffering much, and studying much, are the three pillars of learning." — Disraeli

"There is no royal road to learning." — Proclus

"As we live, so we learn." — Jewish proverb

"Learning is only remembering." — "The learning and knowledge that we have, is, at the most, but little compared with that of which we are ignorant." — Plato

"Wear your learning, like your watch, in a private pocket: and do not pull it out and strike it, merely to show that you have one." — Philip Stanhope

"Have you not learned great lessons from those who reject you, and brace themselves against you? Or who treat you with contempt, or dispute the passage with you?" Whitman

"A learned man is not learned in everything; but the capable man is capable in everything, even in what he is ignorant of." — "We should not ask who is the most learned, but who is the best learned." — Montaigne

"A learned blockhead is a greater blockhead than an ignorant one." — "Tim was so learned that he could name a horse in nine languages: so ignorant that he bought a cow to ride on." — Benjamin Franklin

"When Antisthenes was asked what learning was the most necessary, he said, 'Not to unlearn what you have learned.'" Diogenes

Studying

"Study the teachings of the great sages of all sects impartially." — Buddha

"There are more men ennobled by study than by nature." — Cicero

"The more we study the more we discover our ignorance." — Shelley

"What do I know? I do not understand; I pause; I examine." — Montaigne

"There is no study that is not capable of delighting us after a little application to it." — Alexander Pope

"Examine without corruption." — Sophist saying

"He who would leap far must first take a long run." — Danish Proverb

"To be prepared is to have no anxiety." — Korean proverb

"Brains well prepared are the monuments where human knowledge is most surely engraved." — Rousseau

"From contemplation one may become wise, but knowledge comes only from study." — A. Edward Newton

"Of many books there is no end; and much study is a weariness of the flesh." — Bible, Ecclesiastes 7:12

"Impatience of study is the mental disease of the present generation." — "It is by studying little things that we attain the great art of having as little misery and as much happiness as possible." — Samuel Johnson

"The love of study, a passion which derives great vigor from enjoyment, supplies each day, each hour, with a perpetual round of independent and rational pleasure." — Edward Gibbon

"As there is a partiality to opinions, which is apt to mislead the understanding, so there is also a partiality to studies, which is prejudicial to knowledge." — Locke

"If you devote your time to study, you will avoid all the irksomeness of this life, nor will you long for the approach of night, being tired of the day; nor will you be a burden to yourself, nor your society insupportable to others." — Seneca

"Reading maketh a full man, conference a ready man, and writing an exact man." — "I would live to study, and not study to live." — Sir Francis Bacon

"Never regard study as a duty, but as the enviable opportunity to learn to know the liberating influence of beauty in the realm of the spirit for your own personal joy and to the profit of the community to which your later work belongs." — Einstein

Books

"Books are ships which pass through the vast seas of time." — Sir Francis Bacon

"Books must be read as deliberately and reservedly as they were written." — Thoreau

"Books support us in solitude, and keep us from being a burden to ourselves." — Jeremy Collier

"Books give not wisdom where was none before, but where some is, there reading makes it more." — John Harington

"Books are immortal sons deifying their sires." — Plato

"Books [are] the children of the brain." — Swift

"Dreams, books, are each a world; and books, we know, are a substantial world, both pure and good." — Wordsworth

"It is my ambition to say in ten sentences what everyone else says in a whole book." — Nietzsche

"Everyone has a least one book in him." — Abraham Lincoln

"A great book that comes from a great think . . . is a ship of thought, deep-freighted with truth and beauty." — Theodore Parker

"A book must be the ax for the frozen sea inside us." — Franz Kafka

"A book is like a garden carried in the pocket." — Chinese proverb

"Wondrous, indeed, is the virtue of a true book." — J. Montgomery

"In the highest civilization, the book is still the highest delight." — Emerson

"Books are good enough in their own way, but they are a mighty bloodless substitute for life." — Robert Louis Stevenson

"It is with books as with men: a very small number play a great part." — Voltaire

"Beware of the man of one book." — Thomas Aquinas

"Woe be to him who reads but one book." — George Herbert

"We can not learn men from books." — Disraeli

"A man does not become clever by carrying books along." — African proverb

"All books are divisible into two classes: the books of the hour, and the books of all time." — John Ruskin

"'What is the use of a book,' thought Alice, 'without pictures or conversations?'" Lewis Carroll

"There are books of which the backs and covers are by far the best parts." — Dickens

"Don't judge a book by its cover." — Old proverb

"A best-seller is the gilded tomb of a mediocre talent." — Logan Pearsall Smith

"Life is too short for reading inferior books." — James Bryce

"There is no worse robber than a bad book." — Italian proverb

"There is no book so bad but something valuable may be derived from it." — Pliny the Elder

"Would you know whether the tendency of a book is good or evil, examine in what state of mind you lay it down." — Southey

"The man who does not read good books has no advantage over the man who can't read them." — Mark Twain

"Except a living man, there is nothing more wonderful than a book!" Charles Kingsley

"Show me the books he loves and I shall know the man better than through mortal friends." — Silas Weir Mitchell

"Choose an author as you choose a friend." — Wentworth Dillon

"A good book is the best of friends, the same today and forever." — Martin Tupper

"We are as liable to be corrupted by books as by companions." — Henry Fielding

"You can cover a great deal of country in books." — Andrew Lang

"I can not live without books." — Thomas Jefferson

"A room without books is as a body without a soul." — Cicero

"Over the door of a library in Thebes is the inscription, 'Medicine for the Soul'." — Diodorus Siculus

"Man builds no structure which outlives a book." — Eugene Ware

"Literature is the immortality of speech." — August von Schlegel

"Books are the windows through which the soul looks out." — "A library is not a luxury, but one of the necessaries of life." — Henry Ward Beecher

"Books are the masters who instruct us without rods and ferrules, without hard words and anger." — "Whosoever acknowledges himself to be a zealous follower of truth . . . must of necessity make himself a Lover of Books." — Richard de Bury

"There are some books which cannot be adequately reviewed for twenty or thirty years after they come out." — John Viscount Morley

"When you sell a man a book you don't sell him twelve ounces or paper and ink and glue — you sell him a whole new life." — "Since mankind learned print, no night is wholly black." — Christopher Morley

"A good book is the precious lifeblood of a master spirit, embalmed and treasured up on purpose to a life beyond life." — Milton

"We all know that books burn — yet we have the greater knowledge that books cannot be killed by fire. People die, but books never die." — Franklin D. Roosevelt

"A man who has published an injurious book sins, as it were, in his grave; corrupts others, while he is rotting himself." — Robert. South

"What is a great love of books? It is something like a personal introduction to the great and good people of all past times." — "I would prefer to have one comfortable room well stocked with books to all you could give me in the way of decoration which the highest art can supply." — John Bright

"The true university of these days is a collection of good books." — "All that man has done, thought, gained or been: it is lying as in magic preservation in the pages of books." — Carlyle

"The Bookshop has a thousand books, all colors, hues, and tinges, and every cover is a door that turns on magic hinges." — Nancy Byrd Turner

"Cultivate literature and useful knowledge, for the purpose of qualifying the rising generation for patrons of good government, virtue and happiness." — George Washington

"Books alone are liberal and free, they give to all who ask. They emancipate all who serve them faithfully." — Richard de Bury

Stories

"The one who tells the stories rule the world." — Hopi Indian proverb

"A good story cannot be devised; it has to be distilled." — Raymond Chandler

"A good storyteller is a man who has a good memory and hopes other people haven't." — Irvin S. Cobb

"A good writer is basically a story-teller, not a scholar or a redeemer of mankind." — Isaac Singer

"Stories now, to suit a public taste, must be half epigram, half pleasant vice." — James Russell Lowell

"In seeking truth you have to get both sides of a story." — Walter Cronkite

"It's all storytelling, you know. That's what journalism is all about." — Tom Brokaw

"It is not the voice that commands the story: it is the ear." — Italo Calvino

"No story is the same to us after the lapse of time: or rather we who read it are no longer the same interpreters." — George Eliot

"I cannot tell how the truth may be; I say the tale as it was said to me." — Sir Walter Scott

"There is much good sleep in an old story." — German proverb

"There are several kinds of stories, but only one difficult kind — the humorous." — Mark Twain

"A tale never loses in the telling." — S. Harward

"Time is a good story-teller." — Irish proverb

"There is pleasure in hardship heard about." — Euripides

"Mankind's creative struggle, our search for wisdom and truth, is a love story." — Iris Murdoch

"An honest tale speeds best being plainly told." — Shakespeare

"The greatest thing a human being ever does is to see something and tell what he sees in a plain way." — John Ruskin

"A story should have a beginning, a middle, and an end . . . but not necessarily in that order." — Jean Luc Goddard

"All the best stories in the world are but one story in reality — the story of escape. It is the only thing which interests us all and at all times, how to escape." — A. C. Benson

"Every man is necessarily the hero of his own life story." — John Barth

"We spend our years as a tale that is a tale that is told." — Bible, Psalms 90:9

"Everything that has a beginning has an ending. Make your peace with that, and all will be well." — Buddha

Myths

"Myths are not believed in, they are conceived and understood." — Santayana

"A myth is, of course, not a fairy story. It is the presentation of facts belonging to one category in the idioms appropriate to another." — Gilbert Ryle

"All myths come from what was once labeled history." — Anonymous

"Myths tell us how to confront and bear and interpret suffering, but they do not say that in life there can or should be no suffering." — Joseph Campell

Reading

"Reading is a basic tool in the living of a good life." — Mortimer Adler

"Reading is to the mind what exercise is to the body." — Joseph Addison

"Reading is seeing by proxy." — Herbert Spencer

"Reading should be in proportion to thinking, and thinking in proportion to reading." — Nathaniel Emmons

"Reading made Don Quixote a gentleman, but believing what he read made him mad." — George Bernard Shaw

"The reading of good books is like conversation with the finest souls of the past centuries." — Descartes

"The foundation of knowledge must be laid by reading." — Samuel Johnson

"Learn to read slowly: all other graces will follow in their proper places." — William Walker

"A page digested is better than a volume hurriedly read." — Thomas Macaulay

"To read without reflecting, is like eating without digesting." — Edmund Burke

"Force yourself to reflect on what you read, paragraph by paragraph." — Samuel Coleridge

"Pick something valuable out of everything you read." — Pliny the Elder

"No book can be so good as to be profitable when negligently read." — Seneca

"Read, mark, learn, and inwardly digest." — Book of Common Prayer

"It is well to read everything of something, and something of everything." — Lord Brougham

"If you believe everything you read, better not read." — Japanese proverb

"We read too much; we have forgotten how to listen." — Lincoln Steffens

"Reading, after a certain age, diverts the mind too much from its creative pursuits." — Einstein

"Anybody that's got time to read half of the new books has got entirely too much time." — Frank Hubbard

"As I cannot read all books, I will read only the best." — DeQuincey

"Read the best books first, or you may not have a chance to read them all." — Thoreau

"No entertainment is so cheap as reading, nor any pleasure so lasting." — Lady Mary Montagu

"A classic is something that everybody wants to have read and nobody wants to read." — Mark Twain

"I divide all readers into two classes: Those who read to remember and those who read to forget." — William Phelps

"Where the press is free, and everyone is able to read, all is safe." — Thomas Jefferson

"Every man is a volume if you know how to read him." — William Channing

"The wise man reads both books and life itself." — Lin Yutang

"In science, read, by preference, the newest works; in literature, the oldest. The classic literature is always modern." — Bulwer-Lytton

"We should be as careful of the books we read, as of the company we keep. The dead very often have more power than the living." — Tryon Edwards

Practice

"Practice is the best of all instructors." — Publilius Syrus

"Practice makes perfect." — Old proverb

"Practice yourself, for heaven's sake, in little things; and thence proceed to greater things." — Epictetus

"Practice every time you get a chance." — Bill Monroe

"Practice not your art, and it will soon depart." — German proverb

"By nature, men are nearly alike; by practice, they get to be wide apart." — Confucius

"Apelles was not a master-painter in one day." — Anonymous

"A juggler's instant skill hath been long years a learning." — Martin Tupper

"The best colt needs breaking in." — "A man knows no more to any purpose than he practice." — Old proverbs

"An once of practice is worth a pound of precept." — W. Cecil

"An ounce of practice is more than tons of preaching." — Gandhi

"If I don't practice one day, I know it; two days, the critics know it; three days, the public knows it." — Jascha Heifetz

"I know you're heard it a thousand times before. But it's true — hard work pays off. If you want to be good, you have to practice, practice, practice. If you don't love something, then don't do it." — Ray Bradbury

Curiosity

"Curiosity is as much the parent of attention, as attention is of memory." — Richard Whately

"Curiosity in children is but an appetite for knowledge." — Locke

"Curiosity is one of the permanent and certain characteristics of a vigorous mind." — Samuel Johnson

"The first and simplest emotion which we discover in the human mind, is curiosity." — Edmund Burke

"People are more inclined to ask curious questions, than to obtain necessary instruction." — Pasquier Quesnel

"Leave no stone unturned." — Euripides

"Nothing is so difficult but that it may be found out by seeking." — Terence

"Seek not to follow in the footsteps of men of old; seek what they sought." — Matsuo Basho

"The fabled musk deer searches the world over for the source of the scent which comes from itself." — Ramakrisna

"I have no special talents. I am only passionately curious." — "The important thing is not to stop questioning. Curiosity has its own reason for existing." — Einstein

"The over curious are not over wise." — Philip Massinger

"Curiosity killed the cat." — English proverb

Questioning

"Ask, and it shall be given you; seek, and ye shall find; knock, and it shall be opened unto you." — Bible, Matthew 7:7

"To be or not to be . . . that is the question." — "Every why hath a wherefore." — "Answer me in one word." — Shakespeare

"Ask and learn." — Apocrypha, Maccabees 10:72

"Ask no questions and hear no lies." — Goldsmith

"There are two sides to every question, exactly opposite to each other." — Protagoras

"Who fears to ask doth teach to be denied." — Robert Herrick

"No man really becomes a fool until he stops asking questions." — Charles Steinmetz

"A man who asks is a fool for five minutes, but a man who does not ask remains a fool forever." — Chinese proverb

"There's no such thing as a stupid question." — Old proverb

"The 'silly question' is the first intimation of some totally new development." — Alfred North Whitehead

"What is truth? Said jesting Pilate; and would not stay for an answer." — Sir Francis Bacon

"Judge a man by his questions rather than by his answers." — Voltaire

"It is not every question that deserves an answer." — Publilius Syrus

"Don't ask questions of fairy tales." — Jewish proverb

"I don't pretend we have all the answers. But the questions are certainly worth thinking about." — Arthur C. Clarke

"To question a wise man is the beginning of wisdom." — German proverb

"Men are never so likely to settle a question rightly as when they discuss it freely." — Lord Macaulay

"For the believer there are no questions and for the unbeliever there are no answers." — Menachem Mendel

"It is better to know some of the questions than all of the answers." — James Thurber

"An answer is invariably the parent of a great family of new questions." — John Steinbeck

"Lose your questions and you will find your answers." — Old proverb

"Ask the right questions and you get the right answers." — Anonymous

"A man will not live without answers to his questions." — Hans Morgenthau

"Question Authority" "Why be normal?" Anonymous

"Why not? Why not? Why not? Yeah!" Timothy Leary

"What you are looking for is who is looking." — St. Francis of Assisi

"Except for children who don't know enough not to ask the important questions, few of us spend time wondering why nature is the way it is." — Carl Sagan

"Folly's shallow lips can ask the deepest question." — "No man hath guessed his capabilities, nor how he shall expand." — Martin Tupper

"What is the sound of one hand clapping?" "If a tree falls in the forest and there is no one there to hear it, does it make a sound?" "When the Many are reduced to One, to what is the One reduced?" Zen Koans

"Although a cloth be washed a hundred time, how can it be rendered clean and pure if it be washed in water which is dirty?" Buddha

"There are those who see the world as it is and ask, 'Why?' and there are those who see the world as it could be, and ask, 'Why not?'" George Bernard Shaw

"Live your questions now, and perhaps even without knowing it, you will live along some distant day into your answers." — Rainer Maria Rilke

PRUDENCE

"Prudence is the footprint of wisdom." — A. Bronson Alcott

"Prudence looketh unto faith, content to wait solutions." — Martin Tupper

"A prudent man does not make the goat his gardener." — Hungarian proverb

"In matters of conscience first thoughts are best; in matters of prudence last thoughts are best." — Robert Hall

"A prudent question is one half of wisdom." — Sir Francis Bacon

"If thou wilt apply thy mind, thy shalt be prudent." — Apocrypha, Ecclesiasticus

Patience

"Patience is a virtue." — Old proverb

"Patience is the key of being content." — Mohammed

"Patience is the companion of wisdom." — Augustine

"Patience is the art of hoping." — Marquis de Vauvenargues

"Patience is a bitter plant but it has sweet fruit." — German proverb

"Patience is the best remedy for every trouble." — Plautus

"Patience is the key to paradise." — Turkish proverb

"Patience is the ballast of the soul." — Hopkins

"Patience is so like fortitude that she seems either her sister or her daughter." — Aristotle

"Patience is power; with time and patience the mulberry leaf becomes a silk gown." — Chinese proverb

"Patience is passion tamed." — Lyman Abbott

"Patience and time do more than strength or passion." — Fontaine

"Patience and resignation are the pillars of human peace on earth." — Edward Young

"Patience makes lighter what sorrow may not heal." — Horace

"Patience and diligence, like faith, remove mountains." — William Penn

"Patience surpasses learning." — Old proverb

"Patience attains all it strives for." — St. Theresa

"Patience and fortitude conquer all things." — "Adopt the pace of nature, her secret is patience." — Emerson

"Patience, and shuffle the cards." — Miguel de Cervantes

"Patient doth conquer by out-suffering all." — Peel

"Let patience have its perfect work." — Bible, James 1:4

"The greatest prayer is patience." — Buddha

"Whoever has no patience has no wisdom." — Sa'di

"A man that can have patience, can have what he will." — Benjamin Franklin

"A man who has patience may accomplish anything." — Rabelais

"Above all, do not be discouraged; be patient; wait; strive to attain a calm, gentle spirit." — St. Francis de Sales

"If your understanding fail, have patience with them." — Apocrypha, Ecclesiasticus 1:13

"The greatest and sublimest power is often simple patience." — Bushnell

"An once of patience is worth a pound of brains." — Old proverb

"Job was not so miserable in his sufferings, as happy in his patience." — Bible, Job

"When I planted my pain in the field of patience it bore fruit of happiness." — Kahlil Gibran

"Bring forth fruit with patience." — Bible, Luck 8:15

"Be patient toward all men." — Bible, I Thessalonians 5:14

"It's easy finding reasons why other folks should be patient." — George Eliot

"To lose patience is to lose the battle." — Gandhi

"Our patience will achieve more than our force." — Edmund Burke

"Beware the fury of a patient man." — John Dryden

"Go not for every grief to the physician, for every quarrel to the lawyer, nor for every thirst to the pot." — Italian proverb

"Tribulation worketh patience, and patience hope." — Bible, Romans 5:3

"There is no great achievement that is not the result of patient working and waiting." — Josiah Holland

"If we hope for that we see not, then do we with patience wait for it?" Bible, Romans 8:24

"How poor are they who have not patience! What wound did ever heal but by degrees." — Shakespeare

"Patience with deserving ever winneth due reward." — "The daily martyrdom of patience shall not be wanting of reward." — "Life's trials may be hard to bear, but patience can outlive them." — Martin Tupper

"Patience leads to power; but eagerness in greed leads to loss." — "To enjoy the day of plenty, you must be patient in the day of want." — Far Eastern sayings

"If we could have a little patience, we should escape much mortification; time takes away as much as it gives." — Marquise de Sevigne

"It is not necessary for all men to be great in action. The greatest and sublimest power is often simple patience." — Horace Bushnell

"Good things come to those who wait." — "All things come to those who wait." — Old proverbs

Waiting

"Everything comes to those who hustle while they wait." — Thomas Edison

"Things may come to those who wait, but only the things left by those who hustle." — Abraham Lincoln

"Who waits upon the when and how remains forever in the rear." — Wilber Nesbit

"Delay always brings danger." — Miguel de Cervantes

"Delay is ever fatal to those who are prepared." — Lucan

"Delay is preferable to error." — Thomas Jefferson

"The sooner the better — delay is a fetter." — Old proverb

"It's good to hope, it's the waiting that spoils it." — Jewish proverb

"Men count up the faults of those who keep them waiting." — French proverb

"Everything comes too late for those who only wait." — Elbert Hubbard

"He who hesitates is lost." — Addison

"All is not lost that is delayed." — Old proverb

"Long is not forever." — German proverb

"If you wait, there will come nectar like fair weather." — Japanese proverb

"They also serve who only stand and wait." — Milton

"I rave no more against time or fate. For, lo! Mine own shall come to me." — John Burroughs

"I can cheerfully take it now, or with equal cheerfulness I can wait." — Whitman

"We hate delay, yet it makes us wise." — Old proverb

"To know how to wait is the great secret of success." — Joseph de Maistre

"How much human life is lost in waiting?" "The philosophy of waiting is sustained by all the oracles of the universe." — Emerson

"Let us, then, be up and doing, with a heart for any fate; Still achieving, still pursuing, learn to labor and to wait." — "All things come round to those who will wait." — Longfellow

Tolerance

"Tolerance is the only real test of civilization." — Sir Arthur Helps

"Toleration is a good thing in its place; but you cannot tolerate what will not tolerate you, and is trying to cut your throat." — James Froude

"Tolerance cannot afford to have anything to do with the fallacy that evil may convert itself to good." — Freya Stark

"The tolerance of all religions is a law of nature, stamped on the hearts of all men." — Voltaire

"When a person grows to like himself, he becomes more tolerant of others." — Lao Wei

"The longer I live, the larger allowances I make for human infirmities." — John Wesley

"Travel teaches toleration." — Disraeli

"Tolerance is the positive and cordial effort to understand another's beliefs, practices and habits, without necessarily sharing or accepting them." — Joshua Liebman

"The test of courage comes when we are in the minority; the test of tolerance comes when we are in the majority." — Ralph W. Sockman

Economy

"The most important element in success is economy — economy of money and time." — Anonymous

"Thrift is a great revenue." — Cicero

"Keep adding little by little and you will soon have a big hoard." — Latin proverb

"Men that don't save pennies will never save dollars." — "A man who saves in little things can be liberal in great ones." — Old proverbs

"What is enough was never little." — Thomas Lynch

"Whatever you have, spend less." — Samuel Johnson

"A hunter who has only one arrow does not shoot with careless aim." — African proverb

"Keep a thing for seven years and you'll find use for it." — Irish proverb

"The question is not so much what money you have in your pocket, as what you will buy with it." — Ruskin

"A man is rich whose income is more than his expenses; and a man is poor whose expenses exceed his income." — La Bruyère

"When a man is rich, he begins to save." — German proverb

"Use it up, wear it out; Make it do, or do without." — American proverb

"Pay as you go — unless you are going for good." — Anonymous

"If a little does not go, much cash will not come." — "He who restrains his appetite avoids debt." — Chinese proverbs

"A penny saved is a penny earned." — "Waste not, want not; willful waste makes woeful want." — "Make no expense, but to do good to others or yourself; that is, waste nothing." — "Beware of little expenses; a small leak will sink a great ship." — Benjamin Franklin

"Everything in excess is opposed to nature." — Hippocrates

"The harvest and vintage come not every day, therefore be provident." — "From saving comes having." — "A man's purse will never be bare, if he knows when to buy, to spend, and to spare." — Thomas Fuller

"You never miss the water till the well runs dry." — Rowland Howard

"A creative economy is the fuel of magnificence." — Emerson

Moderation

"Moderation is best." — Cleobulus

"Moderation is best, so avoid all extremes." — Plutarch

"Moderation is the silken string running through the pearl-chain of all virtues." — Thomas Fuller

"Moderation is the inseparable companion of wisdom." — Charles Colton

"Moderation is commonly firm, and firmness is commonly successful." — Samuel Johnson

"Moderation in temper is always a virtue; but moderation in principle is always a vice." — Thomas Paine

"Moderation in all things." — Hesiod

"Moderation, the noblest gift of Heaven." — Euripides

"Ask the gods, nothing excessive." — Aeschylus

"Nothing in excess." — Pittacus

"Everything that exceeds the bounds of moderation, has an unstable foundation." — Seneca

"Avoid extremes; forbear resenting injuries." — Benjamin Franklin

"The frog does not drink up the pond in which he lives." — Native American proverb

"Rule lust, temper and tongue, and bridle the belly." — Old proverb

"To go beyond the bounds of moderation is to outrage humanity." — Pascal

"Be moderate in the use of everything, except fresh air and sunshine." — Elbert Hubbard

"In adversity assume the countenance of prosperity, and in prosperity moderate the temper and desires." — Livy

"Let your moderation be known among all men." — Bible, Philippians 4:5

"A reasonable man needs only to practice moderation to find happiness." — Goethe

"The choicest pleasures of life lie within the ring of moderation." — "All excess is bad — abstinence, as intemperance." — Martin Tupper

"Avoid these two extremes . . . which two? On the one hand, low, vulgar, ignoble, and useless indulgence in passion and luxury; and on the other, painful, ignoble and useless practice of self-torture and mortification. Take the Middle Path for it leads to insight and peace, wisdom and enlightenment, and to Nirvana." — "Everything in moderation, including moderation." — Buddha

Temperance

"Temperance is the lawful gratification of a natural and healthy appetite." — John Gough

"Temperance gives nature her full play, and enables her to exert herself in all her force and vigor." — Joseph Addison

"Fools! Not to know how health and temperance bless the rustic swain, while luxury destroys her pampered train." — Hesiod

"Every man that striveth for mastery is temperate in all things." — Bible, I Corinthians 9:25

"Abstinence is easier than temperance." — Seneca

"The best medicine is temperance." — Old proverb

"Add to your knowledge temperance." — Bible, St. Peter

"The temperate are the most truly luxurious. By abstaining from most things, it is surprising how many things we enjoy." — Simms

"Temperance puts wood on the fire, meal in the barrel, flour in the tub, money in the purse, credit in the country, contentment in the house, clothes on the children, vigor in the body, intelligence in the brain, and spirit in the whole constitution." — Benjamin Franklin

"Temperance and industry are man's true remedies; work sharpens his appetite and temperance teaches him to control it." — Rousseau

"Measure thrice before you cut once." — "If you walk on a tight rope, you'll need a balancing pole." — English proverbs

"I have four good reasons for being an abstainer — my head is clearer, my health is better, my heart is lighter, and my purse is heavier." — Thomas Guthrie

Caution

"Caution is the parent of safety." — Old proverb

"It is well to learn caution by the misfortunes of others." — Publilius Syrus

"The policy of being too cautious is the greatest risk of all." — Nehru

"Deliberating is not delaying." — Apocrypha, Ecclesiasticus

"A full cup must be carried steadily." — "If thou canst not see the bottom, wade not." — English proverbs

"No man tests the depth of a river with both feet." — Ashanti proverb

"Don't think there are no crocodiles because the water is calm." — Malayan proverb

"Think of the going out before you enter." — Arabian proverb

"Forewarned is forearmed." — J. Arderne

"When the old dog barks it is time to watch." — Latin proverb

"A little fore-talk may save much after-talk." — "Never assume." — "Be slow in choosing, but slower in changing." — "Be slow enough to be sure." — Old proverbs

"Be not afraid of going slowly; be afraid of standing still." — "A man should be just as careful in choosing his pleasures as in avoiding calamities." — Chinese proverbs

"Cautious, careful people, always casting about to preserve their reputations . . . can never effect a reform." — Susan B. Anthony

Safety

"By falling we learn to go safely." — "It is best to be on the safe side." — Old proverbs

"It is better to be safe than sorry." — American proverb

"Obscurity often brings safety." — Aesop

"There is safety in numbers." — Bible, Proverbs 11:14

"When one has no lust, no hatred, a man walks safely among the things of lust and hatred." — Bhagavad-gita

"Keep the common road and you are safe." — Old proverb

"In skating over thin ice our safety is in our speed." — Emerson

"Don't burn the candle at both ends." — "It's best not to burn your bridges." — Old proverbs

"Don't keep your coals in a volcano." — Publilius Syrus

"Don't put all your eggs in one basket." — Italian proverb

"Don't try to fly before you have wings." — "Better an egg today than a hen tomorrow." — French proverbs

Secrets

"Secrecy is the chastity of friendship." — Jeremy Taylor

"The things most people want to know about are usually none of their business." — Shaw

"None can be so true to your secret as yourself." — Sa'di

"Who shall be true to us, when we are so unsecret to ourselves?" Shakespeare

"Keep no secrets of thyself from thyself." — Greek proverb

"Nothing is so burdensome as a secret." — French proverb

"There are no secrets better kept than the secrets that everybody guesses." — George Bernard Shaw

"Declare no secrets." — Sophist saying

"Walls have ears." — G. Gascoigne

"Loose lips sink ships." — Old proverb

"Do not speak of secret matters in a field that is full of little hills." — Hebrew proverb

"None are so fond of secrets as those who don't mean to keep them." — Old proverb

"It is said that a man who admits the possession of a secret, has already half revealed it." — William Simms

"We dance round in a ring and suppose, but the Secret sits in the middle and knows." — Robert Frost

"Trust those not with your secrets, who, when left alone in your room, turns over your papers." — Johann Kaspar Lavater

"Never confide your secrets to paper; it is like throwing a stone in the air, you do not know where it may fall." — Pedro la Barca

"There is as much responsibility in imparting your own secrets as in keeping those of your neighbor." — George Darley

"There is a skeleton in every closet." — "The only way to keep a secret is to say nothing." — Old proverbs

"To keep your secret is wisdom; but to expect others to keep it is folly." — Oliver Wendell Holmes

"The truly wise man should have no keeper of his secret but himself." — François Guizot

"To me it is enough to wonder at the secrets." — Einstein

"If you would keep your secret from an enemy, tell it not to a friend." — "Three may keep a secret, if two of them are dead." — Benjamin Franklin

"Love, pain, and money cannot be kept secret. They soon betray themselves." — "To whom you tell your secrets, to them you resign your liberty." — Spanish proverbs

FAITH

"Faith is the substance of things hoped for, the evidence of things not seen." — Bible, Hebrews 11:1

"Faith is courage; it is creative, while despair is always destructive." — David Muzzey

"Faith is a restraint against all violence. Let no Moslem commit violence." — Mohammed

"Faith without works is dead." — Bible, James 2:26

"Faith without good works is dead." — Miguel de Cervantes

"Faith may be defined briefly as an illogical belief in the occurrence of the improbable." — Henry Mencken

"Faith must have adequate evidence, else it is mere superstition." — Archibald Hodge

"Faith is not something to grasp, it is a state to grow into." — "Faith knows no disappointment." — Gandhi

"A man consists of the faith that is in him. Whatever your faith is, you are." — Bhagavad-gita 17

"A faithful man will abound in blessings" Bible, Proverbs 28:20

"We walk by faith not by sight." — Bible, II Corinthians 5:7

"A string of opinions no more constitutes faith, than a string of beads constitutes holiness." — J. Wesley

"What is subject of faith should not be submitted to reason, and much less should bend to it." — Pascal

"The errors of faith are better than the best thoughts of unbelief." — Thomas Russell

"If a man has a strong faith, he can indulge in the luxury of skepticism." — Nietzsche

"If weak thy faith, why choose the harder side?" Edward Young

"Why are you fearful? Have you no faith?" Bible, Mark 4:40

"The only known cure for fear is faith." — Lena Sadler

"Be thou faithful unto death." — Bible, Revelations 2:10

"When faith is lost, when honor dies, the man is dead!" John Greenleaf Whittier

"Talk faith. The world is better off without your uttered ignorance and morbid doubt." — Ella Wheeler Wilcox

"All the scholastic scaffolding falls, as a ruined edifice, before one single word — faith." — Napoleon

"We must have infinite faith in each other." — Thoreau

"Semper Fi — Ever Faithful." — Motto of the U.S. Marines

"The great doers in history have always been men of faith." — Edwin Chapin

"Faith is a knowledge within the heart, beyond the reach of proof." — "Faith perceives Truth sooner than Experience can." — Kahlil Gibran

"Faith is to believe what you do not yet see; the reward for this faith is to see what you believe." — "Faith opens a way for the understanding, unbelief closes it." — St. Augustine

"In the worst is ample hope, if only thou hast charity and faith." — "Never was a marvel done upon the earth, but it had sprung of faith." — "In faith Columbus found a path across untried waters." — Martin Tupper

"Speculate not too much on the mysteries of truth or providence. The effort to explain everything sometimes may endanger faith." — Tryon Edwards

"I tell you the truth, if you have faith as small as a mustard seed, you can say to this mountain, 'Move from here to there,' and it will move. Nothing will be impossible for you." — Bible, Matthew 17:20

"Hope looks for unqualified success; but Faith counts certainly on failure, and takes honorable defeat to be a form of victory." — Robert Louis Stevenson

"Our faith comes in moments . . . yet there is a depth in those brief moments which constrains us to ascribe more reality to them than to all other experiences." — Emerson

"You can do very little with faith, but you can do nothing without it." — Samuel Butler

Believing

"Believe that life is worth living, and your belief will help create the fact." — William James

"Believe not all you hear." — English proverb

"Believe nothing of what you hear, and only half of what you see." — Old proverb

"As a man believes so he becomes." — Bhagavad-gita 17.3

"All things are possible to those who believe." — Bible, Mark 9:23

"It is better to Believe than to Disbelieve, in so doing you bring everything to the realm of possibility." — Einstein

"A great mind is ready to believe, for he hungers to feed on facts." — Martin Tupper

"I can believe anything, provided it is incredible." — Oscar Wilde

"I make it a rule only to believe what I understand." — Disraeli

"Blessed are they that have not seen, and yet have believed." — Bible, John 20:29
"A man must not swallow more beliefs than he can digest." — Havelock Ellis

"A man who is always ready to believe what is told him will never do well." — Petronius

"Do not believe hastily." — "Where belief is painful, we are slow to believe." — "Believe! No storm harms a man who believes." — Ovid

"Nothing is so firmly believed as what we least know." — Montaigne

"As long as people believe in absurdities they will continue to commit atrocities." — Voltaire

"To believe with certainty we must begin with doubting." — Stanislaus I of Poland

"We are inclined to believe those whom we do not know because they have never deceived us." — Samuel Johnson

"I always prefer to believe the best of everybody; it saves so much trouble." — Kipling

"It is always easier to believe than to deny. Our minds are naturally affirmative." — John Burroughs

"Men do not believe that do not live according to their belief." — Thomas Fuller

"Loving is half of believing." — Victor Hugo

"While men believe in the infinite, some ponds will be thought to be bottomless." — Thoreau

"Belief consists in accepting the affirmations of the soul; unbelief, in denying them." — "We are born believing. A man bears beliefs, as a tree bears apples." — Emerson

"I taught you not to believe merely because you have heard, but when you believed of your consciousness, then to act accordingly and abundantly." — Buddha

"It is your own assent to yourself, and the constant voice of your own reason, and not of others, that should make you believe." — Pascal

Promise

"Promise is most given when the least is said." — George Chapman

"A promise is a cloud; fulfillment is rain." — Arabian proverb

"A promise should be given with caution and kept with care." — Socrates

"A promise is the offspring of the intention, and should be nurtured by recollection." — Anonymous

"A promise should be made by the heart and remembered by the hand." — "Promise makes debts and debts promises." — Old proverbs

"A man who promises runs in debt." — The Talmud

"A promise made is a debt unpaid." — Robert William Service

"A promise delayed is justice deferred." — "A promise against law or duty is void in its own nature." — Old proverbs

"Magnificent promises are always to be suspected." — Theodore Parker

"The Promised Land always lies on the other side of a wilderness." — Havelock Ellis

"Vows made in storms are forgot in calms." — English proverb

"Every man is a millionaire where promises are concerned." — Ovid

"A man who promises too much means nothing." — Thomas Fuller

"A man must have a good memory to be able to keep the promises he makes." — Nietzsche

"A man who is most slow in making a promise is the most faithful in its performance." — Rousseau

"A little thing in hand is worth more than a great thing in prospect." — Aesop

"Every brave man is a man of his word." — Pierre Corneille

"Breach of promise is a base surrender of truth." — Gandhi

"Neither promise wax to the saint, nor cakes to the child." — Greek proverb

"Better is it that thou shouldest not vow, than that thou shouldest vow and not pay." — Bible, Ecclesiastes 5:5

"Better to deny at once than to promise long." — "No greater promisers than they who have nothing to give." —

"Things promised are things due." — Old proverbs

"Who promises much and does little, dines a fool on hope." — "Yesterday's promise, like tomorrow's, never comes." — German proverbs

"The highest compact we can make with our fellow is, — 'Let there be truth between us two forevermore.'" Emerson

Hope

"Hope is the pillar that holds up the world." — Pliny the Elder

"Hope is the dream of a soul awake." — French proverb

"Hope is a waking dream." — "Hope is the dream of a waking man." — Aristotle

"Hope is like the sun, which, as we journey toward it, casts the shadow of our burden behind us." — Samuel Smiles

"Hope is the only tie which keeps the heart from breaking." — Thomas Fuller

"Hope is the only good that is common to all men; those who have nothing else possess hope still." — Thales

"Hope springs eternal in the human breast." — Alexander Pope

"Hope to the end." — Bible, I Peter 1:13

"Hope deferred maketh the heart sick." — Bible, Proverbs 13:12

"Hope has as many lives as a cat or king." — Longfellow

"Where there is life there is hope." — Cicero

"Where there is no hope there can be no endeavor." — Samuel Johnson

"Vain hopes cut one off from every good." — Far Eastern saying

"Things which you do not hope happen more frequently than things which you do hope." — Plautus

"It is only for the sake of those without hope that hope is given to us." — Walter Benjamin

"One who lives on hopes will die fasting." — Benjamin Franklin

"A man who lives only by hope will die with despair." — Italian proverb

"In all things it is better to hope than to despair." — Goethe

"There are no hopeless situations; there are only men who have grown hopeless about them." — Clare Booth Luce

"A man who wants hope is the poorest man alive." — Old proverb

"At first we hope too much, later on, not enough." — Joseph Roux

"We should not let our fears hold us back from pursuing our hopes." — John F. Kennedy

"We judge a man's wisdom by his hope." — Emerson

"A man's worth shines forth the brightest, who in hope confides." — "Ten thousand men possess ten thousand hopes." — Euripides

"A good hope is better than a bad possession." — Old proverb

"In the kingdom of hope there is no winter." — Russian proverb

"The natural flights of the human mind are not from pleasure to pleasure, but from hope to hope." — Dr. Johnson

"The mighty hopes that makes us human." — Tennyson

"Before you give up hope, turn back and read the attacks that were made on Lincoln." — Bruce B. Barton

"We shall meanly lose or nobly save the last hope of earth." — Abraham Lincoln

"We are saved by hope." — Bible, Romans 8:24

"Hope and be happy that all's for the best!" "Never go gloomily, man with a mind! Hope is a better companion than fear." — Martin Tupper

"There is no happiness which hope cannot promise, no difficulty which it cannot surmount, no grief which it cannot mitigate." — Cuyler

"You cannot put a great hope into a small soul." — Jenkin Jones

"The sun shines upon all alike." — English proverb

Wishing

"Wish chastely and love dearly." — Persian proverb

"Wishes are like prayers." — Anonymous

"Wishes won't wash dishes." — American proverb

"Wishing of all employments is the worst." — "What ardently we wish we soon believe." — Edward Young

"We easily believe that which we wish." — Pierre Corneille

"If a man could have half of his wishes he would double his troubles." — Benjamin Franklin

"We would often be sorry if our wishes were gratified." — Aesop

"Be careful what you wish for, you just might get it." — Old proverb

"Do not ask for what you will wish you had not got." — Seneca

"If things do not turn out as we wish, we should wish for them as they turn out." — Aristotle

"Things don't change, but by and by our wishes change." — Marcel Proust

"If wishes were horses, beggars might ride." — English proverb

"Few wishes come true by themselves." — June Smith

"A man will sometimes devote all his life to the development of only one part of his body — the wishbone." — Robert Frost

"Wishers and Woulders are never good householders." — "Wishes never filled the bag." — "Many of our wishes have been and will be thwarted." — Thomas Lynch

"Of all amusements for the mind, from logic down to fishing, there isn't one that you can find so very cheap as 'wishing.'" John Godfrey Saxe

"Many of us spend half our time wishing for things we could have if we didn't spend half our time wishing." — Alexander Woollcott

"Those who cannot tell what they desire or expect, still sigh and struggle with indefinite thoughts and vast wishes." — Emerson

"You can't cross the sea merely by standing and staring at the water. Don't let yourself indulge vain wishes." — Rabindranath Tagore

"A man is his own easiest dupe, for what he wishes to be true he generally believes to be true." — Demosthenes

"One must be aware that one is continually being tested in what one wishes most in order to make clean whether one's heart is on earth or in heaven." — Inayat Khan

"The best wishes that can be forged in your thoughts be servants to you." — "A wish is father to the thought." — Shakespeare

"Always leave something to wish for; otherwise you will be miserable from your very happiness." — Baltasar Gracian

"You must go after your wish. As soon as you start to pursue a dream, your life wakes up and everything has meaning." — Barbara Sher

Vision

"Vision is the art of seeing things invisible." — Swift

"Seeing is believing." — S. Harward

"What I can't see, I never will believe in!" Samuel Stone

"One eye-witness is of more weight than ten hearsays." — Plautus

"Eyes are more accurate witnesses than ears." — Heraclitus

"One single glance will conquer all descriptions." — Martin Tupper

"Take no one's word for it; see for yourself." — "A picture is worth a thousand words." — Old proverbs

"One picture is worth more than ten thousand words." — Chinese proverb

"Every picture tells a story." — C. Brontë

"To see sad sights moves more than hear them told." — Shakespeare

"Every man takes the limits of his own field of vision for the limits of the world." — Schopenhauer

"You can not see the mountain near." — "Men only see what they are prepared to see." — Emerson

"It is sure to be dark if you shut your eyes." — Old proverb

"The most pathetic man in the world is someone who has sight, but has no vision." — Helen Keller

"A man may have good eyes and yet see nothing." — Italian proverb

"A man has the biggest blind side who thinks he has none." — Dutch proverb

"There are none so blind as they that won't see." — English proverb

"A blind man who sees is better than a seeing man who is blind." — Persian proverb

"As a rule, men worry more about what they can't see than about what they can." — Julius Caesar

"A guest sees more in an hour than the host in a year." — Polish proverb

"It is not events that disturb the minds of men, but the view they take of them." — Epicetus

"Where the telescope ends, the microscope begins. Which of the two has the grander view?" Victor Hugo

"The real voyage of discovery consists not in seeking new landscapes but in having new eyes." — Marcel Proust

"He who does not look ahead always remains behind." — African proverb

"A man who does not open his eyes must open his purse." — German proverb

"What the eye doesn't see, the heart doesn't grieve over." — St. Bernard

"Have a vision not clouded by fear." — Cherokee Indian proverb

"As you see yourself, I once saw myself; as you see me now, you will be seen." — Mexican proverb

"Other people can't make you see with their eyes. At best they can only encourage you to use your own." — Aldous Huxley

"I shut my eyes in order to see." — Gauguin

"We do not see things as they are. We see things as we are" The Talmud

"Inner freedom is not guided by our efforts; it comes from seeing what is true." — Buddha

"Let the water settle; you will see the moon and stars mirrored in your being." — Rumi

"Things are not what they seem, nor are they otherwise." — Zen proverb

"The things that are seen are temporal; but the things that are not seen are eternal." — Bible, II Corinthians 4:18

"Sight not what's near, when aiming at what's far." — Euripides

"Who lives well sees far off." — Spanish proverb

"The adult looks to deed, the child to love." — Hindustani proverb

"Where there is no vision the people shall perish." — Bible, Proverbs 29:18

"The eyes of other people are the eyes that ruin us. If all but myself were blind, I should want neither fine clothes, fine houses, nor fine furniture." — Benjamin Franklin

"For every man the world is as fresh as it was at the first day, and as full of untold novelties for he who has the eyes to see them." — Thomas Huxley

"You must take the beam from your eye before you can see well enough to remove the splinter from your brother's." — Bible, Matthew 7:3

"It is one of the commonest of mistakes to consider that the limit of our power of perception is also the limit of all there is to perceive." — C. W. Leadbeater

"Throughout the centuries there were people who took first steps down new roads armed with nothing but their own vision." — Ayn Rand

Dreaming

"Dreams are true while they last, and do we not live in dreams?" Tennyson

"Dreams come true; without that possibility, nature would not incite us to have them." — John Updike

"Dreams are illustrations from the book your soul is writing about you." — Marsha Norman

"Dreams that do come true can be as unsettling as those that don't." — Brett Butler

"Dreams have as much influence as actions." — Stephane Mallarme

"Nothing happens, unless first a dream." — Carl Sandburg

"In dreams begins responsibility." — Edna O'Brien

"If you can dream it, you can do it." — "All our dreams can come true, if we have the courage to pursue them." — Walt Disney

"Existence would be intolerable if we were never to dream." — Anatole France

"A man must have something to dream of." — Nikolai Lenin

"If you don't have a dream, how are you going to make a dream come true?" Oscar Hammerstein

"I have a dream . . ." Martin Luther King Jr.

"A man whom a dream hath possessed knoweth no more of doubting." — Shaemas O'Sheel

"A dreamer lives forever, while the toiler dies in a day." — John Boyle O'Reilly

"Ground not upon dreams; you know they are ever contrary." — Thomas Middleton

"Like all dreamers, I mistook disenchantment for truth." — Sartre

"Do not mock our dreamers . . . their words become the seeds of freedom." — Heinrich Heine

"Reality can destroy the dream; why shouldn't the dream destroy reality?" George Moore

"Nothing so much convinces me of the boundlessness of the human mind as its operations in dreaming." — William Clulow

"The significance of a man is not what he attains, but rather in what he longs to attain." — Kahlil Gibran

"Where all is but dream, reasoning and arguments are of no use, truth and knowledge nothing." — Locke

"I am a practical dreamer. I want to convert my dreams into realities, as far as possible." — Gandhi

"I like the dreams of the future better then the history of the past." — Thomas Jefferson

"The future belongs to those who believe in the beauty of their dreams." — Eleanor Roosevelt

"For I see now that I am asleep that I dream when I am awake." — Pedro Calderon de la Barca

"A man is not old until regrets take the place of dreams." — John Barrymore

"If you want your dreams to come true, don't over sleep." — Hebrew proverb

"All dreams spin out from the same web." — Hopi Indian proverb

"A dream is the bearer of a new possibility, the enlarged horizon, the great hope." — Howard Thurman

"Saddle your dreams before you ride them." — Mary Webb

"It has never been my object to record my dreams, just the determination to realize them." — Man Ray

"Castles in the air — they are so easy to take refuge in. And so easy to build too." — Henrik Ibsen

"If a little dreaming is dangerous, the cure for it is not to dream less but to dream more, to dream all the time." — Marcel Proust

"Our dreams drench us in senses, and senses steps us again in dreams." — Amos Bronson Alcott

"Myths are public dreams, dreams are private myths." — Joseph Campbell

"Dare to be wrong, and to dream." — "Keep true to the dreams of thy youth." — Schiller

"Greatness is the dream of youth realized in old age." — Alfred Victor Vigny

"The beautiful is less what one sees than what one dreams." — Belgium proverb

"Few have greater riches than the joy that comes to us in visions, in dreams which no man can take away." — Euripides

"The dream, alone, is of interest. What is life, without a dream?" Edmond Rostand

"Life, what is it but a dream?" Lewis Carroll

"Deserve your dream." — Octavio Paz

"Dreams are the touchstones of our characters." — "I do not know how to distinguish between our waking life and a dream. Are we not always living the life that we imagine we are?" "Go confidently in the direction of your dreams. Live the life you've imagined." — Thoreau

"Dreams do come true, if we only wish hard enough, you can have anything in life if you will sacrifice everything else for it." — Sir James Matthew Barrie

"Those who dream by day are cognizant of many things which escape those who dream only by night." — "Deep into that darkness peering, long I stood there, wondering, fearing, doubting, dreaming dreams no mortal ever dared to dream before." — "All that we see or seem is but a dream within a dream." — Edgar Allan Poe

"The dreamers of the day are dangerous men, for they may act their dream with open eyes, to make it possible." — "All men dream; but not equally." — T. E. Lawrence

"A dreamer is man who can find his way by moonlight, and his punishment is that he sees the dawn before the rest of the world." — Oscar Wilde

"We often forget our dreams so speedily: if we cannot catch them as they are passing out at the door, we never set eyes on them again." — William Hazlitt

"All of us failed to match our dreams of perfection. So I rate us on the basis of our splendid failure to do the impossible." — William Faulker

"As soon as we see our dreams betrayed we realize that the intensest joys of our lives have nothing to do with reality, and we are consumed with regret for the time when they glowed within us. And in this succession of hopes and regrets our life slips by." — Natalia Ginsburg

"The problems of the world cannot possibly be solved by skeptics or cynics whose horizons are limited by the obvious realities. We need men who can dream of things that never were." — John F. Kennedy

"Cherish your visions and your dreams, as they are the children of your soul, the blueprints of your ultimate achievements." — "Man, alone has the power to transform thoughts into physical reality; man, alone, can dream and make dreams come true." — Napoleon Hill

"Dreams are necessary to life." — "Dreams pass into the reality of action. From the action stems the dream again; and this interdependence produces the highest form of living." — "The dream was always running ahead of one. To catch up, to live for a moment in union with it, that was the miracle." — Anais Nin

"Ah, great it is to believe the dream as we stand in youth by the starry stream; but a greater thing is to fight life through and say at the end, the dream is true!" Edwin Markham

Miracles

"Miracles happen, not in opposition to nature, but in opposition to what we know of nature." — St. Augustine

"To me every hour of the light and dark is a miracle, every cubic inch of space is a miracle." — Whitman

"Could a greater miracle take place than for us to look through each other's eyes for an instant?" Thoreau

"Where there is great love there are always miracles." — Willa Cather

"The works that I do shall he do also; and greater works than these shall he do." — Bible, John 14:12

"You know not where a blessing may light." — Old proverb

"Between two Saturday's happen many marvels." — Spanish proverb

"Miracles are propitious accidents, the natural causes of which are too complicated to be readily understood." — Santayana

"Every thread and every ray is a miracle of care; a miracle of mercy too, unless thy folly scorn it; a miracle of wisdom, whatever be thy thought." — Martin Tupper

"We must not allow the clock and the calendar to blind us to the fact that each moment of life is a miracle and mystery." — H. G. Wells

Optimism

"Optimism is the faith that leads to achievement. Nothing can be done without hope and confidence." — Helen Keller

"For myself, I am an optimist — it does not seem to be much use being anything else." — Churchill

"In these times you have to be an optimist to open your eyes when you awake in the morning." — Carl Sandburg

"The optimist sees a glass half full, a pessimist a glass half empty." — Old proverb

"Those who wish to sing always find a song." — Swedish proverb

"Every cloud has a silver lining." — English proverb

"The flower that follows the sun does so even in cloudy days." — Robert Leighton

"Turn your face to the sun and the shadows fall behind you." — Maori proverb

"I count only the sunny hours." — Latin proverb

"Everyday is a good day to be alive, whether the sun's shining or not." — Marty Robbins

"There are two ways of spreading light: to be the candle or the mirror that reflects it." — Edith Wharton

"It is better to light a candle than to curse the darkness." — Eleanor Roosevelt

"Give light, and the darkness will disappear of itself." — Erasmus

"However long the moon disappears, someday it must shine again." — African proverb

"We are all in the gutter, but some of us are looking at the stars." — Oscar Wilde

"Two men look out through the same bars: one sees the mud, the other the stars." — Frederick Langbridge

"Even a small star shines in the darkness." — Danish Proverb

"There's a light at the end of the tunnel." — "Look on the bright side." — "Pluck the rose and leave the thorns." — Old proverbs

"They fish on who catch one." — French proverb

"A propensity to hope and joy is real riches" Hume

"For all right judgment of any man or thing, it is useful, nay essential, to see their good qualities before pronouncing on their bad." — Carlyle

"The people whom I have seen succeed best in life have always been cheerful and hopeful people, who went about their business with a smile on their faces." — Charles Kingsley

"How you think about a problem is more important than the problem itself — so always think positively." — Norman Vincent Peale

WILL

"Will is character in action." — William McDougall

"Will and Intellect are one and the same thing." — Spinoza

"Good will is the mightiest practical force in the universe." — Charles Fletcher Dole

"The good or ill of a man lies within his own will." — "There is nothing good or evil save in the will." — Epictetus

"It is the will that makes the action good or bad." — Robert Herrick

"Great souls have wills; feeble ones have only wishes." — Chinese proverb

"Where there's a will, there's a way." — Aesop

"We will either find a way, or make one." — Hannibal

"A man that doth what he will oft doth what he ought not." — Old proverb

"Our will is truly free, when it serves neither vice nor sin." — Augustine of Hippo

"Nothing is troublesome that we do willingly." — Thomas Jefferson

"Free will is the ability to do gladly that which I must do." — Carl Jung

"To deny the freedom of the will is to make morality impossible." — James Froude

"A man who is firm and resolute in will molds the world to himself." — Goethe

"I wish it, I command it. Let my will take the place of reason." — Juvenal

"Our will grows stronger every time we fight." — Helen Mocksett Stork

"Practically all of us are capable of practically anything." — Aldous Huxley

"When the willingness is great, the difficulties cannot be great." — Machiavelli

"Resolve to perform what you ought; perform without fail what you resolve." — Benjamin Franklin

"Joy is the will which labors, which overcomes obstacles, which knows triumph." — Yeats

"There is no such thing as a great talent without great willpower." — Balzac

"People do not lack strength; they lack will." — Victor Hugo

"The difference between a successful man and others is not a lack of strength, not a lack of knowledge, but rather a lack of will." — Vince Lombardi

"Will is the exclusive possession of mankind. It divides men from the brute, in whom instinctive desire only is active." — Far Eastern saying

"Strength does not come from physical capacity. It comes from an indomitable will." — "If we develop the force of will, we shall find that we do not need the force of arms." — Gandhi

"The will is one of the chief factors in belief, not that it creates belief, but because things are true or false, according to the aspect in which we look at them." — Pascal

"We know that the will seeks itself, and finds itself in itself, and its seeking is a desire, and its finding is the essence of the desire, wherein the will finds itself." — Bohme

Desire

"Desire is the essence of man." — Spinoza

"Want of desire is the greatest of riches." — Louis Jean Baptiste

"The desire accomplished is sweet to the soul." — Bible, Proverbs 13:19

"Lord, grant that I may always desire more than I can accomplish." — Michelangelo

"Men freely believe that which they desire." — Julius Caesar

"I have as much as most, if I have as much as I desire." — Warwick

"When desire dies, fear is born." — Gracian

"A man begins to die who quits his desires." — George Herbert

"The desire for imaginary benefits often involves the loss of present blessings." — Aesop

"We desire nothing so much as what we ought not have." — Publilius Syrus

"In moderating, not in satisfying desires, lies peace." — Reginald Heber

"It is much easier to suppress a first desire than to satisfy those that follow." — La Rochefouculd

"It is hard to fight against impulsive desire; whatever it wants it will buy at the cost of the soul." — Heraclitus

"Where does the ant die except in sugar." — Malayan proverb

"The sea has an enormous thirst and an insatiable appetite." — French proverb

"The thirst of desire is never filled, nor fully satisfied." — Cicero

"Great desire obtains little." — Burmese proverb

"Alas! What a number of desires have come to nothing!" Anonymous

"If you desire many things, many things will seem few." — Benjamin Franklin

"The abstinent run away from what they desire, but carry their desires with them." — Bhagavad-gita 2

"We do not succeed in changing things according to our desire, but gradually our desire changes." — Marcel Proust

"What you can't acquire, don't desire." — Hebrew proverb

"Desire blinds us, like the pickpocket who sees only the saint's pockets." — "Not getting what you desire and getting what you desire can both be disappointing." — Buddha

"Life contains but two tragedies. One is not to get your heart's desire; the other is to get it." — Socrates

"A life directed chiefly toward the fulfillment of personal desires sooner or later always leads to bitter disappointment." — Einstein

"The desire of power in excess caused the angels to fall; the desire of knowledge in excess caused man to fall." — Sir Francis Bacon

"Those who cannot tell what they desire or expect, still sigh and struggle with indefinite thoughts and vast wishes." — Emerson

"Do not spoil what you have by desiring what you have not; but remember that what you now have was once among the things only hoped for." — Epicurus

"Vehement desires about any one thing render the soul blind with respect to other things." — "A man consists of desires. And as his desire, so is his will; and as his will, so is his deed; and whatever deed he does, that he shall reap." — Far Eastern sayings

"Follow your desire as long as you live; do not lessen the time of following desire, for the wasting of time is an abomination to the spirit." — Ptahotep

"Desire is the starting point of all achievement, not hope, not a wish, but a keen pulsating desire which transcends everything." — Napoleon Hill

Wanting

"A man who wants a great deal must not ask for little." — Italian proverb

"He can feel no little wants who is in pursuit of grandeur." — Johann Kaspar Lavater

"It is not from nature, but from education and habits, that our wants are chiefly derived." — Henry Fielding

"Those who want fewest things are nearest to the gods." — Socrates

"Choose rather to want less, than to have more." — Thomas à Kempis

"Nothing in the world is so incontinent as man's accursed appetite." — Homer

"Life is a progress from want to want, not from enjoyment to enjoyment." — Samuel Johnson

"All things that are, are with more spirit chased than enjoyed." — Shakespeare

"The more you get, the more you want." — Horace

"Those who want much are always in need." — Mohammed

"Our necessities are few but our wants are endless." — Josh Billings

"Willful waste brings woeful want." — "Much would have more, but often meets with less." — Thomas Fuller

"If the camel once get his nose in the tent, his body will soon follow." — Arabian proverb

"Possession is the grave of bliss. No sooner do we own some great book than we want another." — A. Edward Newton

"For want of a nail the shoe is lost, for want of a shoe the horse is lost, for want of a horse the rider is lost." — Benjamin Franklin

"Men want to live the way they want instead of how they should." — Anonymous

"Nothing is so hard for those who abound in riches as to conceive how others can be in want." — Swift

"I have everything, yet have nothing; and although I possess nothing, still of nothing am I in want." — Terence

"Want a thing long enough, and you don't." — Chinese proverb

"Our chief want in life is somebody who shall make us do what we can." — Emerson

"We do not want riches, we want peace and love." — Red Cloud

"When Alexander the Great asked Diogenes whether he wanted anything, 'Yes,' said he, 'I would have you stand from between me and the sun.'" Plutarch

"Every man is poorer in proportion as he has more wants, and counts not what he has, but wishes only for what he has not." — Manilius

"No man can have all he wants, but a man can refrain from wanting what he has not, and cheerfully make the best of a bird in the hand." — Seneca

"Try to want what you have, instead of spending your strength trying to get what you want." — Abraham L. Feinberg

Passion

"Passion is the great mover and spring of the soul." — Thomas Sprat

"Passion, though a bad regulator, is a powerful spring." — Emerson

"Passions make us feel, but never see clearly." — Montesquieu

"Our passions are ourselves." — Anatole France

"Only passions, great passions, can elevate the soul to great things." — Denis Diderot

"Nothing great in the world has been accomplished without passion." — Hegel

"All passions are good or bad, according to their objects." — Francis Quarles

"The passions are like fire, useful in a thousand ways and dangerous only in one, through their excess." — Christian Bovee

"When passions become masters, they are vices." — Pascal

"The vicious obey their passions as slaves do their masters." — Diogenes

"Serving one's own passions is the greatest slavery." — Thomas Fuller

"A man in a passion rides a mad horse." — Benjamin Franklin

"We must feel as well as control our passions." — Jean Richter

"Subdue your passion or it will subdue you." — Horace

"A man only employs his passion who can make no use of his reason." — Cicero

"The ruling passion, be it what it will, the ruling passion conquers reason still." — Alexander Pope

"A man submits to be seen through a micro-scope who suffers himself to be caught in a passion." — Johann Kaspar Lavater

"Chastise your passions, that they may not chastise you." — Epictetus

"The passionate are like men standing on their heads; they see all things the wrong way." — Plato

"It may be called the Master Passion, the hunger for self-approval." — Mark Twain

"The mind is the soul's eye, not its source of power. That lies in the heart, in other words, in the passions." — Marquis de Vauvenargues

"A strong passion for any object will ensure success, for the desire of the end will point out the means." — William Hazlitt

"A man that would be superior to external influences must first become superior to his own passions." — Samuel Johnson

"True passion is a consuming flame, and either it must find fruition or it will burn the human heart to dust and ashes." — William Winter

"Our passions are like convulsion fits, which, though they make us stronger for the time, leave us the weaker ever after." — Swift

"Men spend their lives in the service of their passions, instead of employing their passions in the service of their life." — Sir Richard Steele

"In the human heart there is a ceaseless birth of passions, so that the destruction of one is almost always the establishment of another." — La Rochefoucauld

"What profits us, that we from heaven derive a soul immortal, and with looks erect survey the stars, if, like the brutal kind, we follow where passions lead the way?" Claudian

"To conquer the subtle passion seems to me to be harder far than the physical conquest of the world by the force of arms." — Gandhi

"When you have found the master passion of a man, remember never to trust to him where that passion is concerned." — Lord Chesterfield

"Give me that man that is not passion's slave, and I will wear him in my heart's core." — "The mind by passion driven from its firm hold, becomes a feather to each wind that blows." — Shakespeare

"The passions are the winds that fill the sails of the vessel. They sink it at times; but without them it would be impossible to make way. Many things that are dangerous here below, are still necessary." — Voltaire

"The way to avoid evil is not by maiming our passions, but by compelling them to yield their vigor to our moral nature." — Henry Ward Beecher

Goals

"Goals help you overcome short-term problems." — Hannah More

"A goal is a dream with a deadline." — Napoleon Hill

"If your only goal is to become rich, you will never achieve it." — John D. Rockefeller

"Because our goals are not lofty but illusory, our problems are not difficult, but nonsensical." — Wittgenstein

"Before you can score you must first have a goal." — Greek proverb

"The man who has the will to undergo all labor may win any goal." — Menander

"Do not turn back when you are just at the goal." — Publilius Syrus

"If you want to live a happy life, tie it to a goal, not to people or things." — Einstein

"You need to overcome the tug of people against you as you reach for high goals." — Gen. George S. Patton

"Aim at heaven and you will get earth thrown in. Aim at earth and you will get neither." — C. S. Lewis

"We need to learn to set our course by the stars, not by the lights of every passing ship." — Gen. Omar Bradley

"Climb high, climb far, your goal the sky your aim the stars." — Old proverb

"One that would eat the fruit must climb the tree." — J. Grange

"The ripest peach is highest in the tree." — James Whitcomb Riley

"Man is a goal seeking animal. Our life only has meaning if we are reaching out and striving for our goals." — "First, have a definite, clear practical ideal; a goal, an objective. Second, have the necessary means to achieve your ends; wisdom, money, materials, and methods. Third, adjust all your means to that end." — Aristotle

"The rung of a ladder was never meant to rest upon, but only to hold a man's foot long enough to enable him to put the other foot somewhat higher." — Thomas Henry Huxley

"No matter how carefully you plan your goals they will never be more than pipe dreams unless you pursue them with gusto." — W. Clement Stone

"It is not enough to be industrious; so are the ants. What are you industrious about?" "In the long run, men hit only what they aim at. Therefore, they had better aim at something high." — Thoreau

Ambition

"Ambition is the germ from which all growth of nobleness proceeds." — Thomas Dunn English

"Ambition is a commendable attribute, without which no man succeeds. Only inconsiderate ambition imperils." — Warren Harding

"Ambition is like love, impatient both of delays and rivals." — Sir John Denham

"Once you make a decision, the universe conspires to make it happen." — Emerson

"Ambition is a lust that is never quenched, but grows more inflamed and madder by enjoyment." — Thomas Otway

"Ambition, the last infirmity of noble minds." — Milton

"Ambition [may be] so frenzied that you regard yourself last in the race, if there is anyone in front of you." — Seneca

"Ambition is so powerful a passion in the human breast that however high we reach we are never satisfied." — Machiavelli

"Though ambition may be a fault in itself, it is often the mother of virtues." — Quintilian

"Keep away from men who try to belittle your ambitions." — Mark Twain

"Most people would succeed in small things, if they were not troubled with great ambitions." — Longfellow

"A man may miss the mark by aiming too high as too low." — Thomas Fuller

"One can never consent to creep when one feels an impulse to soar." — Helen Keller

"No bird soars too high, if he soars with his own wings." — William Blake

"A man's worth is no greater than the worth of his ambitions." — Marcus Aurelius Antoninus

"Ambition often puts men upon doing the meanest offices; so climbing is performed in the same posture with creeping." — Swift

"Ambition has its disappointments to sour us, but never the good fortune to satisfy us." — "The early bird catches the early worm." — Benjamin Franklin

"I had no ambition to make a fortune. Mere money-making has never been my goal, I had an ambition to build." — John D. Rockefeller, Jr.

"Fling away ambition. By that sin angels fell. How then can men, the image of their Maker, hope to win by it?" "Virtue is choked with foul ambition." — "'Tis a common proof that lowliness is young ambition's ladder." — "No man's pie is freed from his ambitious finger." — Shakespeare

"Let your ambitions further your accomplishments, not overshadow them." — "A man who would rise in the world should veil his ambition with the forms of humanity." — Chinese proverbs

Perseverance

"Perseverance is the master impulse of the firmest souls." — E. L. Magoon

"Perseverance is a great and necessary virtue." — Louis Brandeis

"Perseverance opens up treasures which bring perennial joy." — Gandhi

"Perseverance is failing nineteen times and succeeding the twentieth." — J. Andrews

"Perseverance and audacity generally win." — Madame Deluzy

"Persistence and determination alone are omnipotent." — Calvin Coolidge

"Persistent men begin their success where others end in failure." — Edward Eggleston

"Persistent work triumphs." — Virgil

"Great works need no great strength, but perseverance." — Far Eastern saying

"A man who persists in genuineness will increase in adequacy." — Thomas Lynch

"The power of a man increases steadily by continuance in one direction." — Emerson

"Not to go back is somewhat to advance." — Alexander Pope

"Even after a bad harvest, there must be sowing." — Seneca

"The soft drops of rain pierce the hard marble; many strokes overthrow the tallest oaks." — John Lyly

"[There's] no rock so hard but that a little wave may beat admission in a thousand years." — Tennyson

"Even in social life, it is persistency which attracts confidence more than talents and accomplishments." — Henry Whipple

"Genius, that power which dazzles mortal eyes, is oft but perseverance in disguise." — Henry Austin

"To persevere, trusting in what hopes one has, is courage in a man. The coward despairs." — Euripides

"Give us grace and strength to forbear and to persevere." — Robert Louis Stevenson

"Anything I have begun is always on my mind, and I am not easy while away from it until it is finished." — Thomas Edison

"Perseverance is a great element of success. If you only knock long enough and loud enough at the gate, you are sure to wake up somebody." — Longfellow

"Perseverance, dear my lord, keeps honor bright." — "And many strokes, though with a little ax, hew down and fell the hardest timbered oak." — Shakespeare

"Perseverance is more prevailing than violence; and many things which cannot be overcome when they are together, yield themselves up when taken little by little." — Plutarch

"Perseverance is the most overrated of traits, if it is unaccompanied by talent; beating your head against a wall is more likely to produce a concussion in the head than a hole in the wall." — Sydney Harris

"The difference between perseverance and obstinacy is, that one often comes from a strong will, and the other from a strong won't." — Henry Ward Beecher

"Austere perseverance, harsh and continuous, may be employed by the least of us and rarely fails of its purpose, for its silent power grows irreversibly greater with time." — Goethe

"If we begin with certainties, we shall end in doubts; but if we begin in doubts, and are patient in them, we shall end in certainties." — Sir Francis Bacon

"Now this is not the end. It is not even the beginning of the end. But it is, perhaps, the end of the beginning." — Churchill

Endurance

"The best way out is always through." — Robert Frost

"He conquers who endures." — Persius

"What cannot be cured must be endured." — Rabelais

"Nothing happens to any man which he is not formed by nature to bear." — Marcus Aurelius

"By bravely enduring, an evil which cannot be avoided is overcome." — Old proverb

"That which was bitter to endure may be sweet to remember." — Thomas Fuller

"A man may go a long way, after he is tired." — "He that survives will see the outcome." — French proverbs

"Men must endure their going hence, even as their coming hither." — Shakespeare

"The bird that flutters least is longest on the wing." — William Cowper

"No tree falls at the first stroke." — German proverb

"Continual dripping wears away the stone." — Lucretius

"A cloak is not made for a single shower of rain." — Italian proverb

"Never say never." — English proverb

"Prolonged endurance tames the bold." — Chinese proverb

"Behold, we count them happy which endure." — Bible, James 5:11

"To endure what is unendurable is true endurance." — Japanese proverb

"Bear all things, believe all things, hope all things, endure all things." — Bible, I Corinthians 13:7

"If you want to get somewhere you have to know where you want to go and how to get there. Then never, never, never give up." — Vincent Norman Peale

"Endure all difficulty." — "Endurance is one of the most difficult disciplines, but it is to the man who endures that the final victory comes." — Buddha

Choice

"The strongest principle of growth lies in human choice." — George Eliot

"The history of free people is never really written by chance but by choice — their choice." — Eisenhower

"A dram of discretion is worth a pound of wisdom." — German proverb

"One should choose one's bedfellow whilst it is daylight." — Swedish proverb

"The difficulty in life is the choice." — George Moore

"You are your choices." — Sartre

Enthusiasm

"Enthusiasm begets heroism." — Semen Dubnov

"Enthusiasm is the life of the soul." — Old proverb

"Enthusiasm is essential to the triumph of truth." — Anonymous

"Enthusiasm is a vital element toward the individual success of every man." — Conrad Hilton

"Enthusiasm is a volcano on whose top never grows the grass of hesitation." — Kahlil Gibran

"Enthusiasm signifies 'God in us.'" Madame de Stael

"Enthusiasts soon understand each other." — Washington Irving

"What a man knows only through feeling can be explained only through enthusiasm." — Joseph Joubert

"The world belongs to the Enthusiast who keeps cool." — William McFee

"Opposition inflames the enthusiast, never converts him." — Schiller

"No wild enthusiast ever yet could rest, till half mankind were, like himself possessed." — William Cowper

"Years wrinkle the skin, but to give up enthusiasm wrinkles the soul." — Anonymous

"Life's blows cannot break a man whose spirit is warmed at the fire of enthusiasm." — Vincent Norman Peale

"The great accomplishments of man resulted from the transmission of ideas of enthusiasm." — Thomas J. Watson

"Every great and commanding movement in the annals of the world is the triumph of enthusiasm. Nothing great was ever achieved without enthusiasm." — Emerson

Attitude

"Adopting the right attitude can convert a negative stress into a positive one." — Hans Selye

"A child's attitude toward everything is an artist's attitude." — Willa Cather

"Life is ten percent what you make it, and ninety percent how you take it." — Irving Berlin

"To different minds, the same world is a hell, and a heaven." — Emerson

"If you can't change your fate, change your attitude." — Amy Tan

"The greatest discovery of my generation is that one can alter one's life simply by altering one's attitude of mind." — William James

"The happiness of this life depends less on what befalls you than the way in which you take it." — Elbert Hubbard

"A great attitude does much more than turn on the lights in our world; it seems to magically connect us to all sorts of serendipitous opportunities that were somehow absent before the change." — Earl Nightingale

Influence

"Blessed is the influence of one true, loving human soul on another." — George Eliot

"The people who influence you are people who believe in you." — Prof. H. Drummond

"Persuasion is better than force." — "Just as the twig is bent, the tree is inclined." — Alexander Pope

"Those who fear influences and avoid them make a tacit avowal of the poverty of their souls." — Andre Gide

"A cock has influence on his own dunghill." — Publilius Syrus

"The smallest hair throws its shadow." — Goethe

"Every human being has influence. Each moral action and utterance is linked to a chain of sequences no mortal can foretell. Each is a vast whispering gallery, where words and actions live on and ring on forever." — Morgan

Inspiration

"Just as appetite comes by eating, so work brings inspiration, if inspiration is not discernible at the beginning." — Igor Stravinsky

"When inspiration does not come to me, I go halfway to meet it." — Sigmund Freud

"You can't wait for inspiration. You have to go after it with a club." — Jack London

"We should be taught not to wait for inspiration to start a thing. Action always generates inspiration. Inspiration seldom generates action." — Frank Tibolt

"Ninety per cent of inspiration is perspiration." — Old proverb

"Do not quench your inspiration and your imagination; do not become the slave of your model." — Vincent van Gogh

"No man is great without divine inspiration." — Khunrath

"There never was a great soul that did not have some divine inspiration." — Cicero

"Inspiration is an awakening, a quickening of all man's faculties, and it is manifested in all high artistic achievements." — Puccini

"Inspiration may be a form of super-consciousness, or perhaps of sub-consciousness — I wouldn't know. But I am sure it is the antithesis of self-consciousness." — Aaron Copland

"Our moments of inspiration are not lost though we have no particular poem to show for them; for those experiences have left an indelible impression, and we are ever reminded of them." — Thoreau

"Who knows where inspiration comes from? Perhaps it arises from desperation. Perhaps it comes from the flukes of the universe, or the kindness of the muses." — Amy Tan

"Inspiration is in seeing a part of the whole with the part of the whole in you." — "To understand the heart and mind of a man, look not at what he has already achieved, but at what he aspires to do." — Kahlil Gibran

Opportunity

"The secret of success in life is for a man to be ready for his opportunity when it comes." — Disraeli

"Opportunity never knocks twice at any man's door." — Old proverb

"Opportunity is missed by most people because it is dressed in overalls and looks like work." — Thomas Edison

"Observe thy opportunity." — Apoccrypha, Ecclesiasticus 4:20

"Know opportunity." — Pittacus

"Watch your opportunity." — Diogenes

"Wait for opportunity." — Sophist saying

"One day your ship will come in." — Old proverb

"Ability is nothing without opportunity." — Napoleon

"Men come to their meridian at various periods of their lives." — John Henry Newman

"He is a good time-server that finds out the fittest opportunity of every action." — Thomas Fuller

"Omit no opportunity of doing good, and you will find no opportunity for doing ill." — Anonymous

"While we stop to think, we often miss our opportunity." — Publilius Syrus

"Four things come not back: The spoken word; The sped arrow; Time past; The neglected opportunity." — Omar Ibn Al Halif

"The Gods cannot help those who do not seize opportunities." — Chinese proverb

"Sail while the breeze blows, wind and tide wait for no one." — "There are plenty more fish in the sea." — English proverbs

"The sure way to miss success is to miss the opportunity." — Philarete Chaskes

"Unused advantages are no advantages." — Old proverb

"The wise will make more opportunities than they find." — Sir Francis Bacon

"Too many men are thinking of security instead of opportunity; they seem more afraid of life than of death." — James Byrnes

"For a dead opportunity, there is no resurrection." — Old proverb

"Strike while the iron is hot." — French proverb

"The sky's the limit." — "In the right place at the right time." — Old proverbs

"Seize the occasion." — Pittacus

"All that is valuable in human society depends upon the opportunity for development accorded the individual." — Einstein

"To be a great man it is necessary to turn to account all opportunities." — La Rochefoucauld

"Every opportunity [presents] an obligation." — John D. Rockefeller, Jr.

"To improve the golden moment of opportunity and catch the good that is within our reach is the great art of life." — Samuel Johnson

"Next to knowing when to seize an opportunity, the most important thing in life is to know when to forego an advantage." — Disraeli

GRATITUDE

"Gratitude is the sign of noble souls." — Aesop

"Gratitude is not only the greatest of virtues, but the parent of all the others." — Cicero

"Gratitude is a fruit of great cultivation; you do not find it among gross people." — Samuel Johnson

"Gratitude is the heart's money." — French proverb

"Gratitude is heaven itself." — William Blake

"Be grateful to all men for the teachings they give, be it in understanding or in tolerance." — Buddha

"Be grateful for what you have, or that will be taken away from you too." — Old proverb

"No office so humble, but it is better than nothing." — Anonymous

"To the generous mind the heaviest debt is that of gratitude, when it is not in our power to repay it." — Benjamin Franklin

"One can never pay in gratitude; one can only pay 'in kind' somewhere else in life." — Anne Morrow Lindbergh

"Never cast dirt into that fountain of which thou hast sometime drank." — Hebrew proverb

"Better is half a loaf than no bread." — English proverb

"Don't bite the hand that feeds you." — Old proverb

"It is better to have a little than nothing." — Publilius Syrus

"Always and in everything let there be reverence." — Confucius

"Reflect on your present blessings, of which every man has many; not on your past misfortunes, of which all men have some." — Dickens

"When we have only a little we should be satisfied; for this reason, that those best enjoy abundance who are contented with the least." — Epicurus

"A man who receives a benefit with gratitude repays the first installment on his debt." — "Unhappy are those men, even though they rule the world, do not consider themselves supremely blest." — Seneca

"Two kinds of gratitude: the sudden kind we feel for what we take, the larger kind we feel for what we give." — Edwin Arlington Robinson

Thankfulness

"First among the things to be thankful for is a thankful spirit." — Far Eastern saying

"Do you count your birthdays thankfully?" Horace

"In everything give thanks." — Bible, I Thessalonians 5:18

"Never take anything for granted." — Disraeli

"Something is better than nothing." — "Enough is as good as a feast." — English proverbs

"When eating bamboo sprouts, remember the man who planted them." — Chinese proverb

"Good health and good sense are two of life's greatest blessings." — Publilius Syrus

"The applause of a single human being is of great consequence." — Samuel Johnson

"O Lord, who lends me life, lend me a heart replete with thankfulness." — Shakespeare

"Do not expect thanks." — "Let us rise up and be thankful, for if we didn't learn a lot today, at least we learned a little, and if we didn't learn a little, at least we didn't get sick, and if we got sick, at least we didn't die; so let us all be thankful." — Buddha

Praise

"Praise like gold and diamonds owes its value only to its scarcity." — Samuel Johnson

"Praise makes good men better and bad men worse." — Thomas Fuller

"Praise undeserved is satire in disguise." — Henry Broadhurst

"Praise to the undeserving is severe satire." — Benjamin Franklin

"Think not those faithful who praise all your words and actions, but those who kindly reprove your faults." — Socrates

"Many men know how to flatter; few know to praise." — Greek proverb

"There's no weapon that slays its victim so surely as praise." — Bulwer-Lytton

"Let my mouth be filled with praise." — Bible, Psalms 70:8

"A runaway monk never praises his monastery." — Italian proverb

"Generally we praise only to be praised." — "Refusal of praise is a desire to be praised twice." — La Rochefoucauld

"It is not one who searches for praise that finds it." — Rivarol

"Those who are greedy of praise prove that they are poor in merit." — Plutarch

"Their praise is lost who waits till all commend." — Alexander Pope

"A man's accusations of himself are always believed, his praises never." — Montaigne

"Never raise thy own praise." — Old proverb

"Let another man praise thee, and not thine own mouth." — Bible, Proverbs 27:2

"A man's praises have very musical and charming accents in the mouth of another, but sound very flat and untunable in his own." — Xenophon

"True praise is frequently the lot of the humble; false praise is always confined to the great." — Henry Home

"The only way to escape the corruption of praise is to go on working . . . there is nothing else." — Einstein

"How a little praise warms out of a man the good that is in him." — Bulwer-Lytton

"We are all excited by the love of praise, and it is the noblest spirits that feel it most." — Cicero

"It is a sign of a good man, if he grows better for commendation." — Old proverb

Pleasing

"Please all, and you please none." — Aesop

"You can't please everyone." — E. Paston

"You can't please everyone all the time." — Old proverb

"It is a very hard undertaking to seek to please everybody." — Publilius Syrus

"If you wish to please people, you must begin by understanding them." — Charles Reade

"Whoever has bitten a sour apple will enjoy a sweet one all the more." — German proverb

"Eat to please thyself, but dress to please others." — Benjamin Franklin

"The way to rise is to obey and please." — Ben Jonson

"I would rather please one good man than many bad." — Pittacus

"Whenever you are sincerely pleased you are nourished." — Emerson

"If you mean to profit, learn to please." — Churchill

Value

"Try not to become a man of success but rather try to become a man of value." — Einstein

"The value of a man can only be measured with regard to other men." — Nietzsche

"All that matters is value — the ultimate value of what one does." — James Hilton

"He who would wish to be valued must make himself scarce." — Old proverb

"A man who dares to waste one hour of time has not discovered the value of life." — Darwin

"What we obtain too cheap, we esteem too lightly; it is dearness only that gives everything its value." — Thomas Paine

"An indispensable thing never has much value." — Russian proverb

"That which cost little is less valued." — Miguel de Cervantes

"One man's junk is another man's treasure." — American proverb

"A bird in the hand is better than two in the bush." — Aesop

"A bird in the hand is worth ten fleeing." — Scottish proverb

"Life has a value only when it has something valuable as its object." — Georg Hegel

"Nowadays we know the price of everything and the value of nothing." — Oscar Wilde

"The wise man is one who knows the relative value of things." — William Inge

"I have three precious things which I hold fast and prize. The first is gentleness; the second is frugality; the third is humility, which keeps me from putting myself before others. Be gentle and you can be bold; be frugal and you can be liberal; avoid putting yourself before others and you can become a leader among others." — Lao-tse

Worth

"Men understand the worth of blessings only when they have lost them." — Plautus

"We'll never know the worth of water till the well go dry." — Scottish proverb

"What costs nothing is worth nothing." — Old proverb

"We must treat each man on his worth and merits as a man." — Theodore Roosevelt

"The worth of a thing is what it will bring." — French proverb

"Which brings more to you . . . .you or what you own?" Lao-tse

"It is quality rather than quantity that matters." — Seneca

"It is not what he has, nor even what he does, which directly expresses the worth of a man, but what he is." — Henri-Frederic Amiel

FORGIVENESS

"Forgiveness is better than revenge." — Pittacus

"Forgiveness is better than punishment." — Epictetus

"Forgive us our debts, as we forgive our debtors." — Bible, Matthew 6:12

"To err is human, to forgive divine." — Alexander Pope

"Love truth, but pardon error." — Voltaire

"Let bygones be bygones." — Old proverb

"Pray you now, forget and forgive." — Shakespeare

"It is a man's peculiar duty to love even those who wrong him." — Marcus Aurelius

"There is nothing so advantageous to a man as a forgiving disposition." — Terence

"Joy to forgive and joy to be forgiven hang level in the balances of Love." — Richard Garnett

"Blessed is the man whose transgression is forgiven, whose sin is covered." — Bible, David

"How unhappy are those who cannot forgive themselves." — Publilius Syrus

"An injury forgiven is better than an injury revenged." — Old proverb

"They who forgive most, shall be most forgiven." — Gamaliel Bailey

"It is only one step from toleration to forgiveness." — Sir Arthur Pinero

"The entire world would perish, if pity and forgiveness were not to limit anger." — Seneca the Elder

"The weak can never forgive. Forgiveness is the attribute of the strong." — Gandhi

"The more we know, the better we forgive. Who ever feels deeply, feels for all that live." — Madame de Stael

"They never pardon who commit the wrong." — John Dryden

"The heart has always the pardoning power." — Anne Sophie Swetchine

"We pardon as long as we love." — La Rochefoucauld

"Be assured that if you knew all, you would pardon all." — Thomas à Kempis

"When it comes to acts of injustice forgive the person, not the act." — 14th Dalai Lama

"Injuries may be forgiven but not forgotten." — Aesop

"To forgive without forgetting, is again to reproach the wrong-doer every time the act comes back to us." — Far Eastern saying

"Forgiveness is primarily for our own sake, so that we no longer carry the burden of resentment. But to forgive does not mean we will allow injustice again." — Buddha

"Ye have heard that it hath been said, An eye for an eye, and a tooth for a tooth: but I say unto you, That ye resist not evil with evil: but whosoever smite thee on thy right cheek, turn to them the other also." — Bible, Matthew 5:38

"How oft shall my brother sin against me, and I forgive him? Till seven times? Jesus saith unto him, I say not unto thee, until seven times: but, until seventy times seven." — Bible, Matthew 18:21

"Offenders never pardon." — "A man who can not forgive others breaks the bridge over which he must pass himself." — George Herbert

Confession

"Confession of our faults is the next thing to innocency." — Publilius Syrus

"Confession is good for the soul." — Scottish proverb

"Confess your sins to one another and pray for one another, that you may be healed." — Bible, James 5:16

"Confess thee freely of thy sin." — "Confess yourself to heaven; Repent what's past; avoid what is to come." — Shakespeare

"Confess that you were wrong yesterday; it will show that you are wise today." — Old proverb

"A man that confesseth his fault shall be preserved from hurt." — Apocrypha, Ecclesiasticus

"We confess our little faults only to persuade others that we have no great ones." — La Rochefoucauld

"Not to repent of a fault is to justify it." — Old proverb

"It takes a big man to admit his mistakes." — Anonymous

"The confession of evil works is the first beginning of good works." — Augustine of Hippo

"There could not be a cleansing without a clean confession." — Gandhi

"A generous confession disarms slander." — "A fault confessed is half redressed." — Old proverbs

"A man should never be ashamed to own that he had been in the wrong, which is but saying, in other words, that he is wiser today than he was yesterday." — Alexander Pope

Mercy

"Mercy and alms are the body and soul of charity." — Sir Richard Steele

"Mercy to them that shows it, is the rule." — William Cowper

"Mercy turns her back to the unmerciful." — Francis Quarles

"Mercifulness makes us equal to the gods." — Claudian

"Blessed are the merciful, for they shall obtain mercy." — Bible, Matthew 5:7

"Sweet mercy is nobility's true badge." — Shakespeare

"Being all fashioned of the self-same dust, let us be merciful as well as just." — Longfellow

"Our sorrows are never so great that they hide our mercies." — A. Maclaren

"Do not judge yourself harshly. Without mercy for ourselves we cannot love the world." — Buddha

"We hand folks over to God's mercy, and show none ourselves." — George Eliot

"The merciful man doeth good to his own soul." — Bible, Proverbs

CHARITY

"Charity is love in action." — Dinah Mulock

"Charity is infinitely divisible. One who has a little can always give a little." — Peter McArthur

"Charity is never lost." — Conyers Middleton

"Charity begins at home." — Terence

"Charity begins at home and justice next door." — Dickens

"Charity never faileth." — Bible, I Corinthians 13:4

"Charity shall cover the multitude of sins." — Bible, I Peter 4:8

"Charity suffereth long and is kind." — Bible, I Corinthians 8:4

"With malice toward none; with charity for all." — Abraham Lincoln

"I deem it the duty of every man to devote a certain portion of his income for charitable purposes." — Thomas Jefferson

"In faith and hope the world will disagree, but all mankind's concern is charity." — Alexander Pope

"A man who has no charity deserves no mercy." — English proverb

"The more charity, the more peace." — Hillel

"And now abideth faith, hope, charity, these three; but the greatest of these is charity." — Bible, I Corinthians 13:13

"Avarice hoards itself poor; charity gives itself rich." — German proverb

"You want to double your wealth without gambling or stock-jobbing? Share it." — J. C. Hare

"The living need charity more than the dead." — George Arnold

"And above all these things put on charity, which is the bond of perfectness." — Bible, Colossians 1:17

"That is the best charity which so relieves another man's poverty it still continues his industry." — Thomas Fuller

"Our true acquisitions lie only in our charities, we gain only as we give." — William Simms

"The charities that soothe, and heal, and bless, lie scattered at the feet of man like flowers." — Wordsworth

"The highest of distinctions is service to others." — King George VI

"It is better to comfort than be comforted." — St. Francis

"Good will is the best charity." — Hebrew proverb

"Every good act is charity." — Mohammed

"Charity cannot dwell with a mean and narrow spirit." — "Charity is praised of all, and fear not thou that praise." — "Charity walketh with a high step and stumbleth not at a trifle." — "The measure of charity thou dealest shall be poured into thine own bosom." — Martin Tupper

"The charitable man is loved by all; his friendship is prized highly; in death his heart is at rest and full of joy, for he suffers not from repentance; he receives the opening flower of his reward and the fruit that ripens from it." — Buddha

"The epitaph of a charitable man: What I spent I lost; what I possessed is left to others; what I gave away remains with me." — Addison

Generosity

"Generosity consists not in the sum given, but in the manner in which it is bestowed." — Nathaniel Hawthorne

"When I give, I give myself." — Whitman

"Purity is best demonstrated by generosity." — Bible, Luke 11:41

"The generous man enriches himself by giving; the miser hoards himself poor." — Old proverb

"The greatest good you can do for another is not just share your riches, but reveal to them their own." — Disraeli

"A man there was, though some did count him mad, the more he cast away, the more he had." — John Bunyan

"A good man showeth favor, and lendeth." — Bible, Psalms 152:5

"A man that hath pity upon the poor lendeth." — Bible, Proverbs 19:17

"A loan though old is not a gift." — Hungarian proverb

"Life is an exciting business and most exciting when it is lived for others." — Helen Keller

"I would so live as if I knew that I received my being only for the benefit of others." — Seneca

"He would share even his share of the sun." — Italian proverb

"One who plants a walnut tree expects not to eat of the fruit." — English proverb

Giving

"Give light, and the darkness will disappear of itself." — Desiderius Erasmus

"Give and it will be given to you . . . for the measure you give will be the measure you get back." — Bible, Luke 6:38

"It is more blessed to give than to receive." — Bible, Acts 20:35

"Not one who has much is rich, but one who gives much." — Erich Fromm

"We are rich only through what we give; and poor only through what we refuse and keep." — Anne Swetchine

"Nothing costs so much as what is given us." — Thomas Fuller

"A man must be poor to know the luxury of giving." — George Eliot

"A man that giveth unto the poor shall not lack." — Bible

"A man gives twice who gives quickly." — Publilius Syrus

"A man that lends, gives." — George Herbert

"A man who loves with purity considers not the gift of the lover, but the love of the giver." — Thomas à Kempis

"The manner of giving shows the character of the giver, more than the gift itself." — Johann Kaspar Lavater

"There can be no greater slight and dishonor to a giver than to have his gifts neglected." — A. Maclaren

"What I gave, that I have; what I spent, that I had; what I left that I lost." — Johnson

"There is no happiness in having or in getting, but only in giving." — Henry Drummond

"You give but little when your give of your possessions. It is when you give of yourself that you truly give." — Kahlil Gibran

"If there be any truer measure of a man than by what he does, it must be by what he gives." — Robert South

"We make a living by what we get, we make a life by what we give." — Churchill

"If thou hast abundance, give alms accordingly: if thou have but a little, be not afraid to give according to that little." — Apocrypha, Tobit 4:8

"You have to accept whatever comes and the only important thing is that you meet it with the best you have to give." — Eleanor Roosevelt

"Giving is the secret of a healthy life. Not necessarily money, but whatever a man has of encouragement and sympathy and understanding." — John D. Rockefeller, Jr.

"There is no happiness in having and getting, but only in giving. Half the world is on the wrong scent in the pursuit of happiness." — F. W. Gunsaulus

"The more fully we give our energy, the more it returns to us." — "Giving brings happiness at every stage of its expression. We experience joy in forming the intention to be generous, we experience joy in the actual act of giving something, and we experience joy in remembering the fact that we have given." — Buddha

Helping

"Help thyself, and God will help thee." — George Herbert

"After the verb 'To Love,' 'To Help' is the most beautiful verb in the world!" Baroness Bertha von Suttner

"When a man is down in the world, an ounce of help is better than a pound of preaching." — Bulwer-Lytton

"A willing helper does not wait until he is asked." — Danish proverb

"It is easy to help him, who is willing to be helped." — "When need is greatest, help is nearest." — German proverbs

"A mouse may help a lion." — Aesop

"You roll my log, and I will roll yours." — Seneca

"If I had not lifted up the stone, you would not have found the jewel." — Hebrew proverb

"You may light a another's candle at your own without loss." — Old proverb

"Let no one ever come to you without leaving better and happier." — Mother Teresa

"Let each man look not only to his own interests but also to the interests of others." — Bible, Philippians 2:4

"'Tis certain gain to help an honest man." — Old proverb

"'Tis not enough to help the feeble up, but to support them after." — Shakespeare

"A little help is better than a lot of pity." — Celtic proverb

"You cannot push anyone up a ladder unless he be willing to climb, himself." — Andrew Carnegie

"When helping out, do not let another's sinking ship take you down, too." — Old proverb

"If every man would sweep his own doorstep the city would soon be clean." — T. Adams

"It is one of the most beautiful compensations of this life that no man can sincerely try to help another without helping himself." — Emerson

"You will find that the mere resolve not to be useless, and the honest desire to help other people, will, in the quickest and delicate ways, improve yourself." — John Ruskin

"We live very close together. So, our prime purpose in this life is to help others. And if you can't help them at least don't hurt them." — The 14th Dalai Lama

"Two are better than one; because they have a good reward for their labor. For if either fall the one will lift the other up." — Bible, Ecclesiastes

"The smallest amount of merit dedicated to the good of others is more precious than any amount of merit devoted to one's own good." — "Help men but don't get in the way of men being able to help themselves." — Buddha

Caring

"Cares are often more difficult to throw off than sorrows; the latter die with time, the former grow." — Jean Paul

"Light cares speak, great ones are dumb." — Seneca

"Be careful or you may be full of cares." — Spurgeon

"Each day has its care, but each care has its day." — Old proverb

"The comforter's head never aches." — Italian proverb

"Blessings come from care, troubles from carelessness." — "If you do not care for each other, who will care for you?" Buddha

"When a man cares he is unafraid, when he is fair he leaves enough for others, when he is humble he can grow." — Lao-tse

Gifts

"Each day provides its own gifts." — Martial

"The greatest gift is a portion of thyself." — Emerson

"'Tis a gift to be simple, 'tis a gift to be free." — Shaker hymn

"I am in the habit of looking not so much to the nature of a gift as to the spirit in which it is offered." — Robert Louis Stevenson

"Every gift, though it be small, is in reality great if given with affection." — Pindar

"A gift with a kind countenance is a double present." — Old proverb

"They were one of those men who possess almost every gift, except the gift of the power to use them." — Charles Kingsley

"A gift in season is a double favor to the needy." — Publilius Syrus

"Liberality consists less in giving a great deal than in gifts well timed." — Bruyère

"Purchase not friends by gifts; when thou ceasest to give, such will cease to love." — Thomas Fuller

"A favor to come is better than a hundred received." — Italian proverb

"For though we may think we are specially blest, we are certain to pay for the favors we get!" John Godfrey Saxe

"You need more tact in the dangerous art of giving presents than in any other social action." — William Bolitho

"I have nothing to offer but blood, toil, tears and sweat." — Churchill

"Each man has his own gift from God; one has this gift, another that." — Bible, I Corinthians 7:7

"A gift is a precious stone in the eyes of those who have it." — Bible, Proverbs 17:9

"No one ought to look a gift horse in the mouth." — English proverb

"The most precious gift received by men on earth is desire for wisdom." — "Of a gift to be received or given, of an act to be done, time drinks up the flavor, unless it be quickly performed." — "Poison is not to be taken even though offered by one's mother or father. But gold is acceptable even from one who is inimical." — Far Eastern sayings

PEACE AND NONVIOLENCE

"Peace is liberty in tranquillity." — "The pursuit, even of the best things, ought to be calm and tranquil." — Cicero

"Peace is such a precious jewel that I would give anything for it but truth." — Matthew Henry

"Peace is rarely denied to the peaceful." — Schiller

"Peace is indivisible." — Maksim Litvinov

"Peace is the happy, natural state of man; war, his corruption and disgrace." — James Thomson

"Peace is not an absence of war, it is a virtue, a state of mind, a disposition of benevolence, confidence, justice." — Spinoza

"Peace cannot be achieved through violence; it can only be attained through understanding." — Einstein

"Peace hath her victories no less renowned than war." — Milton

"Peace has its victories no less than war, but it doesn't have as many monuments to unveil." — Frank Hubbard

"Peace comes not from the absence of conflict, but from the ability to cope with it." — Anonymous

"Peace begins just where ambition ends." — Edward Young

"Peace rules the day, where reason rules the mind." — Wilkie Collins

"Peace in the present time is based more on fear than on friendship." — Paul VI

"Peace cannot suddenly descend from the heavens. It can only come when the root-causes of trouble are removed." — Nehru

"Peace, peace! It is not dead, it doth not sleep — it hath awakened from the dream of life." — Shelley

"Peace I leave with you." — Bible, John 14:27

"Blessed are the peacemakers." — Bible, Matthew 5:9

"Nothing can bring you peace but yourself." — Emerson

"First keep the peace within yourself, then you can also bring peace to others." — Thomas à Kempis

"The wise man looks within his heart and finds eternal peace." — Hindu proverb

"When we do not find peace within ourselves, it is vain to seek for it elsewhere." — La Rochefoucauld

"We cannot find Peace until we enter the Path of Self-sacrificing Usefulness." — Henry Van Dyke

"Learn calm to face what's pressing." — Horace

"Arms alone are not enough to keep the peace. It must be kept by people." — John F. Kennedy

"All we are saying is: give peace a chance." — John Lennon

"Courage is the price that life exacts for granting peace. The soul that knows it not knows no release." — Amelia Earhart

"The ambassadors of peace shall weep bitterly." — Bible, Isaiah 33:7

"Follow peace with all men." — Bible, Hebrews 12:14

"No man can have peace longer than his neighbor pleases." — Dutch proverb

"If peace cannot be maintained with honor, it is no longer peace." — Lord John Russell

"Certain peace is better and safer than anticipated victory." — Livy

"It must be a peace without victory. Only a peace between equals can last." — Woodrow Wilson

"If they want peace, nations should avoid the pin-pricks that precede cannon-shots." — Napoleon

"Blessed is the peacemaker, not the conqueror." — Old proverb

"Better beans and bacon in peace than cakes and ale in fear." — Aesop

"If a man would live in peace, he should be blind, deaf, and dumb." — Turkish proverb

"There is no harbor of peace from the changing waves of joy and despair." — Euripides

"Better keep peace than make peace." — Old proverb

"Let us therefore follow after the things which make for peace." — Bible, Romans 14:19

"To experience is to know, to know is to understand, to understand is to tolerate, to tolerate is to have peace." — Far Eastern saying

"I do not want the peace which passeth understanding, I want the understanding which bringeth peace." — Helen Keller

"'Take it easy' and 'Live long' are brothers." — German proverb

"Blessed are the meek, for they shall inherit the earth." — Bible, Matthew 5:3

"What all men are really after is some form, or perhaps only some formula, of peace." — Joseph Conrad

"If there is to be any peace it will come through being, not having." — Henry Miller

"Peace is not an absence of war, it is a virtue, a state of mind, a disposition for benevolence, confidence, justice." — Baruch Spinoza

"There is no joy like peace." — "The only way to bring peace to the earth is to learn to make our own life peaceful." — "Only by nonviolence is excellence achieved." — Buddha

"Nonviolence has come among people and it will live. It is the harbinger of the peace of the world." — "Love is a rare herb that makes a friend even out of a sworn enemy and this herb grows out of nonviolence." — "Each man has to find his peace from within. And peace to be real must be unaffected by outside circumstances." — "I am fighting for nothing less than world peace." — Gandhi

"Five great enemies to peace inhabit with us; avarice, ambition, envy, anger, and pride. If those enemies were to be banished, we should infallibly enjoy perpetual peace." — Petrarch

"A wise man in a crowded street winneth his way with gentleness, not by rudely pushing aside the stranger that standeth in his path." — Martin Tupper

"Until you have become really, in actual fact, a brother to every one, brotherhood will not come to pass." — Dostoyevsky

"For ye shall go out with joy, and be led forth with peace: the mountains and hills shall break forth before you into singing, and all the trees of the field clap their hands." — Bible, Isaiah 55:11

"When monarchs through their bloodthirsty commanders lay waste a country, they dignify their atrocity by calling it making peace." — "They make a desert and call it peace." — Tacitus

"More than an end to war, we want an end to the beginnings of all wars — yes, an end to this brutal, inhuman and thoroughly impractical method of settling the differences between governments." — Franklin D. Roosevelt

"If man does find the solution for world peace it will be the most revolutionary reversal of his record we have ever known." — George Marshall

"Since wars begin in the minds of men, it is in the minds of men that the defenses of peace must be constructed." — United Nations Constitution

"Universal peace will be realized, not because mankind will become better, but because a new order of things, a new science, new economic necessities, will impose peace." — Anatole France

Contentment

"Contentment wears the hues of joy." — "Our content is our best having." — Shakespeare

"Contentment is natural wealth." — "A man is richest who is content with the least, for content is the wealth of nature." — Socrates

"Content is the true riches, for without it there is no satisfying." — Martin Tupper

"Content is health to the sick and riches to the poor." — Old proverb

"I have learned, in whatsoever state I am, therewith to be content." — Bible, Philippians 4:8

"A man has enough who is content." — Old proverb

"A man who is content is rich." — Lao-tse

"A man is not poor that feels content." — Japanese proverb

"Be content with your lot; one cannot be first in everything." — Aesop

"A competence is vital to content." — Edward Young

"If we fasten our attention on what we have, rather than on what we lack, a very little wealth is sufficient." — Francis Johnson

"A happy life consists in tranquillity of mind." — Cicero

"The pleasantest condition of life is in incognito." — Abraham Cowley

"The good and the wise lead quiet lives." — Euripides

"A happy life must be to a great extent a quiet life, for it is only in an atmosphere of quiet that true joy can live." — Bertrand Russell

"If you are but content you have enough to live upon with comfort." — Plautus

"The secret of contentment is the realization that life is a gift, not a right." — Anonymous

"Since we cannot get what we like, let us like what we can get." — "A man who is contented is not always rich." — Spanish proverbs

"When neither their property nor their honor is touched, the majority of men live content." — Niccolo Machiavelli

"Well-being is attained by little and little, and nevertheless it is no little thing itself." — Zeno

"The poor long for riches and the rich for heaven, but the wise long for a state of tranquillity." — Swami Rama

"Tranquillity! Thou better name than all the family of Fame." — Samuel Taylor Coleridge

"To be of service is a solid foundation for contentment in this world." — Charles Eliot

"Leave it if you cannot mend it." — Old proverb

"Let sleeping dogs lie." — English proverb

"You traverse the world in search of happiness, which is within the reach of every man; a contented mind confers all." — Horace

"The wise man is content with half a loaf, or any fraction for that matter, rather than no bread." — Sir Rabindranath Tagore

"Often when Socrates was looking on at auctions he would say, 'How many things there are which I do not need!'" Diogenes

"The noblest mind the best contentment has." — Edmund Spenser

"Nothing will content men who are not content with little." — Greek proverb

"If you know peace, then you thrive; if you know contentment, then you are rich." — Su Shi

"Let life ripen and then fall, will is not the way at all." — Lao-tse

"Let nothing good or bad upset the balance of your life." — Thomas à Kempis

"Contentment consisteth not in heaping more fuel, but in taking away some fire." — "Better a little fire to warm us than a great one to burn us." — Thomas Fuller

"Contentment is the philosopher's stone, which turns all it toucheth into gold; the poor man is rich with it and the rich man is poor without it." — Old proverb

"Possessions, outward success, publicity, luxury — to me these have always been contemptible. I believe that a simple and unassuming manner of life is best for everyone, best both for the body and the mind." — Einstein

"The keen mind, full of thought, rejoiceth in a quiet hour, while dullards hold it irksome, to be killed as best they can." — Martin Tupper

"Do not abandon all the great, pure, calm oceans of the mind and cling to one bubble of confusion and accept it as the whole ocean. Be like the Ocean, which receives all streams and rivers. The Ocean's mighty calm remains unmoved; it feels them not." — Rig-Veda

"The secret of contentment is knowing how to enjoy what you have, and to lose all desire for things beyond your reach." — Lin Yutang

Contemplation

"The ultimate value of life depends upon awareness, and the power of contemplation rather than upon mere survival." — Aristotle

"In order to improve the mind, we ought less to learn than to contemplate." — Descartes

"Often a retrospect delights the mind." — Dante

"A man's greatest strength is shown in standing still." — Edward Young

"When a man goeth forth, let him consider what he is to do; when he returns, examine what he hath done." — Cleobulus

"Let not sleep fall upon thy eyes till thou hast thrice reviewed the transactions of the past day." — Pythagoras

"A rock pile ceases to be a rock pile the moment a single man contemplates it, bearing within him the image of a cathedral." — Saint-Exupéry

"What we plant in the soil of contemplation, we shall reap in the harvest of action." — "What a man takes in by contemplation, that he pours out in love." — Meister Eckhart

Silence

"Silence is golden." — Old proverb

"Silence is wisdom, when speaking is folly." — Thomas Fuller

"Silence is an excellent remedy against slander." — Sir Richard Steele

"Silence is less injurious than a bad reply." — Latin proverb

"Silence is one of the hardest arguments to refute." — Josh Billings

"Silence is the safest course for any man to adopt who distrusts himself." — La Rochefoucauld

"Silence is one great art of conversation." — Williamm Hazlitt

"Silence is one of the virtues of the wise." — Chevalier de Bonnard

"Silence answers much." — "Silence seldom doth harm." — Old proverbs

"Silence never shows itself to so great an advantage as when it is made the reply to calumny and defamation." — Joseph Addison

"Silence, when nothing need be said, is the eloquence of discretion." — Christian Bovee

"Better say nothing than nothing to the purpose." — English proverb

"It is better either to be silent, or to say things of more value than silence." — Pythagoras

"Hear in silence." — Apocrypha, Ecclesiasticus 32:9

"Speech is silver, silence is golden; speech is human, silence is divine." — German proverb

"Good silence is near holiness." — Old proverb

"Many a time the thing left silent makes for happiness." — Pindar

"Talking comes by nature, silence by wisdom." — Old proverb

"A chief fruit on the tree of wisdom is silence." — Schopenhauer

"A man of silence is a man of sense." — "There is a knack of showing we understand the matter, when we hold our peace." — Old proverbs

"They only babble who practice not reflection. I shall think; and thought is silence." — Richard Sheridan

"Better to be silent than to speak ill of another." — African proverb

"Being silent let's me hear other men's imperfections, and conceals my own." — Zeno

"Do you wish people to believe good of you? Don't speak." — Pascal

"Know how to listen, and you will profit even from those who talk badly." — Plutarch

"Blessed is the man who, having nothing to say, abstains from giving in words evidence of the fact." — George Eliot

"Nothing is so good for an ignorant man as silence; if he were sensible of this he would not be ignorant." — Sa'di

"Observe silence and refrain from idle talk." — Baha'u'llah

"If you keep your mouth shut you will never put your foot in it." — Austin O'Mally

"I have often regretted my speech, never my silence." — Publilius Syrus

"The right word may be effective, but no word was ever as effective as a rightly timed pause." — Mark Twain

"Drawing on my fine command of language, I said nothing." — Robert Benchley

"In the company of strangers silence is safe." — Bible, Proverbs

"Next to entertaining or impressive talk, a thoroughgoing silence manages to intrigue most people." — Mrs. J. Borden Harriman

"A silent man's words are not brought into court." — Old proverb

"The silent bear no witness against themselves." — Aldous Huxley

"A judicious silence is always better than truth spoken without charity." — François de Sales

"You have not converted a man because you have silenced him." — John Viscount Morley

"True silence is the rest of the mind; it is the spirit what sleep is to the body, nourishment and refreshment." — William Penn

"Do not the most moving moments of our lives find us all without words?" Marcel Marceau

"Every sound shall end in silence, but the silence never dies." — Samuel Miller Hageman

"Silence is the perfectest herald of joy." — "The silence often of pure innocence persuades when speaking fails." — Shakespeare

"Silence is the element in which great things fashion themselves together." — "Speech is of time, silence is of eternity." — Carlyle

"I think the first virtue is to restrain the tongue; a man approaches nearest to the gods who knows how to be silent, even though he is in the right." — Cato the Elder

"Every man who delights in a multitude of words, even when he says admirable things, is empty within. If you love truth, be a lover of silence." — Isaac of Niniveh

"The first evil that attends those who know not how to be silent, is, that they hear nothing." — "A sage thing is timely silence, and better than any speech." — Plutarch

"Well-timed silence hath more eloquence than speech." — "How oftentimes is silence the wisest of replies." — "Few affections can endure determined dogged silence." — "In the cause of good be wise, and in a case indifferent, keep silence." — Martin Tupper

COURAGE

"Courage is that virtue which champions the cause of right." — Cicero

"Courage is a virtue only in proportion as it is directed by prudence." — Salignac

"Courage is the thing. All goes if courage goes." — Joseph Addison

"Courage is grace under pressure." — Hemingway

"Courage is like love; it must have hope for nourishment." — Napoleon

"Courage is to feel the daily daggers of relentless steel and keep on living." — Douglas Malloch

"Courage is resistance to fear, mastery of fear — not absence of fear." — Mark Twain

"Courage consists not in hazarding without fear, but being resolutely minded in a just cause." — Plutarch

"Courage is doing what you're afraid to do. There can be no courage unless you're scared." — Capt. Eddie Rickenbacker

"Courage in danger is half the battle." — Plautus

"Courage from hearts and not from numbers grows." — John Dryden

"Courage without conscience is a wild beast." — Robert G. Ingersoll

"Courage, which is the sixth sense, finds the shortest way to triumph." — Kahlil Gibran

"Courage conquers all things." — Ovid

"Courage! That is the hue of virtue." — Diogenes

"A man with outward courage dares to die, one with inward courage dares to live." — Lao-tse

"A man of courage never wants weapons." — Thomas Fuller

"One man with courage makes a majority." — Andrew Jackson

"This is courage in a man to bear unflinchingly what heaven sends." — Euripides

"There is plenty of courage among us for the abstract but not for the concrete." — Helen Keller

"We can never be certain of our courage till we have faced danger." — La Rochefoucauld

"If we survive danger it steels our courage more than anything else." — Barthold Niebuhr

"'Tis true that we are in great danger; the greater therefore should our courage be." — Shakespeare

"People with courage and character always seem sinister to the rest." — Hermann Hesse

"One must have the courage to say 'no,' even at the risk of displeasing others." — Fritz Kunkel

"It is from numberless diverse acts of courage and belief that human history is shaped." — Robert F. Kennedy

"Life shrinks or expands according to one's courage." — Anais Nin

"It requires moral courage to grieve; it requires religious courage to rejoice." — Kierkegaard

"A great deal of talent is lost in the world for want of a little courage." — Sydney Smith

"To see what is right and not do it is want of courage, or of principle." — Confucius

"A man without courage is a knife without an edge." — Benjamin Franklin

"Who has not courage should have legs." — English proverb

"One that loses money loses much; one who loses a friend loses more; but one who loses courage loses all." — Spanish proverb

"Recall your courage, and lay aside sad fear." — Virgil

"A peculiar kind of fear they call courage." — Charles Rann Kennedy

"Alertness and courage are life's shield." — Philippine proverb

"'Tisn't life that matters! It's the courage you bring to it." — Hugh Walpole

"Where is your ancient courage?" Bible, Corinthians 4:1

"Naught venture naught have." — Thomas Tusser

"Be of good courage." — Bible, Isaiah 41:6

"Courage is the greatest of all the virtues. Because if you haven't courage, you may not have an opportunity to use any of the others." — Samuel Johnson

"Courage leads starward, fear toward death." — "Sometimes even to live is an act of courage." — "There is nothing in the world so much admired as a man who knows how to bear unhappiness with courage." — Seneca

"Courage is a kind of salvation." — "Courage is a special kind of knowledge: the knowledge of how to fear what ought to be feared and how not to fear what ought not to be feared." — Plato

"Courage is the first of the human qualities because it is the quality which guarantees all the others." — "Without courage, all other virtues lose their meaning." — Churchill

"Courage is poorly housed that dwells in numbers; the lion never counts the herd that are about him, nor weighs how many flocks he has to scatter." — Aaron Hill

"There is more courage in facing the world with undisguised truth than in descending into a wild beast's den." — Far Eastern saying

"The courage of life is often a less dramatic spectacle than the courage of a final moment; but it is no less a magnificent mixture of triumph and tragedy." — John F. Kennedy

"Courage charms us, because it indicates that a man loves an idea better than all things in the world, that he is thinking neither of his bed, nor his dinner, nor his money, but will venture all to put in act the invisible thought of his mind." — "Every man has his own courage, and is betrayed because he seeks in himself the courage of other persons." — "The charm of the best courages is that they are inventions, inspirations, flashes of genius." — "Whatever you do, you need courage." — Emerson

Bravery

"Brave men are brave from the very first." — Pierre Corneille

"Bravery is the capacity to perform properly even when scared half to death." — Gen. Omar Bradley

"Bravery never goes out of fashion." — Thackeray

"None but the brave deserves the fair." — John Dryden

"Danger gleams like sunshine to a brave man's eyes." — Euripides

"The truly brave are soft of heart and eyes, and feel for what their duty bids them to do." — Byron

"The bravest are the tenderest." — Bayard Taylor

"Who bravely dares must sometimes risk a fall." — Tobias Smollett

"A brave man struggling in the storms of fate, and greatly falling with a falling state." — Alexander Pope

"It is easy to be brave from a safe distance." — Aesop

"To the brave man every land is a native country." — Greek proverb

"When were the good and the brave ever in a majority?" Thoreau

"One who doesn't risk never gets to drink champagne." — Russian proverb

"It is not because things are difficult that we do not dare, it is because we do not dare that they are difficult." — Seneca

"A hero is no braver than an ordinary man, but he is brave five minutes longer." — Emerson

"I prefer to strive in bravery with the bravest, rather than in wealth with the richest, or in greed with the greediest." — Marcus Caro

"Live as brave men; and if fortune is adverse, front its blows with brave hearts." — "No man can be brave who thinks pain the greatest evil; nor temperate, who considers pleasure the highest good." — Cicero

"Let us all be brave enough to die the death of a martyr, but let no one lust for martyrdom." — "He who perishes sword in hand is no doubt brave; but he who faces death without raising his little finger and without flinching is braver." — Gandhi

Boldness

"Boldness has genius, power, and magic to it." — Goethe

"Boldness is a mask for fear, however great." — Lucan

"Boldness is the fruit of hope." — Philippine proverb

"Boldness is ever blind, for it sees not dangers and inconveniences; whence it is bad in council though good in execution." — Sir Francis Bacon

"Show boldness and aspiring confidence." — Shakespeare

"No man reaches a high position without boldness." — Publilius Syrus

"What kind of man would live a life without daring?" Charles Lindberg

"The only hope for safety was in boldness." — Tacitus

"A decent boldness ever meets with friends." — Horace

"Venus favors the bold." — Ovid

"We make way for the man who boldly pushes past us." — Christian Bovee

"It is a bold mouse that nestles in the cat's ear." — "Nothing ventured, nothing gained." — English proverbs

"Confidence is conqueror of men; victorious both over them and in them." — Martin Tupper

"No man falls low unless he attempts to climb high." — Danish Proverb

"The heart assured by the truth — this is confidence." — Thomas Lynch

"The bold attempt is half success." — Danish proverb

"Few things seem so possible as they are till they are attempted." — Thomas Lynch

"Write on your doors the saying wise and old: 'Be bold! Be bold! And everywhere — Be bold! But not too bold.'" Longfellow

"It is better by a noble boldness to run the risk of being subject to half of the evils we anticipate than to remain in cowardly listlessness for fear of what may happen." — Herodotus

Valor

"Valor would cease to be a virtue if there were no injustice." — Agesilaus II

"True valor is like honesty; it enters into all that a man sees and does." — Josh Billings

"True valor, on virtue founded strong, meets all events alike." — David Mallet

"Dare to do your duty always; this is the height of true valor." — Charles Simmons

"The iron will of one stout heart shall make a thousand quail." — Martin Tupper

"The valiant never taste of death but once." — Shakespeare

"Discretion is the better part of valor." — Euripides

"It is said of untrue valors, that some men's valors are in the eyes of them that look on." — Sir Francis Bacon

"None sends their arrow to the mark in view whose hand is feeble or their aim untrue." — William Cowper

"Hidden valor is as bad as cowardice." — Latin proverb

"The best lightning-rod for your protection is your own spine." — Emerson

"Fear to do base and unworthy things is valor; if they be done us, to suffer them is also valor." — Ben Jonson

"The meaning of true valor lies between the extremes of cowardice and rashness." — Cervantes

"It is a brave act of valor to contemn death; but where life is more terrible than death, it is then the truest valor to dare to live." — Sir Thomas Browne

Heroism

"Heroism feels and never reasons and therefore is always right." — "Self-trust is the essence of heroism." — Emerson

"Heroism, the Caucasian mountaineers say, is endurance for one moment more." — George F. Kennan

"Heroes are made in the hour of defeat." — Gandhi

"Where there are no heroes, strive to be one." — The Talmud

"A hero who will not flee will make his foes flee." — Old proverb

"Show me a hero and I will write you a tragedy." — F. Scott Fitzegerald

"Take away ambition and vanity, and where will be your heroes and patriots?" Seneca

"Worship your heroes from afar; contact withers them." — Albertine de Saussure

"We can't all be heroes, because someone has to sit on the curb and clap." — Will Rogers

"The hero is a man who has fought impressively for a cause of which we approve." — Dumas Malone

"Nurture your mind with great thoughts; to believe in the heroic makes heroes." — Disraeli

"A hero, in living his own life, in being true to himself — radiates a light by which others may see their own way." — Laurence G. Boldt

"The beauty of the soul shines out when a man bears with composure one heavy mischance after another, not because he does not feel them, but because he is a man of high and heroic temper." — Aristotle

"The hero is the champion not of things become, but of things becoming; the dragon to be slain by him is precisely the monster of the status quo: Hold fast the keeper of the past." — "The hero symbolizes our ability to control the irrational savage within us." — "The courage to face the trials and to bring a whole new body of possibilities into the field of interpreted experience for other people to experience — that is the hero's deed." — Joseph Campbell

"Life, misfortunes, isolation, abandonment, poverty, are battlefields which have their heroes; obscure heroes, sometimes greater than the illustrious heroes." — Victor Hugo

"The world's battlefields have been in the heart chiefly; more heroism has been displayed in the household than on the most memorable battlefields of history." — Beecher

"The age of chivalry is never past, so long as there is a wrong left unredressed on earth, or a man or woman left to say, 'I will redress that wrong, or spend my life in the attempt.'" Kingsley

Strength and Weakness

"A chain is no stronger than its weakest link." — "Only the strongest will survive." — Old proverbs

"Everything nourishes what is strong already." — Jane Austen

"If the sky falls, hold up your hands." — Spanish proverb

"The ready back gets all the loads." — Latvian proverb

"Put a stout heart to a steep hill." — Thomas Lynch

"Tall trees catch more wind." — "Not to break is better than to mend." — English proverbs

"Diamond cuts diamond." — Old proverb

"A single arrow is easily broken, but not ten in a bundle." — Japanese proverb

"The anvil lasts longer than the hammer." — Italian proverb

"If you are strong, behave mildly that you may be respected rather than feared." — Chilon

GENIUS

"Genius is one per cent inspiration and ninety-nine per cent perspiration." — Thomas Edison

"Genius is infinite painstaking." — Longfellow

"Genius is the infinite art of taking pains." — Carlyle

"Genius is nothing but a great aptitude for patience." — Georges de Buffon

"Genius is sorrow's child." — John Adams

"Genius is the gold in the mine; talent is the miner who works and brings it out." — Lady Blessington

"Genius is talent provided with ideals." — Maugham

"Genius does what it must, talent does what it can." — Owen Meredith

"Genius is only a superior power of seeing." — Ruskin

"Genius, in truth, means little more than the faculty of perceiving in an unhabitual way." — William James

"Genius must be born; it never can be taught." — John Dryden

"Genius at first is little more than a great capacity for receiving discipline." — Eliot

"Towering genius disdains a beaten path. It seeks regions hitherto unexplored." — Abraham Lincoln

"Common sense is instinct. Enough of it is genius." — Shaw

"A genius is a man who does unique things of which nobody would expect him to be capable." — Edward Verrall Lucas

"Everyone is a genius at least once a year; a real genius has his original ideas closer together." — G. C. Lichtenberg

"The first and last thing required of genius is the love of truth." — Goethe

"Since when was genius found respectable?" Elizabeth Barrett Browning

"No great genius has ever been without some madness." — Aristotle

"The difference between a genius and a lunatic is that the genius has proof." — Dominique Bouchard

"How glorious it is — and also how painful — to be an exception." — Alfred de Musset

"The persecution of genius fosters its influence." — Tacitus

"Talent is a cistern; genius a fountain." — Edwin Whipple

"Talent is that which is in a man's power; genius is that in whose power a man is." — James Russell Lowell

"Fortune has rarely condescended to be the companion of genius." — Isaac E'Israeli

"Even genius is tied to profit." — Pythia

"A man of genius makes no mistakes. His errors are volitional and are the portals of discovery." — James Joyce

"One science only will one genius fit." — Alexander Pope

"There has been no man of pure genius; as there has been none wholly destitute of genius." — Thoreau

"A work which is destined to live must have genius." — Martial

"Genius finds its own road, and carries its own lamp." — "Genius lights its own fire, but it is constantly collecting materials to keep alive the flame." — Robert Wilmott

"Genius borrows nobly." — "In every work of genius we recognize our own rejected thoughts." — "Genius always finds itself a century too early." — "Genius is sacrificed to talent every day." — "Great geniuses have the shortest biographies." — "To believe your own thought, to believe that what is true for you in your private heart is true for all men — that is genius." — Emerson

"Men of genius do not excel in any profession because they labor in it, but they labor in it because they excel." — Hazlitt

"It will be found, in fact, that the ingenious are always fanciful, and the truly imaginative never otherwise than analytic." — Edgar Allan Poe

"Every production of genius must be the production of enthusiasm." — "Patience is a necessary ingredient of genius." — "The man who anticipates his century is always persecuted when living, and is always pilfered when dead." — Disraeli

"When a true genius appears in this world, you may know him by this sign, that the dunces are all in confederacy against him." — Swift

"I have known no one of genius who had not to pay, in some affliction or defect either physical or spiritual, for what the gods had given him." — Sir Max Beerbohm

"Talent may be in time forgiven, but genius never!" Byron

"To do easily what is difficult for others is the mark of talent. To do what is impossible for talent is the mark of genius." — Henri-Frederic Amiel

Mastery

"The wiser and mightier a master is, the more spontaneously is carried out his work and the simpler it is." — Meister Eckehart

"One eye of the master sees more than four of the servant's." — Italian proverb

"The eye of a master will do more work than both his hands." — Benjamin Franklin

"No man can serve two masters." — Bible, Matthew 6:24

"A man who serves two masters has to lie to one." — Portuguese proverb

"As the master, so the work." — German proverb

"We cannot all be masters." — Shakespeare

"One can have no smaller or greater mastery than mastery of oneself." — Leonardo da Vinci

"The measure of a master is his success in bringing all people round to his opinions twenty years later." — Emerson

"What the caterpillar calls the end of the world, the master calls a butterfly." — Richard Bach

Talent

"Our opportunities to do good are our talents." — Cotton Mather

"There is no substitute for talent. Industry and all the virtues are of no avail." — Aldous Huxley

"It is a very rare thing for a man of talent to succeed by his talent." — Joseph Roux

"The same man cannot be skilled in everything; each has his own special excellence." — Euripides

"Every man must row with the oars he has." — English proverb

"I am not bound to succeed, but I am bound to live by the light that I have." — Abraham Lincoln

"Hide not your talents, they for use were made. What's a sundial in the shade?" Benjamin Franklin

"Talent working with joy in the cause of universal truth lifts the possessor to new power as a benefactor." — "Everyone has a vocation. The talent is the call." — Emerson

"Talent is the capacity of doing anything that depends on application and industry; it is a voluntary power, while genius is involuntary." — Hazlitt

"Talent is only a starting point in this business. You're got to keep on working that talent. Someday I'll reach for it and it won't be there." — Irving Berlin

"Talent is like money: you don't have to have some to talk about it." — "Talent is a question of quantity. Talent does not write one page: it writes three hundred." — Jules Renard

"The superior man is distressed by the limitations of his ability; he is not distressed by the fact that men do not recognize the ability he has." — Confucius

"Everybody is so talented nowadays that the only people I care to honor as deserving real distinction are those who remain in obscurity." — Thomas Hardy

"If a man has a talent and cannot use it, he has failed. If he has a talent and uses only half of it, he has partly failed. If he has a talent and learns somehow to use the whole of it, he has gloriously succeeded, and won a satisfaction and a triumph few men have ever know." — Thomas Wolfe

Invention

"Invention is the talent of youth, as judgment is of age." — Swift

"Invention is nothing more than a fine deviation from, or enlargement on a fine model." — Bulwer-Lytton

"Necessity is the mother of invention." — Plato

"Name the greatest of all the inventors? . . . accident." — Mark Twain

"Whenever someone comes up with a better mousetrap, nature immediately comes up with a better mouse." — James Carswell

"Where we cannot invent, we may least improve." — Charles Colton

"He that invents a machine augments the power of a man and the well-being of mankind." — Beecher

"Someone invented the telephone, and interrupted a nation's slumbers — ringing wrong but similar numbers." — Ogden Nash

"The art of invention grows young with the things invented." — Sir Francis Bacon

"Invention breeds invention." — "If a man can write a better book, preach a better sermon, or make a better mouse-trap than his neighbor, though he build his house in the woods, the world will make a beaten path to his door." — Emerson

"Inventors and men of genius have almost always been regarded as fools at the beginning — and very often at the end — of their careers." — Dostoevsky

"'What is the use of this new invention?' someone once asked me. And my reply was, 'What is the use of a new-born child?'" Benjamin Franklin

"The inventor tries to meet the demand of a crazy civilization." — "There ain't no rules around here! We're trying to accomplish something." — "There is always a better way." — Thomas Edison

"When someone invents a machine, he runs it; then the machine begins to run him, and he becomes the slave of his slave." — "Man merely discovers; we never can and never will invent." — Kahlil Gibran

"I wish to avail myself of all that is already known and then if possible add my might to help the future worker who will attain final success." — Wilbur Wright

"What this power is I cannot say; all I know is that it exists and it becomes available only when a man is in that state of mind in which he knows exactly what he wants and is fully determined not to quit until he finds it." — "Great discoveries and improvements invariably involve the cooperation of many minds." — Alexander Graham Bell

Creativity

"Creativity is merely a plus name for regular activity. . . any activity becomes creative when the doer cares about doing it right, or better." — John Updike

"Creation is a drug I can't do without." — Cecil De Mille

"If you would create something, you must be something." — Goethe

"It is better to create than to be learned; creation is the true essence of life." — Barthold Niebuhr

"Every creator painfully experiences the chasm between his inner vision and its ultimate expression." — Isaac Singer

"The measure of the creator is the amount of life he puts into his work." — Carl Van Doren

"The essential thing in form is to be free in whatever form is used." — Wallace Stevens

"Progress is not created by contented men." — Frank Tyger

"Nothing can be created out of nothing." — Lucretius

"Nothing can come out of nothing, any more than a thing can go back to nothing." — Marcus Aurelius

"The secret to creativity is knowing how to hide your sources." — Einstein

"The creative process requires more than reason." — "Few of the great creators have bland personalities." — David Ogilvy

"I am looking for a lot of men who have an infinite capacity to not know what can't be done." — Henry Ford

"'Tis wise to learn; 'tis God-like to create." — John Saxe

"The creative process is like music which takes root with extraordinary force and rapidity, shoots up through the earth, puts forth branches, leaves, and finally blossoms." — Peter Tchaikovsky

"No man ever forgot the visitations of that power to his heart and brain, which created all things new; which was the dawn in him of music, poetry, and art." — Emerson

"In art, truth and reality begin when one no longer understands what one is doing or what one knows, and when there remains an energy that is all the stronger for being constrained, controlled and compressed." — Matisse

"Everything vanishes around me, and works are born as if out of the void. Ripe, graphic fruits fall off. My hand has become the obedient instrument of a remote will." — Paul Klee

"Oh! Speculators on things, boast not of knowing the things that nature ordinarily brings about; but rejoice if you know the end of those things which you yourself devise." — Leonardo da Vinci

"Happiness lies not in the mere possession of money; it lies in the joy of achievement, in the thrill of creative effort." — Franklin D. Roosevelt

Imagination

"Imagination is the eye of the soul." — Joubert

"Imagination is more important than knowledge." — Einstein

"Imagination rules the world." — Napoleon

"Imagination is as good as many voyages — and how much cheaper." — George Curtis

"Imagination disposes of everything; it creates beauty, justice, and happiness, which are everything in this world." — Pascal

"The lunatic, the lover, and the poet are of imagination all compact." — Shakespeare

"You can't depend on your judgment when your imagination is out of focus." — Mark Twain

"Do not build up obstacles in your imagination." — Norman Vincent Peale

"We are never so happy nor so unhappy as we imagine." — La Rochefoucauld

"I am certain of nothing but of the holiness of the heart's affections, and the truth of Imagination." — Keats

"The greatest instrument of moral good is the imagination." — Percy Shelly

"To know is nothing at all; to imagine is everything." — Anatole France

"What is now proved was once only imagined." — William Blake

"Imagination is not the talent of some men, but is the health of man." — "There are no days in life so memorable as those which vibrated to some stroke of the imagination." — Emerson

"Imagination grows by exercise, and contrary to common belief, is more powerful in the mature than in the young." — Maugham

"Only in men's imagination does every truth find an effective and undeniable existence. Imagination, not invention, is the supreme master of art as of life." — Joseph Conrad

"All the breaks you need in life wait within your imagination, imagination is the workshop of your mind, capable of turning mind energy into accomplishment and wealth." — Napoleon Hill

"One supreme fact which I have discovered is that it is not willpower, but fantasy-imagination that creates. Imagination is the creative force. Imagination creates reality." — Richard Wagner

Originality

"Originality is simply a pair of fresh eyes." — Thomas Higginson

"Originality depends only on the character of the drawing and the vision peculiar to each artist." — Georges Seurat

"All good things which exist are the fruits of originality." — John Stuart Mill

"The originality of a subject is in its treatment." — Disraeli

"The merit of originality is not novelty, it is sincerity." — Carlyle

"As many men, so many minds; every one their own way." — Terence

"What I do you cannot do; but what you do, I cannot do." — Mother Teresa

"There never were, since the creation of the world, two cases exactly parallel." — Chesterfield

"None but oneself can be his parallel." — Lewis Theobald

"You cannot put the same shoe on every foot." — Publilius Syrus

"There is nothing new except what is forgotten." — Mademoiselle Bertin

"A man is great who is what he is from nature and who never reminds us of others." — Emerson

"Every human being is intended to have a character of his own; to be what no other is, and to do what no other can do." — William Channing

"If a man does not keep pace with his companions, perhaps it is because he hears a different drummer. Let him step to the music which he hears, however measured or far away." — Thoreau

ACTION

"Action is eloquence." — "Suit the action to the word, the word to the action." — Shakespeare

"Actions speak louder than words." — Terence

"Act so in the valley that you need not fear those who stand on the hill." — Danish proverb

"The beginning is the half of every action." — Greek proverb

"The excessive increase of anything causes a reaction in the opposite direction." — Plato

"To every action there is an equal opposite reaction." — Sir Isaac Newton

"What so ever a man sows, that shall he also reap." — Bible, Galatians 6:7

"The end of all is an action, not a thought, though it were of the noblest." — J. Montgomery

"The great end of life is not knowledge but action." — Thomas Henry Huxley

"The end of all knowledge should be in virtuous action." — Philip Sydney

"Words show the wit of a man, but actions his meaning." — Old proverb

"The actions of men are the best interpreters of their thoughts." — John Locke

"It is by acts and not by ideas that men live." — Anatole France

"We inherit nothing truly, but what our actions make us worthy of." — George Chapman

"Only the actions of the just smell sweet and blossom in the dust." — James Shirley

"Abundance is from activity." — Turkish proverb

"It is not how much we do . . . but how much love we put in that action." — Mother Teresa

"A good action is never thrown away." — Old proverb

"Not the cry, but the flight of the wild duck, leads the flock to fly and follow." — Chinese proverb

"If you don't touch the rope, you won't ring the bell." — English proverb

"It is better to have less thunder in the mouth and more lightning in the hand." — Native American proverb

"It is well to think well; it is Divine to act well." — Horace Mann

"Our acts our angels are, of good or ill, our fatal shadows that walk by us still." — John Fletcher

"That action is best which procures the greatest happiness for the greatest numbers." — Francis Hutcheson

"This is a world of action, and not for moping and droning in." — Charles Dickens

"The greatest pleasure I know is to do a good action by stealth and have it found out by accident." — Charles Lamb

"One will rarely err if extreme actions be ascribed to vanity, ordinary actions to habit, and mean actions to fear." — Nietzsche

"Be intent on action, not on the fruits of action; avoid attraction to the fruits and attachment to inaction." — Bhagavad-gita II:47

"It is circumstance and proper measure that give an action its character, and make it either good or bad." — Plutarch

"It is a very waste of life to be and not to do." — "Be discreet, but with discretion urge to quickest action." — Martin Tupper

"Begin at the beginning and go till you come to the end; then stop." — Lewis Carroll

"Learn to respond, not react." — "Observe proper action at all times, even at the risk of your own life." — Buddha

"Execute every act of thy life as though it were thy last." — Marcus Aurelies

"Action without thought is like shooting without aim." — "It's better to wear out than to rust out." — "The golden rule of life is: make a beginning." — American proverbs

"Action may not always bring happiness, but there is no happiness without action." — "Act as if what you do makes a difference. It does." — William James

"Action should culminate in wisdom." — "No man shall escape from acting." — "No man ever remains, even for an instant, without performing action. Every man is will-lessly forced to act, by the primary energies." — Bhagavad-gita

"In the area of human life the honors and rewards fall to those who show their good qualities in action." — "Every action must be due to one or other of seven causes: chance, nature, compulsion, habit, reasoning, anger, or appetite." — Aristotle

"It is vain to say human beings ought to be satisfied with tranquillity: they must have action; and they will have it if they cannot find it." — Eliot

"Zeuzidamus, to one who asked him why the Lacedemonians did not commit their constitutions of chivalry to writing, and deliver them to their young people to read, made answer that it was because they would inure them to action and not to words." — Montaigne

"A man walks on, and Karma, the 'law of action' follows him along with his shadow." — "An act may seem right, but it is by its results that its purpose is shown." — "Let every action be done with perfect gravity, humanity, freedom, and justice, and perform it as though that action were your last." — "A man's actions are divided, as regards to his object into four classes; purposeless, unimportant, vain, or good." — Far Eastern sayings

"He who has put forth his total strength in fit actions has the richest return of wisdom." — "Do not be too timid and squeamish about your actions. All life is an experiment." — Emerson

"The difficulty is — as in so many other cases — not for the understanding, but for the will; not to know, but to execute." — Thomas DeQuincey

Doing

"Do not wait for leaders; do it alone, person to person." — Mother Teresa

"It is wonderful how much may be done if we are always doing." — Thomas Jefferson

"Let us not be weary in doing well." — Bible, Galatians 6:9

"No sooner said than done — so acts your man of worth." — Quintus Ennius

"I never notice what has been done. I only see what remains to be done." — Madame Curie

"Better to be done than wish it had been done." — Old proverb

"Well done is better than well said." — Benjamin Franklin

"What is done by night appears by day." — English proverb

"The world is blessed most by men who do things, and not by those who merely talk about them." — James Oliver

"As I grow older, I pay less attention to what men say. I just watch what they do." — Andrew Carnegie

"We learn to do by doing." — John Dewey

"Skill to do comes of doing." — Emerson

"It is easier to know how to do a thing than to do it." — Chinese proverb

"Do not let what you cannot do interfere with what you can do." — John Wooden

"Focus on what you can do, not on what you can't do." — Anonymous

"You must do the thing you think you cannot do." — Eleanor Roosevelt

"What one does one becomes." — Spanish proverb

"He does much who does a little well." — Old proverb

"A man who begins many things finishes but few." — Italian proverb

"A man cannot manage too many affairs: like pumpkins in the water, one pops up while you try to hold down the other." — Chinese proverb

"What you do may not seem important, but it is very important that you do it." — Gandhi

"One must learn by doing the thing; for though you think you know it you have no certainty, until you try." — Sophocles

"The good you do is not lost, though you forget it." — Old proverb

"Striving and struggling is the worst way you could set about doing anything." — Shaw

"Doing well depends upon doing completely." — Persian proverb

"I hate to see a thing done by halves; if it be right, do it boldly; if it be wrong, leave it undone." — Gilpin

"If a thing's worth doing, it's worth doing well." — Chesterfield

"Just do it." — Anonymous

"All we do is done with an eye to something else." — Aristotle

"We all can't do everything." — Virgil

"So many worlds, so much to do, so little done, such things to be." — Tennyson

"What we hope ever to do with ease, we must learn first to do with diligence." — Samuel Johnson

"Start by doing what's necessary; then do what's possible; and suddenly you are doing the impossible." — St. Francis

"Striving to do better, oft we mar what's well." — "Things won are done; joy's soul lies in the doing." — Shakespeare

"Let all things be done decently and in order." — Bible, I Corinthians 14:40

"The way to do is to be." — Lao-tse

"To do is to be." — Socrates

"What thou knowest, do." — Sophist saying

"Whatever you can do, or dream you can, begin it." — "It is better to be doing the most insignificant thing than to reckon even a half-hour insignificant." — Goethe

"Don't think. Thinking is the enemy of creativity. It's self-conscious, and anything self-conscious is lousy. You can't 'try' to do things. You simply 'must' do things." — Ray Bradbury

"To do two things at once is to do neither." — "It is no profit to have learned well, if you neglect to do well." — Publilius Syrus

"In order to do it is necessary to be. And it is necessary first to understand what to be means." — P. D. Ouspensky

"It is not sufficient to have great qualities; we must be able to make proper use of them." — La Rochefoucauld

"The world cares very little about what a man knows; it is what a man is able to do that counts." — Booker T. Washington

"Determine that the thing can and shall be done, and then we shall find the way." — "I do the very best I know how — the very best I can; and I mean to keep doing so until the end." — Abraham Lincoln

Deeds

"Deeds are fruits, words are but leaves." — English proverb

"Deeds are love and not fine phrases." — Old proverb

"Deeds, not words, shall speak for me." — John Fletcher

"Let deeds match words." — Plautus

"Let us not love in word, neither in tongue; but in deed." — Bible, I John 3:18

"We should believe only in deeds; words go for nothing everywhere." — Fernando de Rojas

"Men are all alike in their promises. It is only in their deeds that they differ." — Montaigne

"An acre of performance is worth the whole world of promise." — Howell

"One has half the deed done, who has made a beginning." — Horace

"A small deed may grow to become a large reward." — Anonymous

"As you make your bed, so you must lie upon it." — G. Harvey

"A good deed is never lost." — Basil the Great

"Your own deeds will long be baptized on you." — Irish proverb

"Good actions ennoble us, and we are the sons of our own deeds." — Cervantes

"No man gives joy or sorrow. . . we gather the consequences of our own deeds." — Garuda Purana

"Knowledge, teaching and words may be deeds." — Spanish proverb

"Each small task of everyday life is part of the total harmony of the universe." — St. Theresa of Lisieux

"How far that little candle throws its beam! So shines a good deed in a naughty world." — Shakespeare

"A life spent worthily should be measured by deeds, not years." — Richard Sheridan

"Our deeds are seeds of fate, sown here on earth, but bringing forth their harvest in eternity." — Boardman

"Our deeds still travel with us from afar, and what we have been makes us what we are." — "Our deeds determine us, as much as we determine our needs." — Eliot

"The smallest good deed done unselfishly is more precious than innumerable good deeds done selfishly." — "Neither fire nor wind, birth nor death can erase our good deeds." — Buddha

"A man makes no noise over a good deed, but passes on to another as a vine to bear grapes again in season." — Marcus Aurelius

"Let not any man, though pained, be sour-tempered, nor devise a deed of mischief to another." — "Do not let good deeds be motivated by the ego or the clinging to this world." — "Even a good man sees evil days, as long as his good deeds have not ripened; but when they have ripened, then does the good man see happy days." — Far Eastern sayings

Duty

"Duty only frowns when you flee from it; follow it, and it smiles upon you." — Anonymous

"Duty is a power which rises with us in the morning, and goes to rest with us in the evening." — W. E. Gladstone

"But what is your duty? The demands of every day." — "Do the duty that lies nearest thee." — Goethe

"The path of duty lies in the thing that is nearby, but men seek it in things far off." — Chinese proverb

"Our grand business is not to see what lies dimly in the distance, but to do what lies clearly at hand." — Carlyle

"A man who does what he can do, does what he ought to." — "Do what you ought, come what may." — Old proverbs

"I ought, therefore I can." — Kant

"When Duty whispers low, Thou must, the youth replies, I can." — Emerson

"It is our duty as men and women to proceed as though the limits of our abilities do not exist." — Teilhard de Chardin

"Think ever that you are born to perform great duties." — Disraeli

"There is no duty we so much understand as the duty of being happy." — Robert Louis Stevenson

"The consciousness of duty performed gives us music at midnight." — George Herbert

"A man who has well considered his duty will at once carry his conviction into action." — Samuel Smiles

"Every duty we omit obscures some truth we should have known." — Ruskin

"Every duty that is bidden to wait comes back with seven fresh duties at its back." — Charles Kingsley

"A sense of duty pursues us ever." — Webster

"Without duty, life is soft and boneless." — Joubert

"Consult duty, not events." — W. S. Landor

"It is your duty to use your talents." — Zollars

"Do your duty, and leave the rest to heaven." — Pierre Corneille

"Every man's task is his life preserver." — "You will always find those who think they know what is your duty better than you know it." — Emerson

"It is better to do your duty, however imperfectly, than to assume the duties of another man, however successfully." — "Prefer to die doing your own duty: the duty of another will bring you into great spiritual danger." — Bhagavad-gita

"The life of duty, not the life of mere ease or mere pleasure; that is the kind of life which makes the great man, as it makes the great nation." — Theodore Rossevelt

"The reward of one duty done is the power to fulfill another." — "We must find our duties in what comes to us, not in what might have been." — Eliot

Motivation

"The morality of an action depends upon the motive from which we act." — Samuel Johnson

"It is motive alone that gives character to actions of men." — La Bruyère

"The noblest motive is the public good." — Virgil

"What makes life dreary is the want of a motive." — Eliot

"The moment there is suspicion about a man's motives, everything he does becomes tainted." — Gandhi

"The road is long from the intention to the completion." — Molière

"We would often be ashamed of our noblest actions if the world were acquainted with the motives that impelled us." — La Rochefoucauld

"The four great motives which move men to social activity are hunger, love, vanity, and fear of superior powers." — William Sumner

Habit

"Habit is second nature." — Montaigne

"Habit ever remains." — Old proverb

"Habit is the deepest law of human nature." — Carlyle

"Habit, if not resisted, soon becomes necessity." — Augustine of Hippo

"Habit is stronger than reason." — Santayana

"Habits work more constantly and with greater force than reason." — John Locke

"Habits change into character." — Ovid

"Powerful indeed is the empire of habit." — Publilius Syrus

"How use doth breed a habit in a man!" Shakespeare

"The wisest habit is the habit of care in the formation of habits." — Thomas Lynch

"All in men is association and habit." — Sir Richard Steele

"Nothing so needs reforming as other people's habits." — Mark Twain

"In the great majority of things, habit is a greater plague than ever afflicted Egypt." — Foster

"Reason stands small show against the entrenched power of habit." — Elbert Hubbard

"We cannot, in a moment, get rid of habits of a lifetime." — Gandhi

"Habits are at first cobwebs, then cables." — "Growing old is no more than another bad habit." — "Live with wolves, and you will learn to howl." — Spanish proverbs

"The chains of habit are generally too small to be felt until they are too strong to be broken." — Samuel Johnson

"Good habits are worth being fanatical about." — John Irving

"Habits are soon assumed; but when we strive to strip them off, 'tis being flayed alive." — "Ill habits gather by unseen degrees, as brooks make rivers, rivers to the seas." — William Cowper

"Man is a bundle of habits." — "There is not a quality of function either of body or mind which does not feel the influence of habit." — Paley

"Old habits die hard." — "Each year, one vicious habit rooted out, in time ought to make the worst man good." — Benjamin Franklin

Experience

"Experience is not what happens to you; it is what you do with what happens to you." — Aldous Huxley

"Experience is the child of thought, and thought is the child of action." — Disraeli

"Experience is a comb which nature gives us when we are bald." — Chinese proverb

"Experience is the only prophecy of wise men." — Alphonse de Lamartine

"Experience is the best teacher." — Latin proverb

"Experience is the fool's best teacher; the wise do not need it." — Welsh proverb

"Experience is a hard teacher because she gives the test first, the lesson afterwards." — Vernon Law

"Experience is not always the kindest of teachers, but it is surely the best." — Spanish proverb

"Experience is the only teacher, and we get this lesson indifferently in any school." — Emerson

"Experience is a good school, but the fees are high." — Heinrich Heine

"Experience is good, if not bought too dear." — "Only the wearer knows where the shoe pinches." — English Proverbs

"Smooth seas do not make skillful sailors." — African proverb

"Experience is the Father of Wisdom." — Alcman

"Experience, the universal Mother of Sciences." — Cervantes

"All experience is an arch to build upon." — Henry Adams

"Nothing is a waste of time if you use the experience wisely." — Rodin

"Nothing has happened to you unless you make much of it." — Menander

"Every man's experience is a lesson for us all." — Martin Tupper

"Each man can interpret another's experience only by his own." — Thoreau

"The spectacles of experience; through them you will see clearly a second time." — Ibsen

"Practical wisdom is only to be learned in the school of experience." — Samuel Smiles

"What you learn to your cost you remember long." — Danish proverb

"An expert is a man who knows more and more about less and less." — Nicholas Murray Butler

"Some people have nothing else but experience." — Don Herold

"Every man is a prisoner of his own experience." — Edward Murrow

"People are wise in proportion, not to their experience, but to their capacity for experience." — Shaw

"A man who neglects to drink of the spring of experience is likely to die of thirst in the desert of ignorance." — Ling Po

"A man who has burnt his mouth always blows his soup." — German proverb

"A man who has been bitten by a snake fears a piece of string." — Persian proverb

"Only when you have crossed the river can you say the crocodile has a lump on its snout." — Ashanti proverb

"I know by my own pot how the others boil." — French proverb

"I have but one lamp by which my feet are guided and that is the lamp of experience." — Patrick Henry

"Each man believes only his experience." — Empedocles

"Without experience, nothing can be sufficiently known." — Roger Bacon

"Ask the experienced rather than the learned." — Arabian proverb

"Outward circumstances are no substitute for inner experience." — Carl Jung

"No man's knowledge here can go beyond his experience." — John Locke

"The most instructive experiences are those of everyday life." — Nietzsche

"Progress comes from the intelligent use of experience." — Elbert Hubbard

"Experience does not ever err, it is only your judgment that errs in promising itself results which are not caused by your experiments." — Leonardo da Vinci

"Experience is the name every man gives to his mistakes." — "To deny one's own experiences is to put a lie into the lips of one's own life." — Oscar Wilde

"Nothing ever becomes real till it is experienced — even a proverb is no proverb to you till your life has illustrated it." — Keats

"No man was ever so completely skilled in the conduct of life as not to receive new information from age and experience." — Terence

"We are not human-beings having a spiritual experience. Rather we are spiritual-beings having a human-experience." — Teilhard de Chardin

"We ought not to look back unless it is to derive useful lessons from past errors, and for the purpose of profiting by dear bought experience." — George Washington

WORK

"Works — not words — are the proof of love." — Old proverb

"Work is work if you're paid to do it, and it's pleasure if you pay to be allowed to do it." — Finley Dunne

"Work is something you want to get done; play is something you just like to be doing." — Harry Wilson

"The working man is still greater than his work." — Menander

"Men are workers. If they are not, they are nothing." — Joseph Conrad

"It is your work in life that is the ultimate seduction." — Picasso

"If you enjoy what you do, you'll never work another day in your life." — Confucius

"Let us work without disputing; it is the only way to render life tolerable." — Voltaire

"No man is born into the World whose Work is not born with him." — J. R. Lowell

"Everything depends on work. We owe it everything; it regulates our lives." — Jules Renard

"The finest blessing of life is systematic, useful work." — W. Morris

"Plow deep while sluggards sleep." — Benjamin Franklin

"Everything under the sun is work. We sweat, even in our sleep." — Georg Buchner

"A man who does not rise early never does a good day's work." — Old proverb

"A man goeth forth unto his work and to his labor until evening." — Bible, Psalms 104:23

"He who works achieves and he who sows reaps." — Arabian proverb

"All work is an act of philosophy." — Ayn Rand

"Thunder is good, thunder is impressive; but it is lightning that does the work." — Mark Twain

"What a man does not have in the head, a man must have in the legs." — German proverb

"An ill workman always blames his tools." — English proverb

"Not by my sins wilt Thou judge me, but by the work of my hands." — Robert William Service

"Many hands make light work." — Erasmus

"The beginning is the most important part of the work." — Plato

"The work which is begun well is half done." — Lady Fanshawe

"They whose work hath no delay achieve Herculean labors." — Martin Tupper

"Far and away the best prize that life offers is the chance to work hard at work worth doing." — Theodore Roosevelt

"Without work, all life is rotten. But when work is soulless, life stifles and dies." — Camus

"All work and no play makes Jack a dull boy." — J. Howell

"No life can be dreary when work is a delight." — F. R. Havergal

"It's all in a day's work." — Old proverb

"If you don't work, neither shall you eat." — Bible, Thessalonians II, 3:10

"By works a man is justified, and not by faith only." — Bible, James 2:24

"Thou renderest to every man according to his work." — Bible, Psalms 62:12

"By their fruits ye shall know them." — Bible, Matthew 7:20

"By the work one knows the workman." — La Fontaine

"No race can prosper till it learns there is as much dignity in tilling the field as in writing the poem." — Booker T. Washington

"We work to become, not to acquire." — Elbert Hubbard

"There is no substitute for hard work." — Thomas Edison

"Work is love made visible." — "All work is empty save when there is love." — "When you work you fulfill a part of earth's furthest dream, assigned to you when that dream was born." — Kahlil Gibran

"Work is our sanity, our self respect, our salvation. So far from being a curse, work is the greatest blessing." — "Any man who would really benefit mankind must reach them through his work." — Henry Ford

"Do not draw attention to yourself as you perform good works." — "Do not make someone else do the work that you should be doing." — Buddha

"The world is moved not only by the mighty shoves of the heroes, but also by the aggregate of the tiny pushes of each honest worker." — Helen Keller

"For anything worth having one must pay the price; and the price is always work, patience, love and self-sacrifice." — John Burroughs

"A man's work is a day's work, neither more nor less, and the man who does it needs a day's sustenance, a night's repose, and due leisure, whether he be painter or ploughman." — Shaw

"If you do your fair day's work, you are certain to get your fair day's wage — in praise or pudding, whichever happens to suit your taste." — Alexander Smith

"Hard work, moreover, not only tends to give us rest for the body, but what is even more important, peace to the mind." — Sir John Lubbock

"Good for the body is the work of the body, good for the soul is the work of the soul, and good for either the work of the other." — Thoreau

"Oh, give us the soul who sings at his work." — "Blessed is the man who has found his work; let him ask no other blessedness." — "He that can work is a born King of something." — Carlyle

"What is work? And what is not work? Are questions that perplex the wisest of men." — "He who does the work he is missioned to do, not craving the fruits of his action, is the authentic illuminate and not the man who, averse to action, lights not the sacred fire." — "Desire for the fruits of work must never be your motive in working." — Bhagavad-gita

"The joy and moral stimulation of work no longer must be forgotten in the mad chase of evanescent profits." — Franklin D. Roosevelt

"The man who does not work for the love of work but only for money is not likely to make much money nor to find much fun in life." — Charles M. Schwab

"Not to oversee your workers is to leave them your purse open." — "When you obey your superior, you instruct your inferior." — Old Proverbs

"By working faithfully eight hours a day you may eventually get to be a boss and work twelve hours a day." — Robert Frost

"In order that men may be happy in their work, these three things are needed: They must be for it: They must not do too much of it: And they must have a sense of success in it." — Ruskin

"Every really able man, if you talk sincerely with him, considers his work, however much admired, as far short of what it should be." — "Progress is the activity of today and the assurance of tomorrow." — Emerson

"Every man's work, whether it be literature or music or pictures or architecture or anything else, is always a portrait of himself." — Butler

"If people only knew how hard I worked they wouldn't be so surprised at what I have accomplished." — Leonardo da Vinci

"I acquired all the talent I have by working hard; and all who like to work as hard will succeed just as I have done." — Johann Sebastian Bach

Labor

"Labor overcometh all things." — Thomas Fuller

"Labor is the great producer of wealth; it moves all other causes." — Webster

"Labor preserves us from three great evils — boredom, vice, and want." — Voltaire

"Labor is superior to capital, and deserves much the higher consideration." — Abraham Lincoln

"Labor disgraces no man; unfortunately you occasionally find men disgracing labor." — Ulysses S. Grant

"Labor, the symbol of man's punishment; Labor, the secret of man's happiness." — James Montgomery

"Labor — all labor is noble and holy." — Scott

"To labor is to pray." — St. Benedict

"In all labor there is profit." — Bible, Proverbs 14:23

"Without labor nothing prospers." — Sophocles

"Honest Labor bears a lovely face." — Thomas Dekker

"We put our love where we have put our labor." — Emerson

"A man is not idle because he is absorbed in thought. There is visible labor and there is an invisible labor." — Victor Hugo

"Men are made that they can only find relaxation from one kind of labor by taking up another." — Anatole France

"It is weariness to keep toiling at the same things so that a man becomes ruled by them." — Heraclitus

"When one man builds and another tears down, what do they gain but toil?" Apocrypha, Ecclesiasticus 34:23

"Toil, says the proverb, is the sire of fame." — Euripides

"By labor fire is got out of stone." — Dutch proverb

"Put your shoulder to the wheel." — Aesop

"Elbow-grease is the best polish." — English proverb

"The ass will carry its load, but not a double load; ride not a free horse to death." — Cervantes

"Some do the sowing, others the reaping." — Italian proverb

"A man who begins and does not finish loses his labor." — Old proverb

"A man that gathereth by labor shall increase." — Bible, Proverbs

"A laborer is worthy of his hire." — Bible, Luke 10:7

"Genius begins great works; labor alone finishes them." — Joubert

"Alas! We reap what seed we sow; the hands that smite us are often our own." — Far Eastern saying

"If you sow thorns, you will not reap roses." — Old proverb

"Better is the end of a thing than the beginning thereof." — Bible, Ecclesiastes 7:8

"The time to repair the roof is when the sun is shining." — John F. Kennedy

"Whoever can put a good finish on his undertaking is said to have placed a golden crown to the whole." — Eustachius

"The fruit derived from labor is the sweetest of all pleasures." — Marquis de Vauvenargues

"No labor, however humble, is dishonoring." — "Greater is a man who enjoys the fruits of his labor than a man who fears heaven." — The Talmud

"Excellence in any department can be attained only by the labor of a lifetime; it is not to be purchased at a lesser price." — Samuel Johnson

"Even in the meanest sorts of Labor, the whole soul of a man is composed into a kind of real harmony the instant he sets himself to work." — Carlyle

"A man should inure himself to voluntary labor, and not give up to indulgence and pleasure, as he beget no good constitution of body nor knowledge of mind." — Socrates

"Alexander the Great, reflecting on his friends degenerating into sloth and luxury, told them that it was the most slavish thing to luxuriate, and a most royal thing to labor." — Isaac Barrow

Employment

"Employment is Nature's physician." — Galen

"When men are employed, they are best contented; for on idle days they are mutinous and quarrelsome." — Benjamin Franklin

"He is not the best carpenter that makes the most chips." — Old proverb

"A man who qualifies himself well for his calling, never fails of employment." — Thomas Jefferson

"The vocation of every man is to serve other people." — Tolstoy

"Whatsoever thy hand findeth to do, do it with all thy might." — Bible, Ecclesiastes 9:10

"The test of a vocation is the love of the drudgery it involves." — Logan Pearsall Smith

"Vocations which we wanted to pursue, but didn't, bleed, like colors, on the whole of our existence." — Balzac

"The high prize of life, the crowning fortune of a man, is to be born to some pursuit which finds him in employment and happiness, whether it be to make baskets, or broadswords, or canals, or statues, or songs." — Emerson

Occupation

"Occupation is the necessary basis of all enjoyment." — Leigh Hunt

"Occupation is the scythe of time." — Napoleon

"No thoroughly occupied man was ever yet very miserable." — Letitia Landon

"It is neither wealth nor splendor, but tranquillity and occupation, which give happiness." — Thomas Jefferson

"Absence of occupation is not rest, a mind quite vacant is a mind distressed." — William Cowper

"Constant occupation prevents temptation." — Italian proverb

"Let thine occupations be few, said the sage, if thou wouldst lead a tranquil life." — Marcus Aurelius

"O let us love our occupations. Live upon our daily rations, and always know our proper stations." — Charles Dickens

"Every Egyptian was commanded by law annually to declare by what means he maintained himself; and if he omitted to it, or gave no satisfactory account of his way of living, he was punished with death." — Herodotus

"A musician must make music, an artist must paint, a poet must write, if they are to be ultimately at peace with themselves. What a man is, he must be." — Maslow

"When men are rightly occupied, their amusement grows out of their work, as the color-petals out of a fruitful flower." — Ruskin

Business

"Business is a fight — a continual struggle — just as life is." — Edward Young

"Business is a combination of war and sport." — Maurois

"Business is like riding a bicycle. Either you keep moving or you fall down." — John Wright

"Business before pleasure." — T. Hutchinson

"Business today, tomorrow never." — Spanish proverb

"Business? It's quite simple. It's other men's money." — Alexandre Dumas the Younger

"Boldness in business is the first, second, and third thing." — Thomas Fuller

"Merchants have no country." — Thomas Jefferson

"Time is the measure of business." — Sir Francis Bacon

"Punctuality is the soul of business." — Thomas Haliburton

"Let your discourse with men of business be short and comprehensive." — George Washington

"The customer is always right." — Carl Sandburg

"A dinner lubricates business." — William Scott Stowell

"Live together like brothers, and do business like strangers." — Arabian proverb

"A man who is always ready to believe what is told him will never do well, especially a businessman." — Petronius

"There are two fools in every market: one asks too little, one asks too much." — Russian proverb

"The market is a place set apart where men may deceive each other." — Diogenes

"A show of a certain amount of honesty is in any profession of business the surest way of growing rich." — La Bruyère

"The gambling known as business looks with austere disfavor on the business known as gambling." — Bierce

"The business of America is business." — Calvin Coolidge

"Corporations have neither bodies to be punished nor souls to be damned." — E. Bulstrode

"A man who cannot command his temper should not think of being a man of business." — Chesterfield

"A man without a smiling face must not open a shop." — "To open a shop is easy, to keep it open is an art." — Chinese proverbs

"Everybody's business is nobody's business." — Izaak Walton

"Let every man mind his own business." — Cervantes

"When every man minds his own business, the work is done." — Danish proverb

"'If everybody minded their own business,' said the Duchess in a hoarse growl, 'the world would go round a great deal faster than it does.'" Lewis Carroll

"Study to be quiet, and to do your own business." — Bible, I Thessalonians 4:2

"In business, reinvest a portion of all you make, keep a portion for your use, and save a portion for those in need." — Buddha

"How happy the life unembarrassed by the cares of business!" Publilius Syrus

"Drive thy business, or it will drive thee." — "He that speaks ill of the mare will buy her." — "Let all your things have their place; let each part of your business have its time." — "Keep thy shop, and thy shop will keep thee." — Benjamin Franklin

"It is far more important that they should conduct their business affairs decently than that they should spend the surplus of their fortunes in philanthropy." — Theodore Roosevelt

"Perpetual devotion to what a man calls his business is only to be sustained by perpetual neglect of many other things." — Robert Louis Stevenson

"To business that we love, we rise betimes, and go to it with delight." — "An enterprise, when fairly begun, should not be left till all that ought is won." — Shakespeare

Trade

"Trading is thieving, unless it is barter." — Kahlil Gibran

"There are tricks in every trade." — M. Parker

"Two of a trade never agree." — Dekker

"He who pays the piper may call the tune." — English proverb

"Buy when it is market time." — German proverb

"Good ware makes a quick market." — Old proverb

"Pleasing ware is half sold." — "The buyer needs a hundred eyes, the seller not one." — George Herbert

"Let the buyer beware." — Latin maxim

"We wisely strip the steed we mean to buy." — Edward Young

"He who findeth fault meaneth to buy." — Old proverb

"Nothing is to be had for nothing." — Epictetus

"Never buy what you do not want, because it is cheap; it will be dear to you." — Thomas Jefferson

"What is bought is cheaper than a gift." — Portuguese Proverb

"A miser and a liar bargain quickly." — Greek proverb

"He would sell even his share of the sun." — Italian proverb

"Never offer your hen for sale on a rainy day." — Spanish proverb

"The barber learns his trade on the orphan's chin." — Arabic proverb

"A fair change is no robbery." — J. Heywood

"Everything is worth what its purchaser will pay for it." — Publilius Syrus

"Every man has his price." — W. Wyndham

"If you have to ask the price, you can't afford it." — Anonymous

"A man that never asks will never get a bargain." — French proverb

"A man that resolves to deal with none but honest men must leave off dealing." — "Cheat me in the price but not the goods." — Thomas Fuller

"The wool seller knows the wool buyer." — "In selling a horse praise the bad point, and leave the good ones to look after themselves." — Jewish proverbs

"If I had my life to live over again, I would elect to be a trader of goods rather than a student of science. I think barter is a noble thing." — Einstein

"No nation was ever ruined by trade." — "A man who hath a trade, hath an estate; and a man who hath a calling hath a place of profit and honor. A ploughman on his legs is higher than a gentleman on his knees." — Benjamin Franklin

Profit

"No profit grows where is no pleasure taken." — Shakespeare

"If pains be a pleasure to you profit will follow." — Thomas Fuller

"He profits most who serves best." — Arthur Frederick Sheldon

"More men come to doom through dirty profits than are kept by them." — Sophocles

"Be not greedy of filthy profit." — Bible, I Timothy 3:3

"What's none of my profit shall be none of my peril." — Anonymous

Industry

"Industry is the parent of success." — Elbert Hubbard

"Industry without art is brutality." — Ruskin

"Love of bustle is not industry." — Seneca

"Where there is no desire, there will be no industry." — John Locke

"There can be no persevering industry without a deep sense of the value of time." — Mrs. Siguourney

"When industry goes out of the door poverty comes in at the window." — Dr. Patton

"In industry is all." — Pereiander

GROWTH

"Growth is the only evidence of life." — John Henry Newman

"Growth is gladdening." — Messenger

"We are like new born children, our power is the power to grow." — Rabindranath Tagore

"A point is the beginning of magnitude." — Euclid

"The mass of trifles makes magnitude." — A. Maclaren

"The beginning of all things are small." — Cicero

"Step by step, the ladder is ascended." — George Herbert

"Step by step, one goes far." — "A little each day is much in a year." — Old Proverbs

"Great oaks from little acorns grow." — Chaucer

"Little by little, the bird builds its nest." — French proverb

"Little by little does the trick." — Aesop

"Do little things now; so shall big things come to thee by and by asking to be done." — Persian proverb

"Vast is the mighty ocean, but drops have made it vast." — Martin Tupper

"Like breeds like." — R. Edgeworth

"A pendulum travels much, but it only goes a tick at a time." — "Things to their perfection come, not all at once, but some and some." — Old proverbs

"All that is human must retrograde if it does not advance." — Edward Gibbon

"A man is really alive only when he is moving forward to something more." — Winfred Rhoades

"I am suffocated and lost when I have not the bright feeling of progression." — Margaret Fuller

"Danger and delight grow on one stalk." — English proverb

"The butterfly becomes only when it's entirely ready." — Chinese proverb

"Never discourage any man who continually makes progress, no matter how slow." — Plato

"A man must submit to be slow before he is quick; and insignificant before he is important." — Sydney Smith

"Life is change. Growth is optional. Choose wisely." — Karen Kaiser Clark

"A little and a little, collected together, become a great deal; the heap in the barn consists of single grains, and drop and drop make the inundation." — Sa'di

"The important thing is this: To be able at any moment to sacrifice what we are for what we could become." — Charles du Bois

Discipline

"Discipline is learnt in the school of adversity." — Gandhi

"Apply thyself to discipline." — Sophist saying

"Self-command is the main discipline." — Emerson

"The best discipline, maybe the only discipline that really works, is self discipline." — Walter Kiechel III

"A man must stand erect, and not be kept erect by others." — Marcus Aurelius

"First things first." — Old proverb

"Few things are impossible to diligence and skill." — Samuel Johnson

"Exactitude in some small matters is the very soul of discipline." — Joseph Conrad

"Seek freedom and become captive of your desires. Seek discipline and find your liberty." — Frank Herbert

"We need some discipline to bring us to 'letting be.'" Chogyam Trungpa

"A man who lives without discipline dies without honor." — Icelandic proverb

"The great end of education is to discipline rather than to furnish the mind; to train it to the use of its own powers, rather than fill it with the accumulation of others'." — Tryon Edwards

"Precepts and instruction are useful so far as they go, but without the discipline of real life, they remain of the nature of theory only." — Samuel Smiles

"The purpose of discipline is to promote freedom. But freedom leads to infinity and infinity is terrifying." — Henry Miller

SUCCESS

"Success is the child of Audacity." — Disraeli

"Success is going from failure to failure without losing your enthusiasm." — Churchill

"Success is a series of glorious defeats." — Gandhi

"Success is counted sweetest by those who never succeed." — Emily Dickinson

"Success is the best revenge." — French proverb

"Success is a rare paint, it hides all the ugliness." — Sir John Suckling

"Success covers a multitude of blunders." — Shaw

"Success for the striver washes away the effort of striving." — Pindar

"Success against the odds is the American ideal." — Edwin Embree

"Success 'tis more by fortune than by merit." — Shakespeare

"Success serves men as a pedestal; it makes them look larger, if reflection does not measure them." — Joubert

"Success has many fathers." — Old proverb

"Success doesn't come to those who wait — and it doesn't wait for anyone to come to it." — Anonymous

"Success has a great tendency to conceal and throw a veil over the evil deeds of men." — Demosthenes

"Success makes some crimes honorable." — Seneca

"Nothing succeeds like success." — French proverb

"Nothing recedes like success." — Walter Winchell

"If at first you don't succeed, try, try, try again." — T. H. Palmer

"There is no success without hardship." — Sophocles

"A diligence in all things is the strongest fulcrum of success." — Martin Tupper

"We can do anything we want to do, if we stick to it long enough." — Helen Keller

"Before anything else, getting ready is the secret of success." — Henry Ford

"The success of most things depends upon knowing how long it will take to succeed." — Montesquieu

"There is always room at the top." — Webster

"A man who would climb the ladder must begin at the bottom." — English proverb

"The surest way not to fail is to determine to succeed." — Richard Sheridan

"A minute's success pays the failure of years." — Robert Browning

"No success is worthy of the name unless it is won by honest industry and brave breasting of the waves of fortune." — Huxley

"It's not what you get that makes you successful, it's what you continue to do with what you got." — Anonymous

"The toughest thing about success is that you've got to keep on being a success." — Irving Berlin

"Be satisfied with success in even the smallest matter, and think that even such a result is no trifle." — Marcus Aurelius

"A man who undertakes too much seldom succeeds." — Dutch proverb

"There is only one success — to be able to spend your life in your own way." — Christopher Morley

"When you believe in yourself, you have the first secret of success." — Norman Vincent Peale

"Let man ascertain his special business or calling, and then stick to it, if he would be successful." — Benjamin Franklin

"I believe the true road to preeminent success in any line is to make yourself master of that line." — Andrew Carnegie

"I can give you a six-word formula for success: 'Think things through — then follow through.'" Capt. Eddie Rickenbacker

"The reason some men do not succeed is because their wishbone is where their backbone ought to be." — Anonymous

"Nothing ever succeeds which exuberant spirits have not helped to produce." — Nietzsche

"Vigorous let us be in attaining our ends, and mild in our method of attainment." — Lord Newborough

"All men's gains are the fruit of venturing." — Herodotus

"Everything bows to success, even grammar." — Victor Hugo

"The most important single ingredient in the formula of success is knowing how to get along with people." — Theodore Roosevelt

"The eminently successful man should beware of the tendency of wealth to chill and isolate." — Otto Kahn

"Nothing is more humiliating than to see idiots succeed in enterprises we have failed in." — Flaubert

"Not what men do worthily, but what they do successfully, is what history makes haste to record." — Beecher

"In history as in life it is success that counts." — Hendrik Willen van Loon

"'Tis a man's to fight, but Heaven's to give success." — Homer

"To know even one life has breathed easier because you have lived, this is to have succeeded." — "He has achieved success who has lived well, laughed often, and loved much." — Emerson

"Success seems to be that which forms the distinction between confidence and conceit." — "A man that never knows adversity is but half acquainted with others, or with himself. Constant success shows us but one side of the world." — Charles Caleb Colton

"Success depends on three things: who says it, what they say, how they say it; and of these three things, what they say is the least important." — John Viscount Morley

"Success produces confidence; confidence relaxes industry, and negligence ruins the reputation which accuracy had raised." — Ben Jonson

"Never one thing and seldom one man can make for a success. It takes a number of them merging into one perfect whole." — Marie Dressler

"The talent of success is nothing more than doing what you can do well, and doing well whatever you do, without a thought of fame." — "Always bear in mind that your own resolution to success is more important than any other one thing." — Abraham Lincoln

"The flavor of social success is delicious, though it is scorned by those to whose lips the cup has not been proffered." — Logan Pearsall Smith

"It is success that colors all in life: success makes fools admired, makes villains honest: all the proud virtue of this vaunting world fawns on success and power, how ever acquired." — James Thomson

"Resting on your laurels is as dangerous as resting when you are walking in the snow. You doze off and die in your sleep." — Wittgenstein

"If the day and the night are such that you greet them with joy, and life emits a fragrance like flowers and sweet-scented herbs, is more elastic, more starry, more immortal, — that is your success." — "Men are born to succeed, not to fail." — Thoreau

"The ability to convert ideas to things is the secret of outward success." — "A man's best success comes after his greatest disappointments." — Beecher

"To succeed in the world, we do everything we can to appear successful." — "Few things are impracticable in themselves, and it is for want of application, rather than of means, that men fail of success." — La Rochefoucauld

"Self-reliance is the name we give to the egotism of someone who succeeds." — "Some men succeed by what they know; some by what they do; and a few by what they are." — "Pray that success will not come any faster than you are able to endure it." — Elbert Hubbard

"A man is successful who has lived well, laughed often, and loved much, who has gained the respect of intelligent people and the love of children; who has filled his niche and accomplished his task; who leaves the world better than he found it, whether by an improved poppy, a perfect poem, or a rescued soul; who never lacked appreciation of earth's beauty or failed to express it; who looked for the best in others and gave the best he had." — Robert Louis Stevenson

"Instead of thinking about where you are, think about where you want to be. It takes twenty years of hard work to become an overnight success." — Diana Rankin

Achievement

"The value of achievement lies in the achieving." — Einstein

"What you cannot as you would achieve, you must accomplish as you may." — Shakespeare

"Great achievement is usually born of great sacrifice, and is never the result of selfishness." — Napoleon Hill

"Death comes to all but great achievements raise a monument which shall endure until the sun grows cold." — Georgius Fabricius

"Who faints not, achieves." — Old proverb

"One day's rain makes up for many day's drought." — African proverb

"The three great essentials to achieve anything worthwhile are, first, hard work; second, stick-to-it-iveness; third, common sense." — Thomas Edison

"We never know how high we are till we are called to rise; And then, if we are true to plan, Our statures touch the skies." — Emily Dickinson

"Good to begin well, better to end well." — "All is well that ends well." — English proverbs

"It is amazing what you can accomplish if you do not care who gets the credit." — Truman

Winning

"Win without boasting." — Albert Payson Terhune

"Winning isn't everything." — Old proverb

"If winning isn't everything, why do they keep score?" Vince Lombardi

"You can't win them all." — Old proverb

"You win some and you lose some." — Kipling

"They who lose today may win tomorrow." — Cervantes

"They laugh that win." — "Nothing can seem foul to those that win." — "'Tis deeds must win the prize." — Shakespeare

"Gentleness and kind persuasion win where force and bluster fail." — Aesop

"He may well win the race that runs by himself." — Benjamin Franklin

"It is not enough to aim, you must hit." — Italian proverb

"Nobody has ever bet enough on a winning horse." — American proverb

"When in doubt who will win, be neutral." — Swiss proverb

"To win without risk is to triumph without glory." — Corneille

"Always at it wins the day." — Old proverb

Victory

"Victory belongs to the most persevering." — Napoleon

"Fortitude is victory." — Oliver Goldsmith

"The victor is one who can go it alone!" John Godfrey Saxe

"The race is not to the swift, nor the battle to the strong." — Bible, Ecclesiastes 9:11

"It is not strength, but art, obtains the prize. And to be swift is less than to be wise." — Alexander Pope

"By yielding, you may obtain victory." — Ovid

"On the day of victory, no one is tired." — Arabian proverb

"Forewarned, Forearmed; to be prepared is half the victory." — "They got the better of themselves, and that's the best kind of victory one can wish for." — Cervantes

"With kindness conquer rage; with goodness malice; with generosity defeat all meanness; with the straight truth defeat lies and deceit." — Mahabharata

"The best captain does not plunge headlong nor is the best soldier a man hot to fight. The greatest victor wins without a battle." — Lao-tse

"The problems of victory are more agreeable than those of defeat, but they are no less difficult." — Churchill

WEALTH

"Wealth is not theirs that have it, but those who enjoy it." — Benjamin Franklin

"Wealth is well known to be a great comforter." — Plato

"Wealth is a lot of things that a man can do without." — Socrates

"Wealth is not a matter of intelligence, it's a matter of inspiration." — Jim Rohn

"Wealth is a very dangerous inheritance, unless the inheritor is trained to active benevolence." — Charles Simmons

"Wealth is nothing in itself; it is not useful but when it departs from us." — Saumuel Johnson

"Wealth unused might as well not exist." — Aesop

"Wealth maketh many friends." — Bible, Proverbs 23:5

"Wealth brings many friends, but a poor man's friend deserts him." — Bible, Proverbs 19:4

"Wealth stays with us a little moment if at all; only our characters are steadfast, not our gold." — Euripides

"Without the rich heart, wealth is an ugly beggar." — Emerson

"There is no true wealth beyond a man's need." — Kahlil Gibran

"The greatest wealth is contentment with a little." — Apocrypha, Ecclesiasticus

"There is no Wealth but Life." — Ruskin

"A man's true wealth is the good he does in the world." — Mohammed

"Better to have than to wish." — Old proverb

"Lazy hands make a man poor; but diligent hands bring wealth." — Bible, Proverbs 10:4

"Prefer loss to the wealth of dishonest gain; the former vexes you for a time; the latter will bring you lasting remorse." — Chilon

"It is thinking it is gold that makes it precious and thinking it is precious makes it gold." — Eleanor Slater

"Gold may be bought too dear." — "Light gains make heavy purses." — English proverbs

"Much coin, much care." — Latin proverb

"Superfluous wealth can buy superfluities only." — Thoreau

"With much we surfeit; plenty makes us poor." — Michael Drayton

"Much wealth brings many enemies." — African proverb

"Excess of wealth is cause of covetousness." — Christopher Marlowe

"Do not covet the wealth of any man." — Isa-Upanishad

"The advantages of wealth are greatly exaggerated." — Leland Stanford

"There are those who gain from their wealth only the fear of losing it." — Antoine Rivaroli

"The larger the income, the harder it is to live within it." — Richard Whately

"There's nothing so comfortable as a small bankroll. A big one is always in danger." — Wilson Mizner

"Many a man has found the acquisition of wealth only a change, not an end, of miseries." — Seneca

"The gratification of wealth is not found in mere possession or in lavish expenditure, but in its wise application." — Cervantes

"Make use of thy wealth." — "Confide not in wealth." — Sophist sayings

"The only wealth which you will keep forever is the wealth which you have given away." — Martial

"Wealth consists not in having great possessions, but in having few wants." — "Natural wealth is limited and easily obtained; the wealth defined by vain fancies is always beyond reach." — Epicurus

"Wealth to us is not mere material for vain glory but an opportunity for achievement; and poverty we think it no disgrace to acknowledge but a real degradation to make no effort to overcome." — Thucydides

"Wealth in the hands of a man who thinks not of helping mankind with it is sure to turn one day into dry leaves." — Far Eastern saying

"A man that will not permit his wealth to do any good to others while he is living prevents it from doing any good to himself when he is dead." — Charles Colton

"Surplus wealth is a sacred trust which its possessor is bound to administer in his lifetime for the good of the community." — Andrew Carnegie

"We see how much a man has, and therefore we envy him; if we did see how little he enjoys, we should rather pity him." — Jeremiah Seed

"If you look in a dictionary of quotations you will find few reasons for a sensible man to desire to become wealthy." — Robert Lynd

"The wealth of man is the number of things which he loves and blesses, which he is loved and blessed by." — Carlyle

"Abundance is a blessing to the wise; The use of riches in discretion lies; Learn this, ye people of wealth — a heavy purse in a fool's pocket is a heavy curse." — Richard Cumberland

"A man that cleaves to wealth had better cast it away than allow his heart to be poisoned by it; but a man who does not cleave to wealth, and possessing riches, uses them rightly, will be a blessing unto his fellow humans." — Buddha

Money

"Money is power." — Old proverb

"Money is a handmaiden if thou knowest how to use it; a mistress if thou knowest not." — Horace

"Money is a good servant, but a dangerous master." — Bonhours

"Money is not gained by losing time." — Old proverb

"Money is like a sixth sense — and you can't make use of the other five without it." — Maugham

"Money is the wise man's religion." — Euripides

"Money is not required to buy one necessity of the soul." — Thoreau

"Money is the seed of money and the first guinea is sometimes more difficult to acquire than the second million." — Rousseau

"Money makes money." — T. Wilson

"Money demands that you sell, not your weakness to men's stupidity, but your talent to their reason." — Ayn Rand

"Money often costs too much." — Emerson

"Money isn't everything." — E. O'Neill

"Money answereth all things." — Bible, Ecclesiastes 10:19

"Money alone sets the world in motion." — Publilius Syrus

"Money makes the man." — R. L. Greene

"Money begets money." — "Money talks." — Italian Proverbs

"Money speaks sense in a language all nations understand." — Aphra Behn

"Money brings you food, but not appetite; medicine, but not health; acquaintances, but not friends." — Ibsen

"Money doesn't buy love." — "Money doesn't grow on trees." — Old proverbs

"Money as such is not evil; it is its wrong use that is evil." — Gandhi

"The love of money is the root of all evil." — Bible, Timothy 6:11

"The lack of money is the root of all evil." — "Money is indeed the most important thing in the world." — Shaw

"For money you would sell your soul?" Sophocles

"You can't take it with you when you go." — Old proverb

"They do not own money whose money owns them." — St. Cyprian

"Some men are masters of money, and some its slaves." — Russian proverb

"There are men who are chained to gold and silver." — The Talmud

"Put not your trust in money, but put your money in trust." — Oliver Wendell Holmes

"It takes money to make money." — Old proverb

"No man is hanged who has money in his pocket" "When money speaks, the truth keeps silent." — Russian Proverbs

"Where gold speaks, every tongue is silent." — Italian proverb

"Life is short, and so is money." — Bertolt Brecht

"It is better to have a permanent income than to be fascinating." — Oscar Wilde

"Ready money works great cures." — French proverb

"Make all you can, save all you can, give all you can." — John Wesley

"A fool and his money are soon parted." — "Who heeds not a penny shall never have any." — Old proverbs

"A man that has a penny in his purse is worth a penny; have and you shall be esteemed." — Petronius

"It's a good thing to know how to satisfy your own conscience and make the cash register ring also." — Arthur Brisbane

"To despise money is to dethrone a king." — Sebastien Chamfort

"No man needs money so much as a man who despises it." — Jean Richter

"Virtue has never been as respectable as money." — "All worship money." — Mark Twain

"When it is a matter of money, all men are of the same religion." — Voltaire

"When every man worships gold, all other reverence is done away." — Propertius

"Make money your god, it will plague you like the devil." — Henry Fielding

"For money has a power above the stars and fate, to manage love." — Butler

"Gold will buy the highest honors; and gold will purchase love." — Ovid

"All love has something of blindness in it, but the love of money especially." — Robert South

"There is no fortress so strong that money cannot take it." — Cicero

"Gold goes in any gate except heaven's." — Old proverb

"He who has plenty of pepper can afford to season his cabbage well." — Latin proverb

"I'd like to live like a poor man, only with lots of money." — Picasso

"Do not work to make money for money's sake." — Buddha

"I find all this money a considerable burden." — J. Paul Getty

"Money is like manure, it's not worth anything unless you spread it around to help young beautiful things grow." — Sir Francis Bacon

"Money is like love, it kills slowly and painfully the man who withholds it, and it enlivens the other who turns it upon his fellow men." — Kahlil Gibran

"Money answers all questions." — "Money won, virtue gone." — "A man who will pay has the say." — "Money attracts money." — "The longest road in the world is the one that leads to the pocket." — "With money in your pocket, you are wise and you are handsome and you sing well, too." — "Sooner ask a man for his life than for his money." — "A penny is a lot of money — if you haven't got a penny." — Jewish proverbs

"Money is the sinew of love as well as of war." — "Money never cometh out of season." — "Muck and money go together." — "So we get the chinks, we will bear the stinks." — English Proverbs

"Money grows on the trees of patience." — "When life is ruined for the sake of money's preciousness, the ruined life cares nought for the money." — Japanese Proverbs

"Money does all things for reward. Some are pious and honest as long as they thrive upon it, but if the devil himself gives better wages, they soon change their party." — Seneca

"There is a vast difference in one's respect for the man who has made himself, and the man who has only made his money." — Dinah Mulock

"A penny saved is a penny gained." — "A moneyless man goes fast through the market." — "Take care of your pennies and your dollars will take care of themselves." — Scottish proverbs

"Never spend your money before you have it." — "Banking establishments are more dangerous than standing armies." — Thomas Jefferson

"A wise man should have money in his head, not in his heart." — "No man will take counsel, but every man will take money. Therefore, money is better than counsel." — "Money is the life blood of the nation." — Swift

"Help me to money and I'll help myself to friends." — "If thou wouldst keep money, save money; If thou wouldst reap money, sow money." — Thomas Fuller

"Only after the last tree has been cut down, Only after the last fish has been caught, Only then will you find that money cannot be eaten." — Cree Indian proverb

"The use of money is all the advantage there is in having it." — "Money never made a man happy yet, nor will it. There is nothing in its nature to produce happiness. The more a man has, the more he wants. Instead of its filling a vacuum, it makes one." — "If you would know the value of money, try and borrow some." — "A man that is of the opinion money will do everything may well be suspected of doing everything for money." — Benjamin Franklin

Riches

"Riches do not consist in the possession of treasures, but in the use made of them." — Napoleon

"Riches are intended for the comfort of life, and not life for the purpose of hoarding riches." — Sa'di

"Riches certainly make themselves wings; they fly away as an eagle toward heaven." — Bible, Proverbs 23:5

"Riches have wings, and grandeur is a dream." — William Cowper

"Riches exclude only one inconvenience, and that is poverty." — "It is better to live rich than to die rich." — Samuel Johnson

"Riches amassed in haste will diminish, but those collected by little and little will multiply." — Goethe

"Riches are not an end of life, but an instrument of life." — Beecher

"Get what you can and keep what you have. That's the way to get rich." — Scottish proverb

"A man that is rich will not be called a fool." — Spanish proverb

"The rich would have to eat money if the poor did not provide food." — "Whoever is rich is my brother." — Russian Proverbs

"Everyone is kin to a rich man." — Old proverb

"The poor is hated even of his own neighbor, but the rich hath many friends." — "The hand of the diligent maketh him rich." — Bible, Proverbs 14:20

"A man who hoards up riches and enjoys them not is like an ass that carries gold and eats thistles." — Burton

"The pride of dying rich raises the loudest laugh in hell." — John Foster

"Public sentiment will come to be that the man who dies rich dies disgraced." — Andrew Carnegie

"How you've got rich, none cares; rich you must be." — Juvenal

"No one gets rich quickly if he is honest." — Menander

"He that maketh haste to be rich shall not be innocent." — Bible, Proverbs 28:20

"A man who wishes to be rich in a day will be hanged in a year." — Leonardo da Vinci

"After a rich man gets rich, his next ambition is to get richer." — American proverb

"For one rich man that is content there are a hundred that are not." — Anonymous

"Although they possess enough, and more than enough, still they yearn for more." — Ovid

"As riches grow, care follows, and a thirst for more and more." — Horace

"A man who multiplies riches multiplies cares." — Benjamin Franklin

"Let us not envy some men's accumulated riches; their burden would be too heavy for us." — La Bruyère

"I have seen many rich burdened with the fear of poverty." — Martin Tupper

"A rich man is nothing but a poor man with money." — William Fields

"A vagabond, when rich, is called a tourist." — Paul Richard

"The embarrassment of riches. . ." — Voltaire

"The virtue of some of the rich is that they teach us to despise wealth." — Kahlil Gibran

"It is the wretchedness of being rich that you have to live with rich people." — Logan Smith

"Every man was not born with a silver spoon in his mouth." — Cervantes

"He who enjoys good health is rich, though he knows it not." — Italian proverb

"It is only when the rich are sick that they fully feel the impotence of wealth." — Charles Colton

"I care for riches, to make gifts to friends, or lead a sick man back to health." — Euripides

"A man is rich who owes nothing." — French proverb

"To know you have enough is to be rich." — Tao saying

"Small riches hath the most rest." — Cornish proverb

"He is only rich who owns the day." — Emerson

"If I keep my good character, I shall be rich enough." — Platonicus

"To whom can riches give repute, or trust, content, or pleasure, but the good and just?" Alexander Pope

"Riches serve a wise man, but command a fool." — "A man is not fit for riches who is afraid to use them." — "A man is rich that is satisfied." — "Riches are like muck, which stink in a heap, but spread abroad, make the earth fruitful." — "Not possession but use is the only riches." — Thomas Fuller

"Riches without charity are nothing worth. They are a blessing only to a man who makes them a blessing to others." — Henry Fielding

"Seek not proud riches, but such as thou mayest get justly, use soberly, distribute cheerfully, and leave contentedly." — Sir Francis Bacon

"To be rich is not everything, but it certainly helps." — "A rich man has no need of character." — "The court is most merciful when the accused is most rich." — Hebrew proverbs

"Of all the riches that we hug, of all the pleasures we enjoy, we can carry no more out of this world than out of a dream." — James Bonnell

"There is a burden of care in getting riches; fear in keeping them; temptation in using them; guilt in abusing them; sorrow in losing them; and a burden of account at last to be given concerning them." — Matthew Henry

"It is no longer a distinction to be rich. . . Men do not care for money as they once did. . . What we accumulate by way of useless surplus does us no honor." — Henry Ford

"If you can actually count your money, then you are not really rich." — "You will never get rich working for someone else." — J. Paul Getty

"If a rich man is proud of his wealth, he should not be praised until it is known how he employs it." — "A man is richest who is content with the least, for content is the wealth of nature." — Socrates

"We make ourselves rich by making our wants few." — "A man is rich in proportion to the number of things which he can afford to let alone." — Thoreau

"There are no riches above the riches of the health of the body." — Apocrypha, Ecclesiasticus 30:16

Prosperity

"Prosperity — the very bond of love." — Shakespeare

"Prosperity lets the bridle go." — Portuguese proverb

"Prosperity is only an instrument to be used, not a deity to be worshiped." — Calvin Coolidge

"A prosperous man is never sure that he is loved for himself." — Lucan

"While prosperous, you may number many friends; but when the storm comes you are left alone." — Ovid

"In prosperity, no altars smoke." — Italian proverb

"Everything in the world can be endured, except continual prosperity." — Goethe

"A man who possesses most must be most afraid of loss." — Leonardo da Vinci

"A comfortable career of prosperity, if it does not make men honest, at least keeps them so." — Thackeray

"In prosperity, let us take great care to avoid pride, scorn, and arrogance." — Cicero

"Watch lest prosperity destroy generosity." — Beecher

"Prosperity discovers vice, adversity discovers virtue." — "Prosperity is not without many fears and distastes; and adversity is not without comforts and hopes." — Sir Francis Bacon

"A man who swells in prosperity will shrink in adversity." — "In prosperity caution — in adversity patience." — Old proverbs

"Take care to be an economist in prosperity: there is no fear of your being one in adversity." — Johann von Zimmermann

"Prosperity is the touchstone of virtue; for it is less difficult to bear misfortunes than to remain uncorrupted by pleasure." — Tacitus

"The mind that is much elevated and insolent with prosperity, and cast down by adversity, is generally abject and base." — Epicurus

"It appears more difficult to find a man that bears prosperity well than a man that bears adversity well; for prosperity creates presumption in most men, but adversity brings sobriety to all." — Xenophon

"As riches and favor forsake a man, we discover him to be a fool, but nobody could find it out in his prosperity." — La Bruyère

"When you ascend the hill of prosperity, may you not meet a friend." — "Few of us can stand prosperity — another man's, I mean." — Mark Twain

"In the day of prosperity, adversity is forgotten and in the day of adversity, prosperity is not remembered." — Apocrypha, Ecclesiasticus 11:25

Luxury

"On the soft bed of luxury most kingdoms have expired." — Edward Young

"All luxury corrupts either the morals or the state." — Joubert

"Contentment is natural wealth; luxury is artificial poverty." — Socrates

"Comfort is not known if poverty does not come before it." — Irish proverb

"Abundance, like want, ruins many." — Romanian proverb

"We can do without any article of luxury we have never had; but when once obtained, it is not in human nature to surrender it voluntarily." — Thomas Chandler Haliburton

"The lust for comfort: that stealthy thing that enters the house a guest, and then becomes a host, and then a master." — Kahlil Gibran

"The man who first brought ruin on the Roman people was a man who pampered them by largenesses and amusements." — Italian proverb

"Most of the luxuries, and many of the so-called comforts, of life are not only not indispensable, but positive hindrances to the elevation of mankind." — Thoreau

POWER

"Power must always feel the check of power." — Louis Brandeis

"Power corrupts." — Trollope

"Power tends to corrupt and absolute power corrupts absolutely." — Lord Acton

"Power does not corrupt men; fools, however, if they get into a position of power, corrupt power." — Shaw

"Power gives no purchase to the hand; it will not hold, soon perishes, and greatness goes." — Euripides

"Power hath ordained nothing which Economy saw not needful." — Martin Tupper

"Use thou thy power." — Ovid

"Self-reverence, self-knowledge, self-control: these three alone lead life to sovereign power." — Tennyson

"The measure of a man is what he does with power." — Pittacus

"The sole advantage of power is that you can do more good." — Gracian

"The property of power is to protect." — Pascal

"It is better to be the head of a mouse than the tail of a lion." — Spanish proverb

"We have more power than will." — La Rochefoucauld

"The worst of poisons: to mistrust one's power." — Heinrich Heine

"What lies in our power to do, it lies in our power not to do." — Aristotle

"To have what we want is riches; but to be able to do without is power." — George McDonald

"If you would be powerful, pretend to be powerful." — Horne Tooke

"A friend in power is a friend lost." — Henry Adams

"The only prize much cared for by the powerful is power." — Oliver Wendell Holmes, Jr.

"The greater the power, the more dangerous the abuse." — Edmund Burke

"Unlimited power is apt to corrupt the minds of those who possess it." — William Pitt

"They will sacrifice everything else to hold their power." — Raymond Clapper

"He who is all-powerful should fear everything." — Pierre Corneille

"All power, even the most despotic, rests ultimately on opinion." — Hume

"What power has the shadow before the sun?" Rumi

"It is not possible to found a lasting power upon injustice, perjury, and treachery." — Demosthenes

"Nearly all men can stand adversity, but if you want to test a man's character, give him power." — Abraham Lincoln

"O, it is excellent to have a giant's strength; but it is tyrannous to use it like a giant." — Shakespeare

"I hope our wisdom will grow with our power, and teach us that the less we use our power, the greater it will be." — "An honest man can feel no pleasure in the exercise of power over his fellow citizens." — Thomas Jefferson

"Power exercised with violence has seldom been of long duration, but temper and moderation generally produce permanence in all things." — Seneca

"Power acquired by guilt has seldom been directed to any good end or useful purpose." — "A man who is the next heir to supreme power is always suspected and hated by those who actually wield it." — Tacitus

"Power, like a desolating pestilence, pollutes whatever it touches; and obedience, bane of all genius, virtue, freedom, truth, makes slaves of men, and, of the human frame, a mechanized automation." — Shelley

"Anarchy is the stepping stone to absolute power." — "Even in war, moral power is to physical as three parts out of four." — Napoleon

"A man attains an elevated position only when his mediocrity prevents him from being a threat to others. And for this reason a democracy is never governed by the most competent, but rather by those whose insignificance will not jeopardize anyone else's self-esteem." — Machiavelli

"Nothing destroys authority so much as the unequal and untimely interchange of power, pressed too far and relaxed too much." — Sir Francis Bacon

"Men entrusted with power will abuse it if not also animated with the love of truth and virtue, no matter whether they be kings, queens, or of the people." — La Fontaine

"Big jobs usually go to the men who prove their ability to outgrow small ones." —

"The task ahead of us is never as great as the power behind us." — Emerson

Fame

"Fame is the perfume of heroic deeds." — Socrates

"Fame is the thirst of youth." — Byron

"Fame is a magnifying glass." — English proverb

"Fame is a fickle food upon a shifting plate." — Emily Dickinson

"Fame is no sure test of merit, but only a probability of such; it is an accident, not a property of a man." — Carlyle

"Fame sometimes hath created something of nothing." — Thomas Fuller

"Toil, says the proverb, is the sire of fame." — Euripides

"Even the best things are not equal to their fame." — Thoreau

"I trust a good deal to common fame, as we all must." — Emerson

"There's not a thing on earth that I can name, so foolish, and so false, as common fame." — John Wilmot

"Common fame is much to blame." — Old proverb

"Fondness for fame is avarice of air." — Edward Young

"Worldly fame is but a breath of wind that blows now this way, and now that, and changes name as it changes direction." — Dante

"Some to the fascination of a name surrender judgment, hoodwinked." — William Cowper

"What a heavy burden is a name that has too soon become famous." — Voltaire

"If I'm such a legend, why am I so lonely?" Judy Garland

"All is temporary and ephemeral — fame and the famous, as well." — Marcus Aurelius

"In the future, everyone will get fifteen minutes of fame." — Andy Warhol

"Let us now praise famous men." — Apocrypha, Ecclesiasticus 44:1

"Famous men have the whole earth as their memorial." — Pericles

"The temple of fame is the shortest passage to riches and preferment." — Anonymous

"The way to fame is like the way to heaven, through much tribulation." — Laurence Sterne

"I would give all my fame for a pot of ale and safety." — Shakespeare

"All the fame you should look for in life is to have lived it quietly." — Montaigne

"If fame is only to come after death, I am in no hurry for it." — Martial

"Blessed are those whose fame does not outshine their truth." — Rabindranath Tagore

"Fame does not always light at random: sometimes she chooses her man." — "Known to others all too well, they die to themselves unknown." — Seneca

"Fame has also this great drawback, that if we pursue it we must direct our life in such a way as to please the fancy of men, avoiding what they dislike and seeking what is pleasing to them." — Spinoza

"Fame is no plant that grows on mortal soil." — "Fame is the spur that the clear spirit doth raise, that last infirmity of noble mind, to scorn delights, and live laborious days." — John Milton

"Fame is like a shaved pig with a greased tail, and it is only after it has slipped through the hands of thousands, that some man, by mere chance, holds on to it!" Davy Crockett

"A celebrated people lose dignity, upon a closer view." — Napoleon

"A celebrity is a person who works hard all his life to become well known, then wears dark glasses to avoid being recognized." — Fred Allen

"What is fame? The advantage of being known by people of whom you yourself know nothing, and for whom you care as little." — Stanislas I

"Nor fame I slight, nor for her favors call; she comes unlooked for, if she comes at all." — "Unblemished let me live or die unknown; Oh, grant an honest fame, or grant me none!" Alexander Pope

"Happy is the man who hath never known what it is to taste of fame — to have it is a purgatory, to want it is a hell." — Bulwer-Lytton

"There is no business in this world so troublesome as the pursuit of fame: life is over before you have hardly begun your work." — La Bruyère

"We are all clever enough at envying a famous man while he is yet alive, and at praising him when he is dead." — Mimnermus

"One of the many distinctions between the celebrity and the hero. . . is that one lives only for himself while the other acts to redeem society." — Joseph Campbell

"Those great obscure momentous souls whom fame does not record, Whose impulse still our fate controls with deathless deed or word. . ." — Arthur Davison Ficke

Popularity

"Popularity is exhausting. The life of the party almost always winds up in a corner with an overcoat over him." — Wilson Mizner

"Popularity? It is glory's small change." — Victor Hugo

"Popular opinion is the greatest lie in the world." — Carlyle

"Whatever is popular deserves attention." — Sir James Mackintosh

"Every dog hath his day." — English proverb

"The dispersing and scattering of our names into many mouths, we call this making us greater?" Montaigne

"Would you be known by everybody? Then you know nobody." — Publilius Syrus

"A little mind courteth notoriety, to illustrate its puny self." — Martin Tupper

"How vain, without the merit, is the name." — Homer

"Put a rogue in the limelight and he will act like an honest man." — Napoleon

"Avoid popularity; it has many snares, and no real benefit." — William Penn

"Everybody wants to be somebody; nobody wants to grow." — Goethe

"Popularity is a crime from the moment it is sought; it is only a virtue where men have it whether they will or not." — Sir George Savile

"A plague on eminence! I hardly dare cross the street any more without a convoy and I am stared at wherever I go like an idiot member of a royal family or an animal in a zoo; and zoo animals have been known to die from stares." — Igor Stravinsky

"False is the praise which says that a man's eminence comes from his noble qualities; for the men of this world as a rule do not care about a man's true nature." — Panchatantra

"I have found some of the best reasons I ever had for remaining at the bottom simply by looking at the men at the top." — Frank Moore Colby

"I am not concerned that I have no place; I am concerned how I may fit myself for one. I am not concerned that I am not known; I seek to be worthy to be known." — Confucius

Glory

"Glory is never where virtue is not." — Jean Lefranc

"Glory lies in the attempt to reach one's goal, not in reaching it." — Gandhi

"Glory ought to be the consequence, not the motive, of our actions." — Pliny the Younger

"Glory arrives too late when it comes only to one's ashes." — Martial

"Glory is fleeting, but obscurity is forever." — Napoleon

"Glory, built on selfish principles, is shame and guilt." — William Cowper

"Our greatest glory is not in never falling, but in rising every time we fall." — Confucius

"The shortest way to glory is to be guided by conscience." — Henry Home

"The only glory most of us have to hope for is the glory of being normal." — Katharine Gerould

"No path of flowers leads to glory." — La Fontaine

"No guts, no glory." — Anonymous

"No pain, no palm; no thorns, no throne; no gall, no glory; no cross, no crown." — William Penn

"The noblest spirit is most strongly attracted by the love of glory." — Cicero

"For the desire for glory clings even to the best of men longer than any other passion." — Tacitus

"Of all the affections which attend human life, the love of glory is the most ardent." — Sir Richard Steele

"There is another sort of glory, which is the having too good an opinion of our own worth." — Montaigne

"Avoid shame, but do not seek glory, — there is nothing so expensive as glory." — Sydney Smith

"Desire of glory is the last garment that even a wise man puts off." — Anonymous

"For men to search their own glory is not glory." — Bible, Proverbs 25:27

"Let not a man glory in this, that he loves his country; let him rather glory in this, that he loves his kind." — Persian proverb

"The man who is completely wise and virtuous has no need of glory, except so far as it disposes and eases his way to action by the greater trust that it procures him." — Plutarch

"How many sacrifice honor, a necessity, to glory, a luxury?" Joseph Roux

Ruling

"The ruler is indeed happy who has made his subjects afraid, not of him, but for him." — Plutarch

"The sultan of sultans is one who has gained the love of the pauper." — Kahlil Gibran

"Every noble crown is, and on earth will forever be, a crown of thorns." — Carlyle

"Kings are never without flatterers to seduce them; ambition to deprave them; and desires to corrupt them." — Plato

"Kings are like stars — they rise and set, they have the worship of the world, but no repose." — Shelley

"Kings have long arms." — Ovid

"The King can do no wrong." — Legal maxim

"To rule is an art, not a science." — Ludwig Borne

"All who know well how to obey will know also how to rule." — Flavius Josephus

"One that will not be ruled by the rudder will be wrecked on the rocks." — English proverb

"Uneasy lies the head that wears a crown." — "Woe to that land that's governed by a child!" Shakespeare

"An army of a thousand is easy to find, but, ah, how difficult to find a general." — Chinese proverb

"A throne is only a bench covered with velvet." — French proverb

"Better in the dust than crawl near the throne." — German proverb

"He who has the gold rules . . . that is the 'Golden Rule.'" Anonymous

"Authority is never without hate." — Euripides

"New lords, new laws." — St. Editha

"Every ruler is harsh whose rule is new." — Aeschylus

"Don't rejoice over them that goes, before you see them that comes." — Japanese proverb

"Only with a new ruler do you realize the value of the old." — Burmese proverb

"Better no rule than cruel rule." — Aesop

"The faults of starving people are the faults of their rulers." — Lao-tse

"Better have as king a vulture advised by swans than a swan advised by vultures." — Panchatantra 1

"When the Czar has a cold, all Russia coughs." — Russian proverb

"Name me an emperor who was ever struck by a cannon-ball?" Charles V

"What millions died, that Caesar might be great." — Thomas Campbell

"Were only kings themselves to fight, there'd be an end of war." — Charles Jefferys

"Of all the evils that infest a state, a tyrant is the greatest; his sole will commands the laws, and lords it over them." — Euripides

"Where law ends, tyranny begins." — William Pitt

"A king ruleth as he ought; a tyrant as the lest; a king to the profit of all, a tyrant only to please a few." — Aristotle

"A despot doesn't fear eloquent writers preaching freedom — he fears a drunken poet who may crack a joke that will take hold." — Elwyan Brooks White

JUSTICE

"Justice is love's order." — Rev. J. M. Gibbon

"Justice is truth in action." — Disraeli

"Justice is itself the great standing policy of civil society." — Edmund Burke

"Justice is the tolerable accommodation of the conflicting interests of society." — Learned Hand

"What is justice? To give every man his due." — Aristotle

"Justice is the constant desire and effort to render every man his due." — Justinian I

"Justice discards party, friendship, and kindred, and is therefore represented as blind." — Joseph Addison

"Justice without wisdom is impossible." — James Froude

"Justice delayed is justice denied." — William Gladstone

"Justice is the great interest of man on earth." — Webster

"Judge the tree by its fruits, man by his deeds." — Far Eastern saying

"Judge the contents, not the bottle." — The Talmud

"Judge not according to the appearance." — Bible, John 7:24

"Judge not, that ye be not judged." — Bible, Matthew 7:1

"Judges must be in number, for few will always do the will of few." — Machiavelli

"Judgment is forced upon us by experience." — Samuel Johnson

"I think the first duty of society is justice." — Alexander Hamilton

"Let us have justice, and then we shall have enough liberty!" Joubert

"An honest man nearly always thinks justly." — Rousseau

"Each man is his own judge." — Shawnee Indian proverb

"Without justice, courage is weak." — Benjamin Franklin

"In a just cause, the weak will beat the strong." — Sophocles

"Don't hear one and judge two." — Greek proverb

"How little do they see what really is, who frame their hasty judgment upon that which seems." — Robert Southey

"Beware, as long as you live, of judging people by appearances." — La Fontaine

"Never judge a day by the weather." — Anonymous

"Never judge any man until you have walked a mile in his moccasins." — Sioux Indian proverb

"Wherein thou judgest another, thou condemnest thyself." — Bible, Romans 2:1

"With what judgment ye judge, ye shall be judged." — Old proverb

"I will judge each of you according to your ways." — Bible, Ezekiel 33:11

"Out of thine own mouth will I judge thee." — Bible, Luke 19:22

"What's fair is fair." — Old proverb

"Four things belong to a judge: to hear courteously, to answer wisely, to consider soberly, and to decide impartially." — Socrates

"The just upright man is laughed to scorn." — Bible, Job 7:4

"They acquit the vultures but condemn the doves." — Juvenal

"The judge is condemned when the criminal is acquitted." — Publilius Syrus

"It is better to risk saving a guilty man than to condemn an innocent one." — Voltaire

"The injuries we do and those we suffer are seldom weighed in the same scales." — Aesop

"When a camel is at the foot of a mountain then judge of his height." — Hindu proverb

"Every man loves justice in the affairs of another." — Italian proverb

"You shall judge a man by his foes as well as by his friends." — Joseph Conrad

"No man should be judge in his own cause." — Legal maxim

"I mistrust the judgment of every man in a case which his own wishes are concerned." — Duke of Wellington

"Human nature is so constituted, that all see, and judge better, in the affairs of other men, than in their own." — Terence

"'Tis with our judgments as our watches; none go just alike, yet each believes his own watch." — Alexander Pope

"The outcome justifies the deeds." — Ovid

"The end justifies the means." — Old proverb

"The end doesn't justify the means." — Anonymous

"The end must justify the means." — Matthew Prior

"As the means, so the end." — Gandhi

"The achievement of justice is an endless process." — John F. Kennedy

"Don't judge a man by the words of his mother, listen to the comments of his neighbors." — "Measure the corn of others with your own bushel." — Jewish proverbs

"I care very little if I am judged by you or by any human; indeed, I do not even judge myself." — Bible, Corinthians 4:3

"Do not be attached to the judgments of others, for your interpretation in the end will be the most important." — Buddha

"A mature man is his own judge." — Dag Hammarskjold

"Knowledge is the treasure, but judgment the treasurer of a wise man." — William Penn

"The path of the just is as the shining light, that shineth more and more unto the perfect day." — Bible, Proverbs 4:18

"Justice and power must be brought together, so that whatever is just may be powerful, and whatever is powerful may be just." — Pascal

"Judge a tree from its fruit; not from the leaves." — "Keep alive the light of justice, and much that men say in blame will pass you by." — Euripides

"Justice is nothing else than the interest of the stronger." — "The judge should not be young; he should have learned to know evil, not from his own soul, but from late and long observation of the nature of evil in others: knowledge should be his guide, not personal experience." — Plato

"As the touchstone which tries gold, but is not itself tried by gold, such is a man who has the true standard of judgment." — "Only the just man enjoys peace of mind." — Epicurus

"Be just, before you're generous." — "The number of those who undergo the fatigue of judging for themselves is very small indeed." — Richard Brinsley Sheridan

"We judge ourselves by what we feel capable of doing; others judge us by what we have done." — Longfellow

"The love of justice is simply, in the majority of men, the fear of suffering injustice." — "Everyone complains of his memory, and no one complains of his judgment." — La Rochefoucauld

"I do not distinguish by the eye, but by the mind, which is the proper judge of a man." — "If you would judge, understand." — Seneca

"No man can justly censure or condemn another, because indeed no man truly knows another. . . . Further, no man can judge another, because no man knows himself." — Sir Thomas Browne

"Men are not to be judged by what they do not know, but by what they know, and by the manner in which they know it." — Marquis de Vauvenargues

"It shall be small care to the high and happy conscience, what jealous friends, or envious foes, or common fools may judge." — "Keep justice, keep generosity, yielding to neither singly." — Martin Tupper

"Why should there not be a patient confidence in the ultimate justice of the people? Is there any better or equal hope in the world?" Abraham Lincoln

Law

"Law is the embodiment of the moral sentiment of the people." — Sir William Blackstone

"Law can discover sin, but not remove it." — John Milton

"Law cannot persuade where it cannot punish." — Thomas Fuller

"Laws grind the poor, and rich men rule the law." — Oliver Goldsmith

"Laws are the sovereigns of sovereigns." — Louis XIV

"Laws are like cobwebs which entangle the weak, but through which the greater break uninjured." — Solon

"Laws are like cobwebs, which may catch small flies, but let wasps and hornets break through." — Swift

"Laws are silent in the midst of arms." — "The good of the people is the chief law." — Cicero

"Law will never be strong or respected unless it has the sentiment of the people behind it." — James Bryce

"Laws too gentle are seldom obeyed; too severe, seldom executed." — American proverb

"The best way to get a bad law repealed is to enforce it strictly." — Abraham Lincoln

"If we desire respect for law, we must first make the law respectable." — Louis Brandeis

"All creation is governed by law." — Sri Yukteswar

"A law is valuable not because it is law, but because there is right in it." — Beecher

"An unjust law is no law at all." — Thomas Aquinas

"An unlawful oath is better broke than kept." — Anonymous

"The greater the number of laws, the greater the number of offenses against them." — Henry Havelock Ellis

"When the state is most corrupt, then the laws are most multiplied." — Tacitus

"A multitude of laws in a country is like a great number of physicians, a sign of weakness and malady." — Voltaire

"The way we escape virtue is by passing more laws." — Anonymous

"Law after law breeds a multitude of thieves. The greater the number of laws and enactments, the more thieves and robbers there will be." — Lao-tse

"The more laws, the less justice." — German proverb

"A state is better governed which has but few laws, and those laws strictly observed." — Descartes

"Rigorous law is often rigorous injustice." — Terence

"Petty laws breed great crimes." — Ouida

"The nets of the law are devised to catch small criminals only." — Kahlil Gibran

"The law itself follows gold." — Propertius

"One law for the rich and another for the poor." — Marryat

"Do you not know that I am above the law?" James II

"They cast their vote, distrusting all the elected but not the law." — Karl Jay Shapiro

"Every land has its own law." — "A man that loves law will get his fill of it." — Scottish proverbs

"Men do not make laws. They do but discover them." — Calvin Coolidge

"Certain laws have not been written, but they are more fixed than all the written laws." — Seneca the Elder

"The people should fight for their law as for their city wall." — Heraclitus

"What is in conformity with justice should also be in conformity to the laws." — Socrates

"Man became free when he recognized that he was subject to the law." — Will Durant

"No man has a more sacred obligation to obey the law than those who make the law." — Sophocles

"The law is good, if a man use it lawfully." — Bible, I Timothy 1:8

"He that keepeth the law, happy is he." — Bible, Proverbs 29:18

"It is impossible for us to break the law. We can only break ourselves against the law." — Cecil B. de Mille

"Possession was the strongest tenure of the law." — Pilpay

"Possession is nine points of the law." — Legal maxim

"Possession is eleven points in law." — Colley Cibber

"A good denial, the best point in law." — Irish proverb

"A man who goes to law for a sheep loses his cow." — Spanish proverb

"A lean compromise is better than a fat lawsuit." — Old proverb

"The greater the truth, the greater the libel." — Burns

"In law nothing is certain but the expense." — Butler

"We must not make a scarecrow of the law." — "The law hath not been dead, though it hath slept." — Shakespeare

"The law is a jealous mistress." — Old proverb

"The law is not concerned with trifles." — Legal Maxium

"Use new diets, but old laws." — Periander

"One precedent creates another. They soon accumulate and constitute law." — Junius

"The good need fear no law; it is their safety, and the bad man's awe." — Philip Massinger

"No law can be sacred to me but that of my nature." — Emerson

"The reason of the law is the law." — Sir Walter Scott

"Good laws make it easier to do right and harder to do wrong." — William Gladstone

"Good laws lead to the making of better ones; bad ones bring about worse." — Rousseau

"When men are pure, laws are useless; when men are corrupt, laws are broken." — Disraeli

"Whenever you speak, remember every cause stands not on eloquence, but stands on laws." — Joseph Story

"The life of the law has not been logic; it has been experience." — Oliver Wendell Holmes, Jr.

"Reason is the life of law; nay, the common law itself is nothing else but reason." — Sir Edward Coke

"Law is reason free from passion." — "Whereas the law is passionless, passion must ever sway the hearts of men." — "Good laws, if they are not obeyed, do not constitute good government." — "Even when laws have been written down, they ought not always to remain unaltered." — Aristotle

"Law is experience developed by reason and applied continually to further experience." — "The law must be stable, but it must not stand still." — Roscoe Pound

"Laws control the lesser man. Right conduct controls the greater one." — "Going to law is losing a cow for the sake of a cat." — Chinese proverbs

"The law is the last result of human wisdom acting upon human experience for the benefit of the public." — "It is one of the maxims of the civil law, that definitions are hazardous." — Samuel Johnson

"The law: It has honored us; may we honor it." — "The criminal law is not founded on the principle of vengeance; it uses evil only as the means of preventing greater evil." — Webster

"An oath is not needed by a good man, nor will it prevent the bad man from perjuring himself." — "An oath demands, 'the truth, the whole truth, and nothing but the truth.'" W. H. Howe

"Ignorance of the law excuses no man; not that all men know the law, but because 'tis an excuse every man will plead, and no one can tell how to refute him." — John Selden

"Our nation is founded on the principle that observance of the law is the eternal safeguard of liberty and defiance of the law is the surest road to tyranny." — John F. Kennedy

"Probably all laws are useless; for good men do not need laws at all, and bad men are made no better by them." — Demonax the Cynic

Lawyers

"Lawyers and painters can soon change white to black." — Danish proverb

"A countryman between two lawyers is like a fish between two cats." — Benjamin Franklin

"It is the trade of lawyers to question everything, yield nothing, and to talk by the hour." — Thomas Jefferson

"A man who is his own lawyer has a fool for his client." — L. Hunt

"A lawyer never goes to law himself." — English proverb

"One lawyer will make work for another." — Spanish proverb

"God wanted to chastise man, so he sent lawyers." — Russian proverb

Government

"The happiness of society is the end of government." — "A government of laws, and not of men." — John Adams

"If men were angels, no government would be necessary." — James Madison

"No government is better than the men who compose it." — "The state is the servant of the citizen." — John F. Kennedy

"A Government can be no better than the public opinion which sustains it." — Franklin D. Roosevelt

"Public office is a public trust." — Grover Cleveland

"The responsibility of the great states is to serve and not to dominate the world." — Truman

"The noblest of all forms of government is self-government, but it is the most difficult." — Theodore Roosevelt

"Good government is no substitute for self-government." — Gandhi

"The best of all governments is that which teaches us to govern ourselves." — Goethe

"Democracy is the recurrent suspicion that more than half of the people are right more than half the time." — E. B. White

"A democracy is better than a tyranny or absolute monarchy." — Periander

"The Constitution does not provide for first and second class citizens." — Wendell Lewis Willkie

"They that govern the most make the least noise." — John Selden

"'Tis skill, not strength, that governs a ship." — Thomas Fuller

"Policy goes beyond strength." — Anonymous

"Diplomacy is to do and say the nastiest thing in the nicest way." — Isaac Goldberg

"People starve if taxes eat their grain." — Lao-tse

"No government can remain stable in an unstable society and an unstable world." — Leon Blum

"The government is influenced by shopkeepers." — Adam Smith

"No man can safely govern that which would not willingly become subject." — Thomas à Kempis

"Let the people think they govern, and they will be governed." — Penn

"It is dangerous to be right when the government is wrong." — Voltaire

"Nothing doth more hurt in state than that cunning men pass for wise." — Sir Francis Bacon

"The final end of Government is not to exert restraint but to do good." — Rufus Choate

"The State is made for man, not man for the State." — Einstein

"The people's government, made for the people, made by the people, and answerable to the people." — Webster

"Government is not mere advice; it is authority, with power to enforce its laws." — "Government is not reason, it is not eloquence, it is force; like fire, a handy servant and a dangerous master. Never for a moment should it be left to irresponsible action." — George Washington

"Government big enough to give you everything you need is government big enough to take away everything you have." — "That government is best which governs the least, because its people discipline themselves." — "Information is the currency of democracies." — Thomas Jefferson

"Governments arise either out of the people or over the people." — "When the government fears the people, it is liberty. When the people fear the government, it is tyranny." — "Society in every state is a blessing, but government, ever in its best state, is but a necessary evil; in its worst state, an intolerable one." — Thomas Paine

"Government is a contrivance of human wisdom to provide for human wants." — "In all forms of government the people are the true legislators." — Edmund Burke

"We admit of no government by divine right . . . the only legitimate right to govern is an express grant of power from the governed." — William Henry Harrison

"It is to be regretted that the rich and powerful too often bend the acts of government to their selfish purposes." — Andrew Jackson

"After order and liberty, economy is one of the highest essentials of a free government . . . economy is always a guarantee of peace." — Calvin Coolidge

"The less government we have, the better — the fewer laws, and the less confided power." — "The State is our neighbors; our neighbors are the State." — Emerson

"No government can long be secure without a formidable opposition." — "The greatest of all evils is a weak government." — Disraeli

"That is the best government which desires to make the people happy, and knows how to make them happy." — Lord Macaulay

"People who want to understand democracy should spend less time in the library with Aristotle and more time on the buses and in the subway." — Simeon Strunsky

"Democracy is the form of government in which the free are rulers." — "The state exists for the sake of a good life, and not for the sake of life only." — "Democracy arose from people who thought that if they are equal in any respect, they are equal absolutely." — Aristotle

"We weed out the darnel from the corn and the unfit in war, but do not excuse evil men from the service of the state." — Antisthenes

"The punishment suffered by the wise who refuse to take part in the government is to live under a government of bad rulers." — Plato

"As soon as public service ceases to be the chief business of the citizens, and they would rather serve with their money than with their persons, the State is not far from its fall." — Rousseau

"No man is good enough to govern another without the other's consent." — "This country, with its institutions, belongs to the people who inhabit it. When ever they shall grow weary of the existing government, they can exercise their constitutional right of amending it, or their revolutionary right to dismember or overthrow it." — "That the government of the people, by the people, for the people, shall not perish from the earth." — Abraham Lincoln

Politics

"Politics is the art of government." — Truman

"Politics is a profession — a serious, complicated and, in its true sense, a noble one." — Dwight D. Eisenhower

"Politics is the science of how who gets what, when and why." — Sidney Hillman

"Politics make strange bedfellows." — Charles Warner

"Politicians are like weather vanes." — French proverb

"Politics is not an exact science." — Bismarck

"I believe that politics is a science. It's a scientific approach to handling human beings." — James Farley

"Knowledge of human nature is the beginning and the end of political education." — Henry Adams

"An independent is a man who wants to take the politics out of politics." — Adlai Stevenson

"They know nothing, and think they know everything. That points clearly to a political career." — Shaw

"The ballot is stronger than the bullet." — Abraham Lincoln

"Bad officials are elected by good citizens who do not vote." — George Nathan

"The average man does not vote for anything, but against something." — William Munro

"It doesn't matter who votes, it matters who counts the vote." — Stalin

"The purification of politics is an iridescent dream." — John Ingalls

"Man is by nature a political animal." — Aristotle

"The basis of our political system is the right of the people to make and to alter their constitutions of government." — George Washington

"Always vote for a principle, though you vote alone, and you may cherish the sweet reflection that your vote is never lost." — John Quincy Adams

"There is no gambling like politics." — "The world is weary of the statesmen whom democracy has degraded into politicians." — Disraeli

"Political language . . . is designed to make lies sound truthful and murder respectable, and to give an appearance of solidity to pure wind." — George Orwell

"The proper memory for a politician is one that knows what to remember and what to forget." — "Those who would treat politics and morality apart will never understand the one or the other." — John Viscount Morley

"I think the political life must be an echo of private life and that there cannot be any divorce between the two." — "The best politics is right action." — Gandhi

Leadership

"That leader of the state gains most glory who first himself obeys the laws of his state." — Bias

"The man who would lift others must be uplifted himself, and he who would command others must learn to obey." — Charles K. Ober

"Those who can command themselves command others." — Hazlitt

"Those who have never learned to obey cannot be a good commander." — Aristotle

"For leadership and learning are indispensable to each other." — John F. Kennedy

"A leader is best when people barely know he exists." — Lao-tse

"The place should not honor the man, but the man the place." — Agesilaus II

"If the blind lead the blind, both shall fall into the ditch." — Bible, Matthew 15:14

"Every man who takes office in Washington either grows or swells." — Woodrow Wilson

"Any man can hold the helm when the sea is calm." — Publilius Syrus

"It is a fine thing to command, even if it only be a herd of cattle." — Cervantes

"And when we think we lead, we are most led." — Byron

"We are the warriors in the battle of Life, but some lead and others follow." — Kahlil Gibran

"For many are called, but few are chosen." — Bible, Matthew 22:14

"Honest statesmanship is the wise employment of individual meannesses for the public good." — Abraham Lincoln

"True statesmanship is the art of changing a nation from what it is into what it ought to be." — William Alger

"We want leaders to rule the nation who care more for and love better the nation's welfare than gold and silver, fame or popularity." — Brigham Young

"The history of the world is full of men who rose to leadership, by sheer force of self-confidence, bravery and tenacity." — Gandhi

"No man is great enough or wise enough for any of us to surrender our destiny to. The only way in which any one can lead us is to restore to us the belief in our own guidance." — Henry Miller

CIVILIZATION

"Civilization commenced when man first dug the earth and sowed seeds." — Kahlil Gibran

"Civilization is the process of reducing the infinite to the finite." — "Taxes are what we pay for civilized society." — Oliver Wendell Holmes

"Civilization is the process of setting men free from men." — Ayn Rand

"Civility costs nothing." — J. Stevens

"Civilized man has exchanged some part of his chances of happiness for a measure of security." — Sigmund Freud

"When tillage begins, other arts follow. The farmers therefore are the founders of human civilization." — Webster

"A decent provision for the poor is the true test of civilization." — Samuel Johnson

"The test of a civilization is in the way that it cares for its helpless members." — Pearl Buck

"Increased means and increased leisure are the two civilizers of man." — Disraeli

"All the citizens of a state cannot be equally powerful, but they may be equally free." — Voltaire

"Property is the pivot of civilization." — Leon Samson

"A great city is when the citizens obey the magistrates, and the magistrates obey the laws." — Solon

"A great city, a great loneliness." — Latin proverb

"The right to be let alone is the right most valued by civilized man." — Louis Brandeis

"I am a citizen, not of Athens or Greece, but of the world." — Socrates

"If a man be gracious and courteous to strangers, it shows he is a citizen of the world." — Sir Francis Bacon

"What is a city but the people?" Shakespeare

"It is the people who make a city." — Greek proverb

"The great fact to remember is that the trend of civilization itself is forever upward." — Franklin D. Roosevelt

"Civilization is not a spontaneous generation with any race or nation known to history, but the torch to be handed down from race to race from age to age." — Kelly Miller

"A great city is that which has the greatest men and women, if it be a few ragged huts, it is still the greatest city in the world." — Walt Whitman

"The true test of a civilization is, not the census, nor the size of cities, nor the crops — no, but the kind of man the country turns out." — "Cities give not the human senses room enough." — "The civilized man has built a coach, but has lost the use of his feet; he has a fine Geneva watch, but cannot tell the hour by the sun." — "As long as our civilization is essentially one of property, of fences, of exclusiveness, it will by mocked by delusions." — Emerson

"Order is the sanctity of the mind, the health of the body, the peace of the city, the security of the state." — Anonymous

"Architecture, sculpture, painting, music, and poetry, may truly be called the efflorescence of civilized life." — Herbert Spencer

"A general definition of civilization: a civilized society is exhibiting the five qualities of Truth, Beauty, Adventure, Art, Peace." — "Without adventure civilization is in full decay." — Alfred North Whitehead

"The measure of civilization is the degree in which the method of cooperative intelligence replaces the method of brute conflict." — John Dewey

"The true way for one civilization to 'conquer' another is for it to be so obviously superior in this or that point that others desire to imitate it." — Goldsworthy Dickinson

"The greatest task before civilization at present is to make machines what they ought to be, the slaves, instead of the masters, of man." — Havelock Ellis

"Civilization begins with order, grows with liberty and dies in chaos." — "A civilization is not destroyed by barbarian invasion from without; it is destroyed by barbarian multiplication within." — "Civilization is a stream with banks. The stream is sometimes filled with blood from people killing, stealing, shouting and doing the things historians usually record; while on the banks, unnoticed, people build homes, make love, raise children, sing songs, write poetry and even whittle statues. The story of civilization is what happened on the banks." — Will Durant

Society

"Society is no comfort to one not sociable." — Shakespeare

"Society is the offspring of leisure." — Henry Tuckerman

"Man was formed for society." — Sir William Blackstone

"Human society is like an arch, kept from falling by the mutual pressure of its parts." — Seneca

"The only worthwhile achievements of man are those which are socially useful." — Alfred Adler

"A society grows great when old men plant trees whose shade they know they shall never sit in." — Greek proverb

"We are more sociable, and get on better with men, by the heart than the intellect." — La Bruyère

"I must try to live in society and yet remain untouched by its pitfalls." — Gandhi

"Men would not live in society long if they were not each other's dupes." — La Rochefoucauld

"To be social is to be forgiving." — Robert Frost

"No man can exist in society without some specialty." — Hippolyte Taine

"I had three chairs in my house: one for solitude, two for friendship, three for society." — Thoreau

"It is a community of purpose that constitutes society." — Disraeli

"Man is an animal which can develop into an individual only in society." — Karl Marx

"Society is a masked ball, where every one hides his real character, and reveals it by hiding." — "Society is always taken by surprise at any new example of common sense." — Emerson

"Human society is founded on mutual deceit; few friendships would endure if each knew what his friend said of him in his absence." — Pascal

"Society has only one law, and that is custom. Even religion is socially powerful only so far as it has custom on its side." — Philip Hamerton

"Society is composed of two great classes: those who have more dinners than appetite, and those who have more appetite than dinners." — Sebastien Chamfort

"When the rich assemble to concern themselves with the business of the poor, it is called charity. When the poor assemble to concern themselves with the business of the rich, it is called anarchy." — Paul Richard

"The test of our progress is not whether we add more to the abundance of those who have much; it is whether we provide enough for those who have too little." — Franklin D. Roosevelt

"No social system will bring us happiness, health, and prosperity unless it is inspired by something greater than materialism." — Clement Atlee

"Among the purposes of a society should be to try to arrange for a continuous supply of work at all times and seasons." — Pope Leo XIII

"To get into the best society nowadays, one has either to feed people, amuse people, or shock people." — "I suppose society is wonderfully delightful. To be in it is merely a bore. But to be out of it is simply a tragedy." — Oscar Wilde

"Men do not enter into society to become worse than they were before, nor to have fewer rights than they had before, but to have those rights better secured." — Thomas Paine

Tradition

"Tradition is a guide and not a jailer." — Maugham

"Tradition does not mean that the living are dead but that the dead are alive." — Gilbert Chesterton

"No way of thinking or doing, however ancient, can be trusted without proof." — Thoreau

"They that reverence too much old times are but a scorn to the new." — Sir Francis Bacon

"You are trying to make that child another you; one is enough." — Emerson

"There is much novelty that is without hope, much antiquity without sacredness." — Thomas Lynch

"Every tradition grows ever more venerable — the more remote is its origin, the more confused that origin is." — Nietzsche

"Remove not the ancient landmark, which the fathers have set." — Bible, Proverbs 22:28

"Tradition is an important help to history, but its statements should be carefully scrutinized before we rely on them." — Joseph Addison

"In this age of great progress and rapid change, experience is not needed so much as is courage to break away from old methods." — Anonymous

Custom

"Custom is the universal sovereign." — John Wolcot

"Nothing is stronger than custom." — Ovid

"Custom reconciles us to everything." — Edmund Burke

"Custom is often only the antiquity of error." — Cyprian of Carthage

"Custom is the law of fools." — Sir John Vanbrugh

"Custom doth make dotards of us all." — Carlyle

"Custom may lead a man into many errors, but it justifies none." — Henry Fielding

"Customs may not be as wise as laws, but they are always more popular." — Disraeli

"National customs are national honors." — Danish proverb

"That which arises from custom is the unwritten law." — Diogenes

"When you enter a city, abide by its customs." — The Talmud

"When in Rome, do as the Romans do." — Old proverb

"Everything unusual frightens us; that is why we have our customs." — Anonymous

"A bad custom is like a good cake, better broken than kept." — "Bad customs are not binding." — Old Proverbs

"Old custom without truth is but old error." — Thomas Fuller

"Be not so bigoted to any custom as to worship it at the expense of truth." — Johann von Zimmermann

"We are all tattooed in our cradles with the beliefs of our tribe; the record may seem superficial, but it is indelible." — Oliver Wendell Holmes

"The laws of conscience, which we pretend to be derived from nature, proceed from custom." — "The way of the world is to make laws, but follow customs." — Montaigne

"Relinquish an evil custom even though it be of thy fathers, mothers and ancestors; Adopt a good custom even though it be established among thine enemies." — Far Eastern saying

Culture

"Culture is the arts elevated to a set of beliefs." — Thomas Wolfe

"No culture can live if it attempts to be exclusive." — Gandhi

"It is proof of high culture to say the greatest matters in the simplest way." — Emerson

"You don't have to burn books to destroy a culture. Just get people to stop reading them." — Ray Bradbury

"A culture is in its finest flower before it begins to analyze itself." — Alfred North Whitehead

"Whoever controls the media — the images — controls the culture." — Allen Ginsberg

"The great law of culture is: Let each become all that he is created capable of being." — Carlyle

"The highest possible stage in moral culture is when we recognize that we ought to control our thoughts." — Darwin

"That is true culture which helps us to work the social betterment of all." — Beecher

"Culture is acquainting ourselves with the best that has been known and said in the world, and thus with the history of the human spirit." — Matthew Arnold

"Noble life demands a noble architecture of noble uses of noble men. Lack of culture means what it has always meant: ignoble civilization and therefore imminent downfall." — Frank Lloyd Wright

Fashion

"Fashion is only the attempt to realize art in living forms and social intercourse." — Oliver Wendell Holmes

"Fashion is more powerful than any tyrant." — "Our last garment is made without pockets." — Latin proverbs

"Fashion is what one wears oneself. What is unfashionable is what other people wear." — Oscar Wilde

"Fashion is the science of appearances; and it inspires one with the desire to seem, rather than to be." — Edwin Chapin

"Fashion is, for the most part, nothing but the ostentation of riches." — Locke

"Fashion must be forever new, or she becomes insipid." — James Lowell

"Fine feathers make fine birds." — English proverb

"No man is esteemed by garments, but by fools." — Sir Walter Raleigh

"Tastes differ." — J. Birderne

"Nine tailors make the man." — N. Ward

"The clothes make the man." — Old proverb

"What is outside yourself does not convey much worth; Clothes do not make the man, the saddle not the horse." — Angelius Silesius

"Excess in apparel is another costly folly. The very trimming of the vain world would clothe all the naked ones." — William Penn

"Conformity is the jailer of freedom and the enemy of growth." — John F. Kennedy

"Every generation laughs at the old fashions, but follows religiously the new." — Thoreau

"Tailors and writers must mind the fashion." — English proverb

"As to matters of dress, I would recommend a man never to be first in the fashion nor the last out of it." — John Wesley

"As good be out of the world as out of the fashion." — Colley Cibber

"An emperor in his night-cap would not meet with half the respect of an emperor with a crown." — Oliver Goldsmith

"Had Cicero himself pronounced one of his orations with a blanket about his shoulders, more people would have laughed at his dress than admired his eloquence." — Joseph Addison

History

"History is a pact between the dead, the living, and the yet unborn." — Edmund Burke

"History hath triumphed over time, which besides it nothing but eternity hath triumphed over." — Sir Walter Raleigh

"History repeats itself." — Old proverb

"History does not repeat itself except in the minds of those who do not know history." — Kahlil Gibran

"History never embraces more than a small part of reality." — Paul Sabatier

"History makes us some amends for the shortness of life." — Philip Skelton

"History is merely a list of surprises. . . It can only prepare us to be surprised yet again." — Kurt Vonnegut, Jr.

"History calls those the greatest . . . who ennobled themselves by working for the universal." — Karl Marx

"The best thing which we derive from history is the enthusiasm that it raises in us." — Goethe

"What is history but a fable agreed upon?" Napoleon

"We read history through our prejudices." — Wendell Phillips

"So very difficult a matter is it to trace and find out the truth of anything by history." — Plutarch

"In analyzing history, do not be too profound, for often the causes are quite superficial." — Emerson

"The historian must have some conception of how people who are not historians behave." — Edward Forster

"A wise man does not try to hurry history." — Adlai Stevenson

"The chief office of history [is] to rescue virtuous actions from the oblivion to which a want of records would consign them." — Tacitus

"The history of the world is but the biography of great men." — Carlyle

"Who has fully realized that history is not contained in thick books but lives in our very blood?" Carl Jung

"There is a history in all men's lives." — Shakespeare

"History is . . . the witness of times, the torch of truth, the life of memory, the teacher of life, the messenger of antiquity." — "Not to know what has been transacted in former times is to be always a child. If no use is made of the labors of past ages, the world must remain always in the infancy of knowledge." — Cicero

"History presents the pleasantest features of poetry and fiction — the majesty of the epic, the moving accidents of the drama, and the surprises and moral of the romance." — Robert Willmott

"Histories make men wise; poets, witty; the mathematics, subtle; natural philosophy, deep; moral, grave; logic and rhetoric, able to contend." — Sir Francis Bacon

"Human history in essence is the history of ideas." — "Human history becomes more and more a race between education and catastrophe." — H. G. Wells

"Many historians take pleasure in putting into the mouths of kings what they have neither said nor ought to have said." — Voltaire

"Ideas are, in truth, forces. Infinite, too, is the power of personality. A union of the two always makes history." — Henry James, Jr.

"The impartiality of history is not that of the mirror, which merely reflects objects but of the judge who sees, listens, and decides." — Alphonse de Lamartine

"The history of mankind is one of continuous development from the realm of necessity to the realm of freedom. This process is never-ending." — Mao Tse-tung

"The so-called lessons of history are for the most part the rationalization of the victors. History is written by the survivors." — Max Lerner

"The years by themselves do not make a place historic. It is people who give the color of history to a place by their deeds there or by merely having lived there." — Simeon Strunsky

Nations

"National honor is national property of the highest value." — James Monroe

"National injustice is the surest road to national downfall." — William Gladstone

"Nationalism is an infantile disease. It is the measles of mankind." — Einstein

"Men and nations behave wisely once they have exhausted all the other alternatives." — Abba Eban

"Peace, commerce, and honest friendship with all nations, — entangling alliances with none." — Thomas Jefferson

"Freeing oppressed nationalities is perhaps the most dangerous of all philanthropic enterprises." — William Bolitho

"A nation is a work of art and a work of time." — Disraeli

"Nations are born out of travail and suffering." — "People are the roots, the state is the fruit. If the roots are sweet, the fruits are bound to be sweet." — Gandhi

"No nation can be destroyed while it possesses a good home life." — Josiah Holland

"The sense of greatness keeps a nation great." — Sir William Watson

"Size is not grandeur, and territory does not make a nation." — Thomas Henry Huxley

"Territory is but the body of a nation. The people who inhabit its hills and valleys are its soul, its spirit, its life." — James Garfield

"The most advanced nations are always those who navigate the most." — Emerson

"By gnawing through a dike, even a rat may drown a nation." — Edmund Burke

"Wealth is the canker that destroys nations." — Anonymous

"The health of nations is more important than the wealth of nations." — Will Durant

"Righteousness exalteth a nation." — Bible, Proverbs 14:34

"The empires of the future are the empires of the mind." — Churchill

"Our true nationality is mankind." — "The crazy combative patriotism that plainly threatens to destroy civilization is very largely begotten by the schoolmaster in his history lessons." — H. G. Wells

"If a nation values anything more than freedom, it will lose its freedom; and the irony of it is that if it is comfort or money that it values more, it will lose that too." — Maugham

"Human kindness has never weakened the stamina or softened the fiber of a free people. A nation does not have to be cruel in order to be tough." — Franklin D. Roosevelt

Country

"Ask not what your country can do for you, but what you can do for your country." — John F. Kennedy

"I do love my country's good with a respect more tender, more holy, more profound, than mine own life." — Shakespeare

"I only regret that I have but one life to lose for my country." — Nathan Hale

"Happy is the country which has no history." — Benjamin Franklin

"You'll never have a quiet world till you knock the patriotism out of the human race." — Shaw

"Our country, right or wrong. When right, to be kept right; when wrong, to be put right." — Carl Schurz

PEOPLE

"People are in general so tricky, so envious, and cruel, that when we find one who is only weak, we are happy." — Voltaire

"People who know little are usually great talkers, while people who know much say little." — Rousseau

"At the bottom of things, most people want to be understood and appreciated." — Buddha

"Never seem wiser, nor more well learned than the people you are with." — Chesterfield

"There are three kinds of people: Those who see, those who see when shown, and those who don't see." — Leonardo da Vinci

"There are too many people, and too few human beings." — Robert Zend

"How great in number are the little-minded people." — Plautus

"It is with rivers as it is with people: the greatest are not always the most agreeable nor the best to live with." — Henry van Dyke

"There is nothing so queer as folk." — Old proverb

"Nobody realizes that some people expend tremendous energy merely to be normal." — Camus

"The real difference between people is not sanity and insanity, but more or less insanity." — Anonymous

"To confront a person with his own shadow is to show him his own light." — Carl Jung

"The public seldom forgives twice." — Johann Kaspar Lavater

"The public must and will be served." — William Penn

"A man ain't got no right to be a public man, unless he meets the public views." — Dickens

"Be humble, be big in mind and soul, be kindly; you will like yourself that way and so will other people." — Norman Vincent Peale

"I don't believe that the public knows what it wants; this is the conclusion that I have drawn from my career." — Charlie Chaplin

"The people are to be taken in small doses." — "The instinct of the people is right." — Emerson

"What the people believe, is true." — Anishinabe Indian proverb

"From people who merely pray we must become people who bless." — Nietzsche

"Half of the secret of getting along with people is consideration of their views; the other half is tolerance in one's own views." — Daniel Frohman

"When dealing with people, remember you are not dealing with creatures of logic, but also with creatures of emotion, creatures bristling with prejudice and motivated by pride and vanity." — Dale Carnegie

"Good people shine from afar like the snowy mountains; bad people are not seen, like arrows shot at night." — Far Eastern sayings

"It is absurd to divide people into good or bad. People are either charming or tedious." — "Most people are other people. Their thoughts are someone else's opinions, their lives a mimicry, their passions a quotation." — Oscar Wilde

"A thankful person is thankful under all circumstances. A complaining soul complains even if he lives in paradise." — Baha'u'llah

"There are three kinds of people in the world; the wills, the won'ts, and the can'ts. The first accomplish everything; the second oppose everything; the third fail in everything." — Anonymous

"People are like stained-glass windows. They sparkle and shine when the sun is out, but when the darkness sets in, their true beauty is revealed only if there is a light from within." — Elisabeth Kubler-Ross

"The majority of people are subjective toward themselves and objective toward all others, terribly objective sometimes; but the real task is, in fact, to be objective toward oneself and subjective toward all others." — Kierkegaard

Humanity

"Humanity is just a work in progress." — Tennessee Williams

"Human nature will not change." — Abraham Lincoln

"Human hopes and human creeds have their root in human needs." — Eugene Ware

"It is best to do things systematically, since we are only human, and disorder is our worst enemy." — Hesiod

"The universal human yearning is for something permanent, enduring, without shadow of change." — Willa Cather

"We are spiritual beings having human experiences." — Anonymous

"For to err in opinion, though it be not the part of wise men, is at least human." — Plutarch

"To err is human." — Sophocles

"I've been mixing with humanity today and feel the less humane, in consequence." — Seneca

"There is no indispensable human." — Franklin D. Roosevelt

"Whoso would be a human must be a non-conformist." — Emerson

"All that is human must retrograde if it does not advance." — Edward Gibbon

"A man must either take interest in the human situation or else parade before the void." — Jean Rostand

"I am a human, and whatever concerns humanity is of interest to me." — Terence

"I know of no great souls except those who have rendered great services to the human race." — Voltaire

"After all there is but one race — Humanity." — George Moore

"All humanity is one undivided and indivisible family, and each one of us is responsible for the misdeeds of all the others." — Gandhi

"We must resemble each other a little in order to understand each other, but we must be a little different to love each other." — Paul Geraldy

"Adam and Eve were but human — this explains it all. They did not want the apple for the apple's sake, they wanted it only because it was forbidden." — Mark Twain

"Human nature is often hidden, sometimes overcome, seldom extinguished." — "Our humanity were a poor thing but for the divinity that stirs within us." — Sir Francis Bacon

Crowds

"Cannot the heart in the midst of crowds feel frightfully alone?" Charles Lamb

"A crowd is not company, and faces are but a gallery of pictures." — Sir Francis Bacon

"I live in the crowd of jollity, not so much to enjoy company as to shun myself." — Samuel Johnson

"A crowd always thinks with its sympathy, never with its reason." — William Alger

"Where everyone goes, the grass never grows." — Irish proverb

"All strangers are relations to each other." — Arabian proverb

"If you stop supporting that crowd, it will support itself." — Seneca

"Two is company, but three's a crowd." — J. Stevens

"Who builds on the mob builds on sand." — Italian proverb

"I am the people — the mob — the crowd — the mass. Do you know that all the great work of the world is done through me?" Carl Sandburg

Mankind

"Man is a social animal." — Seneca

"Man is the cruelest animal." — Nietzsche

"Man is a reasoning animal." — Spinoza

"Man is a reasoning rather than a reasonable animal." — Alexander Hamilton

"Man is a pliable animal, a being who gets accustomed to everything!" Fyodor Dostoyevsky

"Man is a gaming animal. We must be always trying to get the better in something or other." — Charles Lamb

"Man is the most intelligent of the animals — and the most silly." — Diogenes

"Man is the merriest specie of the creation; all above or below us are serious." — Addison

"Man: half dust, half deity, alike unfit to sink or soar." — Byron

"Man plans, God laughs." — Hebrew proverb

"If nature does not have to insist, why should man?" Lao-tse

"Wonders are many, and none is more wonderful than man." — Sophocles

"To me one man is worth ten thousand if he is first-rate." — Heraclitus

"Wit and wisdom are born with a man." — John Selden

"An old young man will become a young old man." — Benjamin Franklin

"In making mankind, the universe presented itself at one stroke with a victim and a judge." — Jean Rostand

"Each man ought to be his own model, however frightful that may be." — Einstein

"A man is infinitely more complicated than his thoughts." — Paul Valéry

"A man is always better than a book." — Charles Townsend Copeland

"It is quite absurd to say that a man is good or bad — he is good and bad." — "We deem those men remarkable who think as we do." — Elbert Hubbard

"My idea of an agreeable man is a man who agrees with me." — Hugo Bohun

"The ablest man I ever met is the man you think you are." — Franklin D. Roosevelt

"A man is not a man, but a wolf to those he does not know." — French proverb

"No man is an island, entire of himself; every man is a piece of the continent." — John Donne

"I never met a man I didn't like." — Will Rogers

"No sadder proof can be given by a man of his own littleness than disbelief in great men." — Carlyle

"Every man has a sane spot somewhere." — Robert Louis Stevenson

"A man hath no better thing under the sun, than to eat, and to drink, and to be merry." — Bible, Ecclesiastes 8:15

"Mankind is earthen jugs with spirits in them." — "When man is a brute, he is the most sensual and loathsome of all brutes." — Nathaniel Hawthorne

"Man is the only animal that eats when he is not hungry, drinks when he is not thirsty, and makes love at all seasons." — Anonymous

"A Man is free the moment he wishes to be." — "The instinct of man is to pursue everything that flies from him, and to fly from all that pursue him." — Voltaire

"Men are their own stars." — John Fletcher

"Men are like wines, age souring the bad, and bettering the good." — Cicero

"Man is like palm-wine: when young, sweet but without strength; in old age, strong but harsh." — Congolese proverb

"Men will lie on their backs, talking about the fall of man, and never make an effort to get up." — Thoreau

"Men must make ever new relationships until finally they achieve universal humanity." — Joseph Hart

"Men, in general, are but great children." — "A true man hates no one." — Napoleon

"Associate with men of good judgment." — Thomas Fuller

"Most men judge others only by their success or their good fortune." — La Rochefoucauld

"Bad men live that they may eat and drink, whereas good men eat and drink that they may live." — Socrates

"As many men, so many minds; every one his own way." — Terence

"It is not titles that reflect honor on men, but men on their titles." — Machiavelli

"Men are not flattered by being shown that there has been a difference of purpose between the Almighty and them." — Abraham Lincoln

"I believe that our Heavenly Father invented mankind because he was disappointed in the monkey." — Mark Twain

"There are but three classes of men, the retrograde, the stationary, and the progressive." — Johann Kaspar Lavater

"Whenever two men meet there are really six men present. There is each man as he sees himself, each man as the other sees him, and each man as he really is." — William James

"Let a man overcome anger by love, evil by good, greediness by liberality, lies by truth." — "The best possession of a man of clay is health; the highest virtue of a man of spirit is truthfulness." — Far Eastern Sayings

"The highest happiness of man . . . is to have probed what is knowable and quietly to revere what is unknowable." — "Treat men as if they were what they ought to be and you help them to become what they are capable of being." — Goethe

"At his best, man is the noblest of all the animals; separated from law and justice he is the worst." — "Wicked men obey from fear; good men, from love." — "Of man in general, the parts are greater than the whole." — Aristotle

"Mankind — beings in search of meaning." — "There are three classes of men — lovers of wisdom, lovers of honor, lovers of gain." — "All men are by nature equal, made all of the same earth by the same Creator, and however we deceive ourselves, as dear to God is the poor peasant as the mighty prince." — Plato

"What a piece of work man is! How noble in reason! How infinite in faculty! In form and moving how express and admirable! In action how like an angel! In apprehension how like a god! The beauty of the world, the paragon of animals!" "Men should be what they seem." — Shakespeare

"Each man is a hero and an oracle to somebody." — "A man is a bundle of relations, a knot of roots, whose flower and fruitage is the world." — "If a man owns land, the land owns him." — "Man is a piece of the universe made alive." — "Men cease to interest us when we find their limitations." — Emerson

"When a man assumes a public trust, he should consider himself as public property." — "We hold these truths to be self-evident, that all men are created equal, that they are endowed by their creator with certain unalienable Rights, that among these are Life, Liberty and the pursuit of Happiness." — Thomas Jefferson

"All mankind is divided into three classes: those that are immovable, those that are movable, and those that move." — "There are four types of men. One who knows not and knows not that he knows not: he is a fool — shun him. One who knows not and knows he knows not: he is simple — teach him. One who knows and knows not he knows: he is asleep — wake him And one who knows and knows he knows: he is wise — follow him." — Arabian proverbs

Men

"It is far easier to know men than to know man." — La Rochefoucauld

"Men are but children, too, though they have gray hairs; they are only of a larger size." — Seneca

"Men do not think of sons, when they fall in love." — Elizabeth Barrett Browning

"The test of a man is how well he is able to feel about what he thinks." — Mary Mcdowell

"Not only is it harder to be a man, it is also harder to become one." — Arianna Stassinopoulos

"A man's best possession is a sympathetic wife." — Euripides

"A good wife and health are a man's best wealth." — Apocrypha, Ecclesiasticus

"Women and God are the two rocks on which a man must either anchor or be wrecked." — Fredrick Robertson

"Women and cats will do as they please. Men and dogs had better get used to it." — Robert Heinlein

"When a man's dog turns against him, it is time for a wife to pack her trunk and go home to mama." — Mark Twain

"'Tis strange what a man may do and a woman yet think him an angel." — Thackeray

"If men were as unselfish as women, women would very soon become more selfish than men." — John Collins

"There are two things a man will not admit he cannot do well: drive, and make love." — Stirling Moss

"A bachelor is a man who comes to work each morning from a different direction." — Sholom Aleichem

"I like a man who grins when he fights." — Churchill

"Boys will be boys." — Old proverb

"Boys will be boys, and so will a lot of middle-aged men." — Kin Hubbard

"A diplomat is a man who always remembers a woman's birthday but never remembers her age." — "A mother takes twenty years to make a man of her boy, and another woman makes a fool of him in twenty minutes." — Robert Frost

"Let men tremble to win the hand of woman, unless they win along with it the utmost passion of her heart." — Nathaniel Hawthorne

"If you have any doubts that we live in a society controlled by men, try reading down the index of contributors to a volume of quotations, looking for women's names." — Elaine Gill

"Too often the great decisions are originated and given form in bodies made up wholly of men, or so completely dominated by them that whatever of special value women have to offer is shunted aside without expression." — Eleanor Roosevelt

"A man who has no office to go to — I don't care who he is — is a trial of which you can have no conception." — Shaw

"Though I've belted you and flayed you, by the livin' Gawd that made you, You're a better man than I am, Gunga Din!" Kipling

"His life was gentle, and the elements so mixed in him that Nature might stand up and say to all the world, this was a man!" Shakespeare

Women

"Women are the poetry of the world." — Hargrave

"Women are poets, by just being women." — Jose Martí

"Women prefer poverty with love to luxury without it." — The Talmud

"Woman prefers a man without money to money without a man." — Greek proverb

"Women are apt to see chiefly the defects of a man of talent and the merits of a fool." — Anonymous

"Women sometimes forgive those who force an opportunity, never those who miss it." — Talleyrand

"Women like not only to conquer, but to be conquered." — Thackeray

"Faint hearts never win fair ladies." — Danish proverb

"Women made us lose paradise, but how frequently we find it again in their arms." — De Finod

"Women — if you are friendly with them, they get out of hand. And if you keep them at a distance, they resent it." — Confucius

"I know the disposition of women; when you will, they won't; when you won't, they set their hearts upon you of their own inclination." — Terence

"Women! Can't live with them, can't live without them." — Old proverb

"Womankind is ever a fickle and changeful thing." — Virgil

"A woman's heart, like the moon, is always changing." — Punch

"Many woman long for what eludes them, and like not what is offered them." — Ovid

"That's the nature of woman, not to love when we love them, and to love when we love them not." — Cervantes

"A sufficient and sure method of civilization is the influence of good women." — Emerson

"Whatever may be the customs and laws of a country, the women of it decide the morals." — Martin

"The society of women is the element of good manners." — Goethe

"Sensibility is the power of woman." — Johann Kaspar Lavater

"Who can find a virtuous woman? For her price is far above rubies." — Bible, Proverbs 31:10

"A handsome woman is a jewel; a good woman is a treasure." — Sa'di

"What is better than gold? Jasper. What is better than Jasper? Wisdom. What is better than Wisdom? Woman. What is better than a good woman? Nothing." — Chaucer

"Dost thou nothing know of this, to be awed at woman's beauty?" Martin Tupper

"To feel, to love, to suffer, to devote herself will always be the text of the life of a woman." — Balzac

"Love's all in all to woman." — "Bearing a child is worse than fighting three battles." — Euripides

"For every woman who makes a fool out of a man there is another woman who makes a man out of a fool." — Samuel Hoffam

"The silliest woman can manage a clever man; but there needs a very clever woman to manage a fool!" Kipling

"Disguise our bondage as we will, 'tis woman, woman, rules us still." — Thomas Moore

"Ye must know that women have dominion over you: do ye not labor and toil, and give and bring all to the woman?" Apocrypha, I Esdras 4:22

"Courtesy wins woman all as well as valor may." — Tennyson

"With women worth being won, the softest lover ever best succeeds." — Aaron Hill

"The test of a woman is how well she is able to think about what she feels." — Mary Mcdowell

"If women are expected to do the same work as men, we must teach them the same things." — Plato

"To call a woman a member of the weaker sex is a libel." — Gandhi

"What will not woman, gentle woman dare, when strong affection stirs her spirit up?" Robert Southey

"Man may work from sun to sun, woman's work is never done." — Old proverb

"No one knows like a woman how to say things which are at once gentle and deep." — Victor Hugo

"Women: the fairer sex." — "There is no jewel in the world so valuable as a chaste and virtuous woman." —

"Women is woman's natural ally." — "Woman brings to man his greatest blessing and his greatest plague." — "There is no worse evil than a bad woman; and nothing has ever been created better than a good one." — Euripides

"Woman learns how to hate in proportion as she forgets how to charm." — "In revenge and in love woman is more barbarous than man." — Nietzsche

"Woman reduces us all to a common denominator." — "Women upset everything. When you let them into your life, you find that the woman is driving at one thing and you're driving at another." — Shaw

"Many of our girls feel that their bodily perfection exempts them from the necessity of developing their inner energies." — James Flagg

"In all societies women have played a much more important role than their menfolk are generally ready to admit." — Ashley Montagu

"All talk of women's rights is moonshine. Women have every right. They have only to exercise them." — Victoria Claffin Woodhull

"The reason firm, the temperate will, endurance, foresight, strength, and skill; A perfect woman, nobly planned, to warn, to comfort, and command." — Wordsworth

"Men always want to be a woman's first love. That is their clumsy vanity. Women have a more subtle instinct about things. What they like is to be a man's last romance." — Oscar Wilde

"A woman's advice is no great thing, but those who will not take it are fools." — "One hair of a woman draws more than a team of oxen." — English proverbs

"A women either loves or hates. There is no intermediate course with her." — "Venus yields to caresses, not to compulsion." — Publilius Syrus

"Kindness in women, not their beauteous looks, shall win my love." — "She's beautiful and therefore to be wooed. She is woman, therefore to be won." — "Let not women's weapons, waterdrops, stain my cheeks." — "A women's age cannot wither her, nor custom stale her infinite variety." — Shakespeare

"Who does not realize that without women we can get no pleasure or satisfaction out of life, which but for them we would lack charm and be more uncouth and savage than that of wild beasts? Only women rid our hearts of all vile and base thoughts, anxieties, and miseries. Far from distracting us, they awaken our minds and hearts." — Castiglione

FAMILY

"The family is the first essential cell of human society." — Pope John XXIII

"The family is the association established by nature for the supply of a man's everyday wants." — Aristotle

"The family is the miniature commonwealth upon whose integrity the safety of the larger commonwealth depends." — Felix Adler

"In a man's family, respect and listening are the source of harmony." — Buddha

"A man's pleasures are in the happiness of a man's family." — Rousseau

"A happy family is but an earlier heaven." — Sir John Bowring

"Where can a man better be than with his family?" Jean Marmontel

"I don't know who my grandfather was; I am much more concerned to know what his grandson will be." — Abraham Lincoln

"It takes three generations to make a gentleman." — J. Kepers

"Every family has a skeleton in the closet." — "There's a black sheep in every flock." — Old proverbs

"Like all the best families, we have our share of eccentricities, of impetuous and wayward youngsters and of family disagreements." — Elizabeth II

"Blood is thicker than water." — German proverb

"An ounce of blood is worth more than a pound of friendship." — Spanish proverb

"The knife of the family does not cut." — "None but a mule denies his family." — Arabian proverbs

"Walnuts and pears you plant for your heirs." — Cicero

"My son is my son till he gets him a wife; but my daughter's my daughter all the days of her life." — English proverb

"A good man leaveth an inheritance to his children's children." — Bible, Proverbs

"Men who provide much wealth for their children but neglect to improve them in virtue, do like those who feed their horses high, but never train them to be useful." — Socrates

"The heart of the family is the mother, because life comes from her." — Native American proverb

"As the family goes, so goes the nation and so goes the whole world in which we live." — John Paul II

"With all beings and all things, we shall be as relatives." — Sioux Indian proverb

"It is easy to govern a kingdom but difficult to rule one's family." — "Govern a family as you would cook a small fish — very gently." — Chinese proverbs

"Live with all — with wife or husband and children, father and mother — and serve them. Treat them as if they are very dear to you, but know in your heart of hearts that they do not belong to you." — Sri Ramakrishna

"Look for the good, not the evil, in the conduct of members of the family." — "One of life's greatest mysteries is how the boy who wasn't good enough to marry your daughter can be the father of the smartest grandchild in the world." — Jewish proverbs

"A man that raises a large family does, indeed, while he lives to observe them, stand a broader mark for sorrow; but then, he stands a broader mark for pleasure too." — Benjamin Franklin

"Call it a clan, call it a network, call it a tribe, call it a family. Whatever you call it, whoever you are, you need one." — Jane Howard

Ancestors

"Crown thy ancestors." — Sophist saying

"To forget a one's ancestors is to be a brook without a source, a tree without a root." — Chinese proverb

"Because they had no root, they withered away." — Bible, Matthew 13:6

"Hereditary honors are a noble and splendid treasure to descendants." — Plato

"Every man is a quotation from all his ancestors." — Emerson

"Men will not look forward to posterity who never look backward to their ancestors." — Edmund Burke

"Some men by ancestry are only the shadow of a mighty name." — Lucan

"It is indeed a desirable thing to be well-descended, but the glory belongs to our ancestors." — Plutarch

"The generations of living things pass in a short time, and like runners hand on the torch of life." — Lucretius

Home

"Home is where the heart is." — J. J. McCloskey

"Home is home, be it never so homely." — "Go abroad and you'll hear news of home." — English proverbs

"Home is the place where, when you have to go there, they have to take you in." — Robert Frost

"Home, the spot of earth supremely blest, a dearer, sweeter spot than all the rest." — Robert Montgomery

"Be it ever so humble, there's no place like home." — Payne

"There is no place more delightful than home." — Cicero

"Love begins at home." — Mother Teresa

"In love of home, the love of country has its rise." — Dickens

"The ruin of a nation begins in the homes of its people." — Ashanti proverb

"The strength of a nation is derived from the integrity of its homes." — Confucius

"Only the home can found a state." — Joseph Cook

"If a house be divided against itself, that house cannot stand." — Bible, Mark 3:25

"Set thine house in order." — Bible, Isaiah 38:1

"They are the happiest, be they king, queen or peasant, who finds peace in their home." — Goethe

"My whinstone house my castle is; I have my own four walls." — Carlyle

"In mine own house I am an emperor and will defend what's mine." — Philip Massinger

"A dog is a lion in his own house." — Persian proverb

"'Tis at sixty a man learns how to value home." — Bulwer-Lytton

"The place to spend a happy day — Home." — "East or West, home is best." — Old proverbs

"In a broken nest there are few whole eggs." — Chinese proverb

"Eighty per cent of our criminals come from unsympathetic homes." — Hans Christian Andersen

"Without hearts there is no home." — Byron

"Strength of character may be learned at work, but beauty of character is learned at home." — Henry Drummond

"Where we love is home. Home that our feet may leave, but not our hearts." — Oliver Wendell Holmes

"There's a magical tie to the land of our home, which the heart cannot break, though the footsteps may roam." — Joseph Conrad

"No man can safely go abroad who does not love to stay at home." — Thomas à Kempis

"'Tis ever common that men are merriest when they are from home." — Shakespeare

"Our home life as we understand it is no more natural to us than a cage is natural to a cockatoo." — Shaw

"They have no home whose home is everywhere." — Martial

"A man travels the world over in search of what he needs and returns home to find it." — George Moore

"There's nothing half so pleasant as coming home again." — Margaret Elizabeth Sangster

"You never really leave the place you love." — Anonymous

"The domestic hearth. There only is real happiness." — Anatole France

"Home's not merely four square walls, though with pictures hung and gilded; Home is where Affection calls, — Filled with shrines the Heart hath builded." — Charles Swain

"Every house where love abides and friendship is a guest, is surely home, and home, sweet home; for there the heart can rest." — Henry van Dyke

"This is the true nature of home — it is the place of Peace; the shelter, not only from all injury, but from all terror, doubt, and division." — Ruskin

"It came to me that reform should begin at home, and since that day I have not had time to remake the world." — Will Durant

Marriage

"Marriage is our last, best chance to grow up." — Joseph Barth

"Marriage is the greatest educational institution on earth." — Channing Pollock

"Marriage is an institution the appreciation of which increases as a man grows older." — Sir Thomas Beecham

"Marriage is like life in this — that it is a battle, and not a bed of roses." — Robert Louis Stevenson

"Marriage has many thorns, but celibacy no roses." — Anonymous

"Marriage is the strictest tie of perpetual friendship." — Samuel Johnson

"Marriage is heaven and hell." — "One marriage is never celebrated but another grows out of it." — German proverbs

"Marriages are made in Heaven." — W. Painter

"Marriages are made in Heaven, but worked out on earth." — Tennyson

"Marriages are best made of dissimilar material." — Theodore Parker

"Marry with your equal, for by matching into a higher family, you procure masters, not kinsfolk." — Cleobulus

"Seek a wife in your own sphere." — Latin proverb

"In marriage, when there are equal partners, I fear not." — Aeschylus

"A happy marriage is the union of two good forgivers." — Robert Quillen

"There is no more lovely, friendly and charming relationship, communion or company than a good marriage." — Martin Lurther

"There is more of good nature than of good sense at the bottom of most marriages." — Thoreau

"Love is an ideal thing; marriage is a real thing. A confusion of the real with the ideal never goes unpunished." — Goethe

"Men dream in courtship, but in wedlock wake." — Alexander Pope

"Don't be in a hurry to tie what you can't untie." — Old proverb

"Thus grief still treads upon the heels of pleasure; Married in haste, we may repent at leisure." — William Congreve

"If they cannot contain their lust, let them marry: for it is better to marry than to burn from desire." — Bible, I Corinthians 7:9

"Humble wedlock is far better than proud virginity." — Augustine of Hippo

"When Socrates was asked whether it was better to marry or not, he replied, 'Whichever you do, you will repent it.'" Diogenes

"'Tis safest in matrimony to begin with a little aversion." — Richard Brinsley Sheriden

"There is no living with thee, nor without thee." — Martial

"A good many things are easier said than done — including the marriage ritual." — Anonymous

"In marriage it is all very well to say that 'the two are made one' — the question is, which one?" Anonymous

"Handsome women generally fall to the lot of ugly men." — Old proverb

"Choose neither a spouse nor linen by candlelight." — Italian proverb

"Talk six times with the same single lady and you may get the wedding-dress ready." — Byron

"One wedding brings another." — M. Parker

"Never marry for money, ye'll borrow it cheaper." — Scottish proverb

"There are no premature babies, only delayed weddings." — American proverb

"There goes more to marriage than four bare legs in bed." — J. Heywood

"It is not every couple that makes a pair." — Old proverb

"The wife is always the last to know." — Marston

"The road to success is filled with wives pushing their husbands along." — Thomas Dewar

"A man's character is but half formed till after wedlock." — Charles Simmons

"Take a vine of good soil, and a daughter of a good mother." — Old proverb

"Whoso findeth a wife findeth a good thing." — Bible, Proverbs 18:22

"Of all the home remedies, a good wife is the best." — Frank Hubbard

"A man who has a good wife can bear any evil." — Old proverb

"Of earthly goods, the best is a good wife; A bad, the bitterest curse of human life." — Simonides

"A man who has a bad wife, his hell begins on earth." — Old proverb

"A man who does not honor his wife dishonors himself." — Spanish proverb

"A man should believe in marriage as in the immortality of the soul." — Balzac

"Domestic happiness, thou only bliss of Paradise that has survived the fall!" William Cowper

"Men marry to make an end; women to make a beginning." — Alexis Dupuy

"A happy marriage is a new beginning of life, a new starting point for happiness and usefulness." — Arthur Stanley

"There is no disparity in marriage like unsuitability of mind and purpose." — Dickens

"Never marry but for love; but see that thou lovest what is lovely." — William Penn

"A man should marry no other woman but the one whom he loves." — Kamasutra

"The wedding should last through wedded life." — Old proverb

"Love is often a fruit of marriage." — Molière

"The ideal is to look upon marriage as a sacrament and therefore to lead a life of self-restraint in the married state." — Gandhi

"An ideal wife is any woman who has an ideal husband." — Booth Tarkington

"The happiness of married life depends upon making small sacrifices with readiness and cheerfulness." — John Selden

"What therefore God hath joined together, let no man put asunder." — Bible, Matthew 19:6

"If you would have the nuptial union last, let virtue be the bond that ties it fast." — Nicholas Rowe

"It is not lack of love but lack of friendship that makes unhappy marriages." — Nietzsche

"Marriage! Nothing else demands so much from someone!" "Marriage is something you have to give your whole heart and mind to." — Henrik Ibsen

"Marriage is that relation between a man and woman in which the independence is equal, the dependence mutual, and the obligation reciprocal." — Louis Anspacher

"Marriage is a lottery." — "The clever wife makes her husband an apron." — "There is no perfect marriage, for there are no perfect men." — French proverbs

"Marriage resembles a pair of shears, so joined that they can not be separated; often moving in opposite directions, yet always punishing anyone who comes between them." — Sydney Smith

"Marriage has a biological basis, and would be far more often a success if its biology were generally understood and the knowledge acted upon." — John Haldane

"Marry, and with luck it may go well. But when marriage fails, then those who marry lie at home in hell." — "It's not beauty but fine qualities, my girl, that keeps a husband." — Euripides

"Marry for money, my little honey, a rich man's joke is always funny." — "They who marry for money earn it." — Hebrew proverbs

"They who marry for wealth sell their liberty." — "A good Jill makes a good Jack." — "Every Jack must have his Jill." — "He that would thrive must first ask his wife." — English proverbs

"A man who marries a woman to educate her falls victim to the same fallacy as the woman who marries a man to reform him." — Elbert Hubbard

"Hasty marriage seldom proveth well." — "For what is wedlock forced, but a hell, an age of discord and continual strife? Whereas the contrary bringeth bliss, and is a pattern of celestial peace." — "Who wooed in haste and means to wed at leisure?" Shakespeare

"Is not marriage an open question, when it is alleged, from the beginning of the world, that such as are in the institution wish to get out, and such as are out wish to get in?" Emerson

"From my experience, not one in twenty marries the first love; we build statues of snow, and weep to see them melt." — Sir Walter Scott

"Seldom, or perhaps never, does a marriage develop into an individual relationship smoothly and without crises." — Carl Jung

"Remember, that if thou marry for beauty, thou bindest thyself all thy life for that which perchance will neither last nor please thee one year; and when thou hast it, it will be to thee of no price at all; for the desire dieth when it is attained, and the affection perisheth when it is satisfied." — Sir Walter Raleigh

"It is a woman's business to get married as soon as possible, and a man's to keep unmarried as long as he can." — Shaw

"Keep your eyes wide open before marriage, half shut afterward." — "You can bear your own faults, why not the faults in your wife?" Benjamin Franklin

"By all means marry. If you get a good wife you will become happy — and if you get a bad one you will become a philosopher." — Socrates

"When a woman marries again it is because she detested her first husband. When a man marries again, it is because he adored his first wife. Women try their luck; men risk theirs." — Oscar Wilde

"If you the sea held, I would follow you, my wife, until me also the sea held." — "If you would marry suitably, marry your equal." — Ovid

"With fifty years between you and your well-kept wedding vow, the Golden Age, old friends of mine, is not a fable now." — John Greenleaf Whittier

"When people marry because they think it's a long-time love affair, they'll be divorced very soon, because all love affairs end in disappointment. But marriage is a recognition of a spiritual identity." — Joseph Campbell

"There is nothing nobler or more admirable than when two people who see eye to eye keep house as man and wife, thus confounding their enemies and delighting their friends." — Homer

"A happy marriage has in it all the pleasures of friendship, all the enjoyments of sense and reason, and, indeed, all the sweets of life." — Joseph Addison

"To have and to hold from this day forward, for better or worse, for richer or poorer, in sickness and in health, to love and to cherish, till death us do part." — Book of Common Prayer, Solemnization of Matrimony

Parents

"Honor thy father and mother." — Bible, Exodus 20:12

"The virtue of parents is in itself a great legacy." — Italian proverb

"For the hand that rocks the cradle is the hand that rules the world." — William Wallace

"You are the bows from which your children, as living arrows, are sent forth." — Kahlil Gibran

"The parent's life is the child's copy-book." — W. S. Partridge

"It is of no consequence of what parents a man is born, so he be a man of merit." — Horace

"To the ass, or the sow, their own offspring appears the fairest in creation." — Latin proverb

"The joys of parents are secret, and so are their griefs and fears." — Sir Francis Bacon

"The principal duty which a parent owes a child is to make him happy." — Anthony Trollope

"He was too experienced a parent ever to make positive promises." — Christopher Morley

"Those parents who are afraid to put their foot down usually have children who step on their toes." — Chinese proverb

"Many a parent spanks his children for things his own parents should of spanked out of him." — Don Marquis

"Before you beat a child, be sure you yourself are not the cause of the offense." — Austin O'Malley

"Every parent who does not teach his child a trade, it is as though he taught him to rob." — The Talmud

"Should parents wonder why the streams are bitter, when they themselves have poisoned the fountain?" Locke

"Oh, what a tangled web do parents weave when they think that their children are naive." — Ogden Nash

"If parents would only realize how they bore their children!" Shaw

"Despise not thy parents when they are old." — Bible, Proverbs 23:22

"We never know the love of our parents for us till we have become parents." — "There is no friendship, no love, like that of the parent for the child." — Beecher

"Hear the instruction of thy father, and forsake not the law of thy mother." — Bible, Proverbs 1:8

"What God is to the world, parents are to their children." — Philo

"There is no school equal to a decent home and no teachers equal to honest virtuous parents." — Gandhi

"Parents can only give advice or put them on the right track, but the final forming of a person's character lies in his own hands." — Anne Frank

"Unblessed is the child who does not honor his parents; but if reverent and obedient to them, the child will receive the same from his own." — "Lucky that parent whose children make them happiness in life and not their grief, the anguished disappointment of their hopes." — Euripides

"The sacred books of the ancient Persians say: If you would be holy, instruct your children, because all the good acts they perform will be imputed to you." — Montesquieu

"If there is anything to reform in public morals, one must begin with domestic morals, and they depend entirely on the fathers and mothers." — Rousseau

Mother

"Mother Love is ever in its spring." — Old proverb

"A mother's love endures all." — Washington Irving

"The mother's heart is the child's schoolroom." — Beecher

"God could not be everywhere, and therefore he made mothers." — Jewish proverb

"O people, respect the women who have born you." — The Koran

"Every mother's child is handsome." — German proverb

"Every beetle is a gazelle in the eyes of its mother." — Moorish proverb

"There is only one pretty child in the world, and every mother has it." — Chinese proverb

"A mother never realizes that her children are no longer children." — Holbrook Jackson

"Maternity is a matter of fact, paternity is a matter of opinion." — American proverb

"This is the reason why mothers are more devoted to their children than fathers: it is that they suffer more in giving them birth and are more certain that they are their own." — Aristotle

"Who takes the child by the hand takes the mother by the heart." — Danish proverb

"If you would reform the world from its errors and vices, begin by enlisting the mothers." — Charles Simmons

"An once of mother is worth a pound of clergy." — Spanish proverb

"Children are what the mothers are." — Walter Landor

"Men are what their mothers made them." — Emerson

"All that I am, or hope to be, I owe to my angel mother." — Abraham Lincoln

"Let France have good mothers, and she will have good sons." — Napoleon

"The future of society is in the hands of the mothers. If the world was lost through woman, she alone can save it." — Louis de Beaufort

"The old-time mother who used to wonder where her child was now has a grandchild who wonders where his mother is." — Frank Hubbard

Father

"One father is worth more than a hundred school-masters." — George Herbert

"It is a wise father that knows his child." — Shakespeare

"Fathers, provoke not your children to anger, lest they be discouraged." — Bible, Colossians 3:21

"I don't want to be my child's pal, I want to be his father." — Clifton Fadiman

"A father is a banker provided by nature." — French proverb

"To a hoarding father succeeds an extravagant son." — Spanish proverb

"The fundamental defect of fathers is that they want their children to be a credit to them." — Bertrand Russell

"Like Father, like son." — Old proverb

"The most important thing a father can do for his children is to love their mother." — Theodore Hesburgh

"Hearken unto the father that begat thee." — Bible, Proverbs 23:22

"When men abandon the upbringing of their children to their wives, a loss is suffered by everyone, but perhaps most of all by themselves. For what they lose is the possibility of growth in themselves for being human which the stimulation of bringing up one's children gives." — Ashley Montagu

Children

"Life's aspirations come in the guise of children." — Rabindranath Tagore

"Where children are, there is the golden age." — Novalis

"A babe in a house is a well-spring of pleasure" Martin Tupper

"A sweet child is the sweetest thing in the world." — Charles Lamb

"Praise the child." — Cobbett

"Children need models rather than critics." — Joseph Joubert

"Feel the dignity of a child. Do not feel superior to him, for you are not." — Robert Henri

"Respect the child. Trespass not on his solitude." — Emerson

"'Tis unto children most respect is due." — Juvenal

"It is better to bind your children to you by respect and gentleness than by fear." — Terence

"Mankind owes to the child the best it has to give." — United Nations Declaration

"It takes a whole village to raise a child." — "A child is what you put into him." — "A man who has children does not die." — African proverbs

"Each day of our lives we make deposits in the memory banks of our children." — Charles Swindoll

"A child educated only at school is an undereducated child." — Santayana

"Train up a child in the way that he should go: and when he is old he will not depart from it." — Bible, Proverbs 22:6

"What is learned in the cradle lasts till the grave." — Old proverb

"Men and women are but children of a larger growth." — John Dryden

"In every man a child is hidden that wants to play." — Nietzsche

"Soft is the heart of a child: Do not harden it." — Lady Wyndham Genconner

"A torn jacket is soon mended; but hard words bruise the heart of a child." — Longfellow

"Children have neither past nor future; and what scarcely ever happens to us, they enjoy the present." — La Bruyère

"Sweet childish days, that were long as twenty days are now." — Wordsworth

"Childhood is the sleep of reason." — Rousseau

"Childhood and youth are vanity." — Bible, Ecclesiastes 11:10

"Children, when they are little, they make parents fools; when great, mad." — English proverb

"Children are completely egoistic; they feel their needs intensely and strive ruthlessly to satisfy them." — Sigmund Freud

"The life of children, as much as that of intemperate men, is wholly governed by their desires." — Aristotle

"When I was a child, I spake as a child, I understood as a child, I thought as a child; but when I became a man, I put away childish things." — Bible, I Corinthians 13:11

"A man's childhood shows the man, as morning shows the day." — John Milton

"Even a child is known by his doings." — Bible, Proverbs 20:11

"The child is the father of the man." — John Milton

"Out of the mouth of babes and sucklings hath thou ordained strength." — Bible, Psalms 8:2

"A baby is an angel whose wings decrease as his legs increase." — "The child may be rocked too hard." — French Proverbs

"The potential possibilities of any child are the most intriguing and stimulating in all creation." — Ray Wilbur

"Of all nature's gifts to the human race, what is sweeter to a parent than his children?" Cicero

"A wise child maketh a glad parent." — "One that begetteth a wise child shall have joy in him." — Bible, Proverbs

"Every one calls his son his son, whether he has talents or has not talents." — Confucius

"A good goose may have an ill gosling." — Old proverb

"Children today are tyrants. They contradict their parent, gobble their food, and tyrannize their teachers." — Socrates

"How sharper than a serpent's tooth it is to have a thankless child." — Shakespeare

"Teach your children to hold their tongues; they'll learn fast enough to speak." — Benjamin Franklin

"Small children give you headache; big children heartache." — Russian proverb

"We are weakest when we are caught contending with our children!" Charles Heavysege

"What the child hears at the fireside is soon known at the parish church." — Old proverb

"When brothers agree, no fortress is so strong as their common life." — Antisthenes

"But what am I? An infant crying in the night: An infant crying for the light: And with no language but a cry." — Tennyson

"As long as a child does not cry it does not matter what pleases him." — Russian proverb

"A baby is an inestimable blessing , and bother." — "Familiarity breeds contempt — and children." — Mark Twain

"Better the children's laughter than a chamber neat. Only in their mirth is home complete." — Walter Smith

"Many children, many cares; no children, no felicity." — Christian Bovee

"Wealth and children are the adornment of life." — The Koran

"Your children are not your children. They are the sons and daughters of life's longing for itself." — Kahlil Gibran

"Here all mankind is equal; rich and poor alike, they love their children." — "A wretched child is one who does not return his parents' care." — Euripides

"Children begin by loving their parents; as they grow older they judge them; sometimes they forgive them." — "The best way to make children good is to make them happy." — Oscar Wilde

"Let a child have its will and it will not cry." — "Give to a pig when it grunts and a child when it cries, and you will have a fine pig and a bad child." — "A rich child often sits in a poor mother's lap." — Danish Proverbs

"Each child carries his own blessing into the world." — "Small children disturb your sleep, big children your life." — "Small children, small joys; big children, big annoys." — "Do not confine your children to your own learning, for they were born in another time." — Hebrew proverbs

"I have found the best way to give advice to your children is to find out what they want and then advise them to do it." — Truman

"Why do I write for children? They still believe in God, the family, angels, witches, goblins, logic, clarity, punctuation and other obsolete stuff." — Isaac Singer

"At every step the child should be allowed to meet the real experience of life; the thorns should never be plucked from his roses." — Ellen Key

"I have seen children successfully surmounting the effects of an evil inheritance. That is due to purity being an inherent attribute of the soul." — Gandhi

"To make your children capable of honesty is the beginning of education." — "Give a little love to a child, and you get a great deal back." — Ruskin

"The child becomes largely what it is taught, hence we must watch what we teach him, and how we live before him." — Jane Adams

"If we had paid no more attention to our plants than we have to our children, we would now be living in a jungle of weeds." — Luther Burbank

"A man who helps a child helps humanity with an immediateness which no other help given to the human creature in any other stage of human life can possibly give again." — Phillips Brooks

FRIENDSHIP

"Friendship is the highest degree of perfection in society." — Montaigne

"Friendship is always a sweet responsibility, never an opportunity." — Kahlil Gibran

"Friendship is one mind in two bodies." — Mencius

"Friendship is the only cement that will ever hold the world together." — Woodrow Wilson

"Friendship is a furrow in the sand." — Tongan proverb

"Friendship is like money, easier made than kept." — Butler

"Friendship is . . . the sort of love one can imagine between the angels." — C. S. Lewis

"Friendship of itself a holy tie, is made more sacred by adversity." — John Dryden

"Friendship admits of difference of character, as love does that of sex." — Joseph Roux

"Friendship may, and often does, grow into love; but love never subsides into friendship." — Byron

"Friendship often ends in love; but love in friendship — never." — Charles Caleb Colton

"Friendship made in a moment is of no moment." — Anonymous

"Friendship without self-interest is one of the rare and beautiful things in life." — James Byrnees

"Friendships multiply joys and divide griefs." — Old proverb

"Friends are born, not made." — "One friend in a lifetime is much; two are many; three are hardly possible." — Henry Adams

"Friends share all things." — Pythagoras

"A friend is another I." — Zeno

"True friendship is an identity of souls rarely to be found in this world." — Gandhi

"Friends are lost by calling often and calling seldom." — French proverb

"Go often to the house of a friend; for weeds soon choke up the unused path." — Scandinavian proverb

"A hedge between keeps friendship green." — French proverb

"The constant friend is never welcome." — Jewish proverb

"Absence strengtheneth friendship, where the last recollections were kindly." — Old proverb

"Friends provoked become the bitterest of enemies." — Gracian

"A blessed thing it is for any man to have a friend." — Kingsley

"A sympathetic friend can be quite as dear as a brother." — Homer

"One loyal friend is worth ten thousand relatives." — Latin proverb

"Old friends are best. King James used to call for his old shoes; they were easiest for his feet." — John Selden

"Forsake not an old friend, for the new is not comparable to them." — Apocrypha, Ecclesiasticus 9:10

"I have no talent for making new friends, but oh, such a genius for fidelity to old ones!" George Louis Palmella

"A man that has a thousand friends has not a friend to spare." — Ali Ibn-Abu-Talib

"A friend to everybody is a friend to nobody." — Old proverb

"Do you want to make friends? Be friendly. Forget yourself." — Dale Carnegie

"Be a friend to yourself, and others will." — "Be slow in choosing friends, but slower in changing them." — Scottish Proverbs

"Choose your friends with care, that you may have choice friends." — Old proverb

"Depth of friendship does not depend upon length of acquaintance." — Sir Rabindranath Tagore

"An acquaintance that begins with a compliment is sure to develop into a real friendship." — Oscar Wilde

"I look upon every day to be lost, in which I do not make a new acquaintance." — Samuel Johnson

"Strangers are friends you have yet to meet." — Roberta Lieberman

"The stranger has no friend, unless it be a stranger." — Sa'di

"Promises may get friends, but 'tis performances that keep them." — Old proverb

"I cannot love a friend whose love is words." — "Find friendship an unstable anchorage." — Sophocles

"Save us from our friends." — A. Wydeville

"Our worst enemies are those friends who have failed to find us profitable." — "False friends are worse than open enemies." — "With friends like these who needs enemies?" Old Proverbs

"O wise man, wash your hands of that friend who associates with your enemies." — Sa'di

"Instead of loving your enemies, treat your friends a little better." — Edgar Howe

"Great men gain doubly when they make foes their friends." — Edward Bulwer Lytton

"Suspicion is the poison of true friendship." — Augustine of Hippo

"He that wrongs his friend wrongs himself more." — Tennyson

"That friendship will not continue to the end which is begun for an end." — Francis Quarles

"He that ceases to be a friend never was a good one." — Old proverb

"Greater love hath no man than this, that he will lay down his life for his friends." — Bible, John 15:13

"The difficulty is not so great to die for a friend, as to find a friend worth dying for." — Henry Home

"Nothing is there more friendly to a man than a friend in need." — Plautus

"A friend in need is a friend indeed." — Ennius

"But in deed, a friend is never known till a man have need." — "An empty purse frightens away friends." — English proverbs

"A poor man being down is thrust away by his friends." — Apocrypha, Ecclesiasticus 8:21

"He is a weak friend who cannot bear with his friend's weakness." — Old proverb

"Two men cannot long be friends if they cannot forgive each other's little failings." — La Bruyère

"He is my friend that helps me, and not he that pities me." — Old proverb

"It is one of the severest tests of friendship to tell a friend his faults." — Beecher

"Only your real friends will tell you when your face is dirty." — Sicilian proverb

"A true friend does sometimes venture to be offensive." — Old proverb

"Iron sharpeneth iron; so a man sharpeneth the countenance of his friend." — Bible

"Reprove thy friend privately; commend him publicly." — Solon

"To your friends be the same in prosperity and in adversity." — Periander

"Adversity is the only balance to weigh friends." — Plutarch

"One should go invited to a friend in good fortune, and uninvited in misfortune." — Swedish proverb

"True friends visit us in prosperity only when invited, but in adversity they come without invitation." — Theophrastus

"Go slowly to the feast of your friends, but go swiftly to their misfortunes." — Chilon

"The road to a friend's house is never long." — "Better a friend's bite than an ememy's caress." — Danish proverbs

"I shall live till all my friends are weary of me." — Swift

"No face is ever hopelessly plain through which a friendly soul looks out upon the world." — Old proverb

"Hold a true friend with both hands." — Nigerian proverb

"Absent or dead, still let a friend be dear." — Alexander Pope

"Each year to ancient friendships adds a ring, as to an oak." — James Russell Lowell

"The best way to keep your friends is not to give them away." — Wilson Mizner

"You must consider every man on earth as a friend." — Baha'u'llah

"The friendships of the world are oft confederacies in vice, or leagues of pleasure." — Joseph Addison

"No man is useless while he has a friend." — Robert Louis Stevenson

"Love friendship." — Sophist saying

"Friendship is a plant of slow growth, and must undergo and withstand the shocks of adversity before it is entitled to the appellation." — George Washington

"Friendship is one soul abiding in two bodies." — "My best friend is one who is wishing me well wishes, it for my sake." — "No man would choose a friendless existence on condition of having all the other things in the world." — "A man with a host of friends who slaps on the back every man he meets is regarded as the friend of nobody." — Aristotle

"Friendship increases in visiting friends, but in visiting them seldom." — "We shall never have friends, if we expect to find them without fault." — "Be a friend to thyself, and others will be so too." — "A friend to all is a friend to none." — "A good friend is my nearest relationship." — "Few there are that will endure a true friend." — "They are my friend who speaks well of me behind my back." — "It is best to live as friends with those in time with whom we would be to all eternity." — Thomas Fuller

"Friendship's the wine of life; but friendship new is neither strong nor pure." — "Judge before friendship, then confide till death." — "Reserve will wound friendship, and distrust will destroy it." — Edward Young

"Friendship is constant in all other things save in the office and affairs of love." — "A friend should bear his friend's infirmities." — "I count myself in nothing else so happy as in a soul remembering my good friends." — "We are advertised by our loving friends." — Shakespeare

"Be civil to all; sociable to many; familiar with few; friend to one; enemy to none." — "There are three faithful friends — an old wife, an old dog, and ready money." — "A false friend and a shadow attend only while the sun shines." — Benjamin Franklin

"The best mirror is an old friend." — "A friend to every man and to no man is the same thing." — "Life without a friend is death without a witness." — Spanish proverbs

"A friend is a man who knows all about you — and still likes you." — "In order to have friends, you must be one." — Elbert Hubbard

"A friend that you buy with presents will be brought from you." — "A friend is easier lost than found." — "A friend's faults may be noticed, but not blamed." — "A friend's frown is better than a fool's smile." — "A faithful friend loves to the end." — "A good friend is better than a near relation." — Old proverbs

"A man that hath friends must show himself friendly." — "A friend loveth at all times." — "Every man is a friend to them who giveth gifts." — "Faithful are the wounds of a friend." — "There is a friend that sticketh closer than any brother." — Bible, Proverbs

"A faithful friend is a strong defense: and a man that hath found such a one hath found a treasure." — Apocrypha, Ecclesiasticus 6:14

"We need new friends; some of us are cannibals who have eaten their old friends up: others must have ever-renewed audiences before whom to re-enact an ideal version of their lives." — Logan Pearsall Smith

"A true friend is a man who likes you despite your achievements." — "It is well, when a man is judging a friend, to remember that he is judging you with the same godlike and superior impartiality." — Arnold Bennett

"The more we love our friends, the less we flatter them; it is by excusing nothing that pure love shows itself." — Molière

"Life is partly what we make it, and partly what it is made by the friends whom we choose." — "When you have tea and wine, you have many friends." — Chinese proverbs

"False friendship, like the ivy, decays and ruins the wall it embraces; but true friendship gives new life and animation to the object it supports." — Burton

"Be slow to fall into friendship; but when thou art in, continue firm and constant." — "Get not your friends by bare compliments, but by giving them sensible tokens of your love." — Socrates

"However rare true love may be, it is still less so than genuine friendship." — "Friendship is only a reciprocal conciliation of interests, and an exchange of good offices; it is a species of commerce out of which self-love always expects to gain something." — La Rochefoucald

"Consult your friend on all things, especially on those in which you respect yourself. Their counsel may then be useful where your own self-love might impair your judgment." — Seneca

"In misfortune, what friend remains a friend?" "Real friendship is shown in times of trouble; prosperity is full of friends." — "Life has no blessing like a prudent friend." — Euripides

"A man cannot be said to succeed in this life who does not satisfy one friend." — "The most I can do for my friend is simply to be his friend." — Thoreau

"Do good to your friend that he may be more your friend, your enemy that he may become your friend: for we should beware of the calumny of friends, of the treachery of enemies." — Cleobulus

"A friend is a man who has the same enemies you have." — "We are not enemies, but friends. We must not be enemies. Though passion may have strained, it must not break our bonds of affection." — Abraham Lincoln

"It is better to decide a difference between our enemies than between our friends, for in the first instance one of our enemies will become a friend, but in the second instance, one of our friends certainly will become an enemy." — Bias

"I have no trouble with my enemies. I can take care of my enemies all right. But my damn friends. . . they're the ones that keep me walking the floors nights!" Warren Harding

"A doubtful friend is worse than a certain enemy." — "He that has many friends, has no friends." — "Little friends may prove great friends." — "Never trust a friend who deserts you in a pinch." — Aesop

"Prosperity makes friends, adversity tries them." — "Confidence is the only bond of friendship." — "A friendship that can come to an end, never really began." — Publilius Syrus

"Honest men esteem and value nothing so much in this world as a real friend. Such a man is as it were another self, to whom we impart our most secret thoughts, who partakes of our joy, and comforts us in our affliction; add to this, that his company is an everlasting pleasure to us." — Pilpay

"When fortune is fickle, the faithful friend is found." — "For how many things, which for our own sake we should never do, do we perform for the sake of our friends." — "He removes the greatest ornament of friendship, who takes away from it respect." — Cicero

"Seek friends who have beliefs and habits like thine own and in whom thou canst place thy trust." — "If you have a friend sober, pure, and wise, let nothing hold you back — find delight and instruction in his company." — Buddha

"Be not a friend to the wicked — charcoal when hot, burns; when cold, it blackens the fingers." — "A man who wants a faultless friend, must remain friendless." — "Eat and drink with your friends, but do not trade with them." — "In health and wealth a man is never in want of friends. True friends, however, are those who remain when they are needed." — Far Eastern sayings

"A friend is a man with whom I may be sincere. Before him, I may think aloud." — "I do then with my friends as I do with my books. I would have them where I can find them, but I seldom use them." — "A day for toil, an hour for sport, but for a friend is life too short." — "It is one of the blessings of old friends that you can afford to be stupid with them." — "Every man passes his life in the search after friendship." — "The condition which high friendship demands is the ability to do without it." — "A true friend is somebody who can make us do what we can." — "The only way to have a friend is to be one." — Emerson

"Don't walk behind me, I may not lead. Don't walk in front of me, I may not follow. Just walk beside me and be my friend." — Camus

Loyalty

"Loyalty means nothing unless it has at its heart the absolute principle of self-sacrifice." — Woodrow Wilson

"To act justly, you have to love loyalty. For how can you act justly if you don't love being loyal?" Katie Gordon

"When young, we are faithful to individuals; when older, we grow more loyal to situations and to types." — Cyril Connolly

"Unless you can find some sort of loyalty, you cannot find unity and peace in your active living." — Josiah Royce

"An ounce of loyalty is worth a pound of cleverness." — Elbert Hubbard

"It is easier for a man to be loyal to his club than to his planet; the by-laws are shorter, and he is personally acquainted with the other members." — Elwyn Brooks White

Neighbors

"You shall love your neighbor as yourself." — Bible, Leviticus 19:18

"Your own safety is at stake when your neighbor's house is in flame." — Horace

"Regard your neighbor's gain as your gain, and your neighbor's loss as your loss." — Taoist proverb

"What a neighbor gets is not lost." — Scottish proverb

"Every man's neighbor is his looking glass." — English proverb

"Don't throw stones at your neighbor's windows if you live in a glass house." — Benjamin Franklin

"We are better able to study our neighbors than ourselves, and their actions than our own." — Aristotle

"Better is a neighbor that is near than a brother far off." — Bible, Proverbs 27:10

"Good fences make good neighbors." — American proverb

"Your neighbor will never make a good boundary fence." — Irish proverb

"Do not hurt your neighbor, for it is not he you wrong but yourself." — Shawnee Indian proverb

"How much time a man gains who does not look to see what his neighbor says or does or thinks, but only at what he does himself, to make it just and holy." — Marcus Aurelius

"Each man takes care that his neighbor shall not cheat him. But a day will come when he begins to care that he does not cheat his neighbor. Then all goes well — he has changed his market cart into a chariot of the sun." — Emerson

Company

"A man is known by his companions." — Latin proverb

"Tell me thy company, and I'll tell thee what thou art." — Cervantes

"Every man is like the company he keeps." — Euripides

"Company, villainous company, hath been the spoil of me." — Shakespeare

"Birds of a feather will flock together." — Old proverb

"Take the tone of the company you are in." — Alexander Pope

"There is no satisfaction in any good without a companion." — Seneca

"A good companion makes good company." — Spanish proverb

"Good company in a journey makes the way seem the shorter." — Italian proverb

"An agreeable companion on a journey is as good as a carriage." — Publilius Syrus

"No camel route is long, with good company." — Turkish proverb

"A merry companion is music in a journey." — English proverb

"Men who know the same things are not long the best company for each other." — Emerson

"The strong and the weak cannot keep company." — Aesop

"They who lie down with dogs shall rise up with fleas." — Latin proverb

"The rotten apple spoils its companions." — Benjamin Franklin

"Shun evil company." — Solon

"By associating with good and evil company a soul acquires the virtues and vices which they possess, even as the wind blowing over different places takes along good and bad odors." — Panchatantra

FREEDOM

"Freedom is nothing else but a chance to be better." — Camus

"Freedom is not worth having if it does not connote freedom to err." — Gandhi

"Freedom is what you do with what's been done to you." — Sartre

"Freedom is in the unknown." — John C. Lilly

"Freedom is participation in power." — Cicero

"Freedom is not deliverance." — Victor Hugo

"Freedom means responsibility. That is why most people dread it." — Shaw

"Freedom breeds freedom. Nothing else does." — Anne Roe

"Freedom can't be bought for nothing. If you hold her precious, you must hold all else of little worth." — Seneca

"Better starve free than be a fat slave." — Aesop

"The freedom of the man who boasts of it is a slavery." — Kahlil Gibran

"No man is free who does not rule over himself." — Claudius

"No man is free who has not obtained the empire of himself." — Far Eastern saying

"There is no need to struggle to be free; the absence of struggle is in itself freedom." — Chogyam Trungpa

"If you can not be free, be as free as you can." — "So far as a man thinks, he is free." — Emerson

"A man is free the moment he wishes to be." — Voltaire

"A man who has self-love is halfway to freedom." — Old proverb

"He hath freedom whoso beareth a clean and constant heart within." — Ennius

"The essence of freedom is the practicability of purpose." — Alfred North Whitehead

"Everything that is really great and inspiring is created by the individual who can labor in freedom." — Einstein

"The freedom now desired by many is not freedom to do and dare but freedom from care and worry." — James Truslow Adams

"Those who expect to reap the blessings of freedom must undergo the fatigue of supporting it." — Thomas Paine

"History does not long entrust the care of freedom to the weak or the timid." — Eisenhower

"We gain freedom when we have paid the full price for our right to live." — Rabindranath Tagore

"To accept a benefit is to sell one's freedom." — Publilius Syrus

"You pay a great deal too dear for what's given freely." — Shakespeare

"There no such thing as a free lunch." — American proverb

"Why buy the cow when you can get the milk for free?" Old proverb

"That man is truly free who only wishes what he is able to accomplish and does what pleases him." — Rousseau

"If the world knew how to use freedom without abusing it, tyranny would not exist." — Chinese proverb

"The history of the world is none other than the progress of the consciousness of Freedom." — Georg Hegel

"Independence now and independence forever." — Webster

"Freedom is not merely a word or an abstract theory, but the most effective instrument for advancing the welfare of man." — "The unity of freedom has never relied on uniformity of opinion." — "I do not say that all men are equal in their ability, character and motivation. I do say that every American should be given a fair chance to develop all the talents he may have." — John F. Kennedy

"In the cause of freedom, we have to battle for the rights of people with whom we do not agree; and whom, in many cases, we may not like. These people test the strength of the freedom as which protect all of us. If we do not defend their rights, we endanger our own." — Truman

"Only free peoples can hold their purpose and their honor steady to a common end, and prefer the interests of mankind to any narrow interest of their own." — Woodrow Wilson

"In giving freedom to the slave we assure freedom to the free, — honorable alike in what we give and what we preserve." — Abraham Lincoln

"None are more hopelessly enslaved than those who falsely believe they are free." —

"He only earns his freedom and existence who daily conquers them anew." — Goethe

Liberty

"Liberty! Eternal spirit of the chainless mind." — Byron

"Liberty is the right to do what the laws permit." — Montesquieu

"Liberty is a beloved discipline." — George Homans

"Liberty, like charity, must begin at home." — James Conant

"Liberation leads to liberation." — G. Gurdjieff

"Give me liberty or give me death!" Patrick Henry

"Lean liberty is better than fat slavery." — Thomas Fuller

"A day, an hour of virtuous liberty is worth a whole eternity of bondage." — Joseph Addison

"I would rather not be a king than to forfeit my liberty." — Phaedrus

"If you would liberate me, you must be free." — Emerson

"I am a lover of my own liberty and so I would do nothing to restrict yours." — Gandhi

"Proclaim liberty throughout all the land unto all the inhabitants." — Bible, Leviticus 25:10

"Give me the liberty to know, to utter, and to argue freely according to conscience, above all liberties." — John Milton

"Abstract liberty, like other mere abstractions, is not to be found." — Edmund Burke

"Not through patience, but through impatience, is man liberated." — Ludwig Borne

"The true character of liberty is independence, maintained by force." — Voltaire

"O Liberty! Liberty! How many crimes are committed in thy name!" Madame Roland

"When liberty destroys order, the hunger for order will destroy liberty." — Will Durant

"Too little liberty brings stagnation, and too much brings chaos." — Bertrand Russell

"A country cannot subsist well without liberty, nor liberty without virtue." — Rousseau

"The human race is in the best condition when it has the greatest degree of liberty." — Dante

"Liberty exists in proportion to wholesome restraint." — "Liberty and union, now and forever, one and inseparable." — Webster

"Liberty requires opportunity to make a living — a living which gives a man not only enough to live by, but something to live for." — Franklin D. Roosevelt

"What is liberty without wisdom and without virtue? It is the greatest of all possible evils, for it is folly, vice, and madness, without tuition or restraint." — "The people never give up their liberties but under some delusion." — Edmund Burke

"In America we believe in Life, Liberty — and the pursuit of happiness." — "They that can give up essential liberty to obtain a little temporary safety deserve neither liberty nor safety." — Benjamin Franklin

"Eternal vigilance is the price of liberty, and the price of wisdom is eternal thought." — "The tree of liberty must be refreshed from time to time with the blood of patriots and tyrants. It is its natural manure." — Thomas Jefferson

"Let every nation know, whether it wishes us well or ill, that we shall pay any price, bear any burden, meet any hardship, support any friend, oppose any foe to assure the survival and the success of liberty." — John F. Kennedy

Differences

"Different strokes for different folks." — English Proverb

"Between saying and doing many a pair of shoes is worn out." — Italian proverb

"Vision without action is a daydream. Action without vision is a nightmare." — Japanese proverb

"Fond of lawsuits, little wealth; fond of doctors, little health." — Jewish proverb

"Rags to riches to rags." — Lancastrian proverb

"Even after a bad harvest there must be sowing." — Latin proverb

"The betrothed of good is evil, the betrothed of life is death, the betrothed of love is divorce." — "Flowers and buds fall, and the old and ripe fall." — "When the curry is good, the rice is half cooked; when the rice is good, the curry is half cooked." — Malayan proverbs

"The one that loves does not hate." — Palestinian proverb

"When roubles falls from heaven there is no sack, when there is a sack roubles don't fall." — "The horses of hope gallop, but the asses of experiences go slowly." — "The coat is quite new, only the holes are old." — "An enemy will agree, but a friend will argue." — Russian proverbs

"Wanton kittens make sober cats." — "Learn young, learn fair; learn old, learn more." — "Spare when you're young, and spend when you're old." — Scottish proverbs

"It is better to conceal one's knowledge than to reveal one's ignorance." — "Better a friendly refusal than an unwilling consent." — "We make more enemies by what we say than friends by what we do." — Spanish proverbs

"Shared joy is a double joy; shared sorrow is half a sorrow." — "Fear less, hope more; Whine less, breathe more; Talk less, say more; Hate less, love more; And all good things are yours." — Swedish proverbs

"Goodness speaks in a whisper, evil shouts." — Tibetan proverb

"The hand that gives is above the hand that takes." — "There's no rose without a thorn, or a love without a rival." — Turkish proverbs

"Different strokes for different folks." — "It takes all kinds, to make the world go 'round." — "One man's ceiling is another man's floor." — "All bread is not baked in one oven." — "All feet cannot wear one shoe." — "Let every bird sing its own note." — "Never go straight; just go forward." — "Variety is the spice of life." — Old proverbs

"One star differeth from another star in glory." — Bible, I Corinthians 15:41

"Extremes meet. . . opposite extremes have much in common." — Pascal

"Necessity reforms the poor, and satiety the rich." — Tacitus

"Rich be not exalted; poor, be not dejected." — Cleobulus

"The rose and the thorn, and sorrow and gladness are linked together." — Sa'di

"Science is organized knowledge. Wisdom is organized life." — Kant

"Science is spectral analysis. Art is light syntheses." — Karl Kraus

"Art is I; science is we." — Claude Bernard

"Art is made to disturb. Science reassures." — Georges Braque

"Our fidelity will not be without failures, nor our confidence without fear." — Thomas Lynch

"Sometimes the idiot and the genius are the same man." — Nietzsche

"One is not a wise man that will quit a certainty for an uncertainty." — Samuel Johnson

"The virtues and vices are all put in motion by interest." — La Rochefoucauld

"You cannot run with the hare and hunt with the hounds." — Lydgate

"Fate makes our relatives, choice makes our friends." — Jacques Delille

"There never was a good war or a bad peace." — Benjamin Franklin

"A reed before the wind lives on, while mighty oaks do fall." — Chaucer

"When things are at the worst they begin to mend." — G. Whetstone

"We think in generalities, but we live in detail." — Alfred North Whitehead

"Ability and necessity dwell near each other." — Pythagoras

"Think first and speak afterwards." — R. Edgeworth

"Saying is one thing, and doing is another." — Montaigne

"Silence is deep as Eternity; speech is shallow as Time." — Carlyle

"Less is more." — Robert Browning

"Nothing is so dangerous as an ignorant friend; a wise enemy is worth much more." — La Fontaine

"What is one man's poison, is another's drink." — Beaumont and Fletcher

"I never dared be radical when young for fear it would make me conservative when old." — Robert Frost

"Better to do a little well, then a great deal badly." — Socrates

"Finite to fail, but infinite to venture." — Emily Dickinson

"Between the idea/And the reality/Between the motion/And the act/Falls the Shadow." — T. S. Eliot

"No thought, no reflection, no analysis, no cultivation, no intention; Let it settle itself." — Tilopa

"The gulf between knowledge and truth is infinite." — Henry Miller

"A door must be shut or open." — Goldsmith

"This life is not for complaint, but for satisfaction." — Thoreau

"The coarseness of some is preferable to the gentleness of others." — Kahlil Gibran

"Science without religion is lame, religion without science is blind." — Einstein

"The study of science teaches young people to think, while study of the classics teaches them to express thought." — John Stuart Mill

"People throw away what they could have by insisting on perfection, which they cannot have, and looking for it where they will never find it." — Edith Schaeffer

"To one who knoweth the true nature of things, what need is there of a teacher? To one who hath recovered from illness, what need is there of a physician? To one who hath crossed the river, what need is a boat?" Nagarjuna

"We can easily forgive a child who is afraid of the dark; the real tragedy of life is when men are afraid of the light." — Plato

"Life does not cease to be funny when people die any more than it ceases to be serious when people laugh." — Shaw

"Laugh and the world laughs with you; weep and you weep alone." — "Lighten grief with hopes of a brighter morrow; temper joy, in fear of a change of fortune." — Horace

"Knowledge is proud that it has learned so much; Wisdom is humble that it knows no more." — William Cowper

"There are some people who live in a dream world, and there are some who face reality; and then there are those who turn one into the other." — Douglas Everett

"Seek not happiness too greedily, and be not fearful of unhappiness." — "Rigidity and hardness are companions of death. Softness and tenderness are companions of life." — Lao-tse

"Simulated disorder postulates perfect discipline; simulated fear postulates courage; simulated weakness postulates strength." — Sun Tzu

"Thought is the blossom; language the bud; action the fruit behind it." — "Every sweet has its sour; every evil its good." — "For everything you have missed, you have gained something else; and for everything you gain, you lose something." — Emerson

BEAUTY

"Beauty is in the eye of the beholder." — "Beauty provoketh thieves sooner than gold." — Shakespeare

"Beauty is the only thing worth living for." — Agatha Christie

"Beauty is eternity gazing at itself in a mirror." — Kahlil Gibran

"Beauty is the lover's gift." — Congreve

"Beauty is not caused. It is." — Emily Dickinson

"Beauty is a good letter of introduction." — German proverb

"Beauty is a greater recommendation than any letter of introduction." — Aristotle

"Beauty is only skin deep." — John Davies

"Beauty is like an almanac: if it lasts a year, it is well." — T. Adams

"Beauty is not immortal. In a day, blossom and June and rapture pass away." — Arthur Stringer

"Beauty is a short reign." — Socrates

"Beauty is a fading flower." — Bible, Isaiah 28:1

"Beauty is the purgation of superfluities." — Michelangelo

"Beauty and folly are old companions." — Benjamin Franklin

"Beauty and wisdom are rarely conjoined." — Petronius

"Beauty gets the best of it in this world." — Don Marquis

"Beauty draws us with a single hair." — Alexander Pope

"Beauty without merit and virtue is a bait for fools." — Sir Richard Steele

"Beauty without virtue is like a rose without scent." — Danish proverb

"Beauty of style and harmony and grace and good rhythm depend on simplicity." — Plato

"Beauty adorns virtue." — Leonardo da Vinci

"Harmony is the basis of all beauty in the world." — Old proverb

"What is beautiful is good, and who is good will soon be beautiful." — Sappho

"Cheerfulness and content are great beautifiers, and are famous preservers of youthful looks." — Dickens

"The best part of beauty is that which no picture can express." — Sir Francis Bacon

"The beauty seen is partly in those who see it." — Christian Bovee

"Everything has its beauty but not every man sees it." — Confucius

"Our hearts were drunk with a beauty our eyes could never see." — George W. Russell

"The beautiful! It is beauty seen with the eye of the soul." — Joseph Joubert

"There is nothing that makes its way more directly to the soul than beauty." — Joseph Addison

"I pray thee, O God, that I may be beautiful within." — Socrates

"A heart in love with beauty never grows old." — Turkish proverb

"Let the beauty we love be what we do." — Rumi

"To make oneself beautiful is an universal instinct." — Sir Max Beerbohm

"Who walks with Beauty has no need of fear." — David Morton

"She that is born a beauty is born betrothed." — Italian proverb

"All heiresses are beautiful." — John Dryden

"Take the advice of light when you're looking at linens or jewels; Looking at faces or forms, take the advice of the day." — Ovid

"Handsome apples are sometimes sour." — Dutch proverb

"It is not only fine feathers that make fine birds." — Aesop

"The handsomest flower is not the sweetest." — Thomas Lynch

"A fair skin often covers a crooked mind." — Old proverb

"Yet hath many an angel shape been tenanted by fiends." — Martin Tupper

"Scandal has ever been the doom of beauty." — Propertius

"Beauty's sister is vanity, and its daughter lust." — Russian proverb

"A handsome shoe often pinches the foot." — Old proverb

"A handsome man is not quite poor." — Spanish proverb

"Loveliness needs not the foreign aid of ornament, but it is when unadorned, adorned the most." — Thomson

"Ideal beauty is a fugitive which is never located." — Marquise de Sevigne

"Those who find beautiful meanings in beautiful things are the cultivated. For these there is hope." — Oscar Wilde

"One cannot collect all the beautiful shells on the beach." — Anne Morrow Lindbergh

"Beauty is truth, truth, beauty. That is all ye know on earth, and all ye need to know." — "A thing of beauty is a joy forever: its loveliness increase; it will never pass into nothingness." — Keats

"Beauty of whatever kind, in its supreme development, invariably excites the sensitive soul to tears." — "That pleasure which is at once the most pure, the most elevating and most intense, is derived, I maintain, from the contemplation of the beautiful." — Edgar Allen Poe

"Beauty as we feel it is something indescribable: what it is or what it means can never be said." — "I like to walk about amidst the beautiful things that adorn the world; but private wealth I should decline, or any sort of personal possessions, because they would take away my liberty." — Santayana

"Beauty without expression tires." — "If eyes were made for seeing, then Beauty is its own excuse for being." — "Beauty without grace is the hook without the bait." — "Though we travel the world over to find beauty, we must carry it with us or we find it not." — Emerson

"The beauty that addresses itself to the eyes is only the spell of the moment; the eye of the body is not always that of the soul." — George Sand

"Socrates called beauty a short-lived tyranny; Plato, a privilege of nature; Theophrastus, a silent cheat; Theocritus, a delightful prejudice; Carneades, a solitary kingdom; Aristotle, that it was better than all the letters of recommendation in the world; Homer, that it was a glorious gift of nature, and Ovid, that it was a favor bestowed by the gods." — Charles Quarles

"When desire, having rejected reason and overpowered judgment which leads to right, is set in the direction of the pleasure which beauty can inspire." — Socrates

"With beauty before me I walk, with beauty behind me I walk. With beauty above me and about me, I walk. It is finished in beauty." — Navaho Indian proverb

Art

"Art is life, not something to be placed in a shrine and substituted for life." — Phillip Youtz

"Art is the accomplice of love. Take love away and there is no longer art." — Remy de Gourmont

"Art is either a plagiarist or a revolutionist." — Paul Gauguin

"Art is a step in the known toward the unknown." — Kahlil Gibran

"Art is an effort to create, beside the real world, a more human world." — Maurois

"Art is animated by invisible forces that rule the universe." — Leopold Senghor

"Art is man's nature; nature is God's art." — Philip James Bailey

"Art is the only clean thing on earth, except holiness." — Joris Huysmans

"Art is the method of levitation, in order to separate one's self from enslavement by the earth." — Anais Nin

"Art is long and life is short." — Hippocrates

"Art is in love with luck, and luck with art." — Agathon

"Art raises its head where creeds relax." — Nietzsche

"Art creates an atmosphere in which the proprieties, the amenities, and the virtues unconsciously grow." — Robert G. Ingesoll

"Art and revolt will die only with the last human." — Camus

"Art must be a true falsehood, and not a false truth." — Jean Rostand

"Artistic growth is, more than it is anything else, a refining of the sense of truthfulness." — Willa Cather

"Art's perfect forms no moral need, and beauty is its own excuse." — John Greenleaf Whittier

"Real art is illumination . . . it adds stature to life." — Brooks Atkinson

"I perhaps owe having become a painter to flowers." — Claude Monet

"As the sun colors the flowers, so does art color life." — Sir John Lubbock

"The mission of art is to represent nature; not to imitate her." — William Hunt

"To whiten ivory with dye is to spoil nature by art." — Latin proverb

"Nothing can come out of an artist that is not in the man." — Henry Mencken

"Let each man exercise the art he knows." — Arisolophanes

"There is no wide road which leads to the Muses." — Propertius

"The great artist is the simplifier." — Amiel

"It is a poor art that maintains not the artisan." — Italian proverb

"An artist's career always begins tomorrow." — Whistler

"When pursing the arts, don't give up your day job." — Anonymous

"All art is ephemeral." — Old proverb

"Architecture in general is frozen music." — Friedrich von Schelling

"Into the statue that breathes, the soul of the sculptor is bidden." — Richard Realf

"The head Sublime, the heart Pathos, the genitals Beauty, the hands and feet Proportion." — Blake

"Brushes and paints are all I have to speak the music of my soul." — Gwendolyn Bennett

"I dream of painting and then I paint my dream." — Vincent van Gogh

"When one is painting one does not think." — Raphael

"Where the spirit does not work with the hand there is no art." — Leonardo da Vinci

"I do not paint a portrait to look like the subject, rather does the person grow to look like his portrait." — Salvador Dali

"An artist who theorizes about his work is no longer artist but critic." — H. G. Wells

"An artist cannot speak about his art any more than a plant can discuss horticulture." — Jean Cocteau

"It's not what you see that is art. Art is the gap." — Marcel Duchamp

"One that sips of many arts drinks of none." — Thomas Fuller

"Half of art is knowing when to stop." — Arthur Radford

"Painting is silent poetry, and poetry is a speaking picture." — Simonides

"A picture is a model of reality." — Wittgenstein

"A picture is a poem without words." — "A fine judgment is discerning art." — Horace

"It's clever, pretty . . . but is it art?" Kipling

"Never judge a work of art by its defects." — Washington Allston

"Competitions are for horses, not artists." — Bela Bartok

"The perfection of art is to conceal art." — Quintilian

"The fine arts once divorcing themselves from truth are quite certain to fall mad, if they do not die." — Carlyle

"Without art, the crudeness of the reality would make the world unbearable." — Shaw

"The cultured man is an artist, an artist in humanity." — Ashley Montagu

"When love and skill work together, expect a masterpiece." — Ruskin

"The aim of art is to represent not the outward appearance of things, but their inward significance." — Aristotle

"Art is a human activity having for its purpose the transmission to others of the highest and best feelings to which men have risen." — Leo Tolstoy

"Art postulates communion, and the artist has an imperative need to make others share the joy which he experiences himself." — Igor Stravinsky

"Art is harmony. Harmony is the analogy of contrary and of similar elements of tone, of color and of line, conditioned by the dominate key, and under the influence of a particular light, in gay, calm, or sad combinations." — Seurat

"Art is contemplation. It is the pleasure of the mind which searches into nature and which there divines the spirit of which Nature herself is animated." — Rodin

"Art is a lie that makes us realize the truth." — "I paint objects as I think them, not as I see them." — "There are painters who transform the sun into a yellow spot, but there are others who, thanks to their art and intelligence, transform a yellow spot into the sun." — "Every child is an artist. The problem is how to remain an artist once he grows up." — Picasso

"Art is unquestionably one of the purest and highest elements in human happiness. It trains the mind through the eye, and the eye through the mind. As the sun colors flowers, so does art color life." — John Lubbock

"Art is the path of the creator to his work." — "Art is a jealous mistress, and, if a man have a genius for painting, poetry, music, architecture, or philosophy, he makes a bad husband, and an ill-provider." — "Artists must be sacrificed to their art. Like bees, they must put their lives into the sting they give." — "In the vaunted works of Art the master-stroke is Nature's part." — "Every genuine work of art has as much reason for being as the earth and the sun." — "Every artist was first an amateur." — "In art, the hand can never execute anything higher than the heart can inspire." — Emerson

"Art is the imposing of a pattern on experience, and our esthetic enjoyment in recognition of the pattern." — Alfred North Whitehead

"Art is long, and Time is fleeting." — "Great is the art of beginning, but greater the art is of ending." — Longfellow

"Artists, like the Greek gods, are only revealed to one another." — "No great artist ever sees things as they really are. I he did he would cease to be an artist." — "The best one can say of modern creative art is that it is just a little less vulgar than reality." — "It is through Art, and through Art only, that we can realize our perfection; through Art and Art only that we can shield ourselves from the sordid perils of actual existence." — Oscar Wilde

"There is nothing more difficult for a truly creative painter than to paint a rose, because before he can do so he has to first forget all the roses that were ever painted." — "Drawing is like making an expressive gesture with the advantage of permanence." — Henri Matisse

"There is a logic of colors, and it is with this alone, and not with the logic of the brain, that the painter should conform." — Cézanne

"When I am in my painting, I am not aware of what I am doing. It is only after a sort of 'get acquainted' period that I see what I have been about." — Jackson Pollock

"There is no must in art because art is free." — "The artist's eye should always be turned in upon his inner life, and his ear should be always alert for the voice of inward necessity. This is the only way of giving expression to what the mystic vision commands." — Kandinsky

"Art does not reproduce what we see; rather, it makes us see." — "My hand is entirely the instrument of more distant spheres. Nor is it my head that functions in my work; it is something else." — "The more horrifying this world becomes the more art becomes abstract; while a world at peace produces realistic art." — Paul Klee

"Everything may change in our demoralized world except the heart, mankind's love, and our striving to know the divine. Painting, like all poetry, has its part in the divine; people feel this today just as much as they used to." — "You cannot explain me with 'isms.' They are very bad for an artist. What one must believe in is color." — Chagall

"Daydreams, as it were . . . I look out the window sometimes to seek the color of the shadows and the different greens in the trees, but when I get ready to paint I just close my eyes and imagine a scene." — Grandma Moses

"The observation of nature is part of an artist's life; it enlarges his form and knowledge, keeps him fresh and from working only by formula, and feeds inspiration." — Henry Moore

"There is no better deliverance from the world than art; and a man can form no surer bond with it than through art." — Goethe

"The artist appeals to that part of our being which is not dependent on wisdom: to that in us which is a gift and not an acquisition — and, therefore, more permanently enduring." — Conrad

"The ordinary true, or purely real, cannot be the object of the arts. Illusion on a ground of truth, that is the secret of the fine arts." — Joseph Joubert

"The painter's true reality lies neither in abstraction nor in realism, but in the reconquest of his weight as a human being." — Alfred Manessier

"The stupid believe that to be truthful is easy; only the artist, the great artist, knows how difficult it is." — Willa Cather

"And moreover, to succeed, the artist must possess the courageous soul . . . the brave soul. The soul that dares and defies." — Kate Chopin

"The artist does not illustrate science but he frequently, however, responds to the same interests that a scientist does." — Lewis Mumford

"We must never forget that art is not a form of propaganda; it is a form of truth." — "For art establishes the basic human truths which must serve as the touchstone of our judgment." — John F. Kennedy

"Nothing is so poor and melancholy as art that is interested in itself and not in its subject." — "If artists and poets are unhappy, it is after all because happiness does not interest them." — Santayana

"In art, economy is always beauty." — "It is art that makes life, makes interest, makes importance, for our consideration and application of these things, and I know of no substitute whatever for the force and beauty of it's process." — Henry James

"Dancing is the loftiest, the most moving, the most beautiful of the arts, because it is no mere translation of abstraction from life; it is life itself." — Havelock Ellis

"All art is but imitation of nature." — "That which takes effect by chance is not an art." — "The artist finds a greater pleasure in painting than in having completed the picture." — Seneca

"To wake the soul by tender strokes of art, to raise the genius, and to mend of heart." — "They can paint them who shall feel them most." — Alexander Pope

"There are three arts which are concerned with all things; one which uses, another which makes, a third which imitates them." — Plato

"No man paints as he likes. All a painter can do is to will with all his might the painting his age is capable of." — "An object awakens our love just because it seems to be the bearer of powers that are greater than itself." — Jean Bazaine

"An artist paints with his brains and not with his hands." — "The more the marble wastes, the more the statue grows." — "I saw the angel in the marble and carved until I set it free." — "The true work of art is but a shadow of the divine perfection." — Michelangelo

Music

"Music is the universal language." — Richard Wagner

"Music is well said to be the speech of angels." — Carlyle

"Music is the language of God." — Old proverb

"Music is a part of us, and either ennobles us or degrades our behavior." — Boethius

"Music is nothing else but wild sounds civilized into time and tune." — Thomas Fuller

"Music is Love in search of a word." — Sidney Lanier

"Music is the fourth great material want of our nature, — first food, then raiment, then shelter, then music." — Christian Bovee

"Music is a friend of labor; it lightens the task by refreshing nerves and spirit." — William Green

"Music is the harmonious voice of creation; an echo of the invisible world." — Giuseppe Mazzini

"Music is an agreeable harmony for the honor of God and the permissible delights of the soul." — J. S. Bach

"Music causes us to think eloquently." — Emerson

"Music must be emotional first and intellectual second." — Maurice Ravel

"Music expresses that which cannot be said and on which it is impossible to be silent." — Victor Hugo

"Music has charms to soothe a savage breast, to soften rocks, or bend a knotted oak." — William Congreve

"Music [is] that moody food of us that trade in love." — "If music be the food of love, play on." — Shakespeare

"Music washes away from the soul the dust of everyday life." — Berthold Auerbach

"Music itself is the purest expression of emotion." — Joshua Logan

"Music does not exist until it is performed." — Benjamin Britten

"Music heard so deeply that it is not heard at all, but you are the music while it lasts." — T. S. Eliot

"Music is perpetual, and only the hearing is intermittent." — Thoreau

"Music and art must have their prominent seats of honor, and not merely a tolerant nod of recognition." — Rabindranath Tagore

"Music, in performance, is a type of sculpture. The air in the performance is sculpted into something." — Frank Zappa

"Musical sound acts directly on the soul and finds an echo there, since music is innate in humans." — Vasily Kandinsky

"The only correct music is that which is beautiful and noble." — Ralph Vaughan Williams

"The choir invisible, whose music is the gladness of the world." — Frederick Delius

"We composers are projectors of the infinite in the finite." — Grieg

"After silence, that which comes nearest to expressing the inexpressible is music." — Aldous Huxley

"For what can wake the soul's strong instinct of another world like music?" Letitia Landon

"Such sweet compulsion doth in music lie, untwisting all the chains that tie the hidden soul of harmony." — John Milton

"Lo, with the ancient roots of man's nature, twines the eternal passion of song." — Sir William Watson

"All art constantly aspires towards the condition of music." — Walter Pater

"Where there's music, there can be love." — French proverb

"Where is music, there can be no evil." — "All music jars when the soul's out of tune." — Cervantes

"Life has its music; let us seek a way not to jangle the chords whereon we play." — Archilochus of Paros

"As poetry is the harmony of words, so music is that of notes." — John Dryden

"Only what I experience do I compose. Only what I compose do I experience." — "If a composer could say what he had to say in words, he would not bother trying to say it in music." — Gustav Mahler

"Composers should write tunes that chauffeurs and errand boys can whistle." — Sir Thomas Beecham

"A song ain't nothin' in the world but a story just wrote with music to it." — Hank Williams, Sr.

"It is always the latest song that an audience applauds the most." — Homer

"True music must repeat the thought and inspirations of the people and the time." — Gershwin

"The history of a country is written in its popular songs." — Sigmund Spaeth

"Give me the making of the songs of a nation, and I care not who makes its laws." — Andrew Fletcher

"Wouldst thou know if a society be well governed, if its laws be good or bad? Examine the music it practices." — Lao-tze

"It's amazing how potent cheap music can be." — Noel Coward

"Every kind of music is good, except the boring kind." — Rossini

"Do not fear mistakes — there are none." — "Don't play what's there, play what's not there." — Miles Davis

"Jazz will endure as long as people hear it through their feet instead of their brains." — John Philip Sousa

"One is scarcely sensible of fatigue while one marches to music." — J. Montgomery

"All music is what awakes from you when you are reminded by the instruments." — Walt Whitman

"Life is like music; it must be composed by ear, feeling, and instinct, not by rule." — "There's many a good tune played on an old fiddle." — Butler

"The older the fiddle, the sweeter the tune." — Irish proverb

"They who dance must pay the fiddler." — J. Taylor

"The man who can't dance says the band can't play." — Jewish proverb

"If you can walk, you can dance. If you can talk, you can sing." — Zimbabwean proverb

"Move your neck according to the music." — Ethiopian proverb

"He was one of those people who say, 'I don't know anything about music really, but I know what I like.'" Sir Max Beerbohm

"I don't know anything about music — in my line, you don't have to." — Elvis Presley

"It is not necessary to understand music; it is only necessary that one enjoy it." — Leopold Stokowski

"I don't sing because I'm happy; I'm happy because I sing." — William James

"In the dark times, will there also be singing? Yes, there will also be singing about the dark times." — Bertolt Brecht

"Those who sing drive away sorrow." — Old proverb

"Music is a safe kind of high." — "Blues is easy to play, but hard to feel." — Jimi Hendrix

"No two people on earth are alike, and it's got to be that way in music or it isn't music." — Billie Holiday

"I was determined to carve out a music of my own. I didn't want to copy anybody." — Bill Monroe

"I don't think anybody steals anything: All of us borrow." — B. B. King

"Before I compose a piece, I walk around it several times, accompanied by myself." — Erik Satie

"To produce music is also in a sense to produce children." — "Without music, life would be a mistake." — Nietzsche

"Let me have music dying, and I seek no more delight." — Keats

"Music, even in situations of the greatest horror, should never be painful to the ear but should flatter and charm it, and thereby always remain music." — "When a man has the spirit of a composer, he writes because he can't help it." — Mozart

"Music — The one incorporeal entrance into the higher world of knowledge which comprehends mankind, but which mankind cannot comprehend." — "Music is the mediator between the spiritual and the sensual life." — "Beethoven can write music, thank God — but he can do nothing else on earth." — Beethoven

"Music is the arithmetic of sounds as optics is the geometry of light." — "The century of aeroplanes deserves its own music. As there are no precedents, I must create anew." — Debussy

"Music resembles poetry; in each are nameless graces which no methods teach." — "What will a child learn sooner than a song?" Alexander Pope

"Music . . . can name the unnamable and communicate the unknowable." — "I'm not interested in having an orchestra sound like itself. I want it to sound like the composer." — Leonard Bernstein

"Music is the universal language of man." — "Yea, music is the prophet's art; among the gifts that God hath sent, one of the most magnificent." — "Thy voice is celestial melody." — Longfellow

"Music has the greatest power over man; for while we are in the terrestrial life we are exiled from our heavenly home and often have forgotten it in our material pursuits, but then comes music as a fragrant odor laden with unspeakable memories." — Max Heindel

"Music is the art of the prophets, the only art that can calm the agitations of the soul." — "Besides Theology, Music is the only art capable of affording peace and joy of the heart like that induced by the study of the science of Divinity." — Martin Luther

"Music is the only sensual gratification in which mankind may indulge to excess without injury to moral or religious feelings." — Joseph Addison

"Music, of all the liberal arts has the greatest influence over the passions, and is that to which the legislator ought to give the greatest encouragement." — Napoleon

"Music is the effort we make to explain to ourselves how our brains work. We listen to Bach transfixed because this is listening to a human mind." — Lewis Thomas

"Music, when soft voices die, vibrates in the memory — Odors, when sweet violets sicken, live within the sense they quicken." — "Our sweetest songs are those that tell of saddest thought." — Shelley

"Musicians don't retire; they stop when there's no more music in them." — "Never play a thing the same way twice." — Louis Armstrong

"Musical harmony is a most powerful conceiver. It allures the celestial influences and changes affections, intentions, gestures, notions, actions and dispositions." — Agrippa

"Music gives a soul to the universe, wings to the mind, and life to everything." — "Musical training is a more potent instrument than any other, because rhythm and harmony find their way into the inward places of the soul and take the strongest hold upon it." — Plato

"The trouble with music appreciation in general is that people are taught to have too much respect for music; they should be taught to love it instead." — "I haven't understood a bar of music in my life, but I've felt it." — Igor Stravinsky

"I adore art . . . when I am alone with my notes, my heart pounds and the tears stream from my eyes, and my emotion and my joys are too much to bear." — Verdi

"If being an egomaniac means I believe in what I do and in my art or my music, then in that respect you can call me that . . . I believe in what I do, and I'll say it." — John Lennon

"Any musician who says he is playing better either on tea, the needle, or when he is juiced, is a plain straight liar . . . You can miss the most important years of your life, the years of possible creation." — Charlie Parker

"All a musician can do is to get closer to the sources of nature, and so feel that he is in communion with the natural laws." — John Coltrane

"I can only think of music as something inherent in every human being — a birthright. Music coordinates mind, body and spirit." — Yehudi Menuhin

"The notes I handle no better than many pianist. But the pauses between the notes, ah, that is where the art resides!" Paul Valéry

"The reality of music is in that vibration that remains in the ear after the singer finishes his song and the player no longer plucks the strings." — Kahlil Gibran

"Open my ears to music; let me thrill with Spring's first flutes and drums — But never let me dare forget the bitter ballads of the slums." — Louis Untermeyer

"If I had my life to live over again, I would have made a rule to read some poetry and listen to some music at least once a week; for perhaps the parts of my brain now atrophied would thus have been kept active through use." — Darwin

"I've never known a musician who regretted being one. Whatever deceptions life may have in store for you, music itself is not going to let you down." — Virgil Thomson

"One and the same thing can at the same time be good, bad, and indifferent; music is good to the melancholy, bad to those who mourn, and neither good nor bad to the deaf." — Spinoza

"O Music! Miraculous art! A blast of thy trumpet and millions rush forward to die; a peal of thy organ and uncounted nations sink down to pray." — Disraeli

"A tone is a living cell . . . It has the power of assimilation, of reproduction, of making exchanges, of growing. It is a microcosmos reflecting faithfully the macrocosmos, its laws, its cycle, its center . . . a tone is a solar system." — Dane Rudhyar

"The rotation of the universe and motion of the planets could neither be nor continue without music." — "Music, to create harmony, must investigate discord." — Plutarch

"There is music wherever there is harmony, order, or proportion; and thus far we may maintain the music of the spheres." — Sir Thomas Browne

"There is geometry in the humming of the strings. There is music in the spacings of the spheres. Study the monochord, the music of the spheres." — Pythagoras

"So long as the human spirit thrives on this planet, music in some living form will accompany and sustain it and give it expressive meaning." — Aaron Copland

"Would you have your songs endure? Build on the human heart." — "There is no truer truth obtainable by man than comes of music." — Robert Browning

NATURE

"Nature is the eternal abundance from which art gains its sustenance." — Edvard Munch

"Nature is the art of God." — Dante

"Nature is the living, visible garment of God." — Goethe

"Nature is commanded by obeying her." — Sir Francis Bacon

"Nature never did betray the heart that loved her." — Wordsworth

"Nature and wisdom always say the same." — "Never does nature say one thing and wisdom another." — Juvenal

"Nature always tends to act in the simplest way." — Bernoulli

"Nature teaches more than she preaches." — John Burroughs

"Nature has always had more power than education." — Voltaire

"Nature speaks in symbols and in signs." — John Greenleaf Whittier

"Nature hath nothing made so base, but can read some instruction to the wisest man." — C. Aleyn

"Nature cannot be fooled." — Richard Feynman

"Nature does not proceed by leaps." — Linnaeus

"Nature is visible thought." — Heinrich Heine

"Nature loves to hide." — Heraclitus

"Nature is an Aeolian harp, a musical instrument, whose tones are the re-echo of the higher strings within us." — Novalis

"Nature requires little — fancy, much." — Alexander Pope

"Who lives to nature rarely can be poor — who lives to fancy never can be rich." — Edward Young

"All art, all education, can be merely a supplement to nature." — Aristotle

"In nature there are no rights; there are only duties." — Anonymous

"The law of nature is the strictest expression of necessity." — Molescholte

"The wolf changes it coat, and the serpent its skin, but not their nature." — Far Eastern saying

"We are more sensible of what is done against custom than against Nature." — Plutarch

"Nothing so much prevents our being natural as the desire of appearing so." — La Rochefoucauld

"All is disgust when a man leaves his own nature and does things that misfit it." — Sophocles

"You might drive out nature with a pitchfork, but she keeps coming back." — Horace

"Sympathy with nature is a part of the good man's religion." — F. H. Hedge

"Our ideas must be as broad as nature if they are to interpret nature." — Arthur Conan Doyle

"The study of nature is intercourse with the highest mind. You should never trifle with nature." — Louis Agassiz

"The wise man marvels at the common; the greatest wonder of all is the regularity of nature." — G. D. Boardman

"Men are very long afraid of being natural, from the dread of being taken for ordinary." — Lord Francis Jeffery

"The instinct of ownership is fundamental in men's nature." — William James

"We heed no instincts but our own." — La Fontaine

"What does reason demand of a man? A very easy thing — to live in accord with his own nature." — Seneca

"A rational nature admits of nothing which is not serviceable to the rest of mankind." — Marcus Aurelius

"Accuse not Nature! She hath done her part; Do thou but thine!" John Milton

"Nature arms each man with some faculty which enables him to do easily some feat impossible to any other." — Emerson

"Nature makes boys and girls lovely to look upon so they can be tolerated until they acquire some sense." — William Phelps

"Nature never deceives us; it is always we who deceive ourselves." — "Everything made by man may be destroyed by man; there are no ineffaceable characters except those engraved by nature; and nature makes neither kings nor rich men." — Rousseau

"Nature's laws affirm instead of prohibiting. If you violate her laws, you are your own prosecuting attorney, judge, jury, and hangman." — Luther Burbank

"It is the marriage of the soul with Nature that makes the intellect fruitful, and gives birth to imagination." — Thoreau

"Whatever you are by nature, keep to it; never desert your own line of talent. Be what intended you for, and you will succeed; be anything else and you will be ten thousand times worse than nothing." — Sydney Smith

"Whether a man is disposed to yield to nature or to oppose her, one cannot do without a correct understanding of her language." — Jean Rostand

"Everything we see in nature is manifested truth; only we are not able to recognize it unless truth is manifest within ourselves." — Jacob Boehme

"Nothing exists from whose nature some effect does not follow." — "It is usually the case with most men that their nature is so constituted that they pity those who fare badly and envy those who fare well." — Spinoza

"It is an inexorable Law of Nature that bad must follow good, that decline must follow a rise. To feel that we can rest on our achievements is a dangerous fallacy. Inner strength can overcome anything that occurs outside." — I-Ching; Book of Changes

"Things perfected by nature are better than those finished by art." — "Never can custom conquer nature, for she is ever unconquered. This law then, was not written, but born. It is a law which we have not learned, received from others or read, but which we have derived, absorbed and copied from nature itself." — "I follow nature as the surest guide, and resign myself, with implicit obedience, to her sacred ordinances." — Cicero

"We would be happy if we studied nature more in natural things; and acted according to nature, whose rules are few, plain, and most reasonable." — William Penn

"Nature goes her own way." — "'Sail!' quoth the king; 'Hold!' saith the wind." — "The owl is the kind of the night." — English proverbs

"For Art may err, but Nature cannot miss." — John Dryden

"Know, then, nature is art." — Bhagavad-gita

"All of nature is in us, all of us is in nature." — Native American proverb

"The day, water, sun, moon, night — I do not have to purchase these things with money." — Plautus

"When a man moves away from nature, his heart becomes hard." — Lakota Indian proverb

"Does the song of the seas end at the shore or in the hearts of those who listen to it?" Kahlil Gibran

"The summer's flower is to the summer sweet, though to itself it only live and die." — Shakespeare

"Look upon the rainbow, and praise them that made it." — Apocrypha, Ecclesiasticus 43:11

"Seek the fresh air of the forest and the fields and there in the midst of them shall you find angel air." — "Put off your shoes and your clothing and have the angel of Sunlight embrace you, all your body." — Essene Gospel of Jesus

"There's no music like a little river's. It plays the same tune over and over again, and yet does not weary of it like fiddlers." — Robert Louis Stevenson

"In wilderness I sense the miracle of life, and behind it our scientific accomplishments fade to trivia." — Charles Lindbergh

"I wish I were with some of the wild people that run in the woods, and know nothing about accomplishments!" Joanna Baillie

"I lived in solitude in the country and noticed how the monotony of a quiet life stimulates the creative mind." — Einstein

"Why, one day in the country is worth a month in the town." — Christina Rossetti

"Living Nature, not dull Art, shall plan my ways and rule my heart." — John Henry Newman

"It is possible to make a garden from a wilderness quickly; but it is not easy to re-convert the wilderness from a garden." — Nehru

"Love thou the rose, yet leave it on its stem." — Owen Meredith

"An elemental force is ruthlessly frank." — Joseph Conrad

"In nature things move violently to their place, and calmly in their place." — Sir Francis Bacon

"In nature there are neither rewards nor punishments — there are consequences." — Robert Ingersoll

"Let us a little permit Nature to take her own way; she better understands her own affairs than we." — Montaigne

"Everything in Nature contains all the powers of Nature." — Emerson

"Nature is man's teacher. She unfolds her treasures to his search, unseals his eye, illumines the mind, and purifies his heart; an influence breathes from all the sights and sounds of her existence." — Street

"Nature gives to every time and season some beauties of its own; and from morning to night, as from the cradle to the grave, is but a succession of changes so gentle and easy that we can scarcely mark their progress." — Dickens

"Nature abhors a vacuum, and if I can only walk with sufficient carelessness I am sure to be filled." — "I went to the woods because I wished to live deliberately, to front only the essential facts of life, and see if I could not learn what it had to teach, and not, when I came to die, discover that I had not lived." — Thoreau

"There is however, a true music of Nature — the song of the birds, the whisper of leaves, the ripple of waters upon a sandy shore, the wail of wind or sea." — Lubbock

"There is no lover like an island shore for lingering embrace; no tryst so faithful as the turning tide at its accustomed place." — Elizabeth Cutter

"Sunshine is delicious, rain is refreshing, wind braces up, snow is exhilarating; there is no such thing as bad weather, just different kinds of good weather." — Ruskin

"There is a pleasure in the pathless woods. There is a rapture on the lonely shore. There is society, where none intrudes. By the deep sea, and music in its roars; I love not man the less, but nature more." — Byron

"The use of the sea and air is common to all; neither can a title to the ocean belong to any people or private man, forasmuch as neither nature nor public use and custom permit any possession thereof." — Queen Elizabeth

"You must not know too much, or be too precise or scientific about birds and trees and flowers and water-craft; a certain free margin, and even vagueness — perhaps ignorance, credulity — helps your enjoyment of these things." — Walt Whitman

"The only words that ever satisfied me as describing Nature are the terms used in fairy books, 'charm,' 'spell,' 'enchantment.' They express the arbitrariness of the fact and its mystery." — G. K. Chesterton

"Everything is fruit to me that thy seasons bring, O Nature. All things come of thee, have their being in thee, and return to thee." — Marcus Antoninus

Earth

"Earth, when I am in life, I depend on you." — Ashanti proverb

"Earth laughs in flowers." — Emerson

"Earth knows no desolation. She smells regeneration in the moist breath of decay." — George Meredith

"The Earth has music for those who will listen." — O. W. Holmes

"The poetry of earth is never dead." — Keats

"Speak to the earth, and it shall teach thee." — Bible, Job 12:8

"Through woods and mountain passes the winds, like anthems roll." — Longfellow

"The winds and the waves are always on the side of the ablest navigators." — Edward Gibbon

"My soul can find no staircase to heaven unless it be through earth's loveliness." — Michelangelo

"Occupy the land with character." — Robert Frost

"The land is a mother that never dies." — Maori proverb

"One generation passeth away, and another generation cometh: but the earth abideth for ever." — Bible, Ecclesiastes 7:4

"The supreme reality of our time is . . . the vulnerability of our planet." — John F. Kennedy

"The miracle is not to fly in the air, or to walk on the water, but to walk on the earth." — "When drinking water, remember its source." — Chinese proverbs

"If we dig precious things from the land, we will invite disaster." — "We don't inherit the land from our ancestors, we borrow it from our children." — Native American proverb

"The Earth does not belong to man: man belongs to the Earth." — "Please take care of this land, or living will become survival." — Chief Seattle

"Forget not that the earth delights to feel your bare feet and winds long to play with your hair." — "How can we hear the song of the field while our ears have the clamor of the city to swallow?" Kahlil Gibran

"It is a wholesome and necessary thing for us to turn again to the earth and in the contemplation of her beauties to know the sense of wonder and humility." — Rachel Carson

"No house should ever be on any hill or on anything. It should be of the hill, belonging to it, so hill and house could live together each the happier for the other." — Frank Lloyd Wright

"The Earth viewed from above resembles a ball sewn from twelve pieces of skin." — Plato

"The earth is a living organism, the body of a higher individual who has a will and wants to be well." — Rolling Thunder

Trees and Flowers

"The clearest way into the Universe is through a forest wilderness." — "Going to the woods is going home." — John Muir

"The tree casts its shade upon all, even the woodcutter." — Hindu proverb

"If a tree dies, plant another in its place." — Linnaeus

"Holy is the forest. Holy is that place where the senses are at peace." — Buddha

"A forest is in an acorn." — Old proverb

"These trees shall be my books." — Shakespeare

"I live too near the woods to be scared by owls." — Greek proverb

"Nothing is more beautiful than the loveliness of the woods before sunrise." — Washington Carver

"Stop and smell the roses." — Old proverb

"Every blade of grass has its angel that bends over and whispers, 'Grow, Grow.'" The Talmud

"[There is a] murmur that springs from the growing of grass." — Edgar Allan Poe

"I believe a leaf of grass is no less than the journey-work of the stars." — Walt Whitman

"I have need of the sky, I have business with the grass." — Richard Hovey

"The trees, like the longings of the earth, stand a-tiptoe to peep at the heaven." — Sir Rabindranath Tagore

"I think that I shall never see a poem lovely as a tree — a tree whose hungry mouth is pressed against the earth's sweet flowing breast." — Joyce Kilmer

"There is . . . a certain respect, and a general duty of humanity, that ties us, not only to beasts that have life and sense, but even to trees and plants." — Montaigne

"Men who plant trees love others besides themselves." — "Some men go through a forest and see no firewood." — "Many eyes go through the meadow, but few see the flowers." — "Fields have eyes and woods have ears." — English proverbs

"And 'tis my faith, that every flower enjoys the air it breathes." — "To me the meanest flower that blows can give thoughts that do often lie too deep for tears." — "One impulse from a vernal wood may teach you more of man, of moral evil and of good, than all the sages can." — Wordsworth

Animals

"Animals are such agreeable friends — they ask no questions, they pass no criticisms." — Eliot

"Animals don't look like people, but they think like people, and they really are people under their pelts." — Hopi Indian proverb

"Animals share with us the privilege of having a soul." — Pythagoras

"Animals aren't wild, they're just free." — "Every animal knows more than you do." — Native American proverb

"There is no fundamental difference between man and the higher animals in their mental faculties." — Darwin

"O to be a frog, my lads, and live aloof from care." — Theognis

"Though the boys throw stones at frogs in sport, yet the frogs do not die in sport but in earnest." — Plutarch

"He who is cruel to animals becomes hard also in his dealings with men." — Kant

"Dog is man's best friend." — Old proverb

"Love me, love my dog." — St. Bernard

"A barking dog is often more useful than a sleeping lion." — Washington Irving

"The biggest dog has been a pup." — Joaquin Miller

"A cat has nine lives." — Old proverb

"In a cat's eyes, all things belong to cats." — English proverb

"Well knows the cat whose ear he licks." — French proverb

"When I play with my cat, who knows whether I do not make her more sport than she makes me?" Michel de Montague

"Consider the little mouse, how sagacious an animal it is which never entrusts its life to one hole only." — Plautus

"They say the first inclination which an animal has is to protect itself." — Diogenes Laertius

"If there were no elephant in the jungle, the buffalo would be a great animal." — Ghanan proverb

"He who mounts a wild elephant goes where the wild elephant goes." — Randolph Bourne

"You can take the animal out of the wild but you can't take the wild out of the animal." — Old proverb

"A good horse can not be a bad color." — J. Carmichaell

"A good horse should be seldom spurred." — "A man that will not be merciful to his beast is a beast himself." — Thomas Fuller

"Give me the ass that carries me, in preference to the horse that throws me." — Old proverb

"The cock, that is the trumpet of the morn." — Shakespeare

"I heard a bird at break of day sing from the autumn trees a song so mystical and calm, so full of certainties." — William Percy

"All animals except man know that the principal business of life is to enjoy it." — Butler

"It is much easier to show compassion to animals. They are never wicked." — Haile Selassie

"Forgive us all our trespasses, little creatures, everywhere!" James Stephens

"I am in favor of animal rights as well as human rights. That is the way of a whole human being." — Abraham Lincoln

"Compassion for animals is intimately connected with goodness of character; and it may be confidently asserted that he who is cruel to animals cannot be a good man." — Arthur Schopenhauer

"If you have men who will exclude any of God's creatures from the shelter of compassion and pity, you will have men who will deal likewise with their fellow humans." — "Not to hurt our humble brethren the animals is our first duty to them." — St. Francis

"If the animals had intelligent speech at their command, they would state a case against man that would stagger humanity." — "The greatness of a nation and its moral progress can be judged by the way its animals are treated." — Gandhi

"The birds I heard today, which did not come within the scope of my science, sang as freshly as if it had been the first morning of creation." — "The blue-bird carries the sky on his back." — Thoreau

"When a man wants to murder a tiger he calls it sport: when the tiger wants to murder a man, he calls it savagery." — Shaw

"What is man without the animals? If all the animals were gone, men would die from a great loneliness of spirit. For whatever happens to the animals, soon happens to us. All things are connected." — Chief Seattle

"Let dogs delight to bark and bite, for God hath made them so; Let bears and lions growl and fight, for 'tis their nature too." — Isaac Watts

"Recollect that the Almighty, who gave the dog to be companion of our pleasures and our toils, hath invested them with a nature noble and incapable of deceit." — Sir Walter Scott

"The dog has seldom been successful in pulling man up to its level of sagacity, but man has frequently dragged the dog down to his." — James Thurber

"We call them dumb animals, and so they are, for they cannot tell us how they feel, but they do not suffer less because they have no words." — Anna Sewell

"It is just like man's vanity and impertinence to call an animal dumb because it is dumb to his dull perceptions." — "Indecency, vulgarity, obscenity — these are strictly confined to man; we invented them. Among the higher animals there is no trace of them. They hide nothing. They are not ashamed." — "The fact that man knows right from wrong proves our intellectual superiority to the other creatures; but the fact that we can do wrong proves our moral inferiority to any creatures that cannot." — Mark Twain

AGE

"Age is honorable and youth is noble." — Irish proverb

"Age withers only the outside." — Anonymous

"Age gives good advice when it is no longer able to give a bad example." — American proverb

"The essence of age is intellect." — Emerson

"If youth had but the knowledge and old age the strength." — French proverb

"If youth but knew; if old age but could." — Henri Estienne

"It is magnificent to grow old, if a man keeps young." — Harry Emerson Fosdick

"Old age is not a total misery. Experience helps." — Euripides

"The old age of an eagle is better than the youth of a sparrow." — Greek proverb

"From the altar of age the ashes of the fire of youth are gone, but the flame of more earnest feelings remain." — Anonymous

"When grace is joined with wrinkles, it is adorable. There is an unspeakable dawn in happy old age." — Victor Hugo

"For the unlearned, old age is winter; for the learned it is the season of the harvest." — The Talmud

"It is a truth but too well known, that rashness attends youth, as prudence does old age." — Cicero

"At twenty years of age the will reigns; at thirty, the wit; at forty, the judgment." — Benjamin Franklin

"The old believe everything, the middle-aged suspect everything, the young know everything." — Oscar Wilde

"Age carries all things, even the mind, away." — Virgil

"Age is dull and mean. Men creep, not walk." — John Greenleaf Whittier

"Young men think old people are fools; but old men know young men are fools." — George Chapman

"Young folk, silly folk; old folk, cold folk." — Dutch proverb

"Youth looks forward but age looks back." — English proverb

"That sign of old age, extolling the past at the expense of the present." — Sydney Smith

"In youth we run into difficulties, in old age difficulties run into us." — Josh Billings

"Reckless youth makes rueful age." — Thomas Moore

"The passions of the young are vices in the old." — Joseph Joubert

"The first years of a man's life must make provision for the last." — Samuel Johnson

"The young man who has not wept is a savage, and the older man who will not laugh a fool." — Santayana

"The glory of young men is their strength: and the beauty of old men is their gray hair." — Bible, Proverbs 20:29

"Every age has its beautiful moments." — Einstein

"Expect age." — Sophist saying

"Age is opportunity no less than youth itself, though in another dress. And as the evening twilight fades away the sky is filled with stars invisible by day." — Longfellow

"Age in a virtuous person, of either sex, carries in it an authority which makes it preferable to all the pleasures of youth." — Sir Richard Steele

"Age is a bad traveling companion." — "Where old age is evil, youth can learn no good." — English proverbs

"A man who is of a calm and happy nature will hardly feel the pressure of age, but to a man who is of an opposite disposition, youth and age are equally a burden." — Plato

"For honorable age is not that which standeth in length of time, nor that is measured by number of years. But wisdom is the gray hair unto men, and as unspotted life in old age." — Apocrypha, Book of Wisdom

"Youth is a silly, vapid state; Old age with fears and ills is rife; This simple boon I beg of Fate — A thousand years of Middle Life!" Carolyn Wells

"Say what thou wilt, the young are happy never. Give me blessed Age, beyond the fire and fever — Past the delight that shatters, hope that stings, and eager fluttering of life's ignorant wings." — Sir William Watson

"The world's tragedy is that it must be grown up; in other words, that it must be run by men who, though they know much, have forgotten what they were in their youth." — John Brown

"For strength of nature in youth passeth over many excesses, which are owing a man till his age. Discern the coming on of years, and think not to do the same things still; for age will not be defied." — "Men of age object too much, consult too long, adventure too little, repent too soon." — Sir Francis Bacon

"Life is most delightful when it is on the downward slope." — "Nothing is more dishonorable than an old man, heavy with years, who has no other evidence of having lived long except his age." — Seneca

"When the age is in, the wit is out." — "But age, with his stealing steps, hath clawed me in his clutch." — "Crabbed age and youth cannot live together. Youth is full of pleasure, age is full of care." — "To me, fair friend, you never can be old. For as you were when first your eye I eyed, such seems your beauty still." — Shakespeare

Youth

"Youth is the opportunity to do something and to become somebody." — Theodore Munger

"Youth is the best time to be rich; and the best time to be poor." — Euripides

"Youth is wholly experimental." — Robert Louis Stevenson

"Youth is life as yet untouched by tragedy." — Alfred North Whitehead

"Youth is to all the glad season of life, but often only by what it hopes, not by what it attains or escapes." — Carlyle

"Youth smiles without any reason. It is one of its chiefest charms." — Oscar Wilde

"Youth ever thinks that good whose goodness or evil he sees not." — Sir Philip Sidney

"Youth had been a habit of hers for so long that she could not part with it." — Kipling

"Youth will be served." — English proverb

"Youth, even in its sorrows, always has a brilliancy of its own." — Victor Hugo

"Youth's the season made for joys, love is then our duty." — John Gay

"Young men are thoughtless, as a rule." — Homer

"Young men have a passion for regarding their elders as senile." — Henry Adam

"Young man, like the wise, exhort to be sober minded." — Bible, Titus 2:6

"Youth is perpetual intoxication; it is a fever of the mind." — La Rochefoucauld

"The young are permanently in a state resembling intoxication; for youth is sweet and they are growing." — Aristotle

"No young man believes he shall ever die." — William Hazlit

"How long does youth endure? So long as we are loved." — Golden Book of Diana

"When we are young, we long to tread a way none trod before." — Yeats

"Keep true to the dreams of thy youth." — Schiller

"Rejoice, O young man, in thy youth." — Bible, Ecclesiastes 11:9

"Bliss was it in that dawn to be alive, but to be young was very heaven!" Wordsworth

"Two things youth desires beyond all others, freedom from ridicule, and intensity of sensation." — Louis Miles

"To refuse to grow old is the unmistakable sign of youth." — Anonymous

"Our youth we can have but today, we may always find time to grow old." — George Berkeley

"A young branch takes on all the bends that one gives it." — Chinese proverb

"Frustrations and denials which seem to youth cruel and unfair often are important equipment for life." — Bruce Barton

"If you will be cherished when you are old, be courteous while you are young." — John Lyly

"The right way to begin is to pay attention to the young, and make them just as good as possible." — Socrates

"A youth is to be regarded with respect. How do you know that his future will not be equal to our present?" Confucius

"I am not young enough to know everything." — Sir James Matthew Barrie

"Let no one despise thy youth." — Bible, I Timothy 4:12

"It takes a long time to become young." — Picasso

"There is as close a connection between youth and faith as between age and compromise." — Austin O'Malley

"It is an illusion that youth is happy, an illusion of those who have lost it." — Maugham

"Being young is a fault which improves daily." — Swedish proverb

"Better is a poor and wise youth than an old and foolish king." — Bible, Ecclesiastes

"If thou hast gathered nothing in thy youth, how canst thou find anything in thine age?" Old proverb

"It is not possible for civilization to flow backwards while there is youth in the world." — Helen Keller

"Praise the young and they will blossom." — Irish proverb

"The youth of the soul is everlasting, and eternity is youth." — Jean Richter

"Young men are fitter to invent than to judge, fitter for execution than for counsel, fitter for new projects than for settled business." — Sir Francis Bacon

"Young men are as apt to think themselves wise enough, as drunken men are to think themselves sober enough." — Chesterfield

"Don't laugh at a youth for their affectations; they are only trying on one face after another to find a face of their own." — Logan Pearsall Smith

"Then come kiss me, sweet and twenty, youth's a stuff that will not endure." — "I never knew so young a body with so old a head." — "So wise so young, they say, do never live long." — Shakespeare

"Girls we love for what they are; young men for what they promise to be." — "Everyone believes in his youth that the world really began with him, and that all merely exists for his sake." — Goethe

"I remember my youth and the feeling that will never come back anymore — the feeling that I could last forever, outlast the sea, the earth, and all men." — Joseph Conrad

"There is a feeling of Eternity in youth, which makes us amends for everything." — "To be young is to be as one of the Immortal Gods." — Hazlitt

"In youth, we clothe ourselves with rainbows, and go as brave as the zodiac." — "Within, I do not find wrinkles and used heart, but unspent youth." — "It was a high counsel that I once heard given to a young man, 'Always do what you are afraid to do.'" Emerson

"Tell me what are the prevailing sentiments that occupy the minds of your young men, and I will tell you what is to be the character of the next generation." — Edmund Burke

Old Age

"Old age is venerable." — Latin proverb

"Old age is a second childhood." — Arisophanes

"Old men are twice children." — Greek proverb

"Old age and the wear of time teach many things." — "No man loves life like one who is growing older." — Sophocles

"The tragedy of old age is not that one is old, but that one is young." — Oscar Wilde

"All would live long, but none would be old." — Benjamin Franklin

"Few men know how to be old." — La Rochefoucauld

"We do not count a man's years until he has nothing else to count." — Emerson

"The only thing some men do is grow older." — Ed Howe

"Those who have existed only, and not lived, lack wisdom in old age." — Publilius Syrus

"To be mature means to face, and not evade, every fresh crisis that comes." — Fritz Kunkel

"To grow old is to pass from passion to compassion." — Camus

"As we grow old, . . . the beauty steals inward." — Emerson

"The great sin of maturity is losing one's zest for life." — Stanley Hall

"None are so old as those who have outlived enthusiasm." — Thoreau

"A man is never too old to yearn." — Italian proverb

"It is always in season for the old to learn." — Aeschylus

"I grow old learning something new everyday." — Solon

"It is a man's own fault, it is from want of use, if one's mind grows torpid in old age." — Samuel Johnson

"You can't put new wine in old bottles." — Bible, Matthew 9:17

"An old dog can't alter his way of barking." — Thomas Fuller

"A colt you may break, but an old horse you never can." — Old proverb

"When the snake is old, the frog will tease him." — Persian proverb

"It is well known that the older a man grows, the faster he could run when he was young." — Red Smith

"It is the common vice of all, in old age, to be too intent upon our interests." — Terence

"Next to the very young, I suppose the very old are the most selfish." — Thackeray

"How rare to find old age and happiness in one!" Seneca

"'Tis said that wrath is the last thing in a man to grow old." — Alcaeus

"The man is not old until regrets take place of dreams." — John Barrymore

"Those we call the ancients were once really new in everything." — Pascal

"Forty is the old age of youth; fifty the youth of old age." — Victor Hugo

"To be seventy years young is sometimes far more cheerful and hopeful than to be forty years old." — Oliver Wendell Holmes

"I love everything that's old: old friends, old times, old manners, old books, old wines." — Oliver Goldsmith

"We have some salt of our youth in us." — "For you and I are past our dancing days." — Shakespeare

"Gray hairs seem to my fancy like the soft light of the moon, silvering over the evening of life." — Richter

"A hoary head is a crown of glory." — Bible, Proverbs 16:31

"Many blessings do the advancing years bring with them." — Horace

"Miss not the discourse of the elders." — Apocrypha, Ecclesiasticus 8:9

"When an old man dies, a library burns down." — African proverb

"With the ancient is wisdom; and in length of days understanding." — Bible, Job 12:12

"When a noble life has prepared for old age, it is not decline that it reveals, but the first days of immortality." — Madame De Stael

"Not everything connected with old age is bad." — Euripides

"It is difficult to trap an old fox." — Danish proverb

"You're never too old to become younger." — Mae West

"A man is as old as he feels himself to be." — English proverb

"Grow old along with me! The best is yet to be, the last of life, for which the first was made." — Robert Browning

"Men fool themselves. They pray for a long life, and they fear an old age." — "Don't laugh at one who is old; the same will assuredly happen to us." — Chinese proverbs

"Intelligence, and reflection, and judgment, reside in old men, and if there had been none of them, no states could exist at all." — "No man is so old as to think he cannot live one more year." — Cicero

"As we advance in life, we acquire a keener sense of the value of time. Nothing else, indeed, seems of any consequence; and we become misers in this respect." — Hazlitt

"How to save the old that's worth saving, whether in landscape, houses, manners, institutions, or human types, is one of our greatest problems, and the one that we bother least about." — John Galsworthy

"To know how to grow old is the master-work of wisdom, and one of the most difficult chapters in the great art of living." — Henri Frederic Amiel

"Youth, large, lusty, loving — Youth, full of grace, force, fascination. Do you know that Old Age may come after you, with equal grace, force, fascination?" Walt Whitman

HEALTH

"Health is better than wealth." — "Health and cheerfulness make beauty." — Old proverbs

"Health is the vital principle of bliss, and exercise, of health." — James Thomson

"Health that mocks the doctor's rules, knowledge never learned of schools." — John Greenleaf Whittier

"If you don't have your health . . . you don't have anything." — Old proverb

"Good health and good sense are two of life's greatest treasures." — Publilius Syrus

"It is health which is real wealth and not pieces of gold and silver." — Gandhi

"The first wealth is health." — "The best part of health is a fine disposition." — Emerson

"The groundwork of all happiness is health." — Leigh Hunt

"There's no joy even in beautiful Wisdom, unless one have holy Health." — Simonides of Ceos

"A sound mind in a sound body is the blessedness of creatures." — Old proverb

"There are no riches above the riches of the health of the body." — Bible

"To become a thoroughly good man is the best prescription for keeping a sound mind in a sound body." — Francis Bowen

"Joy, moderation, and repose slam the door on the doctor's nose." — Longfellow

"Shut the door on the sun and you will open it to the doctor." — Seneca

"Fresh air impoverishes the doctor." — Danish proverb

"Half the spiritual difficulties that men and women suffer arise from a morbid state of health." — Beecher

"Every abuse of health hastens death!" F. G. Welch

"If you go long enough without a bath, even the fleas will let you alone." — Ernie Pyle

"Talk health. The dreary, never-ending tale of mortal maladies is more than stale." — Ella Wheeler Wilcox

"It is no petty moral to preserve thy body's health." — Martin Tupper

"It is a wearisome disease to preserve health by too strict a regimen." — La Rochefouauld

"If you would live in health, be old early." — Spanish proverb

"A healthy man is a successful man." — French proverb

"Take care of thy body and soul." — Cleobulus

"Gold that buys health can never be ill spent; nor hours laid out in harmless merriment." — Jean Webster

"Without health life is not life." — Rabelais

"Life is not living but living in health." — Martial

"One must pay Health its tithes." — "No time for your health today: no health for your time tomorrow." — Irish proverbs

"The ingredients of health and long life are great temperance, open air, easy labor, and little care." — Philip Sidney

"The three central forces of health — Motion, Moderation and Rest." — Thomas DeQuincey

"Eat well, drink in moderation, and sleep sound, in these three good health abound." — Latin proverb

"The most fruitful of all the arts [is] the science of living well." — Cicero

"To run away is not glorious, but very healthy." — Russian proverb

"A man who has health has hope; and a man who has hope, has everything." — Arabian proverb

"For where there is love for mankind, there is also love of the art of healing." — "A wise man should consider that health is the greatest of human blessings. And learn how, by his own thought, to derive benefit from his illnesses." — Hippocrates

"Early to bed, and early to rise, makes a man healthy, wealthy, and wise." — "Be sober and temperate, and you will be healthy." — Benjamin Franklin

"When Health is absent Wisdom cannot reveal itself, Art cannot become manifest, Strength cannot be exerted, Wealth is useless and Reason is powerless." — Herophilies

"To preserve health is a moral and religious duty, for health is the basis of all social virtues. We can no longer be useful when not well." — Samuel Johnson

"Take care of your health; you have no right to neglect it, and thus become a burden to yourself, and perhaps to others." — William Hall

"The health of the people is really the foundation upon which all their happiness and all their powers as a State depend." — Disraeli

"What medicine can procure digestion? Exercise. What will recruit strength? Sleep. What will alleviate incurable evils? Patience." — Voltaire

"The surest guide to health, say what they will, is never to suppose we shall be ill; Most of those evils we poor mortals know, from doctors and imagination flow." — Churchill

"The secret of health for both mind and body is not to mourn for the past, worry about the future, or anticipate troubles, but to live in the present moment wisely and earnestly." — Buddha

The Body

"Every man is a builder of a temple called his body." — Thoreau

"Our bodies are our gardens, to which our wills are gardeners." — Shakespeare

"The body is a robe stitched together by desire, thought, and action." — Cherokee Indian proverb

"If you regulate your body and unify your attention, the harmony of heaven will come upon you." — Chuang-tzu

"The body is a community made up of its innumerable cells or inhabitants." — Thomas Edison

"The study of the human soul lies within the province of anatomy." — Andreas Vesalius

"A little body doth often harbor a great soul." — Old proverb

"An upright posture and a few relaxed breaths can make a great difference." — Buddha

"Every tooth in one's head is more valuable than a diamond." — Cervantes

"When you fast, do not put on a sad face as the hypocrites do." — Bible, Matthew 6:16

"Wrinkles should merely indicate where smiles have been." — Mark Twain

"Our bodies are apt to be our autobiographies." — Frank Burgess

"You shall not make any cuttings in your flesh for the dead, nor print any tattoos marks upon you." — Bible, Leviticus 19:28

"Though it be disfigured by many defects, to whom is his own body not dear?" Panchatantra

"You attach too much importance to the body." — Sri Ramana

"Our body is a watch, intended to go for a given time." — Napoleon

"Take no thought for your life, what ye shall eat; neither for the body, what ye shall put on. The life is more than meat, and the body is more than raiment" Bible, Luke 13:23

"However broken down is the spirit's shrine, the spirit is there all the same." — Nigerian proverb

"He will be the slave of many masters who is his body's slave." — "No man is free who is a slave to the flesh." — "This body is not a home, but an inn." — Seneca

"The human body is an instrument for the production of art in the life of the human soul." — Alfred North Whitehead

"If anything is sacred, the human body is sacred." — Walt Whitman

"The body is a sacred garment." — "The body says what words cannot." — Martha Graham

"Life is built up by the sacrifice of the individual to the whole. Each cell in the living body must sacrifice itself to the perfection of the whole; when it is otherwise, disease and death enforce the lesson." — Far Eastern saying

"When one no longer thinks of the personal body as self, neither failure nor success can ail him." — Lao-tse

Eating

"Eat at your own table as you would eat at the table of the king." — Confucius

"Eaten bread is forgotten." — Thomas Fuller

"It is hard to pay for bread that has been eaten." — Danish proverb

"Man doth not live by bread alone." — Bible, Deuteronomy 6:5

"Tell me what you eat, and I will tell you what you are." — Anthelme Brillat-Savarin

"A feast is made for laughter." — Bible, Ecclesiastes 10:19

"Be not hasty in a feast." — Apocrypha, Ecclesiasticus 31:17

"Only the pure in heart can make a good soup." — Ludwig von Beethoven

"The proof of the pudding is in the eating." — Cervantes

"After supper, walk a mile." — Beaumont and Fletcher

"Give me a good digestion, Lord, and also something to digest." — A Pilgrim's Grace

"Butter and honey shall they eat, that they may know to refuse the evil, and choose the good." — Bible, Isaiah 8:15

"He who renounces that food for the sake of a weaker man is a god." — Far Eastern saying

"The belly is the commanding part of the body." — Homer

"A hungry stomach has no ears." — La Fontaine

"The eye is bigger than the belly." — George Herbert

"Choose rather to punish your appetites than to be punished by them." — Tyrius Maximus

"Men whose sole bliss is eating can give but that one brutish reason why they live." — Juvenal

"We must eat to live and not live to eat." — Henry Fielding

"Bad men live that they may eat and drink, whereas good men eat and drink that they may live." — Socrates

"Consume your own smoke." — Browning

"Men who are thirsty drink in silence." — Greek proverb

"What reveals a man is his behavior in time of hunger." — African proverb

"An hungry man is an angry man." — Scottish proverb

"Hunger is the teacher of the arts and the bestower of invention." — Persisus

"No matter how much you feed a wolf he will always return to the forest." — "It is not the horse that draws the cart, but the oats." — Russian proverbs

"The way to a man's heart is through his stomach." — "You can't have your cake and eat it too." — English proverbs

"More men are slain by suppers than by the sword." — Old proverb

"Simple diet is best; for many dishes bring many diseases." — Pliny the Elder

"What is food to one man may be fierce poison to others." — Lucretius

"My soul is dark with stormy riot, directly traceable to diet." — Samuel Hoffenstein

"Eat not to dullness; drink not to elevation." — "I saw few die of hunger — of eating, a hundred thousand." — "A full belly makes a dull brain." — "A fat kitchen, a lean will." — "In general, mankind, since the improvement of cookery, eats twice as much as nature requires." — "To lengthen thy life, lessen thy meals." — Benjamin Franklin

"Small cheer and great welcome makes a merry feast." — "Appetite [is] a universal wolf." — "A man may fish with the worm that hath eaten of a king, and eat the fish that hath fed of that worm." — "I marvel how the fishes live in the sea. Why, as men do on land; the great ones eat up the little ones." — Shakespeare

"Better is a dry morsel and quietness therewith, than a house full of feasting with strife." — "Better is a dinner of herbs where love is, than a stalled ox and hatred therewith." — Bible, Proverbs 15:17

"The difference between a rich man and a poor man, is this — the former eats when he pleases, and the latter when he can get it." — Sir Walter Raleigh

"Men dig their graves with their own teeth and die more by those fated instruments than the weapons of their enemies." — Thomas Moffett

"The stomach begs and clamors, and listens to no precepts." — "A great step towards independence is a good-humored stomach." — Seneca

"Now learn what and how great benefits a temperate diet will bring along with it. In the first place, you will enjoy good health." — Horace

"What we eat is radiation; our food is so much quanta of energy." — Dr. Crile

Medicine

"Medicine, to produce health, has to examine disease." — Plutarch

"Medicine is a science of uncertainty and an art of probability." — William Osler

"Medicine is the only profession that labors incessantly to destroy the reason for its own existence." — James Bryce

"The art of medicine consists of amusing the patient while nature cures the disease." — Voltaire

"A merry heart doeth good like a medicine." — Bible, Proverbs 57:22

"Fasting is medicine." — John Chrysostom

"The best of all medicines are rest and fasting." — Benjamin Franklin

"To array a man's will against his sickness is the supreme art of medicine." — Beecher

"One who lives by medical prescriptions lives miserably." — Linnaeus

"More men die of their medicines than their diseases." — Molière

"Water, air, and cleanness are the chief articles in my pharmacy." — Napoleon

"If you cannot heal the wound, do not tear it open." — Danish proverb

"Better use medicines at the outset than at the last moment." — Publilius Syrus

"By medicine life may be prolonged, yet death will seize the doctor too." — Shakespeare

"Medicine is not merely a science but an art. The character of the physician may act more powerfully upon the patient than the drugs employed. It does not consist of compounding pills and plasters; it deals with the very processes of life, which must be understood before they may be guided." — Paracelsus

"Formerly, when religion was strong and science weak, people mistook magic for medicine; now, when science is strong and religion weak, people mistake medicine for magic." — Thomas Szasz

"Individuals who have diseases, nine times out of ten, are suffering from the accumulated evil effects of medication." — Elbert Hubbard

"Three things can never be got with three things: wealth, with wishing for it; youth, with cosmetics; health with medicine." — Far Eastern saying

"Let food be thy medicine and medicine thy food." — "Wherever the art of medicine is loved, there also is love of humanity." — Hippocrates

"The poets did well to conjoin music and medicine, because the office of medicine is but to tune the curious harp of man's body." — Sir Francis Bacon

Physicians

"Physician, heal thyself." — Bible, Luke 4:23

"Honor a physician with the honor due unto him." — Apocrypha, Ecclesiasticus 38:1

"Man's first doctor is God." — Paracelsus

"Every man is his own doctor of divinity, in the last resort." — Robert Louis Stevenson

"Use three physicians: Doctor Quiet; then, Doctor Merriment; and then, Doctor Diet." — Tiberius

"Nature, time, and patience are the three great physicians." — Henry Bohn

"I am dying from the treatment of too many physicians." — Alexander the Great

"Who shall decide when doctors disagree?" Alexander Pope

"Better no doctor at all than three." — Polish proverb

"Many doctors, death accomplished." — Czech proverb

"The doctor is to be feared more than the disease." — Latin proverb

"If the doctor cures, the sun sees it; but if he kills, the earth hides it." — Scotch proverb

"If the patient dies, the doctor has killed him, but if he gets well, the saints have saved him." — Italian proverb

"If you wish to die young, make your physician your heir." — Romanian proverb

"Don't live in a town where there are no doctors." — Jewish proverb

"Life itself still remains a very effective therapist." — Karen Horney

"Great healers, people of divine realization, do not cure by chance but by exact knowledge." — Yogananda

"We have not lost faith, but we have transferred it from God to the medical profession." — Shaw

"God heals, and the doctor takes the fee." — "He's the best physician that knows the worthlessness of most medicines." — Benjamin Franklin

"Physicians faults are covered with earth, and rich men's money." — "The best surgeon is one that hath been hacked himself." — "Better a lucky physician than a learned one." — "A young doctor makes a humpy churchyard." — English proverbs

"There are only two sorts of doctors: those who practice with their brains, and those who practice with their tongues." — Sir William Osler

"He who cures a disease may be the skillfullest, but he that prevents it is the safest physician." — Thomas Fuller

"When Death lurks at the door, the physician is considered as a God. When danger has been overcome, the physician is looked upon as an angel. When the patient begins to convalesce, the physician becomes a mere human. When the physician asks for his fees, he is considered as the devil himself." — Hendrick Goltzius

"The men you see waiting in the lobbies of doctors' offices are, in a vast majority of cases, suffering through poisoning caused by an excess of food." — Elbert Hubbard

"There is no better surgeon than a man with many scars." — "Happy is the doctor who is called in at the decline of an illness." — Spanish Proverbs

"The superior doctor prevents illness; the mediocre doctor cures imminent illness; the inferior doctor treats illness." — Chinese proverb

"No physician, in so far as he is a physician, considers his own good in what he prescribes, but the good of his patient; for the true physician is also a ruler having the human body as a subject, and is not a mere money-maker." — Plato

Remedies

"There is a remedy for everything except death." — Latin proverb

"Our remedies oft in ourselves do lie, which we ascribe to heaven." — Shakespeare

"He that will not apply new remedies must expect new evils." — Sir Francis Bacon

"There are some remedies worse than the disease, for I see that the cure is not worth the pain." — Publilius Syrus

"Most men die of their remedies, not of their diseases." — Molière

"What destroys one man preserves another." — Corneille

"Prevention is better than cure." — Erasmus

"An ounce of prevention is worth a pound of cure." — "An apple a day keeps the doctor away." — Old Proverbs

"Who is to bell the cat? It is easy to propose impossible remedies." — Aesop

"The herb that can't be got is the one that heals." — Irish proverb

"Every illness is a musical problem, and every cure has a musical solution." — Novalis

"The best of healers is good cheer." — Pindar

"Don't find fault, find a remedy." — Henry Ford

"Nature is always and forever trying hard to keep men well, and most so-called 'disease' — which word means merely the lack of ease — is self-limiting, and tends to cure itself." — Elbert Hubbard

"A careful physician, before he attempts to administer a remedy to his patient, must investigate not only the malady of the man he wishes to cure, but also his habits when in health, and his physical constitution." — Cicero

"Extreme remedies are very appropriate for extreme diseases." — "Healing is a matter of time, but it is sometimes also a matter of opportunity." — "To do nothing is also a good remedy." — Hippocrates

SCIENCE

"Science is the father of knowledge, but opinion breeds ignorance." — Hippocrates

"Science is the knowledge of consequences, and dependence of one fact upon another." — Thomas Hobbes

"Science is the great antidote to the poison of enthusiasm and superstition." — Adam Smith

"Science is the refusal to believe on the basis of hope." — C. P. Snow

"Science means simply the aggregate of all the recipes that are always successful. All the rest is literature." — Paul Valéry

"Science is vastly more stimulating to the imagination than are the classics." — J. B. S. Haldane

"Science without conscience is the death of the soul." — Rabelais

"Science has its being in a perpetual mental restlessness." — Sir William Temple

"Science when well digested is nothing but good sense and reason." — Stanislaus I of Poland

"Science does not permit exceptions." — Claude Bernard

"Science must shake the yoke of all philosophies, including the one of which she is leader." — Jean Rostand

"Books must follow sciences, and not sciences books." — Sir Francis Bacon

"Science carries us into zones of speculation, where there is no habitable city for the mind of man." — Robert Louis Stevenson

"Science should leave off making pronouncements: the river of knowledge has too often turned back on itself." — James Jeans

"Science will never be able to reduce the value of a sunset to arithmetic." — Louis Orr

"Measure, time and number are nothing but modes of thought or rather of imagination." — Spinoza

"Every great advance in science has issued from a new audacity of imagination." — John Dewey

"It is tension between creativity and skepticism that has produced the stunning and unexpected findings of science." — Carl Sagan

"Experience is the mother of science." — Old proverb

"Each particle of matter is an immensity; each leaf a world; each insect an inexplicable compendium." — Johann Kaspar Lavater

"Evolution is not a force but a process; not a cause but a law." — John Viscount Morley

"Life is a wave, which in no two consecutive moments of its existence is composed of the same particles." — John Tyndall

"Nothing exists except atoms and empty space: everything else is opinion." — Democritus

"Matter is the embodiment of an idea." — Semjase

"Matter is energy becoming spirit." — Paolo Soleri

"Don't fight forces, use them." — Buckminster Fuller

"Language is only the instrument of science, and words are but the signs of ideas." — Samuel Johnson

"Happiness hates the timid! So does science!" Eugene O'Neill

"The machine, yes the machine, never wastes anybody's time, never watches the foreman, and never talks back." — Carl Sandburg

"Lo! Men have become the tools of their tools." — Thoreau

"Computers are useless. They can only give you answers." — Picasso

"Man is still the most extraordinary computer of all." — John F. Kennedy

"In a few minutes a computer can make a mistake so great that it would have taken many men many months to equal." — Anonymous

"The inability of science to solve life is absolute. This fact would be truly frightening were it not for faith." — Marconi

"Technological progress has merely provided us with more efficient means for going backwards." — Aldous Huxley

"Our scientific power has outrun our spiritual power. We have guided missiles and misguided men." — Martin Luther King, Jr.

"There is no evil in the atom; only in man's soul." — Adlai Stevenson

"The great tragedy of science is the slaying of a beautiful hypothesis by an ugly fact." — T. H. Huxley

"In scientific work, those who refuse to go beyond fact rarely get as far as fact." — Thomas Henry Huxley

"Physical science is truth with her wings clipped." — Austin O'Malley

"In science, error precedes the truth, and it is better it should go first than last." — Horace Walpole

"After all, the ultimate goal of all research is not objectivity, but truth." — Helene Deutsch

"The newest things [are] not always true." — J. Clarke

"One loses science when losing the purity of the heart." — Nicholas Valois

"The highest reach of human science is the scientific recognition of human ignorance." — Sir William Hamilton

"In science, the credit goes to the man who convinces the world, not to the man to whom the idea first occurs." — William Osler

"In science, the important thing is to modify and change one's ideas as science advances." — Herbert Spencer

"Only when genius is married to science can the biggest results be produced." — Herbert Spencer

"It requires a very unusual mind to make an analysis of the obvious." — Alfred North Whitehead

"Observation is a passive science, experimentation an active science." — Claude Bernard

"All life is an experiment. The more experiments you make, the better." — Emerson

"Reason, Observation, and Experience — the Holy Trinity of Science." — Robert G. Ingersoll

"The science of today is the technology of tomorrow." — Edward Teller

"Modern science is standing on tiptoe, ready to open the doors of a golden age." — Churchill

"Science advances through tentative answers to a series of more and more subtle questions which reach deeper and deeper into the essence of natural phenomena." — Louis Pasteur

"Science is a mechanism, a way of trying to improve your knowledge of nature. It's a system for testing your thoughts against the universe, and seeing whether they match." — Isaac Asimov

"Science is built up of facts, as a house is built of stones; but an accumulation of facts is no more a science than a heap of stones is a house." — "Thus be it understood that, to demonstrate a theorem, it is neither necessary nor even advantageous to know what it means. . ." Henri Poincare

"Science does not know its debt to imagination." — "All science is transcendental or else passes away." — "There is a kind of latent omniscience not only in every man, but in every particle." — "'Tis a short sight to limit our faith in laws to those of gravity, of chemistry, of botany, and so forth." — "[There's] no truth so sublime but it may be seen to be trivial tomorrow in the light of new thoughts." — Emerson

"Science and art are only too often a superior kind of dope, possessing this advantage over booze, morphia, and drugs: that they can be indulged in with a good conscience and with the conviction that, in the process of indulging, one is leading the 'higher life.'" Aldous Huxley

"Science is nothing but developed perception, interpreted intent, common sense rounded out and minutely articulated." — Santayana

"Science has not yet mastered prophecy. We predict too much for the next year and yet far too little for the next ten." — Neil Armstrong

"Science may have found a cure for most evils; but it has found no remedy for the worst of them all — the apathy of human beings." — Helen Keller

"Science is purifying religion from error and superstition, and religion is purifying science from idolatry and false absolutes." — Pope Paul II

"Those who speak of the incompatibility of science and religion either make science say that which it never said or make religion say that which it never taught." — Pius XI

"It is wrong to think that the task of physics is to find out how Nature is. Physics concerns what we say about Nature." — "The opposite of a correct statement is a false statement. But the opposite of a profound truth may well be another profound truth." — Niels Bohr

"Let us put these new hypotheses in public appearance among the old ones which are themselves no more probable, especially since they are wonderful and easy and bring with them a vast storehouse of learned observations." — Copernicus

"If I have been able to see farther than others, it was because I stood on the shoulders of giants." — "It is the weight, not numbers, of experiments that is to be regarded." — "If I have ever made any valuable discoveries, it has been owing more to patient attention than any other talent." — Sir Isaac Newton

"School yourself to demureness and patience. Learn to inure yourself to drudgery in science. Learn, compare, collect the facts." — Ivan Pavlov

"Any sufficiently advanced technology is indistinguishable from magic." — "If an elderly but distinguished scientist says that something is possible, he is almost certainly right, but if he says that it is impossible he is very probably wrong." — Arthur C. Clarke

"Any man who has been seriously engaged in scientific work of any kind realizes that over the entrance to the gates of the temple of science are written the words: 'Ye must have faith.' It is a quality which the scientist cannot dispense with." — Max Planck

"All that science can achieve is a perfect knowledge and a perfect understanding of the action of natural and moral forces." — Hermann Helmholtz

"Research is four things: brains with which to think, eyes with which to see, machines with which to measure and, fourth, money." — Albert Szent-Gyorgy

"The question is this: is man an ape or an angel? I am on the side of the angels. I repudiate with indignation and abhorrence these new-fangled theories." — Disraeli

"The progress of science is strewn, like an ancient desert trail, with the bleached skeleton of discarded theories which once seemed to possess eternal life." — Arthur Koestler

"One could not be a successful scientist without realizing that a goodly number of scientists are not only narrow-minded and dull, but also just stupid." — James D. Watson

"If rational men cooperated and used their scientific knowledge to the full, they could now secure the economic welfare of all." — Bertrand Russell

"The social sciences will never help us solve our problems as long as they continue to go on the assumption that whatever is true of a rat is true of man." — "As machines get to be more and more like men, men will come to be more like machines." — Joseph Wood Krutch

"One machine can do the work of fifty ordinary men. No machine can do the work of one extraordinary man." — Elbert Hubbard

"I find it hard to believe that the machine would go into the creative artist's hand even were that magic hand in true place. It has been too far exploited by industrialism and science at expense to art and true religion." — "If automation keeps up, man will atrophy all his limbs but the push-button finger." — Frank Lloyd Wright

"I have seen the science I worshipped, and the aircraft I loved, destroying the civilization I expected them to serve." — Lindbergh

"Have we not learned from a thousand years of experience that things cease to speak the more we hold up to them the visual mirror of their appearance?" Franz Marc

"He who would study organic existence first drives out the soul with rigid persistence. Then the parts in his hand he may hold and class, but the spiritual link is lost, alas!" Goethe

"There is something fascinating about science. One gets such wholesale returns of conjecture out of such a trifling investment of fact." — "All the modern inconveniences." — Mark Twain

"In my mind, the collapse of the atom was the collapse of the whole world: Suddenly the stoutest walls fell. Everything turned unstable, insecure, and soft." — Kandinsky

"It is generally as painful to us to discard old beliefs as for the scientists to discard the old laws of physics and accept new theories." — Lin Yutang

"Every great scientific truth goes through three stages. First, people say it conflicts with the Bible. Next they say it had been discovered before. Lastly, they say they always believed it." — Louis Agassiz

"When a man sits with a pretty girl for an hour, it seems like a minute. But let him sit on a hot stove for a minute — and it's longer than any hour. That's relativity." — "Concerns for man and his fate must always form the chief interest of all technical endeavors. Never forget this in the midst of your diagrams and equations." — Einstein

"The end of science is not to prove a theory, but to improve mankind." — Manly P. Hall

Numbers

"The world is built on the power of numbers." — Pythagoras

"Mathematics possesses not only truth, but supreme beauty." — Edna St. Vincent Millay

"There is measure in all things." — Horace

"Everything is a vibration." — Anonymous

"But the very hairs of your head are all numbered." — Bible, Matthew 10:30

"Even a single hair casts its shadow." — Publilius Syrus

"If sailors becomes too numerous, the ship sinks." — Arabian proverb

"When there are too many chefs in the kitchen, no cooking gets done." — Old proverb

"Too many boatmen will run the boat up to the top of the mountains." — Japanese proverb

"It never troubles the wolf how many the sheep may be." — Virgil

"Do not count your chickens before they are hatched." — Aesop

"I have hardly ever known a mathematician who was capable of reasoning." — Plato

"That which is common to the greatest number has the least care bestowed upon it." — Aristotle

"Who can number the sand of the sea, and the drops of rain, and the days of eternity?" Apocrypha, Ecclesiasticus 1:2

"There is strength in numbers." — "Too many cooks spoil the broth." — Old proverbs

"As related to individuals these each vibrate to certain numbers according to their name and birthday." — "Every individual entity is on certain vibrations. Life is sustained in this cycle of vibration." — Edgar Cayce

"Having established by experience what philosophers have made evident before, it follows immediately that all knowledge here below depends on the power of mathematics." — Roger Bacon

REALITY

"Reality is a sliding door." — Emerson

"Reality is a narrow little house which becomes a prison to those who can't get out of it." — Joyce Cary

"Reality leaves a lot to the imagination." — John Lennon

"Some other faculty than the intellect is necessary for the apprehension of reality." — Henri Bergson

"Set up as an ideal the facing of reality as honestly and as cheerfully as possible." — Karl A. Menninger

"Be it life or death, we seek only reality." — "Being is the great explainer." — Thoreau

"I am seeking only to face realities and to face them without soft concealments." — Woodrow Wilson

"Too many moralists begin with a dislike of reality." — Clarence Day

"We live in a fantasy world, a world of illusion. The great task in life is to find reality." — Isis Murdoch

"Humankind cannot bear very much reality." — T. S. Eliot

"Either you deal with what is the reality, or you can be sure that the reality is going to deal with you." — Alex Haley

"Do not let your fancy make you forget realities." — Aesop

"Your life is no idle dream, but a solemn reality." — Anonymous

"The most beautiful music of all is the music of what happens." — Irish proverb

"That is real which never changes." — Lao-tse

"There is no reality except the one contained within us. That is why so many people live such an unreal life. They take the images outside them for reality and never allow the world within to assert itself." — Hermann Hesse

"Men alone have the power to transform their thoughts into physical reality; men alone can dream and make their dreams come true." — Napoleon Hill

"A very slight change of our habits is sufficient to destroy our sense of our daily reality, and reality of the world around us." — George Moore

"As far as the laws of mathematics refer to reality, they are not certain; and as far as they are certain, they do not refer to reality." — Einstein

"A independent reality in the ordinary physical sense can neither be ascribed to the phenomenon nor to the agencies of observation." — Niels Bohr

"Is not the language of painters but the language of nature which one should listen to . . . the feeling for the things themselves, for reality, is more than the feeling of pictures." — Vincent van Gogh

"A man must be out-of-doors enough to get experience of wholesome reality, as a ballast to thought and sentiment. Health requires this relaxation, this aimless life." — Thoreau

"No matter how hardened to danger a man may be, he always realizes from the pounding of his heart and the shivering of his flesh, the enormous difference there is between a dream and reality, between a plan and its execution." — Alexandre Dumas

"Whatever is a reality today, whatever you touch and believe in and that seems real for you today, is going to be — like the reality of yesterday — an illusion tomorrow." — Luigi Pirandello

"The permanent temptation of life is to confuse dreams with reality. The permanent defeat of life comes when dreams are surrendered to reality." — James Michener

Facts

"Fact is stranger than fiction." — T. C. Haliburton

"Facts speak for themselves." — Plautus

"Facts are stubborn things." — Alain René le Sage

"Facts are facts and will not disappear on account of your likes." — Nehru

"Facts do not cease to exist because they are ignored." — Aldous Huxley

"Facts are apt to alarm us more than the most dangerous principles." — Junius

"You can't argue with the facts." — Anonymous

"There are no facts, only interpretations." — Nietzsche

"My mind is made up, don't try and confuse me with the facts." — Anonymous

"Time dissipates to ether the shining angularity of fact." — "No facts to me are sacred; none are profane." — Emerson

"Rain beats a leopard's skin, but it does not wash off the spots." — Ashanti proverb

"Everything passes, everything wears out, everything breaks." — French proverb

"It is as fatal as it is cowardly to blink at facts because they are not to our taste." — John Tyndall

"Motives and purposes are in the brain and heart of a man. Consequences are in the world of fact." — William Sumner

"The frontiers are not east or west, north or south, but wherever a man fronts a fact." — Thoreau

"There is no good in arguing with the inevitable. The only argument available with an east wind is to put on your overcoat." — James Russell Lowell

"A fact is like a sack — it won't stand up if it's empty. To make it stand up, first you have to put in it all the reasons and feelings that caused it in the first place." — Luigi Pirandello

Necessity

"Necessity is the mother of invention." — "The true creator is necessity." — Plato

"Necessity is the theme and the inventress, the eternal curb and law of nature." — Leonardo da Vinci

"Necessity is a hard nurse, but she raises strong children." — Old proverb

"Necessity is blind until it becomes conscious. Freedom is the consciousness of necessity." — Karl Marx

"Necessity is the argument of tyrants; it is the creed of slaves." — William Pitt

"Necessity never made a good bargain." — Benjamin Franklin

"Necessity dispenseth with decorum." — Thomas Fuller

"Necessity sharpens industry." — Old proverb

"Necessity turns lion into fox." — Persian proverb

"Necessity knows no laws." — Spanish proverb

"Necessity relieves us from the embarrassment of choice." — Marquis de Vauvenargues

"Necessity of action takes away the fear of the act, and makes bold resolution the favorite of fortune." — Francis Quarles

"Necessity unites hearts." — German proverb

"The art of our necessities is strange, that can make vile things precious." — Shakespeare

"Where necessity speaks, it demands." — Russian proverb

"A wise man never refuses anything to necessity." — "Necessity knows no law except to conquer." — Publilius Syrus

"Against necessity, against its strength, no man can fight and win." — Aeschylus

"Nothing has more strength than dire necessity." — Euripides

"Even the gods cannot strive against necessity." — Diogenes

"Toil and pleasure, in their nature opposites, are yet linked together in a kind of necessary connection." — Livy

"Make a virtue of necessity." — Robert Burton

"We give to necessity the praise of virtue." — Quintilian

"It's not enough that we do our best; sometimes we have to do what's required." — Churchill

"What was once to me mere matter of the fancy, now has grown to be the necessity of heart and life." — Tennyson

"Make yourself necessary to somebody. Do not make yourself hard to any." — Emerson

"Men try to run life according to their wishes: life runs itself according to necessity." — Jean Toomer

Circumstances

"Circumstances are the rulers of the weak; they are but the instruments of the wise." — Samuel Lover

"Circumstances rule men; men do not rule circumstances." — Herodotus

"Circumstances! I make circumstances!" Napoleon

"It is futile to rail at circumstances, for they are indifferent." — Plutarch

"Occasions do not make a man either strong or weak, but they show what he is." — Thomas à Kempis

"The wise adapt themselves to circumstances, as water molds itself to the pitcher." — Chinese proverb

"I am bigger than anything that can happen to me." — Charles Lummis

"Make the most of the best and the least of the worst." — Robert Louis Stevenson

"Inconsistencies of opinion, arising from changes of circumstances, are often justifiable." — Webster

"Many a time a man cannot be such as he would be, if circumstances do not admit of it." — Terence

"When men are easy in their circumstances, they are naturally enemies to innovations." — Joseph Addison

"Our first mistake is the belief that the circumstance gives the joy which we give to the circumstance." — Emerson

"Do not wait for extraordinary circumstances to do good; try to use ordinary situations." — Jean Richter

"Ask not that events should happen as you will, but let your will be that events should happen as they do, and you shall have peace." — Epictetus

"Men are the sport of circumstances, when the circumstances seem the sport of men." — Byron

"He who waits until circumstances completely favor his undertaking will never accomplish anything." — Martin Luther

"Wait not, my soul, on circumstance; it does not wait for you." — Mark Van Doren

"The people who get on in this world are the people who get up and look for the circumstances they want, and, if they can't find them, make them." — Shaw

THE WORLD

"The world is a wheel, and it will all come round right." — Disraeli

"The world is a beehive; we all enter by the same door but live in different cells." — African proverb

"The world is a comedy to those who think, a tragedy to those who feel." — Horace Walpole

"The world is fleeting, all things pass away; or is it we that pass and they that stay?" Lucian

"The world is so full of a number of things, I'm sure we should all be happy as kings." — Robert Louis Stevenson

"The world cannot live at the level of its great men." — Sir James Frazer

"The world is a fine place and worth fighting for." — Hemingway

"Every day is a fresh beginning, every morn is the world made new." — Susan Coolidge

"Every individual has a place to fill in the world and is important." — Nathaniel Hawthorne

"The whole world is a man's birthplace." — Statuis

"My country is the world." — Thomas Paine

"All the world is one country." — Italian proverb

"We are citizens of the world; and the tragedy is of our times is that we do not know this." — Woodrow Wilson

"We all, whether we know it or not, are fighting to make the kind of a world that we should like." — Oliver Wendell Holmes, Jr.

"Our thinking in the future must be world-wide." — Wendell Lewis Willkie

"If the world seems cold to you, kindle fires to warm it!" Lucy Larcom

"Never bend your head. Hold it high. Look the world straight in the eye." — Helen Keller

"We ourselves cannot put any magic spells on this world. The world is its own magic." — Suzuki Roshi

"There's nothing wrong with the world. What's wrong is our way of looking at it." — Henry Miller

"Don't go around saying the world owes you a living; the world owes you nothing. It was here first." — Mark Twain

"The world is a strange affair." — Molière

"For you, the world is weird because if you're not bored with it, you're at odds with it." — Don Juan

"Let the world be your teacher, not your adversary." — Anonymous

"The knowledge of the world is only to be acquired in the world, and not in a closet." — Chesterfield

"Where the world rebuketh, there look out for excellent." — Martin Tupper

"One who rebukes the world is rebuked by the world." — Kipling

"All the world is queer save me and thee; and sometimes I think thee is a little queer." — Quaker saying

"The most incomprehensible thing about the world is that it is comprehensible." — Einstein

"The whole visible world is an imperceptible atom in the ample bosom of nature. No idea approaches it." — Pascal

"The world is ruled by letting things take their course. It cannot be ruled by interfering." — Tao Te Ching XLVIII

"As the world leads, we follow." — Seneca

"One half of the world does not know how the other half lives." — Rabelais

"In this world there are only two tragedies. One is not getting what one wants, and the other is getting it." — Oscar Wilde

"The beauty of the world has two edges, one of laughter, one of anguish, cutting the heart asunder." — Virginia Woolf

"Do I believe in Heaven and Hell? I do; We have them here; the world is nothing else." — John Davidson

"Our eagerness for worldly activity kills in us the sense of spiritual awe." — Lahiri Mahasaya

"This world is a round gulf, and those who cannot swim must go to the bottom." — Spanish proverb

"If you wish to be a success in the world, promise everything and deliver nothing." — Napoleon

"There is a sufficiency in the world for man's need but not for man's greed." — Gandhi

"In this world nothing is certain but death and taxes." — Benjamin Franklin

"There is nothing in this world constant but inconstancy." — Swift

"Nothing is certain in this world except uncertainty." — Old proverb

"The children of this world are wiser than the children of light." — Bible, Luke 16:8

"The world belongs to the rascals; Heaven belongs to the good." — Persian proverb

"For what has a man profited if he shall gain the whole world and lose his own soul?" Bible, Matthew 16:26

"What is the use of a house if you haven't got a tolerable planet to put it on?" Thoreau

"Each object in the world is not merely itself but involves every other object, and in fact is every other object." — Rig-Veda

"Vast worlds lie within the hollows of each atom, multifarious as the motes in a sunbeam." — Yoga Vasishtha

"Do not let the ways of the world dismay your heart, being that you are a spiritual warrior of truth." — Ramayana

"This world is a dream within a dream; and as we grow older, each step is an awakening." — Sir Walter Scott

"The world, while I am perceiving it, is being incessantly created for myself in time and space." — Rabinranath Tagore

"Naked came I into the world, and naked must I go out." — Cervantes

"We brought nothing into this world and it is certain we can carry nothing out." — Bible, I Timothy 6:7

"The world is a bridge; pass over it, but build no house upon it." — Agrapha, Jesus Christ

"Ascend above the restrictions and conventions of the World, but not so high as to lose sight of them." — Richard Garnett

"The best thing in the world is to live above it." — H. G. Bohn

"They are not of the world, just as I am not of the world." — Bible, John 17:16

"To be in the world but not of it." — Sufi saying

"Be wisely worldly, be not worldly wise." — Francis Quarles

"With our love, we could save the world." — George Harrison

"Driven by the forces of love, the fragments of the world seek each other so that the world may come to being." — Teilhard de Chardin

"Never doubt that a small group of committed citizens can change the world; indeed, it is the only thing that ever has." — Margaret Mead

"The world will ever bow to those who hold principle above policy, truth above diplomacy, and right above consistency." — Macaulay

"He who would know the world, seek first within his being's depths; he who would truly know himself, develop interest in the world." — Rudolf Steiner

"The world is a looking-glass, and gives back to every man the reflection of his own face. Frown at it, and it in turn will look sourly upon you; laugh at it and with it, and it is a jolly, kind companion." — Thackeray

"The world looks like a mathematical equation, which, turn it how you will, balances itself. Every secret is told, every crime is punished, every virtue rewarded, every wrong redressed, in silence and certainty." — "The world is his, who has money to go over it." — "The world belongs to the energetic." — "The way to mend a bad world is to create the right world." — Emerson

"The world was not built with random bricks of chance, a blind god is not destiny's architect; a conscious power has drawn the plan of life, there is a meaning in each curve and line." — Sri Aurobindo

"This world is like a vestibule before the World to Come. Prepare yourself in the vestibule that you may enter the hall." — The Talmud

"The only effort by any intelligent being in this world is to know something that can not be destroyed by death." — Buddha

"Do not be conformed to this world but be transformed by the renewal of the mind, that you may prove what is good." — Bible, Romans 12:2

"A good man and a wise man may at times be angry with the world, at times grieved for it; but be sure no man was ever discontented with the world who did his duty in it." — Robert Southey

"The reasonable man adapts himself to the world; the unreasonable one persists in trying to adapt the world to himself." — "You don't learn to hold your own in the world by standing on guard, but by attacking, and getting well hammered yourself." — Shaw

"No man lives without jostling and being jostled; in all ways he has to elbow himself through the world, giving and receiving offense." — Carlyle

"This world that we're living in is mighty hard to beat; You get a thorn with every rose, but ain't the roses sweet." — "Worldly wise is but half-witted, at its highest." — Edward Young

"He who imagines he can do without the world deceives himself much; but he who fancies the world cannot do without him is still more mistaken." — La Rochefoucauld

"I begin to understand the promises of this world are for the most part, vain phantoms; and that to confide in one's self and become something of worth and value is the best and safest course." — Michelangelo

"The world is a perpetual caricature of itself; at every moment it is the mockery and the contradiction of what it is pretending to be." — Santayana

"The world-pool of information fathered by electric media — movies, Telstar, flight — far surpasses any possible influence mom and dad can now bring to bear." — Marshall McLuhan

"The softest things in the world overcome the hardest things in the world." — "The biggest problem in the world could have been solved when it was small." — Lao-tse

"It's a mad world. Mad as Bedlam." — "No one is useless in this world who lightens the burden of it to anyone else." — Dickens

"To him who looks upon the world rationally, the world in its turn presents a rational aspect. The relation is mutual." — Hegel

"In spite of the large population of this planet, men and women remain today the most inaccessible things on it." — Frank Moore Colby

"There are two worlds: the world that we can measure with line and rule, and the world that we feel with our hearts and imagination." — Leigh Hunt

"I find the great thing in this world is not so much where we stand, as in what direction we are moving." — Goethe

"The worst cause has often been illustrated with the most heroic virtue, and the world owes some of its greatest debts to men from whose memory it recoils." — William Stubbs

"All the world's a stage and all the men are merely players. They have their entrances and their exits, and one man in his time plays many parts." — Shakespeare

The Universe

"The universe is deathless; deathless because, having no finite self, It stays infinite." — Lao-tse

"The universe comes forth from the Imperishable." — Mundaka-Upanishad

"The universe is not hostile, nor yet is it friendly. It is simply indifferent." — John Haynes Holmes

"I find no hint throughout the Universe of good or ill, of blessing or of curse, I find alone Necessity Supreme." — James Thomson

"The universe is change." — Marcus Aurelius

"The universe is made of stories, not of atoms." — Muriel Rukeyser

"All this visible universe is only an imperceptible point in the vast bosom of nature." — Pascal

"In this orderly universe, everything has its place and its function." — Edgar Cayce

"Everything existing in the universe is the fruit of chance and necessity." — Democritus

"Do I dare disturb the universe?" T. S. Eliot

"Men know the universe, and know not themselves." — La Fontaine

"Everybody is the center of his own universe." — Old proverb

"Man cannot live without seeking to explain the universe." — Isaiah Berlin

"What is it that breathes fire into the equations and makes a universe for them to describe?" Stephen Hawking

"There is a coherent plan in the universe, though I don't know what it's a plan for." — Fred Hoyle

"The human mind is not capable of grasping the Universe." — Einstein

"When we try to pick out anything by itself, we find it hitched to everything else in the universe." — John Muir

"We are an impossibility in an impossible universe." — Ray Bradbury

"With our short sight, we affect to take a comprehensive view of eternity. Our horizon is the universe." — Paul Laurence Dunbar

"The Universe begins to look more like a great thought than a great machine." — Sir James Jeans

"The universe does not jest with us, but is in earnest." — "The universe is represented in every one of its particles. Everything is made of one hidden stuff. The world globes itself in a drop of dew." — "The solar system has no anxiety about its reputation." — "Everything in the universe goes by indirection. There are no straight lines." — Emerson

"In this unbelievable universe in which we live, there are no absolutes. Even parallel lines, reaching into infinity, meet somewhere yonder." — Pearl Buck

"The universe is but one vast Symbol of God." — "It is the first of all problems for man to find out what kind of work he is to do in this universe." — Carlyle

"We are so bound together that no man can labor for himself alone. Each blow he strikes in his own behalf helps to mold the universe." — J. K. Jerome

"A man said to the universe: 'Sir, I exist!' 'However,' replied the universe, 'The fact has not created in me a sense of obligation.'" Stephen Crane

"The universe seems bankrupt as soon as we begin to discuss the characters of individuals." — "The universe is wider than our views of it." — Thoreau

"Knowing the plumbing of the universe, intricate and awe-inspiring though that plumbing might be, is a far cry from discovering its purpose." — Gerald L. Schroeder

"For some curious reason man has always assumed that he is the highest form of life in the Universe. There is, of course, nothing at all with which to sustain this view." — James Thurber

"Sometimes I think we're alone in the universe, and sometimes I think we're not. In either case, the idea is quite staggering." — Maslow

"How unreasonable it would be to suppose that, besides the heavens and earth which we can see, there are no other heavens and no other earths." — Teng Mu

"The most beautiful things in the universe are the starry heavens above us and the feeling of duty within us." — Native American proverb

Unity

"Unity does not imply uniformity." — Sri Aurobindo

"Unity, to be real, must stand the severest strain without breaking." — Gandhi

"United we stand, divided we fall." — Aesop

"Union is strength." — Homer

"There is no strength without unity." — Irish proverb

"With unity, the time is right for great deeds." — I-Ching; Book of Changes

"All is one." — Sai Baba

"One is All." — Alchemist motto

"All for one, and one for all." — Alexandre Dumas the elder

"From many to make one." — St. Augustine

"E Pluribus Unum: Out of Many, One." — Motto of the United States of America

"A mystic bond of brotherhood makes all men one." — Carlyle

"Behold, how good and how pleasant it is for brethren to dwell together in unity." — Bible, Psalms 133:1

"When spider webs unite, they can tie up a lion." — Ethiopian proverb

"Alone we can do so little; together we can do so much." — Helen Keller

"We must all hang together, or assuredly we shall all hang separately." — Benjamin Franklin

"Noble and common blood is of the same color." — German proverb

"I am a part of all that I have met." — Tennyson

"Like a sword that cuts, but cannot cut itself." — Zen proverb

"Everything is related to everything else in a space-time continuum." — Einstein

"We are all related; We are all one." — Sioux Indian proverb

"We are members one of another." — Bible, Ephesians 4:25

"All things are connected." — Chief Seattle

"Independence? That's middle-class blasphemy. We are all dependent on one another, every soul of us on earth." — Shaw

"Nothing in the world is single; all things by a law divine in one spirit meet and mingle." — Shelley

"Truth, and goodness, and beauty are but different faces of the same all." — Emerson

"Wisdom and virtue are like two wheels of a cart." — Japanese proverb

"Let there be spaces in our togetherness." — Kahlil Gibran

"Harmony would lose its attractiveness if it did not have a background of discord." — Chinese proverb

"The least movement is of importance to all nature. The entire ocean is affected by a pebble." — Pascal

"Thou canst not stir a flower without troubling of a star." — Francis Thompson

"The fundamental delusion of humanity is to suppose that I am here and you are out there." — Yasutani Roshi

"Who can determine where one ends and the other begins?" Sun-tzu

"Everything that lives, Lives not alone, nor for itself." — William Blake

"Everyone is a piece of this puzzle called life." — Anonymous

"All are but parts of one stupendous whole, whose body Nature is, and God the soul." — Alexander Pope

"Heaven and earth are threads of one loom." — Shaker saying

"Heaven, Earth and I are living together and all things and I form an inseparable unity." — Chuang-tzu

"Om! That is whole; whole is this; from the Invisible Whole comes forth the visible whole." — Isa-Upanishad

"See one Changeless Life in all that lives, and in the separate, One Inseparable." — Bhagavad-gita 18

"In real existence, there is only unity." — Rumi

"Man and Woman may only enter Paradise hand in hand. Together, the myth tells us, they left it, and together must they return." — Richard Garnett

"What is within us is also without. What is without is also within. One who sees a difference between the two and not the unity wanders on from death to death." — The Upanishads

"Yoga or union is attained from the inhibition of the mental energy and matter. Then the Seer is clothed in his essential nature." — Patanjali

"We are not independent but interdependent." — "Fear is always an anticipation of what has not yet come. Our fear and separation are great, but the truth of our connection is greater still." — Buddha

Mystery

"Mystery is but another name for our ignorance; if we were omniscient, all would be perfectly plain." — Tryon Edwards

"Mysteries are not necessarily miracles." — Goethe

"Everything that is unknown is taken to be grand." — Tacitus

"The mystery of life is certainly the most persistent problem ever placed before the thought of man." — Marconi

"Life is not a problem to be solved but a mystery to be lived." — Thomas Merton

"Each time dawn appears, the mystery is there in its entirety." — René Daumal

"It is the dim haze of mystery that adds enchantment to pursuit." — Antoine Rivarol

"All is mystery; but he is a slave who will not struggle to penetrate the dark veil." — Disraeli

"Every man is a moon, and has a dark side which he never shows to anyone." — Mark Twain

"Put the mysteries of wisdom into practice and all evil will flee from you." — Egyptian saying

"A wonderful fact to reflect upon, that every human creature is constituted to be that profound secret and mystery to every other." — Dickens

"The final mystery is oneself." — Oscar Wilde

"Widely as we stretch our reverent conceptions, there is ever something beyond." — A. Maclaren

"All is riddle, and the key to a riddle is another riddle." — Emerson

"The unknown is ever imagined." — Greek proverb

"The moment one gives close attention to anything, even a blade of grass, it becomes a mysterious, awesome, indescribably magnificent world in itself." — Henry Miller

"The most beautiful thing we can experience is the mysterious. It is the fundamental emotion which stands at the cradle of true art and science." — Einstein

"It was my science that drove me to the conclusion that the world is much more complicated than can be explained by science. It is only through the supernatural that I can understand the mystery of existence." — Alan Sandage

"Essentially there is one truth underlying our attempts to describe what is indescribable." — Dhyani Ywahoo

"The law of analogy is a priceless key to the divine mysteries." — Hermes

"He who knows the secret of the sounds knows the mystery of the whole universe." — Hazrat Inayat Khan

"The hidden harmony is better than the obvious." — "If you do not expect the unexpected, you will not find it; for it is hard to be sought out, and difficult." — Heraclitus

"This creation — how it sprang forth, if it is supported or not. Who its supervisor is in heaven is beyond. Oh! They verily know or know not." — Nasadiya Sukta

"They had lived long enough to know that it is unwise to wish everything explained." — Sir Thomas Coningsby

"Leave a few mysteries to explore in Eternity." — Sri Yukteswar

"We injure mysteries, which are matters of faith, by any attempt at explanation, in order to make them matters of reason. Could they be explained, they would cease to be mysteries." — Charles Colton

"I would rather live in a world where my life is surrounded by mystery than live in a world so small that my mind could comprehend it." — Harry Fosdick

"When all is said and done, all people are confronted with the Great Mystery." — Luther Standing Bear

"As we acquire more knowledge, things do not become more comprehensible, but more mysterious." — Albert Schweitzer